The Hidden Curriculum and Moral Education

Deception or Discovery?

Edited by

Henry Giroux

Boston University

and

David Purpel

University of North Carolina, Greensboro

McCutchan Publishing Corporation
2526 Grove Street
Berkeley, California 94704

ISBN 0-8211-1519-7
Library of Congress Catalog Card Number 82-62034

Cover design by Terry Down, Griffin Graphics
Typesetting composition by The Typehouse

This book is dedicated to teachers everywhere who believe that schooling is inextricably connected with the need to create a more just, free, and rational human existence.

Henry Giroux
David Purpel

Contributors

Jean Anyon, Rutgers University
Michael Apple, University of Wisconsin, Madison
Samuel Bowles, University of Massachusetts, Amherst
Carol Gilligan, Harvard University
Paulo Freire, University of Campinas, Brazil
Herbert Gintis, University of Massachusetts, Amherst
Henry Giroux, Boston University
Maxine Greene, Teachers College, Columbia University
Philip Jackson, University of Chicago
Nancy King, University of Maryland
Lawrence Kohlberg, Harvard University
Ulf Lundgren, Stockholm Institute of Education, Sweden
James Macdonald, University of North Carolina, Greensboro
Jane Martin, University of Massachusetts, Boston
Anthony Penna, Carnegie-Mellon University
David Purpel, University of North Carolina, Greensboro
Kevin Ryan, Boston University
Israel Scheffler, Harvard University
Elizabeth Vallance, Kansas State University

Contents

Section III: From the Hidden Curriculum to Moral Values in Pedagogy

Part A: Education as Liberation

Part B: Curriculum and Liberation

Preface

Since Philip Jackson's *Life in Classrooms* appeared in 1968, a heated debate among curriculum theorists and other educators has developed over the issue of what schools do and do not do, particularly with respect to the overt and tacit teaching that takes place at the classroom level. While a consensus has grown that schools are indeed agencies of socialization and so do more than simply teach subject matter and technical skills, no such consensus exists regarding the role schools play in the social, moral, and economic reproduction of the existing society. In other words, what is being hotly debated among educators is not whether the hidden curriculum exists so much as the function and consequence of such a curriculum. What has become quite clear is that educators can no longer examine schooling simply through the lens of the formal curriculum; or put another way, educators can no longer ignore the importance and significance of the hidden curriculum as a major dimension of the schooling process, and they will have to provide opportunities for researchers to make a systematic study of the subject.

This book taps some of the best theoretical and ethnographic research that has so far provided a valuable and comprehensive framework for using the concept of the hidden curriculum as a powerful analytical tool in both the development of educational theory and classroom research. In this book, we bring together examples of the most cogent theoretical work available on the hidden curriculum as well as some of the more recent ethnographic studies.

The Hidden Curriculum and Moral Education is divided into three sections. The first, "Search for a Definition," includes a number of articles that attempt to define the notion of the hidden curriculum and its relationship to the process of schooling. This section provides the reader with a diversity of definitions and also demonstrates a range of perspectives and views that have fueled the debate over the issue of the hidden curriculum.

Section II, "Applications of the Concept," is devoted to a number of studies that use and apply the hidden curriculum concept as an analytical tool in examining different aspects of the schooling process. This section covers a wide range of issues including topics such as the hidden function of IQ testing, sexism in the schools, classroom labeling, and the relationship between class and different teaching styles.

Section III, "From the Hidden Curriculum to Moral Values in Pedagogy," points to the possible prescriptive uses the notion of the hidden curriculum might have for classroom teachers. In other words, in this section we provide a theoretical framework grounded in the assumption that schools are in fact social sites deeply involved in the reproduction of social, political, and moral values. If educators are to lend themselves to a notion of emancipation and social justice in their classrooms, they will find in this last section a series of articles that provide the theoretical underpinnings for just such a task.

Introduction

Maxine Greene

At a time of economic stringency and unabashed technological control, the deficiencies and inequities in American society are becoming more evident than ever before. The doors once called "equal opportunity" are closing; the public school coalitions are breaking apart; special interests battle for local influence; education is becoming the target of conservative philosophies. Even as resources dwindle and confidence ebbs, such terms as *cost-benefit, effectiveness, input-output*, and *productivity* are used repeatedly. And, all the while, public debate and dialogue diminish, overwhelmed by the sounds of impersonal expertise.

This is a time when crucial questions must be posed. If not, a terrible silence will overtake us—broken, now and then, by television evangelists and the murmur of prayers in schools. Americans will stop thinking and talking about how they choose to live together and do the work they have to do; they will stop wondering how they ought to teach their children. Instead, they will acquiesce in weariness, apathy, fear, and hopelessness. Clearly, the time has come for beginning again.

This book may constitute just such a beginning because it provokes the crucial questions. Bringing together much of the trail-breaking writing in the areas of curriculum and moral education, it provides an expanded range of vantage points on our social as well as our educational worlds. Because of the diversity of these vantage points, the illusion of an objectively existent or a petrified "reality" can no longer be maintained, certainly not where the schools are concerned. Not only does it become increasingly clear that what we call *reality* is a function of particular interpretations; but it also becomes evident that we must attend to the origin of those interpretations. The readers of these articles and essays are themselves called upon to assemble their own sense of what is called the "hidden curriculum" and their own meaning of moral education against the confused and troubling backgrounds of today. There are no answers here; there are new and often startling perspectives. There is the hope of fresh commitment. There is the hope that we can transform.

Critical investigation of the hidden curriculum began at a moment when the long-standing myth of the American common school was being replaced by images of actuality. Since the days of its founding, the school had been described as the institution that would "equalize the condition of men," ensure upward mobility for those who were fit, provide a "social balance wheel," and sustain progress. The children who voluntarily complied with the "laws of righteousness" and who achieved "self-control" were assured equal opportunity to "create wealth." Moreover, they were promised personal independence and the benefits of liberty. It was argued—and generally believed—that the school would mediate social and economic change and replace class consciousness with social consciousness. It would bring a democracy into being as—to use John Dewey's words—it educated the mass of children "to personal initiative and adaptability." There were, of course, moments when the faith in schools foundered: on occasion, they were accused of laxness and mediocrity; they were attacked for stressing "critical thinking" or for their secular values or for their neglect of the talented or for their inefficiency. But seldom until the 1960s were schools attacked for their racism, their sexism, their "selecting out" practices when it came to the incapacitated, the neglected, the excluded, or the very poor. Below the surface, the assumption continued that the schools were (or ought to be) agents of social improvement and reform, just as they were (or ought to be) promoters of national security and economic prosperity.

In 1965, when the Elementary and Secondary Education Act was passed and federal money began flowing to the schools, a great resurgence of confidence in the social function of public education took place. The schools, it was suggested, would compensate for deprivation, alleviate poverty, end discrimination. No need was seen for major structural change, for all the revelations forced on the attention of the public by the Civil Rights movement, the community organizers, and the rest. Almost immediately, however, the Coleman Report was commissioned; and people were forced to recognize that gaps in achievement—considered the touchstone—would not be remedied by changes in the school alone. At the same time, the campuses began to stir, the Blacks began calling for basic structural changes and the Vietnamese War provoked widespread disgust and outrage. Protesting students were articulating their own fundamental disillusionment at the spectacle of the "military-industrial establishment" and the "power elite" working their will through higher education. The so-called romantic critics were attracting public attention with their exposures and dramatizations of coercion and manipulation within ostensibly benevolent public schools. Revisionist historians were retelling and recasting the story of education in America, disclosing the ways in which the schools had served the capitalist system through their bureaucratic arrangements, their tracking devices, their testing procedures. Rather than equalizing, it appeared schools had more often than not legitimated class distinctions, stratified the young, frozen people into place.

Equally important was the emerging recognition that in the postindustrial, technological society (responsible not merely for a murderous war but for the first nuclear holocaust in human history), the sciences had lost their innocence and their humanity as well. "Technological" or "functional" rationality had replaced what was once thought of as scientific or experimental intelligence; the growth of positivism had split values off from empirical inquiry and technical expertise. The increasingly potent mass media was reinforcing a false public consciousness of an independently existent, predefined "reality," which then became no longer susceptible to ordinary interpretation or to change.

In the sciences and the social sciences, there were splits and stirrings. Reliance on empiricist norms, on single paradigms, on quantitative measures was challenged here and there in the fields of scholarship. Qualitative methodologies were developed; ethnographic approaches were explored; phenomenological ways of seeing were tried. It was by dint of these nonpositivist and nontechnical modes of inquiry that the glassy and mythicized surfaces of schooling were penetrated and the hidden curriculum disclosed. The discussions that compose this book make clear the meaning and the importance of what was found, as they also make clear the reconceptualizations entailed. Again, the approaches taken are richly diverse, but all appear to be responsive to a "shock of awareness" with respect to the surface structures and, yes, the underlying structures of American society.

The shock was, in part, due to the recognition that the traditional claims —of the equalizing function, as well as the releasing capacities of schools to educate for personal initiative and adaptability—were deceptive. The hidden curriculum—whether it involves what Jane Roland Martin calls "unintended learning states" or is linked to what Elizabeth Vallance calls "social control" or to the "types of work tasks and interactions" that Jean Anyon finds connected to "the unequal structure of economic relationships"—always has a normative or "moral" component. Values, virtues, desirable ways of behaving—these are, intentionally or not, conveyed through social structures, settings, and the ways in which knowledge is distributed. This accounts for the association of moral education with the matter of the hidden curriculum in these pages. It must be said, in addition, that Lawrence Kohlberg's concern for moral reasoning and Carol Gilligan's for the nature of women's moral development, like David Purpel's and Kevin Ryan's, are themselves responses to the fact-value split produced by positivism. If, indeed, the communication of norms is inevitable in the schools of a society, attention ought to be deliberately paid to the kind of teaching that stimulates moral thought and growth rather than fixating it, as some hidden curricula are wont to do. This would make it possible for the young themselves to choose in accord with an ethic of rights and responsibilities—to be actively valuing persons in their interrelationships rather than passive objects of a controlling society.

This comes close to suggesting why most of the writers in this book resist what is often taken for granted in classrooms, wherever they exist. Once children move from the intimacies of family life into the impersonality and organization associated with life in classrooms, they cannot help becoming subject to the pressures of the prevailing ideology, to socialization in its varied forms. In the first place, many of the contributors appear to believe that the norms communicated by the hidden curriculum—because unacknowledged, often more powerful than what is explicitly taught—are in conflict with the values publicly affirmed by an ostensibly free society. Instead of nurturing rational and reflective action, current norms of the hidden curriculum maintain what Paulo Freire calls a "banking" approach to education; they compel an unthinking, nonreflective acceptance of what is presented as a social destiny, even if it is a destiny of failure, deprivation, and powerlessness. In the second place, according to a number of the writers here, there is a political aspect of the phenomenon that has to be confronted. For Henry Giroux and Michael Apple, among others, the hidden curriculum is not unintended, accidental, or simply intrinsic to schooling. They view the familiar functionalist approaches, professionalized knowledge, and even empirical research as mystifying, stultifying, and (crucially) nondialectical. These approaches, knowledge, and research deliberately serve, in consequence, the interests of a materialistic and exploitative society. They are not neutral in the manner claimed; they actually close off discussion of alternative modes of structuring; and, in effect, they give rise to the hidden curriculum.

Is it enough to promote a critical consciousness of the "learning states" or the norms being conveyed? Is it sufficient to work for what James Macdonald calls "liberating growth"? Will "conscientization" empower persons to resist hegemony and gain perspective on control? How much institutional change, how much structural change are required if the schools are to become liberating places with a central and valid moral concern? Henry Giroux, calling for a redefinition of educational theorizing and the development of new political and social theory, joins those who draw ideas from critical theory for emancipation and transformation. In conclusion, a consciousness of possibility informs intentional critique.

This book, then, poses the problems; it is itself a mode of pedagogy. If readers engage with it as colearners, they may find themselves liberated. They may even be empowered to transform.

Search for a Definition

1

Hiding the Hidden Curriculum:
An Interpretation of the Language of Justification in Nineteenth-Century Educational Reform

Elizabeth Vallance

There is a curious discontinuity in the history of educational rhetoric, one that to my knowledge has not yet been seriously explored. The discontinuity appears toward the beginning of the twentieth century as a sudden shift in the ways that schoolpeople and others have justified public schooling in America. Exploring this shift may shed considerable light on a current issue in education, the issue of the schools' "hidden curriculum."

Recently we have witnessed the discovery—or, rather, we have heard the allegation, for the issue is cast most often as criticism—that schools are teaching more than they claim to teach, that they are doing it systematically, and doing it well. A pervasive hidden curriculum has been discovered in operation. The functions of this hidden curriculum have been variously identified as the inculcation of values, political socialization, training in obedience and docility, the perpetuation of traditional class structure— functions that may be characterized generally as social control. Critics allege that, although this function of social control is not acknowledged openly, it is performed nevertheless, perhaps more effectively than the deliberate teaching of intellectual content and skill, the function in whose name we explicitly justify schooling.

But if social control is now called a hidden function of the school, it cannot be called an unfamiliar one. Even the recent literature of discovery

Reprinted from *Curriculum Theory Network* 4:1 (1973/1974): 5-21. Reprinted by permission of John Wiley & Sons, Inc.

and exploration conveys no astonishment at what it has found.[1] The functions of the hidden curriculum are performed openly, sometimes by the most mundane and venerable practices of the schools. If these practices constitute a hidden curriculum, it is hidden only in the sense that the function of social control goes unacknowledged in current rationales for public education. The schools' social-control function has been hidden from the language of justification. Indeed, it has vanished from that language, for much that is today called a hidden function of the schools was previously held to be among the prime benefits of schooling. Until the end of the nineteenth century, American educators argued the case for public education precisely in terms of social control.

This paper is an attempt to understand the hidden curriculum from a historical perspective through a survey of the language of justification for schooling in America. I shall attempt to demonstrate by sketching the development of reform rhetoric up to the end of the nineteenth century that the function of the hidden curriculum had been explicit from the beginning, that it gained in salience as formal education became legitimatized and institutionalized, and that it went underground only when schooling as a social institution was secure enough to turn for its justification from the control of groups to the welfare of individuals. The hidden curriculum became hidden only when schoolpeople were satisfied that it was working.

The [questions are], then: When did reference to the function of the hidden curriculum drop out of the public rationales for schooling and what contributed to this apparent shift in focus? What hid the hidden curriculum?

The Concept of the Hidden Curriculum

The great deal of attention given in recent years to the hidden curriculum has done more to establish the legitimacy of the concept than to clarify its specific referents. That the concept itself is still somewhat loose is apparent in the number of satellite labels that attach themselves to it—including the "unstudied curriculum," the "covert" or "latent" curriculum, the "nonacademic outcomes of schooling," the "by-products of schooling," the "residue of schooling," or simply "what schooling does to people."[2] Each label carries a set of connotations as to what the hidden curriculum is presumed to mean. Let me suggest three dimensions along which these various labels may be read: (1) Hidden curriculum can refer to any of the *contexts* of schooling, including the student-teacher interaction unit, classroom structure, the whole organizational pattern of the educational establishment as a microcosm of the social value system. (2) Hidden curriculum can bear on a number of *processes* operating in or through schools, including values acquisition, socialization, maintenance of class structure. (3) Hidden curric-

ulum can embrace differing *degrees of intentionality* and depth of hiddenness as perceived by the investigator, ranging from incidental and quite
unintended by-products of curricular arrangements to outcomes more
deeply embedded in the historical social function of education. The position that any given conception occupies along these or other continuums
will likely reflect the academic discipline from which the investigator
comes and, not infrequently, his or her political orientation as a critic.

The notion of hidden curriculum used here is a composite of some of the
more salient perspectives on the topic. Dreeben focuses on "what is learned
in school" as a function of the social structure of the classroom and of the
teacher's exercise of authority.[3] Kohlberg identifies the hidden curriculum
as it bears on moral education and the role of the teacher in transmitting
moral standards.[4] Jackson distinguishes the "secondary consequences" of
schooling, the broad range of outcomes that the formal curriculum may
hope to bring about, from the "primary consequences," the lasting impressions that children pick up from the school environment as though by os-
mosis.[5] Henry attends to the relationship between student and teacher, the
rules governing it, and the role of these rules in "educating for docility."[6]
Social critics such as Goodman, Friedenberg, Reimer, and Illich use a conception of the hidden curriculum in order to identify and account for the
schools' reinforcement of the class structure and of certain social norms.[7]
Bowles draws similar inferences with reference to Cuban society.[8] The
notion of hidden curriculum used here borrows from each of these accounts
as well as from other similar accounts of schooling that do not treat the issue
of the hidden curriculum directly.[9] In general, I use the term to refer to those
nonacademic but educationally significant consequences of schooling that
occur systematically but are not made explicit at any level of the public
rationales for education. This usage is intended to include, for example,
both the "Pygmalion effect" of teacher expectations[10] and coming to believe
that art is something one does only on rainy days. It refers broadly to the
social-control function of schooling.

It is difficult, then—and perhaps unwise in the earliest stages of investigation—to be too precise about the meaning of the hidden curriculum. The
very fluidity of the notion offers a rich perspective from which to analyze
the phenomenon of schooling. The idea of a hidden curriculum functions most usefully as a device for identifying those systematic side effects
of schooling that we sense but which cannot be adequately accounted for
by reference to the explicit curriculum. To grapple with the notion at all
is to adopt a critical attitude toward schooling and to allow ourselves to
ask what the institution's nonacademic functions and effects really are.

The Language of Justification: A Historical Overview

There are three major reasons for the focus here on nineteenth-century
rationales for schooling: (1) The nineteenth century offers in microcosm the
range of social conditions that have characterized American society from its

beginnings to the modern era; it witnessed the shift from a predominantly rural to a highly urbanized industrial society. (2) More specifically, the century was an urbanizing one and the history of the hidden curriculum appears to be closely tied to the changing demands of an urban society. (3) Since, as I shall try to demonstrate, the hidden curriculum went underground around the turn of the century, it is important to trace developments up to that time. Because the hidden curriculum can be traced even farther back, I shall make frequent reference to its background in the colonial period. I leave it for another study to trace the career of the hidden curriculum during the twentieth century.

The history of public education in America can be divided roughly into periods. Those established here correspond approximately to quantitative differences in the sheer size of the educational establishment, to significant shifts in patterns of organization, and most pertinently to corresponding shifts in the rhetoric of reform efforts. These periods are: (1) *Prior to the 1830s.* This embraces the colonial period and continues through the era of the common school crusade, when the form of public education was irregular. Schooling was predominantly a rural institution, it was not universal nor compulsory, and it served a very limited population. (2) *Mid-nineteenth century.* The period from the 1830s to the Civil War included the common school reform movement, and the extension of the village school pattern across both the rural society and the gradually growing towns and cities where large numbers of immigrants had begun to settle. The pattern of the district school developed and was extended into the context of cultural diversity that was developing in the cities. (3) *Post-Civil War.* The period from the end of the Civil War to 1900 saw vast industrial expansion and the swelling of the cities by both rural migration and a second wave of immigrants from abroad. During this period the urban school systems became centralized and their control was shifted from the community to the professionals. Also during this period the high school began to come into its own. I shall examine in turn the rationales for schooling characteristic of each period.

Prior to the 1830s: From the Colonial Period

America in the long period preceding and the period immediately following the Revolution was a rural society organized around self-sufficient farms and villages. Its social structure was tied to the small local community struggling for survival in virgin territory; social organization of the territory was without a center. Within each community the burden of socialization fell heavily on the family unit tightly bound by local mores. Formal education in the early part of the period was extremely limited; moral standards and the necessary skills for survival were transmitted through the institutions of family and church. Formal schooling was unsystematic, a rare elite function restricted to the upper classes and reflecting most often the classical and nonutilitarian orientation of the private academy, as in New England, or of the tutor system, as in the South. *Public* schooling did not exist.

Yet the beginnings of a need for social control were there. Bailyn argues that the stable socializing family structure began to break down not long into the colonial period.[11] The wilderness setting proved inadequate to maintain the constraints that had held European society together. In the course of adjusting to new demands, the family structure shifted. Children gained a measure of independence, and changing work patterns and the rising status of women tended to reduce the traditional authority of the male-dominated family unit. Socialization by family and church weakened as the pattern of social contact shifted from the patriarchal kinship group to the more heterogeneous and functionally differentiated village community. By the end of the colonial period, Bailyn maintains, the "once elaborate interpenetration of family and community [had] dissolved" and the child's transition from family to society had lost its "naturalness."[12] Socialization as a smooth, automatic process had lost its traditional base; family and community as educational institutions were no longer adequate.

Early rationales for public schooling were phrased in these terms. Public education was urged as an antidote to this breakdown in the socialization process. Increasing economic complexity made skill learning imperative, and a pattern of independent village schools emerged as a functional response to the needs for socialization and mastery of the three Rs—mastery through the explicitly moral medium of the Bible and the social catechisms of spellers and readers.[13] Thus the 1642, 1647, and 1648 education laws of Massachusetts were an attempt to fill the gap created by rapid social changes in the colony; the "ould deluder Satan" had disrupted a heretofore stable social pattern and created new needs. Because of "the great neglect of many parents and masters in training up their children," and amid allegations of excessive indulgence,[14] public schools were established to restore the pervasively educational climate that children had traditionally enjoyed. Schooling was clearly closing a breach. The earliest public—and denominational—schools in the colonies were largely an adaptive response to recently developed gaps in the traditional process of education.

By the mid-eighteenth century the spirit of nationalism was growing and schooling was coming to be seen as more than a stopgap measure. In addition to assuming the socialization responsibilities borne previously by family and church, schools were called upon to actively form a national character.[15] The language of educational reform preached by those leaders attempting to define and consolidate a new nation was dominated by reference to the need to inculcate a spirit of nationalism, and thereby to establish social control from above. If the states and local communities had earlier seen the need to fill a gap, those intent on creating from these communities a single unified nation saw a broader need. More than simply supplementing the traditional training of the young, the function of education was to actively create what Benjamin Franklin called a "Publick Religion."[16] The generation spanning George Washington, Thomas Jefferson, Benjamin Rush, Benjamin Franklin, and Noah Webster, deliberately engaged in unifying an ethnically and socially diverse population, turned to education for the creation of a homogeneous American public.

Homogeneity was explicitly cited as a goal. Washington advocated public higher education on the grounds that "the more homogeneous our citizens can be made . . . the greater will be our prospect of permanent union."[17] Jefferson argued against foreign education of Americans, preferring a system that would "educate men to manners, morals, and habits perfectly homogeneous with those of the country."[18] Benjamin Rush of Pennsylvania sought to reinforce the "prejudices in favor of our country" through his proposed "one general and uniform system of education" that would "render the mass of the people more homogeneous and thereby fit them more easily for uniform and peaceable government."[19] This demand for the free and uniform republican citizen was echoed by Noah Webster, who called for an education that would produce an "inviolable attachment" to country.

Insofar as it embodied the intent of these educator-statesmen, the pattern of American schooling prior to the 1830s was designed to serve two purposes. First, it was intended to transmit the traditional culture. But the need to perform such a function had become apparent only in the light of unsettling changes in the social structure; family and church were no longer carrying their old share of the educational burden. The pattern of schooling that had been urged as a remedy to this breakdown of the socialization process represented an adaptive, but also a conservative, response. Second, the pattern of schooling had come to serve as a means of creating a specifically national and uniform culture. Schools as agencies of social reform were to inculcate the standards of a public morality and to reinforce the legitimacy of established authority.

Interestingly, this seeking after a homogeneous national character was not seen to demand a leveling of the class structure. In fact, it often sought specifically to maintain what was presumed an inevitable pattern of class differences, but to maintain it peaceably. The rhetoric of justification did not refer to individual betterment as such, nor to the amelioration even of so gross a social difference as that between the aristocracy and the laboring classes. With the provisions of his bill for the greater diffusion of knowledge, Jefferson hoped to "rake a few geniuses from the rubbish" while providing the laboring classes with the basic three Rs. Although a public academy had been established by Franklin to foster the mobility of lower-class youth, its curriculum maintained implicitly the distinction between the practical education that it offered its students and the classical one customarily offered the upper class. Class structure, though acknowledged, was not an issue, and the language of justification could effectively remain at the undifferentiated level of a public morality applicable to all. The rationale for schooling invoked the welfare not of individuals but of the public at large.

Mid Century: The Common Schools and Beyond

The period from the 1830s to the Civil War marks the beginning of urban education in America and, as the era of the common school crusade and the establishment of public school systems, it fixes the emerging rhetoric of the hidden curriculum in the context of a more systematic policy.

This was the era when urban growth became problematic. During the 1830s, the first great wave of post-Revolutionary immigration profoundly changed the established social fabric. The spirit of nationalism engendered in the period of the Revolution (and propounded, as some allege, largely by the elite and educated classes anyway)[20] was threatened by new social turbulence. The patchwork pattern of educational institutions—some supported publicly, some by religious institutions, others by charitable free school societies and private enterprise, and all reflecting the division between elite classical and quasi-public functional schooling—appeared too fragile in the eyes of the 1830s reformers to deal with the new and conflicting needs. The drive to create truly common schools, a move that was to define the system of nationwide public education, began in the settled regions of the East where the threat of conflict and diversity was most keenly felt.

Whereas the Revolutionary generation had felt a need to create a national character, the reformers of the mid-century period were not at all sure that this national character could withstand the onslaught of cultural diversity. It was clear to the common school crusaders that the national character was basically "Anglo-American";[21] the problem facing that character was now one of self-preservation. "To sustain an extended republic like our own," wrote Calvin Stowe in 1836, "there must be a *national* feeling, a national assimilation. . . . It is altogether essential to our national strength and peace that the foreigners should cease to be Europeans and become Americans. Let them be like grafts which become branches of the parent stock."[22] Dr. Daniel Drake described the schoolhouse hopefully as "the crucible of social amalgamation."[23] Conservative support of the common school saw education as a peacekeeping agency, "a wise and liberal system of police, by which property, and life, and the peace of society are secured," thereby purifying "the whole moral atmosphere."[24]

There certainly was concern for the individual child. During this period a genuine compassion for the victims of social inequities appears in the rhetoric for the first time. Horace Mann's passionate humanism and his devotion to the plight of the urban workers is unquestionable.[25] His abiding dedication to equality of opportunity and to the inherent "capability of man for self-government" was a motivating force behind the common school movement. But the persuasive arguments for free public education were presented less on grounds of compassion for individuals than on the basis that the alternative to free public education was a general moral degeneracy and loss of the public peace. Mann himself "overemphasized the effectiveness of morality implanted by education" and "entirely approved of indoctrination" that would prevent the masses from resort to violence; he was "hardly free to think out either an educational or a social philosophy that could challenge the status quo in any fundamental way."[26] Though he welcomed diversity, at the same time he feared "the mob" and the accompanying conflict of values.[27] His work was a move against what he perceived as two dangers, ignorance and vice, and in its course he hoped to stave off the "increasing darkness and degeneracy" threatened by the complex new national situation.

Henry Barnard, after Mann the second great reformer for the cause of the common school, was even less equivocal in his view of its moral function, which he saw as "the first essential" of education.[28] He, too, believed "that the status quo might be preserved if the worst abuses were removed" and seems to have sanctioned "what was virtually the indoctrination of the teachers of youth with capitalistic theory."[29] Whether these and other reformers genuinely desired the well-being of the masses is not at issue here; what is significant is the tone of the language in which the case was argued.

The rationales of the common school reformers in the decades around mid century were at least in part a call, in the name of self-preservation, to assimilate aliens into the national character. The language of justification in this era both continued and extended that of the Revolutionary generation. School was still seen as a supplementary nurturing institution; but it was seen also, now that a national character could be identified, as an active socializing agent to guarantee stability in the face of the growing diversity of the populace. A society newly in conflict over its own identity could respond to such an appeal. Education continued to be justified more as a means of social control than as an instrument of individual betterment.

Post-Civil War: Urbanism and Centralization

The common school crusade won its major battle, of course, and by the period following the Civil War the district-school pattern had become, as much as anything could, a nationwide institution.[30] It was carried from New England westward in virtually the same form it had known in its northeastern origins.

It should be remembered, however, that assertive socialization remained a more prominent feature of urban than of rural schooling. In the simpler and less diverse rural communities, control of the schools still lay largely in the hands of the communities; social control was not commonly cited as a rationale for reform until later in the century, when nostalgia for a vanishing ruralism would prompt educators to advocate consolidating the schools as a means of preserving the rural tradition. A concern for moral conservation continued to dominate rationales for rural schooling.

In urban areas the situation was quite different. The village-school pattern emerging from the previous reform era had been transposed into urban areas as well, and here community control meant immersion of the schools in the baroque machinations of ward politics.[31] Precisely at the moment when there again seemed an urgent need to Americanize and assimilate, local control in urban areas spelled control by ethnic and special interest factions. The cities were a patchwork of ethnic groupings living under volatile slum conditions.[32] A generation of reformers nurtured in the production ethic and confronted by the success of bureaucratic organization in industry found the local politics of urban education maddeningly inefficient. City school boards were vast operations with memberships numbering into the hundreds;[33] they assumed such diverse responsibilities as responding to constituent interests, controlling policy, appointing teachers, and making purchases.[34]

As the sheer size and complexity of urban educational machinery continued to increase, the language of educational reform began to focus more on the organizational structure than on the moral content of schooling. Moral content itself remained undiminished certainly. But in counterpoint with the deliberate Americanizing of the textbooks and the literal washing of the unwashed immigrants, there was a vigorous structural move to centralize. Tyack, Schrag, and Katz have amply documented this movement toward centralization in cities in every corner of the country;[35] by the 1870s and 1880s the pattern was virtually fixed from Portland to Boston.

Implications of centralization. Centralization had clear implications for the curricular and social experiences offered to the children. It is evident from muckraking reports of that era, from reports by the children themselves,[36] and from public documents on educational policy that the standardization and efficiency of both process and product that dominated the public rhetoric had to filter down to affect the classroom experience. Superintendent John Philbrick of Boston, leading an army of vociferous professionals in centralizing and professionalizing the schools, had asserted in 1885 that "the best is the best everywhere" and that movement toward greater centralization would surely be "in the direction of progress and improvement."[37] The quest for the one best system precluded any acknowledgement of local differences and aspired instead to a uniformity of experience.

That the standardization of organizational structure was paralleled by a focus on homogeneity, efficiency, and obedience to authority is clear in an 1874 statement describing the theory and practice of American education. The statement was signed by seventy-seven leading educators, and it held that: (1) a system of public education was necessary to the existence of the "modern industrial community," because (2) the "peculiarities of civil society" in America weaken the family's role in initiating the young into society and "the consequence of this is the increased importance of the school in an ethical point of view," (3) the functions of the school therefore include the development of discipline and the "moral phase" of education must necessarily coincide with "the commercial tone prevalent in the city," which stresses "military precision in the maneuvering of classes. Great stress is laid on punctuality, regularity, attention, and silence, as habits necessary through life" for success in an industrial civilization.[38] The schools, under this description, offered skill training and initiation into the prevailing mode of social organization. Socialization into the industrial mode was the express purpose of the curricular and organizational structure of schools and remained so through the end of the century. In 1891 the Commissioner of Education, William Torrey Harris, frankly admitted that a major purpose of schools was to teach respect for authority and that forming the "habits of punctuality, silence, and industry" was more important than understanding the reasons for good behavior.[39]

That the production-model approach to cultural assimilation did prevail is crucial. Its success is indicated in the numerous muckracking reports issued toward the end of the century as well as in the criticisms of overstandardization made by educators a decade later. Writing in the 1890s, Joseph Mayer Rice vigorously attacked the automatized, regimented, and dehumanized instruction carried out in classrooms dominated by a compulsion to "save the minutes," where children responded in rote manner to a teacher who stood as the unquestioned source of wisdom "giving the child ready-made thoughts"; Rice described the schools of New York as places of mechanical drudgery where "the laws of mental development are entirely ignored."[40] By 1916, the critics of Ellwood P. Cubberley's generation could decry the outcome of this orientation. In that year Cubberley described the Portland public school system as one offering a "rigidly prescribed, mechanical" schooling in which "all must be made as nearly alike as possible."[41]

The painful accounts by social critics and parents at the end of the nineteenth century, and later recollections by students, indicate the bitterness of the conflict induced by the moral domination of the school's culture over the traditional European family norms. Americanization was difficult, but it was leveling out some of the differences and wrenching children away from the inefficiency of cultural diversity. Both those children who hoped only to survive in the public schools and those who actively sought to succeed and thrive followed the schools' dicta and adapted to the norms of obedience. Homogeneity was as much a goal of schooling as it had been over a century before; it was now buttressed by a standardized organizational mode that strengthened the means to that end.

Some Generalizations

At this point let me offer four generalizations about the arguments for education during the period when the present urban orientation of schooling was established. First, public schooling evolved as a response to the declining role of the family and local community. The weakening of traditional educative processes had been the initial impetus to public schooling; rhetoric throughout the nineteenth century continued to claim that training in the home was inadequate and consequently that the school must assume a compensatory burden. Second, the notion of schooling as supplementary socialization becomes altered with reference to the Revolutionary generation. During that period educator-statesmen turned to the schools less to maintain a stable traditional value system than to create a national character where none had existed. In both arguments, the function of education is still cast in moralistic terms. Schools are an agency of undifferentiated social control. Third, the prevalence of social over individual concerns runs consistently through the nineteenth-century language of justification, emerging most strongly in response to the urban developments of that century. The great waves of immigration during the 1830s, the 1880s, and the 1890s produced enormous strains in the cities both on the immigrants themselves and on the Anglo-American character they encountered. Cultural diversity was seen as a problem in both periods of immigration. In both periods schooling was called on actively to socialize and assimilate. But fourth, as Tyack suggests,[42] the bodies of rhetoric in the two immigration periods were different in tone. Though the reformers of the 1830s were more actively oriented toward assimilation and imposition than the Revolutionary generation had had to be, schooling was still viewed as a nurturing agency. By the end of the century the language of justification had become more strident; the element of coercive detention had been added.

Thus the nineteenth century is a significant period in the history of the hidden curriculum. One major characteristic of the period—the growing diversity of cultural and political structures—pushed educators to resume with renewed vigor the language of social control and homogenization that had dominated educational rhetoric from the earliest colonial period. The language of the hidden curriculum was never more explicit than in this period when the rationales for education began shifting focus from an emphasis on supplementary nurture to one on active molding and imposition of values.

Yet the other major characteristic of the period, the growth of a commer-

cial and industrial production ethic and of a cult of rationalism and efficiency, meant that a concern with inculcating values was no longer
enough. In the fragmented political structure of the cities, and therefore
also of education, the reform rhetoric discovered a salient new need. To
assertive socialization was added a focus on organizational efficiency. The
language of production, economic models, and bureaucratic skills came to
dominate the educational reform movements that had the greatest effect on
schooling at the time. The rationale for change shifted from moralism to
functionalism.

At the same time, of course, functionalism became a demand not only of
the educational organizers but of society as a whole. The pressures of
modernization and industrialization in this post-Civil War period produced new demands for skill training and practical learning. The functionalism and means-ends orientation of the educational reformers reflected a
mode that permeated most of American urban society at the time. The
changes of the industrial era demanded more than training in American
morals. For if Horace Mann had seen the school as fashioning a stable
social order, the generation of William T. Harris had to confirm this social
order in the face of threats from without and from within. As apologists for
industrialism, the late-century reformers had to begin dealing with providing specific skills to large numbers of people, developing the capabilities
that would assure survival of the industrial order. Americanize they must,
and organizational reform helped to standardize the product.

But now for the first time educators began talking of an education that
would "fit" the child "for the active life." The curriculum itself had to be
product-oriented, practical, and useful. Schooling became a functional
creature not only organizationally but in intent. The goals became less
unitary.

Hiding the Hidden Curriculum

It was at this point, when the rationale for schooling began to be argued
in functional as well as moral terms, that what we now call the hidden curriculum could safely lose its saliency in the rhetoric. With a shock of recognition we note today that the schools are educating "for docility,"[43] or that
they operate to reinforce a rigid class structure,[44] or that teaching methods
and curriculum content are saturated with a middle-class value bias.[45] These
are precisely the grounds on which American schooling was initially
justified.

I suggest that the hidden curriculum became hidden by the end of the
nineteenth century simply because by that point the rhetoric had done its
job. Schooling had evolved from a supplementary socializing influence to
an active impositional force. By the turn of the century it could be taken for

granted that the schools offered an experience sufficiently homogeneous and regimented. The hidden curriculum was well ensconced. Only when the view of schooling as molder of a common character was at its height did functionalist reforms in organization open the door to a new rhetoric of justification. Only at this point could the need to provide individuals with the tools of economic and social survival offer a rationale for schooling that would rival, and eventually displace, the need to create a homogeneous populace.

A Parallel Development: The Growth of the High School

The clearest confirmation of this process of hiding the hidden curriculum may be a concurrent phenomenon, the rise of public secondary education. Secondary education had not been a major concern of the early nineteenth-century reformers. Jefferson had never intended that the working classes have more than three years of basic schooling. The reformers of Mann's generation spoke in more egalitarian terms, but the scope of their interest was limited nevertheless and did not extend far beyond the goals of basic literacy. In the 1870s William T. Harris boasted that the greatest achievement of the common schools had been their "transformation of an illiterate population into a population that reads the daily newspapers"[46] —in addition to imparting the necessary urban discipline. As long as schooling was seen primarily as a source of social harmony and stability, and only secondarily as a means of personal advancement, extended education was not only unessential but, insofar as it was oriented to the classical curriculum, not even very useful. In his comprehensive study of the high school, Edward Krug documents the sudden growth of public secondary education in the decades following 1880.[47] Both Krug and Cremin trace the development of a demand for the practical in public education.[48] I offer here only a very brief synopsis of this story.

At the end of the century secondary education was by no means widespread. Krug reports that in 1889 the total number of students enrolled in institutions of secondary education, academies and public high schools alike was less than 1 percent of the total population; though within a decade the number had increased by a factor of two and a half, the numerical reach of secondary education was still very restricted. Changes in the patterns and balance of secondary schooling in this period are, however, quite significant, for they reflect important shifts in the public conception of the function of public education.

Attendance at the private academies had been limited, for the most part, to the children of those who could afford the luxury; and public secondary schooling had not accumulated much momentum, even though the first public high school had opened in Boston as early as 1821. Confined as it was to urban areas where longer schooling could be justified, secondary education retained a flavor of elitism simply by virtue of its limited numbers. In 1890 Harvard President Charles W. Eliot reported that "the mass of the rural population—that is to say three-quarters of the American people—is unprovided with secondary schools."[49] Of the one-quarter that was suitably provided, very few availed themselves of the chance. And though even fewer actually went on to college—less than 10 percent of secondary students—college preparation strongly influenced the curriculum; a secondary education was scarcely a practical one.

In the post-Civil War era, however, there arose a demand for practical education, which a few decades later would reach much greater proportions. In this period, vocationalism as such was not yet a major theme in education, but it was emerging significantly in the establishment of manual training and agricultural programs beginning in the late 1870s, as well as in the growing demand for high school programs offering commercial courses. The public high school grew partially in response to the sheer increase in numbers of children who could afford to extend their education, and partially therefore in response to a need for a more practical education than either the elementary school or the classically oriented secondary curriculums could provide.

The high school developed as an urban institution. It was a creature of late-nineteenth-century urbanization and the new demands it created. By the 1880s public high schools began to outnumber the academies as institutions of secondary education, increasing in number from 2,520 in 1890 to 6,005 ten years later.[50] Reasons for the rise of the high school in this period are varied. One was the sheer increase in urban population as a function of rural migration. Another was the growth of technology and its demand for more advanced occupational skills. The inability of the elementary schools to fully equip students for assimilation into the urban situation was clear; and it is possible that the elementary school's emphasis on homogeneity, and its consequent disinclination to acknowledge individual needs and interests by differentiating its programs, provided the necessary impetus for the growth of secondary education. The explicit social control function assigned to the elementary schools meant that their curriculum was necessarily standardized and uniform, that the products of these schools could be assumed to have certain backgrounds in common, and that any necessary specialized training would have to be provided by an institution other than the elementary school.

Thus the high school, as a relatively novel element in the educational structure, was able to evolve its own rationale. In the role of "the people's college" it assumed responsibilities attendant on it as the highest level of education to which most people could aspire. As chief agent of social mobility it had to be able both to prepare students for higher education and also (mainly) to "prepare for the duties of life," performing "the two-fold function of the 'fitting' and the 'finishing' school."[51] It was thus forced to diversify its curriculum to meet the needs of diverse groups of students. In 1892, Eliot's Committee of Ten, although allegedly prompted by a concern for the lack of articulation between secondary schooling and the colleges, proposed a package of four separate curricula for high schools.[52] The high school was compelled to be responsive to diversity in a way that the elementary school had never been. It became, in a sense, a vehicle by which the explicit curriculum came to be tailored to the needs of the individual. The demands placed on the late-nineteenth-century high school offered a starting point for orienting education as much to the demands of the individual as to the undifferentiated need for societal homogeneity and uniform social control. The high school was made necessary partly, I suggest, by the effectiveness of the hidden curriculum at the elementary level. It was the vehicle for the progressive individualization of the curriculum. As such it helped to accomplish the hiding of the hidden curriculum.

With the rise of public secondary education around 1900, then, we see the clearest indication of the nineteenth-century shift in the rationale for schooling. Education came to be justified less from the top down than from the bottom up. The burden of the argument began to shift from the need to impose homogeneity to the social needs of the individual. Social control was not abandoned as an aim; it simply shifted its visibility as the goals of education came to be phrased in terms of individual development *within* the social content.

Though direct reference to social and moral shaping has occasionally re-emerged in the period since 1900—the public reaction to the Red Scare and McCarthyism is but one example—a progressive personalization of the curriculum and of the goals of education has continued to saturate the language of justification since the turn of the century. By 1918 the Committee on the Reorganization of Secondary Education could state that "education in a democracy . . . should develop in each individual the knowledge, interests, ideals, habits and powers whereby he will find his place and use that place to shape both himself and society toward ever nobler ends."[53] Social control is there, but hidden through reference to the individual. The shift in emphasis is enormous; I suspect it would have been impossible if the hidden curriculum had not been taken for granted.

Rediscovery

It is beyond the scope of this paper to develop the notion that the language of justification of modern education has been phrased increasingly in terms of the welfare of individuals. Some sketchy evidence for the altered emphasis appears in the thrust, and in the very names, of those movements, campaigns, and enthusiasms that have marked the progress of twentieth-century education—the child-study movement and the measurement of individual differences, progressive education and the child-centered school, the development of a psychology of learning, and individualized instruction. Surely the individual has come into his or her own. In 1961 the Educational Policy Commission stated the goals of American education in these terms: "to foster that development of individual capacities which will enable each human being to become the best person he is capable of becoming. . . . The general morality depends on choices made by individuals."[54] The four major goals of schooling were given as "self-realization, human relationship, economic efficiency, and civic responsibility," in that order— which is a long way from creating the "homogeneous American."

That Reimer, Goodman, Friedenberg, and Henry, to name a few, are now criticizing the schools for having succeeded in the very purposes they initially set for themselves is perhaps ironic. But in a sense it is not surprising that growing attention to the individual, and to the role of the social environment in individual growth, should be accompanied by the discovery that a hidden curriculum is operating in the schools. It is tempting to suggest that it was not until the effectiveness of the hidden curriculum could be taken for granted that educators were able to turn their attention to other matters and begin to understand and respond to the unique problems of the learning process itself. That the schooling experience might not be the same for every child was perhaps a discovery that could not have been made until the context of learning had been sufficiently standardized to make such comparisons pertinent. This is not to say that the hidden curriculum's effectiveness was a good thing. It is simply to suggest, and only very tentatively, that there may be a line of development in fact from the explicitness of nineteenth-century educational rhetoric, to its success in establishing social control and a uniform learning context, to the subsequent dropping of the social-control function from the rhetoric, and to the rediscovery of it as an explanation for the peculiarly systematic, though allegedly unintended, outcomes of schooling. Those outcomes may not be nearly as unintended as we think. They may be hidden from the rhetoric precisely because they do work.

What to do with the hidden curriculum now that we have found it is an open question. We can embrace it wholeheartedly once again, attempt to expunge it altogether, or most likely something in between these two extremes. This survey of the language of justification of school reform suggests that the hidden curriculum is so deeply embedded in our whole conception of schooling that while it no longer needs to be made explicit, neither can it merely be washed away. The history of the language of justification throughout the nineteenth century should give us a better idea of what modifying the hidden curriculum might entail.

Notes

1. See, for example, N. Overly, ed., *The Unstudied Curriculum: Its Impact on Children* (Washington, D.C.: Association for Supervision and Curriculum Development, 1970).

2. Ibid.; E. Vallance, "Introduction to the Bibliography: Conceptualizing the Hidden Curriculum" (Unpublished manuscript, 1972).

3. R. Dreeben, "The Contribution of Schooling to the Learning of Norms," *Harvard Educational Review* 37: 2 (Spring 1967): 211–37; id., *On What Is Learned in School* (Reading, Mass.: Addison-Wesley, 1968); id., "Schooling and Authority: Comments on the Unstudied Curriculum," in *The Unstudied Curriculum,* ed. Overly.

4. L. Kohlberg, "The Moral Atmosphere of the School," in *The Unstudied Curriculum,* ed. Overly.

5. P. Jackson, "The Consequences of Schooling," in *The Unstudied Curriculum,* ed. Overly.

6. J. Henry, "Attitude Organization in Elementary School Classrooms," *American Journal of Orthopsychiatry* 27 (1957): 117–33; id., "Docility, or Giving Teacher What She Wants," *Journal of Social Issues* 2: 2 (1955): 33–41.

7. P. Goodman, *Growing Up Absurd* (New York: Random House, 1960); id., *Compulsory Mis-Education* (New York: Horizon Press, 1964); E. Z. Friedenberg, *Coming of Age in America: Growth and Acquiescence* (New York: Random House, 1965); id., "New Value Conflicts in American Education," *School Review* 74: 1 (Spring 1966): 66–94; id., "Curriculum as Educational Process: The Middle Class Against Itself," in *The Unstudied Curriculum,* ed. Overly; E. Reimer, *School Is Dead: Alternatives in Education,* 1st ed. (Garden City, N.Y.: Doubleday, 1971); I. Illich, *Deschooling Society* (New York: Harper & Row, 1971).

8. S. Bowles, "Cuban Education and the Revolutionary Ideology," *Harvard Educational Review* 41: 4 (November 1971): 472–500.

9. Vallance, "Introduction to the Bibliography."

10. R. Rosenthal and Lenore Jacobson, *Pygmalion in the Classroom: Teacher Expectation and Pupils' Intellectual Development* (New York: Holt, Rinehart & Winston, 1968).

11. B. Bailyn, *Education in the Forming of American Society: Needs and Opportunities for Study* (Chapel Hill: University of North Carolina Press, 1960).

12. Ibid., p. 25.

13. C. Johnson, *Old Time Schools and School Books* (New York: Dover, 1963); D. Tyack, *Turning Points in American Educational History* (Waltham, Mass.: Blaisdell, 1967).

14. Tyack, *Turning Points,* pp. 14–16.

15. Ibid.

16. Ibid., p. 75.

17. Ibid., p. 85.

18. Ibid.

19. Ibid., p. 103.

20. C. Beard and M. Beard, *An Economic Interpretation of the Constitution of the United States* (New York: Free Press, 1935).

21. Tyack, *Turning Points.*

22. Ibid., p. 149.

23. Ibid., p. 150.

24. Ibid., p. 126.

25. M. Curti, *The Social Ideas of American Educators* (Paterson, N.J.: Littlefield, Adams, 1959); Tyack, *Turning Points.*

26. Curti, *Social Ideas,* pp. 125–31.

27. Tyack, *Turning Points.*

28. Curti, *Social Ideas,* p. 142.

29. Ibid., pp. 147–54.

30. E. P. Cubberley, *Rural Life and Education* (New York: Houghton Mifflin Co., 1914).

31. M. Katz, *Class, Bureaucracy and Schools: The Illusion of Educational Change in America* (New York: Praeger, 1971); P. Schrag, *Village School Downtown: Politics and Education* (Boston: Beacon Press, 1967); D. Tyack, "Bureaucracy and the Common School: The Example of Portland, Oregon, 1851–1913," *American Quarterly* 19: 3 (Fall 1967); id. *From Village School to Urban System: A Political and Social History* (Washington, D.C.: United States Office of Education, 1972).

32. J. Riis, *How the Other Half Lives* (New York: Hill & Wang, 1957).

33. D. Tyack, *Village School to Urban System;* id., "City Schools: Centralization of Control at the Turn of the Century," in *The Organizational Society,* ed. J. Israel (New York: Free Press, 1972).

34. Schrag, *Village School Downtown;* Tyack, *Village School to Urban System;* Tyack, "City Schools."

35. Tyack, "Bureaucracy and the Common School"; Tyack, *Village School to Urban System;* Tyack, "City Schools"; Schrag, *Village School Downtown;* Katz, *Class, Bureaucracy and Schools.*

36. Tyack, "City Schools."

37. J. D. Philbrick, *City School Systems in the United States,* 1885, reprint, U.S. Bureau of Education, Circulars of Information, no. 1 (Washington, D.C.: U.S. Government Printing Office), p. 19.

38. Tyack, *Turning Points,* pp. 325–26.

39. Curti, *Social Ideas of American Educators,* p. 334.

40. Tyack, *Turning Points,* pp. 329–32.

41. Ibid., p. 333.

42. Tyack, *Village School to Urban System.*

43. Henry, "Giving Teacher What She Wants."

44. Illich, *Deschooling Society;* Reimer, *School Is Dead.*

45. Kohlberg, "Moral Atmosphere of School."

46. Tyack, *Village School to Urban System.*

47. E. A. Krug, *The Shaping of the American High School* (New York: Harper & Row, 1964).

48. L. Cremin, *The Transformation of the School: Progressivism in American Education* (New York: Random House, 1961).

49. Tyack, *Turning Points,* p. 354.

50. Krug, *American High School.*

51. Tyack, *Turning Points,* p. 390.

52. Krug, *American High School.*

53. Tyack, *Turning Points,* p. 399.

54. Ibid., pp. 408–09.

Additional Readings

Easton, D., and J. Dennis, "The Child's Acquisition of Regime Norms; Political Efficacy." *American Political Science Review* 61: 1 (1967): 25–38.

Hays, Samuel P. "The Politics of Reform in Municipal Government in the Progressive Era." *Pacific North-West Quarterly* 55 (October 1964): 157–69.

Henry, Jules. *Culture Against Man.* New York: Random House, 1963.

Hess, Robert D., and David Easton, "The Role of the Elementary School in Political Socialization." *School Review* 70 (Autumn 1952): 257–65.

Hess, Robert D., and Judith V. Torney, *The Development of Political Attitudes of Children.* Chicago: Aldine, 1967.

Jackson, Philip. "The Way Teaching Is." In *The Way Teaching Is,* edited by C. Hitchcock. Washington, D.C.: Association for Supervision and Curriculum Development, 1966.

Tyack, David. "Views From Below." Colloquium on History of American Urban Education, Ed. 302. Stanford University. Mimeographed.

Vallance, Elizabeth. "The Later Case for Consolidation: Romanticism in Rural School Reform." Unpublished manuscript. 1972.

2

The Daily Grind . . .

Philip Jackson

On a typical weekday morning between September and June some 35 million Americans kiss their loved ones goodbye, pick up their lunch pails and books, and leave to spend their day in that collection of enclosures (totaling about one million) known as elementary school classrooms. This massive exodus from home to school is accomplished with a minimum of fuss and bother. Few tears are shed (except perhaps by the very youngest) and few cheers are raised. The school attendance of children is such a common experience in our society that those of us who watch them go hardly pause to consider what happens to them when they get there. Of course our indifference disappears occasionally. When something goes wrong or when we have been notified of his remarkable achievement, we might ponder, for a moment at least, the meaning of the experience for the child in question, but most of the time we simply note that our Johnny is on his way to school, and now it is time for our second cup of coffee.

Parents are interested, to be sure, in how *well* Johnny does while there, and when he comes trudging home they may ask him questions about what happened today or, more generally, how things went. But both their questions and his answers typically focus on the highlights of the school experience—its unusual aspects—rather than on the mundane and seemingly trivial events that filled the bulk of his school hours. Parents are

Reprinted from *Life in Classrooms*, by Philip W. Jackson. Copyright © by Holt, Rinehart and Winston, Inc. Reprinted by permission of Holt, Rinehart and Winston.

interested, in other words, in the spice of school life rather than in its substance.

Teachers, too, are chiefly concerned with only a very narrow aspect of a youngster's school experience. They, too, are likely to focus on specific acts of misbehavior or accomplishment as representing what a particular student did in school today, even though the acts in question occupied but a small fraction of the student's time. Teachers, like parents, seldom ponder the significance of the thousands of fleeting events that combine to form the routine of the classroom.

And the student himself is no less selective. Even if someone bothered to question him about the minutiae of his school day, he would probably be unable to give a complete account of what he had done. For him, too, the day has been reduced in memory into a small number of signal events—"I got 100 on my spelling test," "A new boy came and he sat next to me"—or recurring activities—"We went to gym," "We had music." His spontaneous recall of detail is not much greater than that required to answer our conventional questions.

This concentration on the highlights of school life is understandable from the standpoint of human interest. A similar selection process operates when we inquire into or recount other types of daily activity. When we are asked about our trip downtown or our day at the office we rarely bother describing the ride on the bus or the time spent in front of the watercooler. Indeed, we are more likely to report that nothing happened than to catalog the pedestrian actions that took place between home and return. Unless something interesting occurred there is little purpose in talking about our experience.

Yet from the standpoint of giving shape and meaning to our lives these events about which we rarely speak may be as important as those that hold our listener's attention. Certainly they represent a much larger portion of our experience than do those about which we talk. The daily routine, the "rat race," and the infamous "old grind" may be brightened from time to time by happenings that add color to an otherwise drab existence, but the grayness of our daily lives has an abrasive potency of its own. Anthropologists understand this fact better than do most other social scientists, and their field studies have taught us to appreciate the cultural significance of the humdrum elements of human existence. This is the lesson we must heed as we seek to understand life in elementary classrooms.

I

School is a place where tests are failed and passed, where amusing things happen, where new insights are stumbled upon, and skills acquired. But it is also a place in which people sit, and listen, and wait, and raise their hands, and pass out paper, and stand in line, and sharpen pencils. School is where we encounter both friends and foes, where imagination is unleashed and misunderstanding brought to ground. But it is also a place in which yawns are stifled and initials scratched on desktops, where milk money is collected and recess lines are formed. Both aspects of school life, the celebrated and the unnoticed, are familiar to all of us, but the latter, if only because of its characteristic neglect, seems to deserve more attention than it has received to date from those who are interested in education.

In order to appreciate the significance of trivial classroom events it is necessary to consider the frequency of their occurrence, the standardization of the school environment, and the compulsory quality of daily attendance. We must recognize, in other words, that children are in school for a long time, that the settings in which they perform are highly uniform, and that they are there whether they want to be or not. Each of these three facts, although seemingly obvious, deserves some elaboration, for each contributes to our understanding of how students feel about and cope with their school experience.

The amount of time children spend in school can be described with a fair amount of quantitative precision, although the psychological significance of the numbers involved is another matter entirely. In most states the school year legally comprises 180 days. A full session on each of those days usually lasts about six hours (with a break for lunch), beginning somewhere around nine o'clock in the morning and ending about three o'clock in the afternoon. Thus, if a student never misses a day during the year, he spends a little more than one thousand hours under the care and tutelage of teachers. If he has attended kindergarten and was reasonably regular in his attendance during the grades, he will have logged a little more than seven thousand classroom hours by the time he is ready for junior high school.

The magnitude of seven thousand hours spread over six or seven years of a child's life is difficult to comprehend. On the one hand, when placed beside the total number of hours the child has lived during those years it is not very great—slightly more than one-tenth of his life during the time in question, about one-third of his hours of sleep during that period. On the other hand, aside from sleeping, and perhaps playing, there is no other activity that occupies as much of the child's time as that involved in attending school. Apart from the bedroom (where he has his eyes closed most of the time) there is no single enclosure in which he spends a longer time than he does in the classroom. From the age of six onward he is a more familiar sight to his teacher than to his father, and possibly even to his mother.

Another way of estimating what all those hours in the classroom mean is to ask how long it would take to accumulate them while engaged in some other familiar and recurring activity. Church attendance provides an interesting comparison. In order to have had as much time in church as a sixth grader has had in classrooms we would have to spend all day at a religious gathering every Sunday for more than 24 years. Or, if we prefer our devotion in smaller doses, we would have to attend a one-hour service every Sunday for 150 years before the inside of a church became as familiar to us as the inside of a school is to a twelve-year-old.

The comparison with church attendance is dramatic, and perhaps overly so. But it does make us stop and think about the possible significance of an otherwise meaningless number. Also, aside from the home and the school there is no physical setting in which people of all ages congregate with as great a regularity as they do in church.

The translation of the child's tenure in class into terms of weekly church attendance serves a further purpose. It sets the stage for considering an important similarity between the two institutions: school and church. The inhabitants of both are surrounded by a stable and highly stylized environment. The fact of prolonged exposure in either setting increases in its meaning as we begin to consider the elements of repetition, redundancy, and ritualistic action that are experienced there.

A classroom, like a church auditorium, is rarely seen as being anything other than that which it is. No one entering either place is likely to think that he is in a living room, or a grocery store, or a train station. Even if he entered at midnight or at some other time when the activities of the people would not give the function away, he would have no difficulty understanding what was *supposed* to go on there. Even devoid of people, a church is a church and a classroom, a classroom.

This is not to say, of course, that all classrooms are identical, any more than all churches are. Clearly there are differences, and sometimes very extreme ones, between any two settings. One has only to think of the wooden benches and planked floor of the early American classroom as compared with the plastic chairs and tile flooring in today's suburban schools. But the resemblance is still there despite the differences, and, more important, during any particular historical period the differences are not that great. Also, whether the student moves from first to sixth grade on floors of vinyl tile or oiled wood, whether he spends his days in front of a black blackboard or a green one, is not as important as the fact that the environment in which he spends these six or seven years is highly stable.

In their efforts to make their classrooms more homelike, elementary school teachers often spend considerable time fussing with the room's decorations. Bulletin boards are changed, new pictures are hung, and the seating arrangement is altered from circles to rows and back again. But these

are surface adjustments at best, resembling the work of the inspired house-
wife who rearranges the living room furniture and changes the color of the
drapes in order to make the room more "interesting." School bulletin
boards may be changed but they are never discarded, the seats may be
rearranged but thirty of them are there to stay, the teacher's desk may have a
new plant on it but there it sits, as ubiquitous as the roll-down maps, the
olive drab wastebasket, and the pencil sharpener on the window ledge.

Even the odors of the classroom are fairly standardized. Schools may use
different brands of wax and cleaning fluid, but they all seem to contain
similar ingredients, a sort of universal smell which creates an aromatic background that permeates the entire building. Added to this, in each classroom,
is the slightly acrid scent of chalk dust and the faint hint of fresh wood from
the pencil shavings. In some rooms, especially at lunch time, there is the
familiar odor of orange peels and peanut butter sandwiches, a blend that
mingles in the late afternoon (following recess) with the delicate pungency
of children's perspiration. If a person stumbled into a classroom blind-
folded, his nose alone, if he used it carefully, would tell him where he was.

All of these sights and smells become so familiar to students and teachers
alike that they exist dimly, on the periphery of awareness. Only when the
classroom is encountered under somewhat unusual circumstances, does it
appear, for a moment, a strange place filled with objects that command our
attention. On these rare occasions when, for example, students return to
school in the evening, or in the summer when the halls ring with the
hammers of workmen, many features of the school environment that have
merged into an undifferentiated background for its daily inhabitants suddenly stand out in sharp relief. This experience, which obviously occurs in
contexts other than the classroom, can only happen in settings to which the
viewer has become uncommonly habituated.

Not only is the classroom a relatively stable physical environment, it also
provides a fairly constant social context. Behind the same old desks sit the
same old students; in front of the familiar blackboard stands the familiar
teacher. There are changes, to be sure—some students come and go during
the year and on a few mornings the children are greeted at the door by a
strange adult. But in most cases these events are sufficiently uncommon to
create a flurry of excitement in the room. Moreover, in most elementary
classrooms the social composition is not only stable, it is also physically
arranged with considerable regularity. Each student has an assigned seat
and, under normal circumstances, that is where he is to be found. The
practice of assigning seats makes it possible for the teacher or a student to
take attendance at a glance. A quick visual sweep is usually sufficient to
determine who is there and who is not. The ease with which this procedure
is accomplished reveals more eloquently than do words how accustomed
each member of the class is to the presence of every other member.

An additional feature of the social atmosphere of elementary classrooms deserves at least passing comment. There is a social intimacy in schools that is unmatched elsewhere in our society. Buses and movie theaters may be more crowded than classrooms, but people rarely stay in such densely populated settings for extended periods of time and while there, they usually are not expected to concentrate on work or to interact with each other. Even factory workers are not clustered as close together as students in a standard classroom. Indeed, imagine what would happen if a factory the size of a typical elementary school contained three or four hundred adult workers. In all likelihood the unions would not allow it. Only in schools do thirty or more people spend several hours each day literally side by side. Once we leave the classroom we seldom again are required to have contact with so many people for so long a time. This fact will become particularly relevant [when] we treat the social demands of life in school.

A final aspect of the constancy experienced by young students involves the ritualistic and cyclic quality of the activities carried on in the classroom. The daily schedule, as an instance, is commonly divided into definite periods during which specific subjects are to be studied or specific activities engaged in. The content of the work surely changes from day to day and from week to week, and in this sense there is considerable variety amid the constancy. But spelling still comes after arithmetic on Tuesday morning, and when the teacher says, "All right class, now take out your spellers," his announcement comes as no surprise to the students. Further, as they search in their desks for their spelling textbooks, the children may not know what new words will be included in the day's assignment, but they have a fairly clear idea of what the next twenty minutes of class time will entail.

Despite the diversity of subject matter content, the identifiable forms of classroom activity are not great in number. The labels: "seatwork," "group discussion," "teacher demonstration," and "question-and-answer period" (which would include work "at the board"), are sufficient to categorize most of the things that happen when class is in session. "Audio-visual display," "testing session," and "games" might be added to the list, but in most elementary classrooms they occur rarely.

Each of these major activities is performed according to rather well-defined rules which the students are expected to understand and obey—for example, no loud talking during seatwork, do not interrupt someone else during discussion, keep your eyes on your own paper during tests, raise your hand if you have a question. Even in the early grades these rules are so well understood by the students (if not completely internalized) that the teacher has only to give very abbreviated signals ("Voices, class." "Hands, please.") when violations are perceived. In many classrooms a weekly time schedule is permanently posted so that everyone can tell at a glance what will happen next.

Thus, when our young student enters school in the morning he is entering an environment with which he has become exceptionally familiar through prolonged exposure. Moreover, it is a fairly stable environment— one in which the physical objects, social relations, and major activities remain much the same from day to day, week to week, and even, in certain respects, from year to year. Life there resembles life in other contexts in some ways, but not all. There is, in other words, a uniqueness to the student's world. School, like church and home, is someplace special. Look where you may, you will not find another place quite like it.

There is an important fact about a student's life that teachers and parents often prefer not to talk about, at least not in front of students. This is the fact that young people have to be in school, whether they want to be or not. In this regard students have something in common with the members of two other of our social institutions that have involuntary attendance: prisons and mental hospitals. The analogy, though dramatic, is not intended to be shocking, and certainly there is no comparison between the unpleasantness of life for inmates of our prisons and mental institutions, on the one hand, and the daily travails of a first or second grader, on the other. Yet the schoolchild, like the incarcerated adult, is, in a sense, a prisoner. He too must come to grips with the inevitability of his experience. He too must develop strategies for dealing with the conflict that frequently arises between his natural desires and interests on the one hand and institutional expectations on the other. Several of these strategies will be discussed in the chapters that follow. Here it is sufficient to note that the thousands of hours spent in the highly stylized environment of the elementary classroom are not, in an ultimate sense, a matter of choice, even though some children might prefer school to play. Many seven-year-olds skip happily to school, and as parents and teachers we are glad they do, but we stand ready to enforce the attendance of those who are more reluctant. And our vigilance does not go unnoticed by children.

In sum, classrooms are special places. The things that happen there and the ways in which they happen combine to make these settings different from all others. This is not to say, of course, that there is no similarity between what goes on in school and the students' experiences elsewhere. Classrooms are indeed like homes and churches and hospital wards in many important respects. But not in all.

The things that make schools different from other places are not only the paraphernalia of learning and teaching and the educational content of the dialogues that take place there, although these are the features that are usually singled out when we try to portray what life in school is really like. It is true that nowhere else do we find blackboards and teachers and textbooks in such abundance and nowhere else is so much time spent on reading, writing, and arithmetic. But these obvious characteristics do not constitute all that is unique about this environment. There are other features, much less obvious though equally omnipresent, that help to make up "the facts of life," as it were, to which students must adapt. From the standpoint of understanding the impact of school life on the student, some features of the classroom that are not immediately visible are fully as important as those that are.

The characteristics of school life to which we now turn our attention are not commonly mentioned by students, at least not directly, nor are they apparent to the casual observer. Yet they are as real, in a sense, as the unfinished portrait of Washington that hangs above the cloakroom door. They comprise three facts of life with which even the youngest student must learn to deal and may be introduced by the key words: *crowds, praise,* and *power.*

Learning to live in a classroom involves, among other things, learning to live in a crowd. This simple truth has already been mentioned, but it requires greater elaboration. Most of the things that are done in school are done with others, or at least in the presence of others, and this fact has profound implications for determining the quality of a student's life.

Of equal importance is the fact that schools are basically evaluative settings. The very young student may be temporarily fooled by tests that are presented as games, but it doesn't take long before he begins to see through the subterfuge and comes to realize that school, after all, is a serious business. It is not only what you do there but what others think of what you do that is important. Adaptation to school life requires the student to become used to living under the constant condition of having his words and deeds evaluated by others.

School is also a place in which the division between the weak and the powerful is clearly drawn. This may sound like a harsh way to describe the separation between teachers and students, but it serves to emphasize a fact that is often overlooked, or touched upon gingerly at best. Teachers are indeed more powerful than students, in the sense of having greater responsibility for giving shape to classroom events, and this sharp difference in authority is another feature of school life with which students must learn how to deal.

In three major ways then—as members of crowds, as potential recipients of praise or reproof, and as pawns of institutional authorities—students are confronted with aspects of reality that at least during their childhood years are relatively confined to the hours spent in classrooms. Admittedly, similar conditions are encountered in other environments. Students, when they are not performing as such, must often find themselves lodged within larger groups, serving as targets of praise or reproof, and being bossed around or guided by persons in positions of higher authority. But these kinds of experiences are particularly frequent while school is in session and it is likely during this time that adaptive strategies having relevance for other contexts and other life periods are developed.

In the sections of this chapter to follow, each of the three classroom qualities that have been briefly mentioned will be described in greater detail. Particular emphasis will be given to the manner in which students cope with
these aspects of their daily lives. The goal of this discussion . . . is to deepen
our understanding of the peculiar mark that school life makes on us all.

II

Anyone who has ever taught knows that the classroom is a busy place,
even though it may not always appear so to the casual visitor. Indeed, recent
data have proved surprising even to experienced teachers. For example, we
have found in one study of elementary classrooms that the teacher engages
in as many as one thousand interpersonal interchanges each day.[1] An
attempt to catalog the interchanges among students or the physical movement of class members would doubtlessly add to the general impression that
most classrooms, though seemingly placid when glimpsed through the
window in the hall door, are more like the proverbial beehive of activity.
One way of understanding the meaning of this activity for those who
experience it is by focusing on the teacher as he goes about channeling the
social traffic of the classroom.

First, consider the rapidity of the teacher's actions. What keeps him
hopping from Jane to Billy to Sam, and back again, in the space of a few
seconds? Clearly, much of this activity is done in the interest of instruction.
Teaching commonly involves talking, and the teacher acts as a gatekeeper
who manages the flow of the classroom dialogue. When a student wishes to
say something during a discussion it is usually the teacher's job to recognize
his wish and to invite his comment. When more than one person wishes to
enter the discussion or answer a question at the same time (a most common
event), it is the teacher who decides who will speak and in what order. Or we
might turn the observation around and say that the teacher determines who
will *not* speak, for when a group of students have signaled the desire to
enter the dialogue, several of them may be planning to say the same thing.
Therefore, if Johnny is called on first, Billy, who also had his hand raised,
may now find himself without anything to say. This fact partially explains
the urgency with which the desire to speak is signaled to the teacher.

Another time-consuming task for the teacher, at least in the elementary
school, is that of serving as supply sergeant. Classroom space and material
resources are limited and the teacher must allocate these resources judici-
ously. Only one other student at a time can borrow the big scissors, or look
through the microscope, or drink from the drinking fountain, or use the
pencil sharpener. And broken pencil points and parched throats obviously
do not develop one at a time or in an orderly fashion. Therefore, the number
of students desiring to use various classroom resources at any given moment

is often greater than the number that can use them. This explains the lines of students that form in front of the pencil sharpener, the drinking fountain, the microscope, and the washroom door.

Closely related to the job of doling out material resources is that of granting special privileges to deserving students. In elementary classrooms it is usually the teacher who assigns coveted duties, such as serving on the safety patrol, or running the movie projector, or clapping the erasers, or handing out supplies. In most classrooms volunteers are plentiful, thus the jobs are often rotated among the students. (A list of current job-holders is a familiar item on elementary school bulletin boards.) Although the delegation of these duties may not take up much of the teacher's time, it does help to give structure to the activities of the room and to fashion the quality of the total experience for many of the participants.

A fourth responsibility of the teacher, and one that calls our attention to another important aspect of classroom life, is that of serving as an official timekeeper. It is he who sees to it that things begin and end on time, more or less. He determines the proper moment for switching from discussion to workbooks, or from spelling to arithmetic. He decides whether a student has spent too long in the washroom, or whether those who take the bus may be dismissed. In many schools he is assisted in this job by elaborate systems of bells and buzzers. But even when the school day is mechanically punctuated by clangs and hums, the teacher is not entirely relieved of his responsibility for watching the clock. The implications of the teacher clock-watching behavior for determining what life in school is like are indeed profound. This behavior reminds us, above all, that school is a place where things often happen not because students want them to, but because it is time for them to occur.

All of the teacher's actions described so far are bound together by a common theme. They are all responsive, in one way or another, to the crowded condition of the classroom. If the teacher dealt with one student at a time (as does happen in tutorial settings), most of the tasks that have been mentioned would be unnecessary. It is, in part, the press of numbers and of time that keeps the teacher so busy. But our ultimate concern, it must be remembered, is with the student and the quality of *his* life in the classroom. Therefore, the frenetic activity of the teacher as he goes about calling on students, handing out supplies, granting privileges, and turning activities on and off is of interest, within the present context, only insofar as that behavior tells us something about what school is like for those who are at the receiving end of the teacher's action.

The things the teacher does as he works within the physical, temporal, and social limits of the classroom have a constraining effect upon the events that might occur there if individual impulse were allowed free reign. If everyone who so desired tried to speak at once, or struggled for possession of the big scissors, or offered a helping hand in threading the movie projector, classroom life would be much more hectic than it commonly is. If students were allowed to stick with a subject until they grew tired of it on their own, our present curriculum would have to be modified drastically. Obviously, some kinds of controls are necessary if the school's goals are to be reached and social chaos averted. The question of whether the teacher should or should not serve as a combination traffic cop, judge, supply sergeant, and timekeeper is somewhat irrelevant to the present discussion, but the fact that such functions must be performed, even if the responsibility for performing them falls upon individual students, is far from irrelevant. For a world in which traffic signs, whistles, and other regulatory devices abound is quite different from one in which these features are absent.

One of the inevitable outcomes of traffic management is the experiencing of delay. In crowded situations where people are forced to take turns in using limited resources, some must stand by until others have finished. When people are required to move as a group toward a goal, the speed of the group is, necessarily, the speed of its slowest member. Almost inevitably, therefore, in such situations some group members are waiting for the others to catch up. Moreover, whenever the future is thought to be more attractive than the present—a common perception among schoolchildren—slow movement can sometimes seem like no movement at all.

All of these different kinds of delay are commonplace in the classrooms. Indeed, when we begin to examine the details of classroom life carefully, it is surprising to see how much of the students' time is spent in waiting. The most obvious examples are to be found in the practice of lining up that has already been mentioned. In most elementary schools, students stand in line several times a day. The entire class typically lines up during recess, lunch, and dismissal, and then there are the smaller lines that form sporadically in front of the drinking fountains, pencil sharpeners, and the like. Furthermore, it is not uncommon for teachers to hold these lines motionless until talking has ceased and some semblance of uniformity and order has been achieved.

Nor does the waiting end when the line has disappeared. Even when students are sitting in their seats they are often in the same position, psychologically, as if they were members of a line. It is not uncommon, for example, for teachers to move down rows asking questions or calling for recitations or examining seatwork. Under these conditions students interact with the teacher in a fixed order with the consequence of each student waiting until his turn arrives, speaking his piece, and then waiting for the teacher to get to him again in the next round. Even in rooms where teachers do not operate "by the numbers," as it were, the idea of taking turns during discussion and recitation periods is still present. After a student has made a contribution in a more informally run class, the teacher is less likely to call on him again, at least for a brief period of time. Conversely, a student who has said nothing all period is more likely to have his raised hand recognized than is a student who has participated several times in the lesson. Unusual variations from this procedure would be considered unfair by students and teachers alike. Thus, even during so-called free discussion invisible lines are formed.

In rooms where students have considerable freedom to move about on their own during seatwork and study periods, the teacher himself often becomes the center of little groups of waiting students. One of the most typical social arrangements in such settings is that in which the teacher is chatting with one student or examining his work while two or three others stand by, books and papers in hand, waiting to have the teacher evaluate their work, give them further direction, answer their questions, or in some other fashion enable them to move along. At such moments it is not unusual for one or two of the seated students also to have their hands raised, propped at the elbow, waiting patiently for the teacher to get around to them.

A familiar arrangement in the lower grades is for the teacher to work with a part of the class, usually a reading group, while the remainder engage in seatwork. Not uncommonly the students working by themselves finish their assignments before the teacher is finished with the group with which he is working. Under such circumstances it is not uncommon for the teacher to admonish the students to "find something to do" until it is time for a new activity to begin. These students may obey the teacher and thus appear to be busy, but their busyness is analogous to that of patients who read the old magazines in the doctor's waiting room.

A final example of the kinds of delay to be observed in the classroom involves the situation in which the group is given a problem to solve or an exercise to complete and some students complete the work long before others. At such times the teacher may be heard to ask, "How many need more time?" or to command, "Raise your hand when you have finished." This type of delay may only last a few seconds, but it occurs very frequently in some classrooms. Further, it is a kind of delay that is not experienced equally by all students, as are some of the others that have been mentioned, but tends, instead, to be encountered most frequently by students who are brighter, faster, or more involved in their work.

Thus, in several different ways students in elementary classrooms are required to wait their turn and to delay their actions. No one knows for certain how much of the average student's time is spent in neutral, as it were, but for many students in many classrooms it must be a memorable portion. Furthermore, delay is only one of the consequences of living in a crowd and perhaps not even the most important one from the standpoint of constraining the individual. Waiting is not so bad, and may even be beneficial, when the things we are waiting for come to pass. But waiting, as we all know, can sometimes be in vain.

The denial of desire is the ultimate outcome of many of the delays occurring in the classroom. The raised hand is sometimes ignored, the question to the teacher is sometimes brushed aside, the permission that is sought is sometimes refused. No doubt things often have to be this way. Not everyone who wants to speak can be heard; not all of the student's queries can be answered to his satisfaction; not all of their requests can be granted. Also, it is probably true that most of these denials are psychologically trivial when considered individually. But when considered cumulatively their significance increases. And regardless of whether or not they are justified, they make it clear that part of learning how to live in school involves learning how to give up desire as well as how to wait for its fulfillment.

Interruptions of many sorts create a third feature of classroom life that results, at least in part, from the crowded social conditions. During group sessions irrelevant comments, misbehavior, and outside visitors bearing messages often disrupt the continuity of the lesson. When the teacher is working individually with a student—a common arrangement in elementary classrooms—petty interruptions, usually in the form of other students coming to the teacher for advice, are the rule rather than the exception. Thus, the bubble of reality created during the teaching session is punctured by countless trivial incidents and the teacher must spend time patching up the holes. Students are expected to ignore these distractions or at least to turn quickly back to their studies after their attention has been momentarily drawn elsewhere.

Typically, things happen on time in school and this fact creates interruptions of another sort. Adherence to a time schedule requires that activities often begin before interest is aroused and terminate before interest disappears. Thus students are required to put away their arithmetic book and take out their spellers even though they want to continue with arithmetic and ignore spelling. In the classroom, work is often stopped before it is finished. Questions are often left dangling when the bell rings.

Quite possibly, of course, there is no alternative to this unnatural state of affairs. If teachers were always to wait until students were finished with one activity before they began another, the school day would become interminable. There seems to be no other way, therefore, but to stop and start things by the clock, even though this means constantly interrupting the natural flow of interest and desire for at least some students.

Another aspect of school life, related to the general phenomena of distractions and interruptions, is the recurring demand that the student ignore those who are around him. In elementary classrooms students are frequently assigned seatwork on which they are expected to focus their individual energies. During these seatwork periods talking and other forms of communication between students are discouraged, if not openly forbidden. The general admonition in such situations is to do your own work and leave others alone.

In a sense, then, students must try to behave as if they were in solitude, when in point of fact they are not. They must keep their eyes on their paper when human faces beckon. Indeed, in the early grades it is not uncommon to find students facing each other around a table while at the same time being required not to communicate with each other. These young people, if they are to become successful students, must learn how to be alone in a crowd.

Adults encounter conditions of social solitude so often that they are likely to overlook its special significance in the elementary classroom. We have learned to mind our own business in factories and offices, to remain silent in libraries, and to keep our thoughts to ourselves while riding public conveyances. But there are two major differences between classrooms and most of these other settings. First, except for the first few days of school, a classroom is not an ad hoc gathering of strangers. It is a group whose members have come to know each other quite well, to the point of friendship in many cases. Second, attendance in the room is not voluntary, as it is in many other social situations. Students are there whether they want to be or not and the work on which they are expected to concentrate also is often not of their own choosing. Thus, the pull to communicate with others is likely somewhat stronger in the classroom than in other crowded situations.

Here then are four unpublicized features of school life: delay, denial, interruption and social distraction. Each is produced, in part, by the crowded conditions of the classroom. When twenty or thirty people must live and work together within a limited space for five or six hours a day, most of the things that have been discussed are inevitable. Therefore, to decry the existence of these conditions is probably futile, yet their pervasiveness and frequency make them too important to be ignored. One alternative is to study the ways in which teachers and students cope with these facts of life and to seek to discover how that coping might leave its mark on their reactions to the world in general.

First, we must recognize that the severity of the conditions being described is to some extent a function of social tradition, institutional policy, and situational wealth and poverty. In some schools daily schedules are treated casually and in others they are rigidly adhered to. In some classrooms a rule of no talking is in force almost all of the time, while a steady murmur is tolerated in others. In some classrooms there are forty or more students, in others, at the same grade level, there are twenty or less. Some teachers are slow to recognize an upraised hand, others respond almost immediately. Some rooms are equipped with several pairs of big scissors, others have only one.

Despite these differences, however, it is doubtful that there is any class-room in which the phenomena we have been discussing are uncommon. Space, abundant resources, and a liberal attitude toward rules and regula-tions may reduce the pressure of the crowd somewhat but it certainly does not eliminate it entirely. Indeed, most of the observations on which the present analysis is based were made in so-called advantaged schools whose teachers were proud of their "progressive" educational views.

Second, as we begin to focus on the ways of coping with these institu-tional demands, it should be recognized at once that adaptive strategies are idiosyncratic to individual students. We cannot predict, in other words, how any particular student will react to the constraints imposed on him in the classroom. We can only identify major adaptive styles that might be used to characterize large numbers of students.

The quintessence of virtue in most institutions is contained in the single word: *patience*. Lacking that quality, life could be miserable for those who must spend their time in our prisons, our factories, our corporation offices, and our schools. In all of these settings the participants must "learn to la-bour and to wait." They must also, to some extent, learn to suffer in silence. They are expected to bear with equanimity, in other words, the continued delay, denial, and interruption of their personal wishes and desires.

But patience is more of a moral attribute than an adaptive strategy. It is what a person is asked to "be" rather than what he is asked to "do." More-over, when we consider how a person *becomes* patient—that is, the behav-iors he must engage in in order to earn the title—it becomes apparent that patience is more clearly determined by what a person does *not* do than by what he does. A patient man is one who does not act in a particular way, even though he desires to. He is a man who can endure the temptation to cry out or to complain, even though the temptation is strong. Thus patience has to do principally with the control of impulse or its abandonment.

Returning to the situation in our schools, we can see that if students are to face the demands of classroom life with equanimity, they must learn to be patient. This means that they must be able to disengage, at least temporarily, their feelings from their actions. It also means, of course, that they must be able to re-engage feelings and actions when conditions are appropriate. In other words, students must wait patiently for their turn to come, but when it does they must still be capable of zestful participation. They must accept the fact of not being called on during a group discussion, but they must con-tinue to volunteer.

Thus, the personal quality commonly described as patience—an essential quality when responding to the demands of the classroom—represents a balance, and sometimes a precarious one, between two opposed tendencies. On the one hand is the impulse to act on desire, to blurt out the answer, to push to the front of the line, or to express anger when interrupted. On the other hand is the impulse to give up the desire itself, to stop participating in the discussion, to go without a drink when the line is long, or to abandon an interrupted activity.

Whether or not a particular student acquires the desirable balance between impulsive action and apathetic withdrawal depends in part, as has been suggested, on personality qualities that lie outside the scope of the present discussion. In most classrooms powerful social sanctions are in operation to force the student to maintain an attitude of patience. If he impulsively steps out of line, his classmates are likely to complain about his being selfish or pushy. If he shifts over into a state of overt withdrawal, his teacher is apt to call him back to active participation.

But the fact that teachers and peers help to keep a student's behavior in line does not mean that the demands themselves can be ignored. Regardless of his relative success in coping with it, or the forces, personal or otherwise, that might aid in that coping, the elementary school student is situated in a densely populated social world. As curriculum experts and educational technologists try to experiment with new course content and new instructional devices, the crowds in the classroom may be troublesome. But there they are. Part of becoming a student involves learning how to live with that fact.

III

Every child experiences the pain of failure and the joy of success long before he reaches school age, but his achievements, or lack of them, do not really become official until he enters the classroom. From then on, however, a semipublic record of his progress gradually accumulates, and as a student he must learn to adapt to the continued and pervasive spirit of evaluation that will dominate his school years. Evaluation, then, is another important fact of life in the elementary classroom.

As we all know, school is not the only place where a student is made aware of his strengths and weaknesses. His parents make evaluations of him in the home and his friends do likewise on the playground. But the evaluation process that goes on in the classroom is quite different from that which operates in other settings. Accordingly, it presents the student with a set of unique demands to which he must adapt.

The most obvious difference between the way evaluation occurs in school and the way it occurs in other situations is that tests are given in school more frequently than elsewhere. Indeed, with the exception of examinations related to military service or certain kinds of occupations, most people seldom encounter tests outside of their school experience.[2] Tests are as indigenous to the school environment as are textbooks or pieces of chalk.

But tests, though they are the classic form of educational evaluation, are not all there is to the process. In fact, in the lower grades formal tests are

almost nonexistent, although evaluation clearly occurs. Thus the presence
of these formal procedures is insufficient to explain the distinctively evaluative atmosphere that pervades the classroom from the earliest grades onward. There is more to it than that.

The dynamics of classroom evaluation are difficult to describe, principally because they are so complex. Evaluations derive from more than one
source, the conditions of their communication may vary in several different
ways, they may have one or more of several referents, and they may range in
quality from intensely positive to intensely negative. Moreover, these variations refer only to objective or impersonal features of evaluation. When the
subjective or personal meanings of these events are considered, the picture
becomes even more complex. Fortunately, for purposes of the present discussion, we need to focus only on the more objective aspects of the student's
evaluative experiences.

The chief source of evaluation in the classroom is obviously the teacher.
He is called upon continuously to make judgments of students' work and
behavior and to communicate that judgment to the students in question
and to others. No one who has observed an elementary classroom for any
length of time can have failed to be impressed by the vast number of times
the teacher performs this function. Typically, in most classrooms students
come to know when things are right or wrong, good or bad, pretty or ugly,
largely as a result of what the teacher tells them.

But the teacher is not the only one who passes judgment. Classmates
frequently join in the act. Sometimes the class as a whole is invited to
participate in the evaluation of a student's work, as when the teacher asks,
"Who can correct Billy?" or "How many believe that Shirley read that poem
with a lot of expression?"[3] At other times the evaluation occurs without any
urging from the teacher, as when an egregious error elicits laughter or an
outstanding performance wins spontaneous applause.

There is a third source of evaluation in the classroom that is more difficult to describe than are the positive or negative comments coming from
teachers and peers. This type of evaluation, which entails self-judgment,
occurs without the intervention of an outside judge. When a student is unable to spell any of the words on a spelling test he has been apprised of his
failure even if the teacher never sees his paper. When a student works on an
arithmetic example at the blackboard he may know that his answer is correct even if the teacher does not bother to tell him so. Thus, as students respond to test questions, complete exercises in their workbooks, or solve
problems at the blackboard, they inevitably obtain some information about
the quality of their performance. The information is not always correct and
may have to be revised by later judgments (not everyone who thinks he has
the right answer really has it!), but even when wrong, evaluation can leave
its mark.

The conditions under which evaluations are communicated add to the complexity of the demands confronting the student. He soon comes to realize, for example, that some of the most important judgments of him and his work are not made known to him at all. Some of these "secret" judgments are communicated to parents; others, such as IQ scores and results of personality tests, are reserved for the scrutiny of school officials only. Judgments made by peers often circulate in the form of gossip or are reported to persons of authority by "tattle-tales." Before he has gone very far in school the student must come to terms with the fact that many things are said about him behind his back.

Those judgments of which the student is aware are communicated with varying degrees of privacy. At one extreme is the public comment made in the presence of other students. In the elementary classroom in particular, students are often praised or admonished in front of their classmates. Perfect papers or good drawings are sometimes displayed for all to see. Misbehavior evokes negative sanctions—such as scolding, isolation, removal from the room—that are frequently visible. Before much of the school year has gone by the identity of the "good" students and the "poor" students has become public knowledge in most classrooms.

A less public form of evaluation occurs when the teacher meets privately with the student to discuss his work. Sometimes the student is called to the teacher's desk and sometimes the teacher walks around the room and chats with individuals while the class is engaged in seatwork. Often, however, these seemingly private conferences are secretly attended by eavesdroppers. Thus, it is quite probable, although it might be difficult to prove, that a student's nearest classmates are more intimately aware of the teacher's evaluation of him than are students sitting at a greater distance.

Writing is an even more private means of communicating evaluations than is the spoken word. The terse comment on the margin of a student's paper is the classic form of written evaluation. A variant of this situation occurs when the student answers a self-quiz in his workbook or textbook but does not report his score to anyone. On occasions such as these the student confronts the evaluation of his work in solitude.

Logically, evaluation in the classroom might be expected to be limited chiefly to the student's attainment of educational objectives. And clearly these limits seem to hold insofar as most of the official evaluations go—the ones that are communicated to parents and entered on school records. But there are at least two other referents of evaluation quite common in elementary classrooms. One has to do with the student's adjustment to institutional expectations; the other with his possession of specific character traits. Indeed, the smiles and frowns of teachers and classmates often provide more information about these seemingly peripheral aspects of the student's behavior than they do about his academic progress. Moreover, even when the student's mastery of certain knowledge or skills is allegedly the object of evaluation, other aspects of his behavior commonly are being judged at the same time.

As every schoolchild knows, teachers can become quite angry on occasion. Moreover, every schoolchild quickly learns what makes teachers angry. He learns that in most classrooms the behavior that triggers the teacher's ire has little to do with wrong answers or other indicators of scholastic failure. Rather, it is violations of institutional expectations that really get under the teacher's skin. Typically, when a student is scolded by the teacher it is not because he has failed to spell a word correctly or to grasp the intricacies of long division. He is scolded, more than likely, for coming into the room late, or for making too much noise, or for not listening to directions, or for pushing while in line. Occasionally, teachers do become publicly vexed by their students' academic shortcomings, but to really send teachers off on a tirade of invective, the young student soon discovers nothing works better than a partially suppressed giggle during arithmetic period.

The teacher, of course, is not the only source of nonacademic judgments. Evaluation that focuses on a student's personal qualities is as likely to come from his classmates as from anyone else. The student's classroom behavior contributes in large measure to the reputation he develops among his peers for being smart or dumb, a sissy or a bully, teacher's pet or a regular guy, a cheater or a good sport. Most students are fully aware that their behavior is being evaluated in these terms because they judge others in the same way. Classroom friendships and general popularity or unpopularity are based largely on such assessments.[4] Although some of these judgments are instantly communicated to the person being evaluated, others are relayed through intermediaries or friends. Some are so secret that even best friends won't tell.

The teacher's evaluation of the personal qualities of his students typically deals with such matters as general intellectual ability, motivational level, and helpfulness in maintaining a well-run classroom. Such qualities are commonly mentioned on cumulative record folders in terse but telling descriptions. "Johnny has some difficulty with third-grade material, but he tries hard," or "Sarah is a neat and pleasant girl. She is a good helper," or simply, "William is a good worker," are typical of the thumbnail sketches to be found in abundance in school records. Some teachers, particularly those who pride themselves on being "psychologically sophisticated," also evaluate their students in terms that relate more closely than do the ones already mentioned to the general concept of psychopathology. Aggressiveness and withdrawal are among the traits most frequently mentioned in this connection. Teachers also use the general labels of "problem child" or "disturbed child" for this purpose.

Quite naturally most of the evaluations that have to do with the student's psychological health are not communicated to the student and often not even to the child's parents. Less severe judgments, however, are often made publicly. In the lower grades it is not at all uncommon to hear the teacher, as she gazes over her class, say things like, "I see that John is a good worker," or "Some people (their identities obvious) don't seem to know how to follow directions," or "Lisa has a listening face."

The separation of classroom evaluations into those referring to academic attainment, those referring to institutional adjustment, and those referring to possession of personal qualities should not obscure the fact that in many situations all three kinds of assessment are going on at one time. For example, when a student is praised for correctly responding to a teacher's question it may look as though he is simply being rewarded for having the right answer. But obviously there is more to it than that. If the teacher discovered that the student had obtained the answer a few seconds before by reading from a neighbor's paper, he would have been punished rather than praised. Similarly, if he had blurted the answer out rather than waiting to be called on, he might have received a very different response from the teacher. Thus, it is not just the possession of the right answer but also the way in which it was obtained that is being rewarded. In other words, the student is being praised for having achieved and demonstrated intellectual mastery in a prescribed, legitimate way. He is being praised, albeit indirectly, for knowing something, for having done what the teacher told him to do, for being a good listener, a cooperative group member, and so on. The teacher's compliment is intended to entice the student (and those who are listening) to engage in certain behaviors in the future, but not simply in the repeated exposure of the knowledge he has just displayed. It is intended to encourage him to do again what the teacher tells him to do, to work hard, to master the material. And so it is with many of the evaluations that appear to relate exclusively to academic matters. Implicitly, they involve the evaluation of many nonacademic aspects of the student's behavior.

Evaluations, by definition, connote value. Accordingly, each can be described, at least ideally, according to the kind and degree of value it connotes. Some are positive, others are negative. Some are *very* positive or negative, others are less so. In the classroom, as everyone knows, both positive and negative assessments are made and are communicated to students. Teachers scold as well as praise, classmates compliment as well as criticize.

The question of whether smiles are more frequent than frowns and compliments more abundant than criticisms depends in part, of course, on the particular classroom under discussion. Some teachers are just not the smiling type; others find it difficult to suppress their grins. The answer also varies dramatically from one student to the next. Some youngsters receive many more negative sanctions than do others, and the same is true with respect to rewards. Conditions also vary for the sexes. From the early grades onward, boys are more likely than are girls to violate institutional regulations and, thus, to receive an unequal share of control messages from the teacher. All of these inequalities make it difficult to describe with great accuracy the evaluative setting as it is experienced by any particular child. All that can be said with assurance is that the classroom environment of most students contains some mixture of praise and reproof.

Because both the teacher and his fellow classmates may evaluate a student's behavior, contradictory judgments are possible. A given act may be praised by the teacher and criticized by peers, or vice versa. This may not be the normal state of affairs, to be sure, but it does happen frequently enough to bear comment. A classic example of this kind of a contradiction was observed in one second-grade classroom in which a boy was complimented by his teacher for his gracefulness during a period of creative dancing while, at the same time, his male classmates teased him for acting like a sissy. This example calls attention to the fact that students are often concerned with the approval of two audiences whose tastes may differ. It also hints at the possibility that the conflict between teacher and peer approval might be greater for boys than for girls. Many of the behaviors that the teacher smiles upon, especially those that have to do with compliance to institutional expectations (for example, neatness, passivity, cleanliness), are more closely linked·in our society with feminine than with masculine ideals.

From all that has been said it is evident that learning how to live in a classroom involves not only learning how to handle situations in which one's own work or behavior are evaluated, but also learning how to witness, and occasionally participate in, the evaluation of others. In addition to getting used to a life in which their strengths and weaknesses are often exposed to public scrutiny, students also have to accustom themselves to viewing the strengths and weaknesses of their fellow students. This shared exposure makes comparisons between students inevitable and adds another degree of complexity to the evaluation picture.

The job of coping with evaluation is not left solely to the student. Typically the teacher and other school authorities try to reduce the discomfort that might be associated with some of the harsher aspects of meting out praise and punishment. The dominant viewpoint in education today stresses the pedagogical advantages of success and the disadvantages of failure. In short, our schools are reward-oriented. Thus, teachers are instructed to focus on the good aspects of a student's behavior and to overlook the poor. Indeed, even when a student gives a wrong answer, today's teacher is likely to compliment him for trying. This bias toward the positive does not mean, of course, that negative remarks have disappeared from our schools. But there are certainly fewer of them than there might be if teachers operated under a different set of educational beliefs.

When harsh judgments have to be made, as they often must, teachers often try to conceal them from the class as a whole. Students are called up to the teacher's desk, private conferences are arranged before or after school, test papers are handed back with the grades covered, and so on. Sometimes when the judgments are very harsh, they are not reported to the student at all. Students are rarely told, for example, that they have been classified as slow learners or that the teacher suspects them of having serious emotional problems. Such evaluations, as has been pointed out, are usually the carefully guarded secrets of the school authorities.

School practices covering the communication of positive evaluations are probably less consistent than are those covering negative judgments. Although there is a common tendency to praise students whenever possible, this tendency is usually tempered by the teacher's desire to be fair and "democratic." Thus the correct answers and perfect papers of students who almost always do good work may be overlooked at times in the interest of giving less able students a chance to bask in the warmth of the teacher's admiration. Most teachers are also sensitive to the fact that lavish praise heaped upon a student may arouse negative evaluations ("teacher's pet, eager beaver") from his classmates.

Although the student's task in adjusting to evaluation is made easier by common teaching practices, he still has a job to do. In fact, he has three jobs. The first and most obvious is to behave in such a way as to enhance the likelihood of praise and reduce the likelihood of punishment. In other words, he must learn how the reward system of the classroom operates and then use that knowledge to increase the flow of rewards to himself. A second job, although one in which students engage with differing degrees of enthusiasm, consists of trying to publicize positive evaluations and conceal negative ones. The pursuit of this goal leads to the practice of carrying good report cards home with pride, and losing poor ones along the way. A third job, and again, one that may be of greater concern to some students than to others, consists of trying to win the approval of two audiences at the same time. The problem for some is how to become a good student while remaining a good guy, how to be at the head of the class while still being in the center of the group.

Most students soon learn that rewards are granted to those who lead a good life. And in school the good life consists principally of doing what the teacher says. Of course the teacher says many things, and some of his directions are easier to follow than others, but for the most part his expectations are not seen as unreasonable and the majority of students comply with them sufficiently well to ensure that their hours in the classroom are colored more by praise than by punishment.

But only in very rare instances is compliance the only strategy a student uses to make his way in the evaluative environment of the classroom. Another course of action engaged in by most students, at least some of the time, is to behave in ways that disguise the failure to comply; in short, to cheat. It may seem unduly severe to label as "cheating" all the little maneuvers that students engage in to cloak aspects of their behavior that might be displeasing to the teacher or to their fellow students. Perhaps the term should be reserved to describe the seemingly more serious behavior of trying to falsify performance on a test. But this restriction bestows greater significance than is warranted to test situations and implies that similar behavior in other settings is harmless or hardly worthy of notice.

Yet why should a student who copies an answer from his neighbor's test paper be considered guilty of more serious misbehavior than the student who attempts to misinform by raising his hand when the teacher asks how many have completed their homework assignment? Why is cheating on a test considered a greater breach of educational etiquette than is faking interest during a social studies discussion or sneaking a peek at a comic book during arithmetic class? The answer presumably is that performance on tests counts for more, in that it is preserved as a lasting mark on the student's record. And that answer might justify the differences in our attitudes toward these various practices. But it should not permit us to overlook the fact that copying an answer on a test, feigning interest during a discussion, giving a false answer to a teacher's query, and disguising forbidden activities are all of a piece. Each represents an effort to avoid censure or to win unwarranted praise. Such efforts are far more common in the classroom than our focus on cheating in test situations would have us believe. Learning how to make it in school involves, in part, learning how to falsify our behavior.

There is another way of coping with evaluations that warrants mention even though it is not deserving of the term "strategy." This method entails devaluing the evaluations to a point where they no longer matter very much. The student who has adopted this alternative over those of complying or cheating has learned how to "play it cool" in the classroom. He is neither elated by success nor deflated by failure. He may indeed try to stay out of trouble in the classroom and thus comply with the teacher's minimal expectations, but this is principally because getting into trouble entails further entanglements and involvement with school officials and other adults, a situation that he would prefer to avoid.

This brief description of emotional detachment from school affairs has two shortcomings. It makes the process sound more rational than it probably is and it focuses on a rather extreme form of the condition. Students do not likely *decide* to become uninvolved with school in the same way that they decide to collect baseball cards or to visit a sick friend. Rather, their lack of involvement likely has a causal history of which they are only dimly aware at best. . . . Also, detachment is surely not an either/or state of affairs. Students cannot be sharply divided into the involved and the uninvolved. Rather, all students probably learn to employ psychological buffers that protect them from some of the wear and tear of classroom life. To anyone who has been in a classroom it is also evident that some students end up being more insulated than others.

Before leaving the topic of evaluation in the classroom, attention must be given to a distinction that has enjoyed wide currency in educational discussions. This is the distinction between extrinsic motivation (doing schoolwork for the rewards it will bring in the form of good grades and teacher approval) on the one hand, and intrinsic motivation (doing schoolwork for the pleasure that comes from the task itself) on the other. If we want children to continue to learn after they leave the classroom, so the argument goes, it would be wise gradually to deemphasize the importance of grades and other extrinsic rewards and to concentrate instead on having the student derive his major satisfactions from the learning activities themselves. An illustration often used in making this point involves the child's progress in learning how to play the piano. When piano lessons are first begun the student may have to be forced to practice through the use of external rewards and punishments. But after a time, hopefully, the student will derive such pleasure from the skill itself that rewards and punishments will no longer be very important.

The trouble with the piano-playing illustration and with the whole concept of intrinsic and extrinsic motivation as it relates to classroom activity is that it does not take into account the complexity of the evaluations that occur there. If classroom rewards and punishments only had to do with whether the students practiced their spelling or their arithmetic, life for both the teacher and his students would be much simpler. But, clearly, reality is more complicated than that.

The notion of intrinsic motivation begins to lose some of its power when applied to behaviors other than those that involve academic knowledge or skills. What about behaviors that deal with conformity to institutional expectations? What kind of intrinsic motivation can the teacher appeal to when he wants students to be silent even though they want to talk? It is true that he might make a logical appeal to them rather than merely telling them to shut up, but it is hard to imagine that the students will ever find anything intrinsically satisfying about being silent when they wish to talk. And the same thing is true for many aspects of classroom behavior that arouse evaluative comments from teachers and students. Thus, the goal of making classroom activities intrinsically satisfying to students turns out to be unattainable except with respect to a narrowly circumscribed set of behavior.

IV

The fact of unequal power is a third feature of classroom life to which students must become accustomed. The difference in authority between the teacher and his students is related, quite obviously, to the evaluative aspects of classroom life. But it involves much more than the distribution of praise and reproof. This difference provides the most salient feature of the social structure of the classroom, and its consequences relate to the broader conditions of freedom, privilege, and responsibility as manifest in classroom affairs.

One of the earliest lessons a child must learn is how to comply with the wishes of others. Soon after he becomes aware of the world he is in, the newborn infant becomes conscious of one of the main features of that world—adult authority. As he moves from home to school the authority of parents is gradually supplemented by control from teachers, the second most important set of adults in his life. But early parental authority differs in several important ways from that which he will confront in school, and these differences are important for understanding the character of the classroom environment.

Two of the chief differences between the parent's relationship with his child and the teacher's with his student have to do with the intimacy and duration of the contact. The emotional ties between parents and children are usually stronger and last longer than those between teachers and students. This does not mean, of course, that students never feel close to their teachers, and vice versa. We know that a child's relationship with his teacher can at times rival in intensity the union between him and his mother and father. We also know that teachers are occasionally attracted toward particular students in an intense and personal way. But still the dominant relationship in the classroom is quite impersonal when compared with that which goes on in the home.

The reduced intimacy in the classroom as compared with the home has to do not only with the intensity of feelings among participants but also with the extent to which the participants have been exposed to each other in a variety of poses and guises. Members of a household come to know each other physically as well as psychologically in a way that almost never happens in the classroom. Also, family members share a personal history in a way that members of other groups do not. Consequently, parents and children are likely to have a much more extensive familiarity with each other than are teachers and students.

The relative impersonality and narrowness of the teacher-student relationship has consequences for the way in which authority is handled in the classroom. It is there that students must learn to take orders from adults who do not know them very well and whom they do not themselves know intimately. For the first time in the child's life, power that has personal consequences for the child himself is wielded by a relative stranger.

Perhaps one of the chief differences between the authority of parents and teachers, although not the most obvious, has to do with the purposes for which their power is put to use. Parents, by and large, are principally restrictive. Their chief concern, at least during the child's early years, is with prohibiting action, with telling the child what *not* to do. Parental authority during the preschool years is characterized by the commands, "Stop!" and "Don't!" It is an authority whose chief goal is to place limits on natural impulses and spontaneous interests, particularly when those impulses and interests endanger the child himself or threaten to destroy something of value to the parent. The infant's playpen symbolizes the type of authority with which children must learn to live during their early years. This ubiquitous piece of child-rearing equipment places definite limits on the child's sphere of activity, but within that sphere he is free to do almost anything he wishes.

The teacher's authority, in contrast, is as much prescriptive as restrictive. Teachers are concerned with setting assignments for students rather than with merely curbing undesirable behavior. Their authority is characterized as much by "Do" as by "Don't." Just as the playpen is symbolic of the parent's commands, so is the desk symbolic of the commands issued by teachers. The desk represents not just a limited sphere of activity but a setting specially designed for a very narrow range of behavior. Seated at his desk the student is in the position to do something. It is the teacher's job to declare what that something shall be.

At the heart of the teacher's authority is his command over the student's attention. Students are expected to attend to certain matters while they are in the classroom, and much of the teacher's energies are spent in making sure that this happens. At home the child must learn how to stop; at school he must learn how to look and listen.

Another view of the teacher's authority might focus on the process of substitution by which the teacher's plans for action are substituted for the student's own. When students do what the teacher tells them to do they are, in effect, abandoning one set of plans (their own) in favor of another (their teacher's). At times, of course, these two sets of plans do not conflict and may even be quite similar. But at other times, that which is given up in no way resembles the action called for by the teacher. The lack of resemblance between the teacher's plans and the student's own must partially account for the difficulty some students have in adjusting to the classroom, but the relationship between these two states of affairs is surely not simple. The important point is that students must learn to employ their executive powers in the service of the teacher's desires rather than their own. Even if it hurts.

The distinction between work and play has far-reaching consequences for human affairs, and the classroom is the setting in which most people encounter this distinction in a personally meaningful way. According to one of its many definitions, work entails becoming engaged in a purposeful activity that has been prescribed for us by someone else; an activity in which we would not at that moment be engaged if it were not for some system of authority relationships. As preschoolers the students may have played with the concept of work, but their fanciful enactments of adult work situations usually lack one essential ingredient—namely, the use of some kind of an external authority system to tell them what to do and to keep them at their job. The teacher, with his prescriptive dicta and his surveillance over the students' attention, provides the missing ingredient that makes work real. The teacher, although he may disclaim the title, is the students' first "Boss."

The worker, almost by definition, is a person who is tempted from time to time to abandon his role. Presumably there are other things he would rather be doing, but his boss's eye, or his need for money, or the voice of his inner conscience keep him at the job. Sometimes, of course, he yields to his temptation, either by taking the day off or, when conditions become intolerable, by quitting his job. The right to leave the work situation varies greatly from one job to another, but the ultimate privilege, that of quitting, is open to all adults. Any worker, if he doesn't like his job, can throw down his tools and walk away. He may live to regret his decision, but the decision to leave is his.

But consider the plight of the young student. If a third grader should refuse to obey the system of bells that tell him when to enter and when to leave the classroom, the wheels of retributive justice would begin to grind. And the teacher would sound the alarm that would put them in motion. This fact calls attention to an important aspect of the teacher's use of authority. As has been pointed out, schools resemble so-called total institutions such as prisons, mental hospitals, and the like, in that one subgroup of their clientele (the students) are involuntarily committed to the institution, whereas another subgroup (the staff) has greater freedom of movement and, most important, has the ultimate freedom to leave the institution entirely. Under these circumstances it is common for the more privileged group to guard the exits, either figuratively or literally. Again, teachers may not like this description and may, in protesting, insist that they operate democratic classrooms, but in a very real sense their responsibilities bear some resemblance to those of prison guards. In progressive prisons, as in most classrooms, the inhabitants are allowed certain freedoms, but there are real limits. In both institutions the inmates might be allowed to plan a Christmas party, but in neither place are they allowed to plan a "break."

The starkness of the difference in power between teachers and students may be heightened or subdued depending on school policy and the personal predilections of the teachers. Many of the differences between so-called traditional and progressive institutions derive from the ways in which the teacher's authority is handled. In some schools, for example, students are required to rise when the teacher enters the room, whereas in others they are encouraged to call the teacher by his first name. In some schools students have little or no say in determining the content of the curriculum, whereas in others pupil-planning is used as a procedure for increasing the meaningfulness of the students' experience. But, even in the most progressive environments, the teacher is very much in control and pupils usually are aware of the centrality and power of his position. Even a first grader knows that an absent teacher requires a substitute, whereas an absent student does not.

In the best of all possible worlds it is expected that children will adapt to the teacher's authority by becoming good workers and model students. And, by and large, this ideal comes close to being realized. Most students learn to look and to listen when told to and to keep their private fantasies in check when class is in session. Moreover, this skill in complying with educational authority is doubly important because the student will be called upon to put it to work in many out-of-school settings. The transition from classroom to factory or office is made easily by those who have developed good work habits in their early years.

But not all students become good workers, and even those who do are sometimes forced to employ "shady" practices when dealing with the teacher's authority. Under conditions of grossly unequal power such as exist in classrooms, two types of interpersonal maneuvering almost inevitably arise. The first involves the seeking of special favor. One way of managing life in a total institution is by moving close to the sources of power during the off-hours and behaving in ways that cause authorities to respond favorably. At the more manipulative and cynical extreme this strategy involves fawning, false compliments, and other forms of social dishonesty. These extreme practices, which might be referred to collectively as "apple polishing," are usually accompanied by feelings of cynicism or self-hatred. Less extreme variations include merely being helpful and creating a good impression. In adult society this strategy leads to the practice of bringing the boss home for dinner. The classroom equivalent of dinner for the boss is the traditional apple for the teacher.

A second tactic that is in some ways the reverse of the first involves the practice of hiding words and deeds that might displease the authorities. It takes effort to create a good impression but it also requires work to avoid creating a bad one. Just as some of the pupil's energies are spent in trying to please the teacher, so are others spent in trying to keep out of trouble. The secrecy that frequently develops in total institutions is aligned, at least in part, with the authority structure. Certainly this is true in school. Teachers keep secrets from their principals as do students from their teachers. But not all of these secrets have to do with the avoidance of a negative evaluation from authority figures. Some may have as their goal the manipulation of institutional privileges. When, for example, a teacher asks a student if he has already been to the drinking fountain that morning and he untruthfully says "no," it is not because a truthful answer would provoke the teacher but because it might destroy the chances of his getting a second drink. So it is with many of the minor subterfuges that are commonplace in the classroom.

Because the oppressive use of power is antithetical to our democratic ideals, it is difficult to discuss its normal occurrence in the classroom without arousing concern. The concepts of obedience and of independence are often thought to be antithetical and, in our society, the latter concept is more often the declared objective of our schools than is the former. There-fore, we typically play down or fail to recognize the extent to which students are expected to conform to the expectations of others, and when this state of affairs is called to our attention, the natural response is one of alarm.

Yet the habits of obedience and docility engendered in the classroom have a high payoff value in other settings. So far as their power structure is concerned, classrooms are not too dissimilar from factories or offices, those ubiquitous organizations in which so much of our adult life is spent. Thus, school might really be called a preparation for life, but not in the usual sense in which educators employ that slogan. Power may be abused in school as elsewhere, but its existence is a fact of life to which we must adapt. The process of adaptation begins during the first few years of life, but it is significantly accelerated, for most of us, on the day we enter kindergarten.

V

. . . The crowds, the praise, and the power that combine to give a distinctive flavor to classroom life collectively form a hidden curriculum which each student (and teacher) must master if he is to make his way satisfactorily through the school. The demands created by these features of classroom life may be contrasted with the academic demands—the "official" curriculum so to speak—to which educators have traditionally paid the most attention. As might be expected, the two curricula are related to each other in several ways.

As has already been suggested in the discussion of praise in the class-room, the reward system of the school is linked to success in both curricula. Indeed, many of the rewards and punishments that sound as if they are being dispensed on the basis of academic success and failure are really more closely related to the mastery of the hidden curriculum. Consider as an instance, the common teaching practice of giving a student credit for trying. What do teachers mean when they say a student tries to do his work? They mean, in essence, that he complies with the procedural expectations of the institution. He does his homework (though incorrectly), he raises his hand during class discussion (though he usually comes up with the wrong answer), he keeps his nose in his book during free study period (though he doesn't turn the page very often). He is, in other words, a model student, though not necessarily a good one.

It is difficult to imagine any of today's teachers, particularly those in elementary schools, failing a student who tries, even though his mastery of course content is slight. Indeed, even at higher levels of education rewards sometimes go to the meek as well as to the mighty. It is certainly possible that many of our valedictorians and presidents of our honor societies owe their success as much to institutional conformity as to intellectual prowess. Although it offends our sensibilities to admit it, no doubt that bright-eyed little girl who stands trembling before the principal on graduation day arrived there at least in part because she typed her weekly themes neatly and handed her homework in on time.

This manner of talking about educational affairs may sound cynical and may be interpreted as a criticism of teachers or as an attempt to subvert the virtues of neatness, punctuality, and courteous conduct in general. But nothing of that kind is intended. The point is simply that in schools, as in prisons, good behavior pays off.

Just as conformity to institutional expectations can lead to praise, so can the lack of it lead to trouble. As a matter of fact, the relationship of the hidden curriculum to student difficulties is even more striking than is its relationship to student success. As an instance, consider the conditions leading to disciplinary action in the classroom. Why do teachers scold students? Because the student has given a wrong answer? Because, try as he might, he fails to grasp the intricacies of long division? Not usually. Rather, students are commonly scolded for coming into the room late, or for making too much noise, or for not listening to the teacher's directions, or for pushing while in line. The teacher's wrath, in other words, is more frequently triggered by violations of institutional regulations and routines than by signs of his students' intellectual deficiencies.

Even when we consider the more serious difficulties that clearly entail academic failure, the demands of the hidden curriculum lurk in the background. When Johnny's parents are called in to school because their son is not doing well in arithmetic, what explanation is given for their son's poor performance? Typically, blame is placed on motivational deficiencies in Johnny rather than on his intellectual shortcomings. The teacher may even go so far as to say that Johnny is unmotivated during arithmetic period. But what does this mean? It means, in essence, that Johnny does not even try. And not trying, as we have seen, usually boils down to a failure to comply with institutional expectations, a failure to master the hidden curriculum.

Test makers describe a person as "test-wise" when he has caught on to the tricks of test construction sufficiently well to answer questions correctly even though he does not know the material on which he is being examined. In the same way one might think of students as becoming "school-wise" or "teacher-wise" when they have discovered how to respond with a minimum amount of pain and discomfort to the demands, both official and unofficial, of classroom life. Schools, like test items, have rules and traditions of their own that can only be mastered through successive exposure. But with schools as with tests all students are not equally adroit. All are asked to respond, but not everyone catches on to the rules of the game.

If it is useful to think of there being two curricula in the classroom, a natural question to ask about the relationship between them is whether their joint mastery calls for compatible or contradictory personal qualities. That is, do the same strengths that contribute to intellectual achievement also contribute to the student's success in conformity to institutional expectations? This question likely has no definite answer, but it is thought-provoking, and even a brief consideration of it leads into a thicket of educational and psychological issues.

It is probably safe to predict that general ability, or intelligence, would be an asset in meeting all the demands of school life, whether academic or institutional. The child's ability to understand causal relationships, as an instance, would seem to be of as much service [when] he tries to come to grips with the rules and regulations of classroom life as when he grapples with the rudiments of plant chemistry. His verbal fluency can be put to use as easily in "snowing" the teacher as in writing a short story. Thus, to the extent that the demands of classroom life call for rational thought, the student with superior intellectual ability would seem to be at an advantage.

But more than ability is involved in adapting to complex situations. Much also depends upon attitudes, values, and lifestyle—upon all those qualities commonly grouped under the term *personality*. When the contribution of personality to adaptive strategy is considered, the old adage of "the more, the better," which works so well for general ability, does not suffice. Personal qualities that are beneficial in one setting may be detrimental in another. Indeed, even a single setting may make demands that call upon competing or conflicting tendencies in a person's makeup.

We have already seen that many features of classroom life call for patience, at best, and resignation, at worst. As he learns to live in school, our student learns to subjugate his own desires to the will of the teacher and to subdue his own actions in the interest of the common good. He learns to be passive and to acquiesce to the network of rules, regulations, and routines in which he is embedded. He learns to tolerate petty frustrations and to accept the plans and policies of higher authorities, even when their rationale is unexplained and their meaning unclear. Like the inhabitants of most other institutions, he learns how to shrug and say, "That's the way the ball bounces."

But the personal qualities that play a role in intellectual mastery are very different from those that characterize the "company man." Curiosity, as an instance, that most fundamental of all scholarly traits, is of little value in responding to the demands of conformity. The curious person typically engages in a kind of probing, poking, and exploring that is almost antithetical to the attitude of the passive conformist. The scholar must develop the habit of challenging authority and of questioning the value of tradition. He must insist on explanations for things that are unclear. Scholarship requires discipline, to be sure, but this discipline serves the demands of scholarship rather than the wishes and desires of other people. In short, intellectual mastery calls for sublimated forms of aggression rather than for submission to constraints.

This brief discussion likely exaggerates the real differences between the demands of institutional conformity and the demands of scholarship, but it does serve to call attention to points of possible conflict. How incompatible are these two sets of demands? Can both be mastered by the same person? Apparently so. Certainly not all of our student council presidents and valedictorians can be dismissed as weak-willed teacher's pets, as academic Uriah Heeps. Many students clearly manage to maintain their intellectual aggressiveness while at the same time acquiescing to the laws that govern the social traffic of our schools. Apparently it *is* possible, under certain conditions, to breed docile scholars, even though the expression seems to be a contradiction in terms. Indeed, certain forms of scholarship have been known to flourish in monastic settings, where the demands for institutional conformity are extreme.

Unfortunately, no one seems to know how these balances are maintained, nor even how to establish them in the first place. But even more unfortunate is the fact that few if any schoolpeople are giving the matter serious thought. As institutional settings multiply and become for more and more people the areas in which a significant portion of their life is enacted, we will need to know much more than we do at present about how to achieve a reasonable synthesis between the forces that drive a person to seek individual expression and those that drive him to comply with the wishes of others. Presumably, what goes on in classrooms contributes significantly to this synthesis. The school is the first major institution, outside the family, in which almost all of us are immersed. From kindergarten onward, the student begins to learn what life is really like in "the company."

The demands of classroom life discussed in this chapter pose problems for students and teachers alike. As we have seen, there are many methods for coping with these demands and for solving the problems they create. Moreover, each major adaptive strategy is subtly transformed and given a unique expression as a result of the idiosyncratic characteristics of the student employing it. Thus, the total picture of adjustment to school becomes infinitely complex as it is manifested in the behavior of individual students.

Yet certain commonalities do exist beneath all the complexity created by the uniqueness of individuals. No matter what the demand or the personal resources of the person facing it, there is at least one strategy open to all. This is the strategy of psychological withdrawal, of gradually reducing personal concern and involvement to a point where neither the demand nor one's success or failure in coping with it is sharply felt. . . . In order to better understand student tactics, however, it is important to consider the climate of opinion from which they emerge. Before focusing on what they do in the classroom, we must examine how students feel about school.

Notes

1. P. W. Jackson, "Teacher-Pupil Communication in the Elementary Classroom: An Observational Study" (Paper read at the American Educational Research Association meeting, Chicago, February 1965).

2. There are, of course, the popular quizzes in newspapers and magazines that many people seem to enjoy answering. But these exercises, which might best be called "toy tests," are of little consequence when compared with the real thing that goes on in school.

3. Jules Henry, an anthropologist, has witnessed signs of what he terms "a witch-hunt syndrome" in several elementary classrooms. A chief component of this syndrome is the destructive criticism of each other by the students, egged on, as it were, by the teacher. See his article, "Attitude Organization in Elementary School Classrooms," *American Journal of Orthopsychiatry* 27 (January 1957): 117–33.

4. Watching these evaluations being made in the classroom (through huddled conferences and the surreptitious exchange of notes) one begins to wonder whether friendship is determined by the possession of special qualities, or whether the qualities are ascribed as a rationalization of friendship or enmity that already exists. In many instances it is almost as if the students were saying, "My friends are good guys and my enemies are tattle-tales and cheaters," rather than "Good guys are my friends and tattle-tales and cheaters my enemies." Doubtlessly, both kinds of reasoning are in operation in most classrooms.

3

The Moral Atmosphere of the School

Lawrence Kohlberg

I have to start by saying that Philip Jackson* is responsible for my paper, by which I mean he is "to blame."

First, he is responsible because he invented the term "hidden" or "unstudied curriculum" to refer to 90 percent of what goes on in classrooms. Second, he is responsible because he induced me to speak about the unstudied curriculum when my only qualification to do so is that I have never studied it. While I have done plenty of observing of children in and out of classrooms, such observation has always been with reference to developing personality and behavior, and not in terms of the nature of classroom life and its influence on children. Third, he is to blame because he wrote a book defining the hidden curriculum on which I based this paper, and then he prepared a document . . . defining the unstudied curriculum in a completely different way, leaving me holding the bag.

The Hidden Curriculum and Moral Education

Anyhow, I am going to revenge myself on Dr. Jackson for putting me in this awkward spot by claiming that I am the only person who is really an

---

*Dr. Philip Jackson, Chairman, ASCD Elementary Education Council.

intellectual expert on this problem of the hidden curriculum. I say this because it will be my claim that the only integrated way of thinking about the hidden curriculum is to think of it as moral education, a topic about which few other academicians besides myself are currently concerned. To make educational sense out of the insights of Jackson, Dreeben, Friedenberg, and Rosenthal, I shall claim, you must put them in the framework of the ideas and concerns in *moral* education propounded by such writers as Emile Durkheim, John Dewey, and Jean Piaget.

To make my point, I shall start with the central question most of us have about the hidden curriculum, that of whether it educates, miseducates, or does neither. I shall claim that the answer to this question depends upon a viable conception of moral development. The question itself, that of whether the hidden curriculum educates, is posed by the very phrase, "hidden curriculum." The phrase indicates that children are learning much in school that is not formal curriculum, and the phrase also asks whether such learning is truly educative.

In *Life in Classrooms,* Philip Jackson summarizes three central characteristics of school life: the crowds, the praise, and the power.[1] Learning to live in the classroom means, first, learning to live and to be treated as a member of a crowd of same-age, same-status others.

Second, learning to live in the classroom means learning to live in a world in which there is impersonal authority, in which a relative stranger gives orders and wields power. Robert Dreeben emphasizes similar characteristics—first and foremost, learning to live with authority. Both Jackson and Dreeben stress the fact that the hidden curriculum provides a way station between the personal relations of the family and the impersonal achievement and authority-oriented roles of adult occupational and socio-political life.

The perspectives of Jackson and Dreeben derive from a long and great tradition of educational sociology founded by Emile Durkheim in France at the end of the nineteenth century. According to Durkheim:

There is a great distance between the state in which the child finds himself as he leaves the family and the one toward which he must strive. Intermediaries are necessary, the school environment the most desirable. It is more extensive than the family or the group of friends. It results neither from blood nor free choice but from a meeting among subjects of similar age and condition. In that sense, it resembles political society. On the other hand it is limited enough so that personal relations can crystallize. It is groups of young persons more or less like those of the social system of the school which have enabled the formation of societies larger than the family. Even in simple societies without schools,in the family.[2]

What this sociological tradition of Durkheim and Dreeben is telling us is that you cannot get rid of authority in the classroom, because you need people who can live with it in the bigger society. Edgar Friendenberg starts out with the same Durkheim perspective before turning it on its ear. I hesitate to restate Dr. Friedenberg. I am tempted to say that he is the only person in the world who can state a message in many syllables, and make it come across with one-syllable impact. In *Coming of Age in America* Friedenberg says,

After the family the school is the first social institution an individual must deal with, the place in which he learns to handle himself with strangers. Free societies depend upon their members to learn early and thoroughly that public authority is not like that of the family, but must rely basically on the impersonal application of general formulae.[3]

However, Friedenberg's observations of the hidden curriculum suggest that it is less a vehicle of socialization into a free society than that caricature of socialization we call a jail. Says Friedenberg:

Between classes at Milgrim High, no student may walk down the corridor without a form signed by a teacher, telling where he is coming from, where he is going, and the time to the minute at which the pass is valid. There is no physical freedom whatever in Milgrim, there is no time or place in which a student may simply go about his business. Privacy is strictly forbidden. Toilets are locked. There are more different washrooms than there must have been in the Confederate Navy.[4]

Friedenberg's style of observation of the hidden curriculum is colored by his view that its function of socialization into large-scale society means socialization into a mass middle-class society of mediocrity, banality, and conformity. From this point of view, the hidden curriculum consists of "the ways in which education subverts the highest function of education, which is to help people understand the meaning of their lives and those of others."

I have summarized utterances by our other speakers to indicate how the perceived nature of the hidden curriculum rests on a prior perspective which is both a social theory and a mode of valuing. The fact that this must necessarily be the case in social inquiry, I learned in an illuminating course by Edgar Friedenberg on social science method. The observation and study of a reading curriculum rests on assumptions of both what reading is and what reading as a desirable skill ought to be. The same is true of the hidden curriculum.

Educational Consequences of Moral Education

As the educational philosopher R. S. Peters points out, "the concept 'education' has built into it the criterion that something worthwhile should be achieved. It implies something worthwhile is being transmitted in a morally acceptable manner.''[5] To discuss the educational consequences of the hidden curriculum is to discuss whether it does or can lead to the transmission of something worthwhile in a morally acceptable manner. While Friedenberg assumes this, Dreeben claims a value-neutral stance. Dreeben concludes an earlier article by saying,

> The argument of this paper presents a formulation of how schooling contributes to the emergence of certain psychological outcomes, not to provide an apology or justification for these outcomes on ideological grounds. From the viewpoint of ideological justification, the process of schooling is problematic in that outcomes morally desirable from one perspective are undesirable from another.[6]

It is hard to understand what conclusions to draw from Dreeben's analysis if it is really value-neutral. The analysis points out that authority is necessary in adult society, so it is necessary to have a hidden curriculum by which it is learned in the school.

Nature of School Discipline

If Dreeben's analysis has real educational force, however, it is contained in the implicit value-perspective of functional sociology, the perspective that the invisible hand of societal survival guides the shaping of human institutions and gives them a value or wisdom not apparent at first glance. Durkheim, the founder of functional sociology, understood that functional sociology was not a value-free position, but essentially represented a moral point of view. Durkheim articulately and explicitly argued that the sociologist's definition of the invisible hand of the social system was also the definition of rational or scientific morality. So Durkheim goes further than saying that acceptance of authority is one of the key elements of the child's moral development.

Durkheim argues that the crowds, the praise, and the power, which look so wasteful from the point of view of intellectual development, are the necessary conditions for the moral development of the child. According to Durkheim,

> Morality is respect for rule and is altruistic attachment to the social group. . . . although family education is an excellent preparation for the moral life, its usefulness is restricted, above all with respect to the spirit of discipline. That which is essential to the spirit of discipline, respect for the rule, can scarcely develop in the familial setting, which is not subject to general impersonal immutable regulation, and should have an air of freedom. But the child must learn respect for the rule; he must learn to do his duty because it is his duty, even though the task may not seem an easy one.
> Such an apprenticeship must devolve upon the school. Too often, it is true,

people conceive of school discipline so as to preclude endowing it with such an important moral function. Some see in it a simple way of guaranteeing superficial peace and order in the class. Under such conditions, one can quite reasonably come to view these imperative requirements as barbarous, as a tyranny of complicated rules. In reality, however, school discipline is not a simple device for securing superficial peace in the classroom; it is the morality of the classroom as a small society."[7]

Durkheim's System

I shall not go into Durkheim's system of moral education in detail in this paper except to say it is, in my opinion, the most philosophically and scientifically comprehensive, clear, and workable approach to moral education extant. Its workability has been demonstrated not in France but in Soviet Russia, where it has been elaborated from the point of view of Marxist rather than Durkheimian sociology. Like Durkheim, the Russians hold that altruistic concern or sacrifice, like the sense of duty, is always basically directed toward the group rather than to another individual or to an abstract principle. Durkheim reasons that altruism is always sacrificing the self for something greater than the self, and another self can never be greater than the self except as it stands for the group or for society. Accordingly, a central part of moral education is the sense of belonging to, and sacrificing for, a group. Says Durkheim,

In order to commit ourselves to collective ends, we must have above all a feeling and affection for the collectivity. We have seen that such feelings cannot arise in the family where solidarity is based on blood and intimate relationship since the bonds uniting the citizens of a country have nothing to do with such relationships. The only way to instill the inclination to collective life is to get hold of the child when he leaves his family and enters school. We will succeed the more easily because in certain respects, he is more amenable to this joining of minds in a common consciousness than is the adult. To achieve this tonic effect on the child, the class must really share in a collective life. Such phrases as "the class," "the spirit of the class," and "the honor of the class" must become something more than abstract expressions in the student's mind. A means to awaken the feeling of solidarity is the discreet and deliberate use of collective punishments and rewards. Collective sanctions play a very important part in the life of the classroom. The most powerful means to instill in the children the feeling of solidarity is to feel that the value of each is a function of the worth of all.[8]

A Russian Example

One of the logical but to us rather horrifying innovations in the hidden curriculum Durkheim suggests on this basis is the use of collective responsibility [and] collective punishment and reward. Here is how a Russian moral education manual (quoted by Urie Bronfenbrenner) tells us this and other aspects of moral education are to be done in a third-grade classroom:

Class 3-B is just an ordinary class; it's not especially well disciplined.

The teacher has led this class now for three years, and she has earned affection, respect, and acceptance as an authority from her pupils. Her word is law for them.

The bell has rung, but the teacher has not yet arrived. She has delayed deliberately in order to check how the class will conduct itself.

In the class all is quiet. After the noisy class break, it isn't so easy to mobilize yourself and to quell the restlessness within you! Two monitors at the desk silently observe the class. On their faces is reflected the full importance and seriousness of the job they are performing. But there is no need for them to make any reprimands: the youngsters with pleasure and pride maintain scrupulous discipline; they are proud of the fact that their class conducts itself in a manner that merits the confidence of the teacher. And when the teacher enters and quietly says be seated, all understand that she deliberately refrains from praising them for the quiet and order, since in their class it could not be otherwise.

During the lesson, the teacher gives an exceptional amount of attention to collective competition between "links." (The links are the smallest unit of the Communist youth organization at this age level.) Throughout the entire lesson the youngsters are constantly hearing which link has best prepared its lesson, which link has done the best at numbers, which is the most disciplined, which has turned in the best work.

The best link not only gets a verbal positive evaluation but receives the right to leave the classroom first during break and to have its notebooks checked before the others. As a result the links receive the benefit of collective education, common responsibility, and mutual aid.

"What are you fooling around for? You're holding up the whole link," whispers Kolya to his neighbor during the preparation period for the lesson. And during the break he teaches her how better to organize her books and pads in her knapsack.

"Count more carefully," says Olya to her girl friend. "See, on account of you our link got behind today. You come to me and we'll count together at home."[9]

I do not need to say any more to indicate that Durkheim and the Russians know how to make the hidden curriculum explicit, and how to make it work. Furthermore, it is clear that Durkheim has simply taken to its logical conclusion a justification of the hidden curriculum which many teachers vaguely assume, the justification that the discipline of group life directly promotes moral character. We see, however, that when this line of thinking is carried to its logical conclusion, it leads to a definition of moral education as the promotion of collective national discipline, which most of us feel is neither rational ethics nor the American constitutional tradition.

Valuing the Hidden Curriculum

What I am arguing is that the trouble with Durkheim's approach to the hidden curriculum is not that of starting from a conception of moral development, but of starting from a wrong conception of moral development. Before having the arrogance to present the right conception of moral development, I want to indicate briefly how analyses of the hidden curriculum which do not articulate an explicit conception of the moral fail to provide a framework an educator can really get hold of. We have pointed out that Dreeben sees the hidden curriculum as shaped by the invisible hand of the social system without being willing to say whether what serves the social system is good or bad. In contrast, Friedenberg seems to see the hidden curriculum as shaped by pretty much the same invisible hand of society or lower-middle-class society, but to see this invisible hand as bad, as destroying the hearts and minds of the poor, the aristocrats, and the non-middle class in general. The core difficulty of Friedenberg's analysis is his willingness to call things good or bad without systematic criteria of morality behind his judgments. This is reflected in the question, "If you don't like the values which dominate education, what set of values should dominate education?"

The core badness of the hidden curriculum, in Friedenberg's view, is its injustice, its violation of the rights and dignity of adolescents who do not meet the mass image. One might, therefore, expect Friedenberg to hold that the optimal moral consequence of a good curriculum would be the cultivation of just men, of the sense of justice. Instead he comes out for a bag of aristocratic virtues which are as arbitrary as the middle-class virtues he rejects. Put in different terms, he says, "Leave kids alone. Respect their freedom!" without asking whether an education that leaves them alone will educate them to respect the freedom of others.

The School—Transmitter of Values

If lack of explicitness in moral framework creates confusion in Friedenberg's analysis, Dreeben's and Jackson's moral neutrality presents worse puzzles in interpreting their cogent observations. For instance, Dreeben points out that the school arbitrarily demands independent performance on tasks, while cooperation in tasks is considered a good thing under other circumstances. In school tests and assignments, cooperation is cheating, while it is legitimate on other occasions. Jackson makes a similar point:

Another course of action engaged in by most students at least some of the time is to disguise the failure to comply, that is, to cheat. Learning to make it in school involves, in part, learning how to falsify our behavior.[10]

It is not quite correct to say, as Jackson does, that the hidden curriculum of the school teaches children to cheat. More accurately, the school teaches children about cheating and leads to the development of styles of approach to the issue of cheating. In functional sociology phrases, it prepares children for life in an industrial society in which they will have to decide where and when to cheat and when not to. Recent studies confirm the old findings of Hartshorne and May that schooling does not lead to increased honesty.[11] In experimental situations allowing cheating, older children in a given school are as likely to cheat as younger children. What age and passage through school appear to do is to lead to more generalized strategies about cheating. Some older children are more likely to cheat all the time than younger children, while other older children are more likely to refrain from cheating altogether than younger children. This leaves the mean amount of cheating the same.

The point I am making is that Dreeben's analysis of the hidden curriculum suggests that it has neither the hidden nor the manifest function of developing morality. While it presents moral issues such as whether to cheat, its central norms are not moral norms but norms of independent competition and achievement. Accordingly, while teachers may strive to police cheating, they will not exert any real influence over children's moral values or character. Put in a different way, Dreeben is telling us that the schools are transmitting values. A good functional sociologist might reply that from the social system point of view, cultivating independent competition is more important or more *moral* than cultivating honesty, since our society is built to tolerate a lot of petty cheating but is not built to tolerate a lot of people who are not interested in making it by institutional achievement standards. It is just at this point that we have to go back to a conception of the moral before the implications of Dreeben's sociological analysis can be understood.

The Hidden Curriculum as Freedom

One final example of an approach to the hidden curriculum denies considering its use and value for moral education. This example is that of Summerhill's A. S. Neill, whose solution is to chuck out both the hidden curriculum and the concept of morality from education. Dreeben and Jackson say the hidden curriculum is authority, Neill says chuck it out and make the hidden curriculum freedom. Friedenberg's position seems not too different, if Friedenberg were to start a school as Neill has done. Says Neill,

We set out to make a school in which we should allow children freedom to be themselves. To do this we had to renounce all discipline, all direction, all moral training. We have been called brave but it did not require courage, just a complete belief in the child as a good, not an evil, being. A child is innately wise and realistic. If left to himself without adult suggestion of any kind he will develop as far as he is capable of developing. I believe that it is moral instruction that makes the child bad, not good.[12]

A philosopher could while away a pleasant afternoon trying to find out just what ethical framework Neill is using when he says children are good but morality is bad. It is more instructive, however, to recognize that even at Summerhill moral poblems arise and to see how Neill handles them. Some years ago, Neill says,

We had two pupils arrive at the same time, a boy of seventeen and a girl of sixteen. They fell in love with each other and were always together. I met them late one night and stopped them. "I don't know what you two are doing," I said, "and morally I don't care for it isn't a moral question at all. But economically, I do care. If you, Kate, have a kid my school will be ruined. You have just come to Summerhill. To you it means freedom to do what you like. Naturally, you have no special feeling for the school. If you had been here from the age of seven, I'd never have had to mention the matter. You would have such a strong attachment to the school that you would think of the consequences to Summerhill.[13]

What the quotation makes clear, of course, is that the hidden moral curriculum of Summerhill is the explicit curriculum of Durkheim and the Russians. Unquestioned loyalty to the school, to the collectivity, seems to be the ultimate end of moral education at Summerhill. Surely, however, moral education has some other aims than a loyalty to the school and to other children, which might possibly later transfer to loyalty to the nation and [to] other men. To consider what such aims might be we may start with the observation that all the writers we have discussed so far have assumed that morality is fundamentally emotional and irrational. Neill, Dreeben, and Durkheim agree on this point, differing only in their evaluation of the worth of this irrational part of life. It is assumed that the means and ends of intellectual education are one thing and those of moral education another.

Growth of Moral Character

Durkheim and Dreeben assume that learning to accept rules and authority is a concrete nonrational process based on repetition, emotion, and sometimes sanctions. The assumption is that the child is controlled by primitive and selfish drives he is reluctant to give up and that the steady experience of authority and discipline is necessary to live with rules. The notions of Dewey and Piaget, that the child genuinely learns to accept authority when he learns to understand and accept the reasons and principles behind the rules, leads moral education in a different direction, tied much more closely to the intellectual curriculum of the school.[14] This second direction is supported by many research findings. My research and that of others indicates that the development of moral character is in large part a sequential progressive growth of basic principles of moral reasoning and their application to action.

Moral Stages

In my research, I have longitudinally followed the development of moral thinking of a group of fifty boys, from age ten to age twenty-five, by asking them at each three-year interval how and why they would resolve a set of eleven moral dilemmas. We have found that changes in moral thinking go step by step through six stages, with children's development stopping or becoming fixed at any one of the six stages. These stages are defined in [Appendix A at the end of this chapter]. We have found these same stages in the same order in children in Mexico, Turkey, England, and Taiwan, in illiterate villages, and in the urban middle and lower classes, as Figures 3-1, 3-2, and 3-3 indicate.

Take one dilemma, such as whether a husband should steal a drug to save his dying wife if he could get it no other way. (Sample responses to the dilemma at each stage are presented in [Appendix B].) Stage 1 is obedience and punishment. You should not steal the drug because you will be put in jail. Stage 2 is pragmatic hedonism and exchange. Steal the drug, you need your wife and she may do the same for you someday. Stage 3 is love, happiness, kindness, and approval-oriented. Steal the drug because you want to be a good husband and good husbands love their wives. Stage 4 is the maintenance of the social order, respect for law and order, and the loyalty to the group's goals, the morality of Durkheim and the Russians. Stage 5 is social-contract constitutionalism, the definition of the good as the welfare of society where society is conceived as a set of individuals with equal rights and where rules and obligations are formed by the contractual agreements of free men. Stage 6 is the sense of principled obligation to universal human values and justice even when these are not represented in particular legal agreements and contracts in our society.

Each stage includes the core values of the prior stage but defines them in a more universal, differentiated, and integrated form. To the Stage 4 mind of George Wallace, the concept of justice is a threat to law and order, because he does not really understand the concept of a constitutional democracy in which law and order, the government, is set up to pursue and preserve justice, the equal rights of free men; and in that sense the concept of justice includes the valid elements of the law and order concept.

Let me illustrate Stage 5 and its difference from Stage 6 by a quotation from Earl Kelley's pamphlet *Return to Democracy*.

A simple way to measure our efforts to educate is to judge them in the light of the tenets of democracy. . . . It is the way our forefathers decided that they wanted to live, and it is reaffirmed daily by all kinds of Americans except a very few who belong to the radical right or left. The founding fathers attempted to make the democratic ideal come to life by building our Constitution around these tenets. . . . (a) Every person has worth, has value. . . . He is entitled to be treated as a human being. He has equal rights under the law, without regard to his condition of birth or the circumstances under which he has been obliged to live. (b) The individual counts for everything. The state and school—constructed by individuals to serve individuals— are implementations of the way we want to live. . . . (c) Freedom is a requirement for living in a democracy. . . . This does not mean freedom to do just as one pleases. Nobody has this right if he lives in the vicinity of any other human being, because the other human being has rights which also must be respected. . . . If we are to

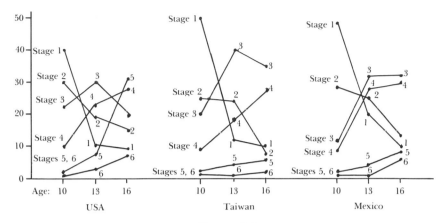

Figure 3-1

Middle-class urban boys in the United States, Taiwan, and Mexico. At age ten, the stages are used according to difficulty. At age thirteen, Stage 3 is most used by all three groups. At age sixteen, United States boys have reversed the order of age ten stages (with the exception of 6). In Taiwan and Mexico, conventional (3–4) stages prevail at age sixteen, with Stage 5 also little used.

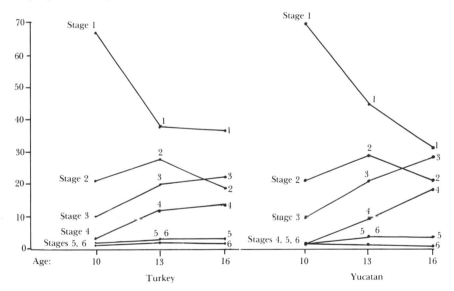

Figure 3-2

Two isolated villages, one in Turkey, the other in Yucatan, show similar patterns in moral thinking. There is no reversal of order, and preconventional (1–2) does not gain a clear ascendancy over conventional stages at age sixteen.

Source: L. Kohlberg and R. Kramer, "Continuities and Discontinuities in Childhood and Adult Moral Development," *Human Development* 12 (1969): 93–120.

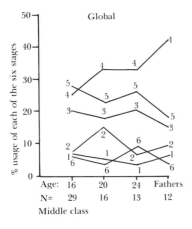

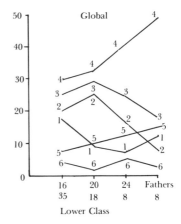

Figure 3-3.

Moral judgment profiles (percentage usage of each stage by global rating method) for middle- and lower-class males at four ages.

Source: L. Kohlberg and R. Kramer, "Continuities and Discontinuities in Childhood and Adult Moral Development," *Human Development* 12 (1969): 93–120.

emphasize the learner himself, there can be no better point of reference than the democratic ideal. It has the advantage of having been agreed upon.[15]

Professor Kelly's statement is clearly not Stage 6, although it contains a recognition of universal human rights and justice. Fundamentally, however, Kelley is arguing that his ideal springs from a ready-made agreed-upon social-constitutional framework, one which permits social change and individual differences, but one which derives its validity from the fact that it is agreed upon, and that it has worked, rather than from the intrinsic universality and morality of its principles. If a man is confronted with a choice of stealing a drug to save a human life, however, Kelley's framework provides no clear ethical solution.

If it is recognized, however, that universal respect for fundamental human rights and for the human personality provides a moral guide defining the way in which any human should act, as well as being the established underlying values of our particular society, we are on the way to Stage 6. It is quite likely that in his personal thinking about moral dilemmas, Kelley would operate in a Stage 6 framework, but that in trying to write a public document that will gain agreement among members of a professional association, he turns to the safer ground of established actual agreement rather than that of Stage 6 principles, which logically are universal though they may not be the basis of historical consensus.

For my purposes, it is not critical whether we take Stage 5 or Stage 6 as defining a desirable level for moral education in the schools. It can safely be said that lower-stage conceptions of morality cannot define the aims of moral education, because the Constitution forbids a type of moral education which involves indoctrination and violation of the rights of individuals and their families to freedom of beliefs. This prevents us from taking the beliefs of the majority as an aim of moral education in the schools, partly because the majority has no consensus on moral issues, partly because studies show majority beliefs are grounded more on Stage 3 beliefs in conforming virtues and Stage 4 conceptions of law and order than upon Stage 5 awareness of justice and constitutional democracy.

An example of a school principal who expressed the Stage 4 beliefs of the majority has been provided by Friedenberg. The principal told his high school students they could not have a radical speaker because the speaker was against the government and the school was an agency of the government. If he had understood our constitutional system at the Stage 5 level, he would have recognized that the school as an agent of the government has a responsibility for communicating conceptions of individual rights which the government was created to maintain and serve. I am not arguing that the principal had a Stage 6 moral obligation to defy heroically an angry community of parents to see that a given radical speaker was heard. He was failing as a moral educator, however, if all he could transmit was Stage 4 moral messages to students, many of whom were quite likely already at a Stage 5 level. Let us assume that all of the readers of this paper are at Stage 5 or Stage 6. What should your moral messages to children be?

Moral Comprehension of Children

A series of carefully replicated experimental studies demonstrate that children seldom comprehend messages more than one stage above their own, and understand but reject messages below their own level.[16] The studies also indicate that people can comprehend and to some extent use all stages lower than their own. As principled moral educators, you have the capacity to use lower-level as well as higher-level messages when you choose.

With young children, it is clear that we can make the mistake of [being at] both too high and too low a level. It is worse to make the mistake of being at too low a level because the child loses respect for the message in that case. Yet this is frequently the case. Let me quote an example of a familiar tone of Stage 3, "everything nice," from a magazine called *Wee Wisdom: A Character Building Magazine*:

"Thank you" can just be a polite little word or it can be something warm and wonderful and happy that makes your heart sing. As Boosters let us climb the steps of appreciation on a golden stairway. Let us add that magic ingredient to all our thank yous. Everyone is happier when our thanks express real appreciation.

Won't you join the Boosters to climb the stairway to happiness and success. What a wonderful world it will be if we all do our part.[17]

The quotation is, of course, straight Stage 3, be nice and everyone will be happy. The only person who can sell that message to adolescents is Tiny Tim, and he has to adopt a few unusual mannerisms to do so.

It is, of course, quite necessary to transmit moral messages at Stages 3 and 4 in the elementary school years. Even here, however, it is probably desirable to have these messages under the integrative control of higher levels. Holstein studies a group of middle-class twelve-year-olds who were about equally divided between the preconventional (Stages 1 and 2) and the conventional (Stages 3 and 4) levels.[18]

Principled mothers were more likely to have conventional-level children than conventional mothers. The principled mothers were capable of conventional moral messages and undoubtedly emitted them. However, their integration of them in terms of the higher level made them better moral educators even where the moral educator's task is bringing children to the conventional level.

Developing Moral Education

My research has led my colleagues and me to go on to develop experimental programs of moral education from the intellectual side. Programs center around the discussion of real and hypothetical moral conflicts. We set up arguments between students at one stage and those at the next stage up, since children are able to assimilate moral thinking only one stage above their own. The preliminary results have been encouraging, with most students advancing one stage and maintaining the advance a year later in comparison with a control group.[19] Such procedures form an explicit intellectual curriculum of moral education. Such a curriculum should not exist in abstraction; however, it should exist as a reflection upon the hidden curriculum of school life.

What is the essential nature of the hidden curriculum as a vehicle of moral growth? Our viewpoint accepts as inevitable the crowds, the praise, and the power which the school inevitably contains. How much or little crowd, praise, or discipline, or power is of little interest from our point of view. A generation of child psychology research measuring the effects of amount and type of family authority and discipline on moral character have yielded few substantial results. If these things do not define the moral-educational effects of the family, they are unlikely to define the weaker and more transient moral effects of particular schools.

The Role of the Teacher

We believe what matters in the hidden curriculum is the moral character and ideology of the teachers and principal as these are translated into a working social atmosphere which influences that atmosphere of the children. In the introduction of a recent book presenting portraits of Shapiro, the principal of P.S. 119, and Boyden, the headmaster of Deerfield, Mayerson says, "Each is engaged in a diligent attempt to achieve a consistency between an articulated personal morality and the daily passage of their lives. The two schools are the sites of the working out of this ideal."[20] Shapiro, the Harlem principal, was trained as a clinical psychologist. His ideology is one of empathy, permissiveness, and respect for his deprived children: meeting their needs, trying to keep their liveliness from dying, with no explicit concern for moral education. The ideology is one of warmth and humility and Shapiro is a warm and humble man who is against the crowds, the praise, and the power. How does his ideology, his warmth, and his humility come across to the school? I quote,

A woman announced that the assembly was being dedicated to Dr. Shapiro. He winced. Eleven girls stood and sang in unison: "Oh he is the bravest, Oh he is the greatest, we'll fight before we switch."

"Talk about brainwashing," Shapiro mumbled, slumped in a back row seat.[21]

It is clear that this humble and dedicated believer in permissiveness is in firm control of the crowds, the praise, and the power.

Neill's personal characteristics are quite different from Shapiro's, yet he too has created an effective moral atmosphere. As a character, Neill is obviously dogmatic, self-assured, imposing. One could not want a stronger, more vigorous leader of a *leaderless* school. In character, he is reminiscent of Frank Boyden, the headmaster of Deerfield, who is described as being without contradiction humanitarian, ruthless, loyal, selfish, selfless, stubborn, indestructible, and infallible. Unlike Neill, Boyden believes in discipline and believes that the purpose of his school is moral character-building. Like Neill, Boyden radiates a belief in the value of his school as an end in itself.

In citing Boyden, Shapiro, and Neill as masters of the hidden curriculum, I have tried to indicate that the transformation of the hidden curriculum into a moral atmosphere is not a matter of one or another educational technique or ideology or means, but a matter of the moral energy of the educator, of his communicated belief that his school or classroom has a human purpose. To get his message across, he may use permissiveness or he may use discipline, but the effective moral educator has a believable human message.

The Ends of Moral Education

We have seen, however, that this human message cannot be an ideology of education, or it will end by treating the school as the ultimate value, with the corresponding eventual morality of loyalty to the school or to an ideological doctrine of education in itself. The hidden curriculum of the school must represent something more than the goals and social order of the school itself. Our definition of moral maturity as the principled sense of justice suggests what this end must be. The teaching of justice requires just schools. The crowds, the praise, and the power are neither just nor unjust in themselves. As they are typically used in the schools, they represent the values of social order and of individual competitive achievement. The problem is not to get rid of the praise, the power, the order, and the competitive achievement, but to establish a more basic context of justice which gives them meaning. In our society authority derives from justice, and in our society learning to live with authority should derive from and aid learning to understand and to feel justice.

The need to make the hidden curriculum an atmosphere of justice, and to make this hidden curriculum explicit in intellectual and verbal discussions of justice and morality, is becoming more and more urgent. Our research studies have shown that our Stage 6 or most morally mature college students are the students most active in support of universal civil rights and in support of the universal sacredness of human life as both issues have recently come in clear conflict with authority, law and order, national loyalty, and college administrations. Research also indicates that these mature adolescents are joined by an immature group of rebellious egoistic relativists who think justice means everyone "doing his thing." It seems clear that student-administration confrontations will spread to younger and younger groups who are increasingly confused and immature in their thought about the issues of justice involved.

In the current college confrontations, it has been typical for administrators to harden into poses of what I call Stage 4 law and order thinking, or what I call Stage 5 social-contract legalism. What else can they do? What else are they taught in programs of school administration? This is hard to answer because the world's great moral educators have not run schools. Moral education is something of a revolutionary activity. When Socrates engaged in genuine moral education, he was executed for corrupting the Athenian youth. I mention Socrates to indicate that it is not only America who kills its moral educators, its men like Martin Luther King, Jr., who both talked and lived as drum majors of justice.

These fatalities and many others will continue to go on as long as the dialogue about justice goes on across the barricades. The current fate of the school administrator is to find that if he keeps the dialogue out of the classroom, he will face it across the barricades with students to whom he cannot speak. The educational use of the hidden curriculum is not to prevent the dialogue by calling classroom law and order moral character, nor to cast it out on the ground that the child needs only freedom, but to use it to bring the dialogue of justice into the classroom. It is my hope that our educational research program may find worthwhile ways of doing this in the next five years. It is perhaps less a hope than a dream that the American schools will want to use it.

Appendix A: Definition of Moral Stages

I. Pre-Conventional Level

At this level the child is responsive to cultural rules and labels of good and bad, right or wrong, but interprets these labels in terms of either the physical or the hedonistic consequences of action (punishment, reward, exchange of favors) or in terms of the physical power of those who enunciate the rules and labels. The level is divided into the following two stages:

Stage 1: The punishment and obedience orientation. The physical consequences of action determine its goodness or badness regardless of the human meaning or value of these consequences. Avoidance of punishment and unquestioning deference to power are valued in their own right, not in terms of respect for an underlying moral order supported by punishment and authority (the latter being Stage 4).

Stage 2: The instrumental relativist orientation. Right action consists of that which instrumentally satisfies one's own needs and occasionally the needs of others. Human relations are viewed in terms like those of the marketplace. Elements of fairness, of reciprocity, and of equal sharing are present, but they are always interpreted in a physical pragmatic way. Reciprocity is a matter of "you scratch my back and I'll scratch yours," not of loyalty, gratitude, or justice.

II. Conventional Level

At this level, maintaining the expectations of the individual's family, group, or nation is perceived as valuable in its own right, regardless of immediate and obvious consequences. The attitude is not only one of *conforming* to personal expectations and social order, but of loyalty to it, of actively *maintaining*, supporting and justifying the order and of identifying with the persons or group involved in it. At this level, there are the following two stages:

Stage 3: The interpersonal concordance or good boy—nice girl orientation. Good behavior is that which pleases or helps others and is approved by them. There is much conformity to stereotypical images of what is majority or "natural" behavior. Behavior is frequently judged by intention—"he means well" becomes important for the first time. One earns approval by being "nice."

Stage 4: The law-and-order orientation. There is orientation toward authority, fixed rules, and the maintenance of the social order. Right behavior consists of doing one's duty, showing respect for authority, and maintaining the given social order for its own sake.

III. Post-Conventional, Autonomous, or Princifled Level

At this level, there is a clear effort to define moral values and principles that have validity and application apart from the authority of the groups or persons holding these principles and apart from the individual's own identification with those groups. This level again has two stages:

Stage 5. The social-contract, legalistic orientation. Generally with utilitarian overtones. Right action tends to be defined in terms of general individual rights and in terms of standards which have been critically examined and agreed upon by the whole society. There is a clear awareness of the relativism of personal values and opinions and a corresponding emphasis upon procedural rules for reaching consensus. Aside from what is constitutionally and democratically agreed upon, the right is a matter of personal values and opinion. The result is an emphasis upon the legal point of view, but with an emphasis upon the possibility of changing law in terms of rational considerations of social utility (rather than freezing it in terms of Stage 4 law-and-order). Outside the legal realm, free agreement and contract are the binding elements of obligation. This is the "official" morality of the American government and Constitution.

Stage 6. The universal ethical principle orientation. Right is defined by the decision of conscience in accord with self-chosen *ethical principles* appealing to logical comprehensiveness, universality, and consistency. These principles are abstract and ethical (the Golden Rule, the categorical imperative); they are not concrete moral rules like the Ten Commandments. At heart, these are universal principles of *justice*, of the reciprocity and equality of the human rights, and of respect for the dignity of human beings as individual persons.

Appendix B: A Moral Dilemma and Sample Responses

In Europe, a woman was near death from a special kind of cancer. There was one drug that the doctors thought might save her. It was a form of radium that a druggist in the same town had recently discovered. The drug was expensive to make, but the druggist was charging ten times what the drug cost him to make. He paid $200 for the radium and charged $2,000 for a small dose of the drug. The sick woman's husband, Heinz, went to everyone he knew to borrow the money, but he could only get together about $1,000, which is half of what it cost. He told the druggist that his wife was dying and asked him to sell it cheaper or let him pay later. But the druggist said, "No, I discovered the drug and I'm going to make money from it." So Heinz got desperate and broke into the man's store to steal the drug for his wife.

Should the husband have done that? Why?

Musammer—Age 10   **Stage 1**   **Turkish**

1. No. It's not good to steal. (Why?) If you steal some other's things one day he will steal yours, there will be a fight between the two and they will just put both in prison.

2. (Is it a husband's duty to steal the drug? Would a good husband?) No. He must go and work in order to earn the money for the drug. (If he can't?) One must give him the money. (If nobody gives?) If they don't she will die—he should not steal. (Why not?) If he steals they will put him in prison.

3. (Does the druggist have the right to charge that much for the drug if the law allows him?) No—if he charges so much from the villagemen then they won't have enough money.

4a. (If it were your wife who were dying?) I will not steal. I would let her die.

5a. If I stole they would tell on me and put me in prison—so I would not.

6. They should put him in jail because he stole.

Hamza—Age 12   **Stage 2**   **Turkish**

1. Yes, because nobody would give him the drug and he had no money, because his wife was dying it was right. (Wrong not to?) Yes, because otherwise she would die.

2. (Is it a husband's duty to steal the drug?) Yes—when his wife is dying and he cannot do anything he is obliged to steal. (Why?) If he doesn't steal his wife will die.

3. (Does the druggist have the right to charge that much for the drug?) Cause he is the only store in the village it is right to sell.

4. (Should he steal the drug if he doesn't love his wife?) If he doesn't love his wife he should not steal because he doesn't care for her, doesn't care for what she says.

5. (How about if it is a good friend?) Yes—because he loves his friend and one day when he is hungry his friend would help. (If he doesn't love his friend?) No—when he doesn't love him it means his friend will not help him.

6. (Should the judge punish him?) They should put him in jail because he stole.

Iskender—Age 17   **Stage 4**   **Turkish**

1. He should not have stolen—he should have asked for the drug and they would give him the drug. (They didn't.) He should go somewhere else. (Nowhere else to go.) He should try to work for the drug. (He can't.) Then it would be right to steal and not let his wife die because she will die and for that moment it would be right—he had to steal because his wife would die—he had to steal for the first and last time.

It is all right to steal when he can't do anything else—for the first and last time and then he should go out to work. (His duty?) It's not his duty to steal, but it is his duty to feed her.

(Did the druggist have the right to charge so much?) It's not right—laws are set up to organize people and their living—he charges so much because he is not human—if he thinks of others he must sell things so that everybody can buy.

4. (If he doesn't love her, should he steal the drug?) Because they are married he must—loving and feeling close to her has nothing to do with it. They must be together in bad or good times. Even if it's someone else who is dying he should steal. If I was in his place I would steal if I didn't know the man who was dying. He should do it only once to save somebody's life—if it's a question of death he should steal but not for anything else.

6. (Should the judge send him to jail?) It is up to the judge to decide. If he thinks the man stole just for this once and had to steal to save his wife then he would not put him in jail, but if he thinks the man will do it again and that it will become a habit then he should put him in jail. If the judge is understanding he would find a job for this man who is not working.

James   Stage 5   American College

Heinz did only what he had to. Had I been Heinz, I would probably have done the same thing. In any event, however, Heinz must be prepared to go to jail for breaking into a store. Breaking into the store was not "right," but the lesser of two wrongs.

(Is it his duty?) Every husband must decide which of the two wrongs—letting his wife go without the drug or stealing—is greater *to him.* I would steal.

(Did the druggist have the right to charge that much or keep the drug?) The druggist had the *right* to charge that much, although perhaps he should not have. I consider the druggist a despicable human being, even though he was acting within his rights.

Richard   Stage 6   American Adult

(Should Heinz have done that?) Yes. It was right; human life and the right to it are prior to, and more precious than, property rights.

(Is it a husband's duty to steal the drug for his wife if he can get it no other way?) It is the husband's duty to do so. Any good husband whose ethical values were not confused would do it.

(Did the druggist have the right to charge that much when there was no law actually setting a limit to the price?) In a narrow legal sense, he had such a right. From a moral point of view, however, he had no such right.

(Heinz broke into the store and stole the drug and gave it to his wife. He was caught and brought before the judge. Should the judge send Heinz to jail for stealing, or should he let him go free? Why?) He should suspend the sentence or dismiss the charge since Heinz did no moral wrong.

Notes

1. P. Jackson, *Life in Classrooms* (New York: Holt, Rinehart & Winston, 1968).

2. E. Durkheim, *Moral Education* (New York: Free Press, 1961), p. 231.

3. E. Z. Friedenberg, *Coming of Age in America: Growth and Acquiescence* (New York: Random House, 1963), p. 43.

4. Ibid., p. 29.

5. R. S. Peters, *Ethics and Education* (Chicago: Scott, Foresman & Co., 1967), p. 6.

6. R. Dreeben, "The Contribution of Schooling to the Learning of Norms," *Harvard Educational Review* (Spring 1967): 211–37.

7. Durkheim, *Moral Education*, p. 148.

8. Ibid., p. 239.

9. U. Bronfenbrenner, "Soviet Methods of Character Education, Some Implications for Research," *American Psychologist* 17 (1962): 550–65.

10. Jackson, *Life in Classrooms*, p. 27.

11. H. Hartshorne and M. A. May, *Studies in the Nature of Character*: Vol. I, *Studies in Deceit*; Vol II, *Studies in Self Control*; Vol. III, *Studes in the Organization of Character* (New York: Macmillan, 1928–30).

12. A. S. Neill, *Summerhill: A Radical Approach to Child Rearing* (New York: Hart Publishing Co., 1960), p. 4.

13. Ibid., pp. 57–58.

14. J. Dewey, *Moral Principles in Education* (Boston: Houghton Mifflin Co., 1909); J. Piaget, *The Moral Judgment of the Child* (Glencoe, Ill.: Free Press, 1948).

15. E. Kelley, *Return to Democracy* (Washington, D.C.: American Association of Elementary/Kindergarten/Nursery Educators, National Education Association, Elementary Instructional Service, 1964).

16. E. Turiel, "Developmental Processes in the Child's Moral Thinking," in *New Directions in Developmental Psychology*, ed. P. Mussen, J. Heavenrich, and J. Langer (New York: Holt, Rinehart & Winston, 1969).

17. *Wee Wisdom—A Character Building Magazine*, June 1967, p. 83.

18. C. Holstein, "Parental Determinants of the Development of Moral Judgment" (Ph.D. dissertation, University of California, Berkeley, 1960).

19. M. Blatt and L. Kohlberg, "The Effects of a Classroom Discussion Program upon the Moral Levels of Preadolescents," *Merrill Palmer Quarterly* (1969).

20. N. Hentoff, *Our Children Are Dying*; and J. A. McPhee, *The Headmaster: Frank L. Boyden, of Deerfield* (New York: Four Winds Press, 1966).

21. Ibid., p. 38.

4

What Do Schools Teach?

Michael Apple and Nancy King

Schooling and Cultural Capital

One of the least attractive complaints about schools in recent years has been that they are relatively unexciting, boring, or what have you because of mindlessness.[1] The basis of this argument is that schools covertly teach all those things that humanistic critics of schools like to write and talk about—among them, behavioral consensus, institutional rather than personal goals and norms, alienation from one's products—because teachers, administrators, and other educators do not really know what they are doing. Such a perspective is misleading at best. In the first place, it is thoroughly ahistorical. It ignores the fact that schools were in part designed to teach exactly these things. The hidden curriculum, the tacit teaching of social and economic norms and expectations to students in schools, was not as hidden or "mindless" as many educators believe. Such a perspective also ignores the critical task that schools, as the fundamental set of institutions in advanced industrial societies, do perform in order to certify adult competence, and it pulls schools out of their setting within the larger and much more powerful nexus of economic and political institutions that give schools their meaning. That is, schools seem to do what they are in fact supposed to do, by and large, at least in terms of roughly providing dispositions and propensities that are quite functional to one's later life in a complex and stratified social and economic order.

While there is no doubt that mindlessness does exist outside Charles Silberman's mind, neither it, nor venality, nor indifference are adequate descriptive devices in explaining why schools are so resistant to change or why schools teach what they do.[2] Nor is it an appropriate conceptual tool for use in ferreting out what exact kinds of things are taught in schools or why certain social meanings and not others are used to organize school life. Yet it is not just the critics of schools who tend to oversimplify their analysis of the social and economic meaning of schools.

All too often the social meaning of school experience has been accepted as unproblematic by sociologists of education or as merely engineering problems by curriculum specialists and other programmatically inclined educators. The curriculum field especially, among other educational areas, has been dominated by a perspective that might best be called "technological" in that the major interest guiding its work has involved finding the one best set of means to reach prechosen educational ends.[3] Against this relatively ameliorative and uncritical background, a number of sociologists and curriculum scholars, influenced strongly by the sociology of knowledge in both its Marxist or neo-Marxist and phenomenological variants, have begun to raise serious questions about this lack of attention to the relationship of school knowledge to extraschool phenomena. A fundamental basis for these investigations has been best articulated by Michael F. D. Young. He notes that there is a "dialectical relationship between access to power and the opportunity to legitimize certain dominant categories, and the process by which the availability of such categories to some group enables them to assert power and control over others."[4] In essence, just as there is a relatively unequal distribution of economic capital in society, so, too, is there a similar system of distribution surrounding cultural capital.[5] In advanced industrial societies, schools become particularly important as distributors of this cultural capital and play a critical role in giving legitimacy to certain categories and forms of knowledge. The very fact that certain traditions and normative "content" are construed as school knowledge is prima facie evidence of perceived legitimacy.

The argument in this presentation is that the *problem* of educational knowledge, of what is taught in schools, has to be considered a form of the larger distribution of goods and services in a society. It is not merely an analytic problem (What shall be construed as knowledge?), nor exclusively a technical consideration (How do we organize and store knowledge so that children have access to it and can "master" it?), nor solely a psychological concern (How do we get students to learn X?). Rather, the study of educational knowledge is a study in ideology, the investigation of what is considered legitimate knowledge (be it knowledge of the logical type of "that," "how," or "to") by specific social groups and classes, in specific institutions, at specific historical moments. It is, further, a critically oriented form of investigation in that it chooses to focus on how this knowledge, as distributed in schools, can contribute to cognitive and dispositional development that strengthens or reinforces existing and often problematic institutional arrangements in society. In clearer terms, the overt and covert knowledge found within school settings and the principles of selection, organization, and evaluation of this knowledge are valuative selections from a much larger universe of possible knowledge and collection principles. As valuative selections, they must not be accepted as given, but must be made problematic—bracketed, if you will—so that the social and economic ideologies and the institutionally patterned meanings that stand behind them can be scrutinized. It is the latent meaning, the configuration that lies behind the commonsense acceptability of a position, that may be its most important attribute. And these hidden institutional meanings and relations[6] are almost never uncovered if we are guided only by amelioration. As Daniel Kallos has noted recently, there are both manifest in politico-economic terms. In short, discussions about the quality of educational life are relatively meaningless if the "specific functions of the educational system are unrecognized."[7] If much of the literature on what schools tacitly teach is accurate, then the specific functions may be more economic than "intellectual."

The focus here is on certain aspects of the problem of schooling and social and economic meaning. Schools are viewed as institutions that embody collective traditions and human intentions that are the products of identifiable social and economic ideologies. The starting point might best be phrased as a question: *Whose* meanings are collected and distributed through the overt and hidden curricula in schools? That is, as Marx was fond of saying, reality does not stalk around with a label. The curriculum in schools responds to and represents ideological and cultural resources that come from somewhere. Not all groups' visions are represented and not all groups' meanings are responded to. How, then, do schools act to distribute this cultural capital? Whose reality "stalks" in the corridors and classrooms of American schools? The concern here is, first, to describe the historical process through which certain social meanings became particularly *school* meanings, and thus now have the weight of decades of acceptance behind them. Second, we shall offer empirical evidence of a study of kindergarten experience to document the potency and staying power of these particular social meanings. Finally, we shall raise the question of whether piecemeal reforms, be they humanistically oriented or other, can succeed.

The task of dealing with sets of meanings in schools has traditionally fallen to the curriculum specialist. Historically, however, this concern for meaning in schools by curriculum specialists has been linked to varied notions of social control. This should not be surprising. It should be obvious, though it usually is not, that questions about meanings in social institutions tend to become questions of control.[8] Forms of knowledge—both overt and covert—found within school settings imply relations of power and economic resources and control. The very choice of school knowledge, that is, the act of designing school environments, consciously or unconsciously reflects ideological and economic presuppositions that provide the commonsense rules for educators' thoughts and actions. Perhaps the link between meaning and control in schools can be made clearer by a relatively brief account of curricular history.

Meaning and Control in Curricular History

Bill Williamson, a British sociologist, argues that men and women "have to contend with the institutional and ideological forms of earlier times as the basic constraints on what they can achieve."[9] If one takes this notion seriously in looking at education, what is both provided and taught in schools must be understood historically. Speaking specifically about schools, Williamson notes: "Earlier educational attitudes of dominant groups in society still carry historical weight and are exemplified even in the bricks and mortar of the school buildings themselves."[10]

If we are to be honest with ourselves, the curriculum field itself has its roots in the soil of social control. From its beginnings early in the twentieth century, when its intellectual paradigm took shape and became an identifiable set of procedures for selecting and organizing school knowledge, a set that should be taught to teachers and other educators, the fundamental consideration of the formative members of the curriculum field was that of social control. Part of this concern for social control is understandable. Many historically important figures who influenced the curriculum field (such as Charles C. Peters, Ross Finney, and, especially, David Snedden) had interests that spanned both the field of educational sociology and the more general problem of what should concretely happen in school. Given the growing importance of the idea of social control in the American Sociological Society at the time, an idea that seemed to capture the imagination and energy of so many of the nation's intelligentsia, as well as powerful segments of the business community, it is not difficult to see how it also attracted those people interested in both sociology and curriculum.[11]

Interest in schooling as a mechanism for exerting social control did not have merely sociological origins. Individuals who first called themselves curriculists (men like Franklin Bobbitt and W. W. Charters) were vitally concerned with social control for ideological reasons as well. Influenced strongly by the scientific management movement and the work of social measurement specialists[12] and guided by beliefs that found the popular eugenics movement a "progressive" social force, these men brought social control into the very heart of the field that was concerned with developing criteria to guide selection of those meanings students would encounter in educational institutions.

This is not to say that social control in and of itself is always negative, of course. In fact, it is nearly impossible to envision social life without some element of control, if only because institutions, as such, tend to respond to the *regularities* of human interaction. What strongly influenced early curriculum workers was a historically specific set of assumptions, commonsense rules, about school meanings and control that incorporated not merely the idea that organized society must maintain itself through the preservation of some of its valued forms of interaction and meaning, which implied a quite general and wholly understandable "weak" sense of social control. Deeply embedded in their ideological perspective was a "strong" sense of control wherein education in general and the everyday meanings of the curriculum in particular were seen as essential to the preservation of the existing social privilege, interests, and knowledge of one element of the population at the expense of less powerful groups.[13] Most often this took the form of attempting to guarantee expert and scientific control in society, to eliminate or "socialize" unwanted racial or ethnic groups or characteristics, or to produce an economically efficient group of citizens in order to, as C. C. Peters put it, reduce the maladjustment of workers from their jobs. It is this latter interest, the economic substratum of everyday school life, that will become of particular importance when we look at what schools teach about work and play in a later section of this presentation.

Of course, neither the idea of nor an interest in social control emerged newborn through the early curriculum movement's attempts to use school knowledge for rather conservative social ends. Social control had been the implied aim of a substantial number of ameliorative social and political programs carried out during the nineteenth century by both state and private agencies so that order and stability, and the imperative of industrial growth, might be maintained in the face of a variety of social and economic changes.[14] Walter Feinberg's analysis of the ideological roots of liberal educational policy demonstrates that even in this century many of the proposed "reforms" in schools and elsewhere latently serve the conservative social interests of stability and social stratification.[15]

The argument presented so far is not meant to belittle the efforts of educators and social reformers. Instead, it is an attempt to place the current arguments over the "lack of humaneness in schools," the tacit teaching of social norms and values, and similar considerations within a larger historical context. Without such a context, it is impossible to understand fully the relationship between what schools actually do and an advanced industrial economy. The best example of this context can be found in the changing ideological functions of schooling in general and curricular meanings in particular. Behind much of the argumentation about the role of formal education during the nineteenth century in the United States were concerns about the standardization of educational environments, the teaching through day-to-day school interaction of moral, normative, and dispositional values, and economic functionalism. Today these concerns have been termed the "hidden curriculum" by Philip Jackson[16] and others. But it is the very question of its hiddenness that may help us uncover the historical relationship between what is taught in schools and the larger context of institutions that surround them.

We should be aware that historically the hidden curriculum was not hidden at all; instead, it was the overt function of schools during much of their existence as an institution. During the nineteenth century, the increasing diversity of political, social, and cultural attributes and structures "pushed educators to resume with renewed vigor the language of social control and homogenization that had dominated educational rhetoric from the earliest colonial period."[17] As the century progressed, the rhetoric of reform, of justifying one ideological position against that of other interest groups, did not focus merely on the critical need for social homogeneity. The use of schools to inculcate values, to create an "American community," was no longer sufficient. The growing pressures of modernization and industrialization also created certain expectations of efficiency and functionalism among certain classes and an industrial elite in society as well. As Elizabeth Vallance puts it, "to assertive socialization was added a focus on organizational efficiency." Thus, the reforms having the greatest effect on school organization and ultimately the procedures and principles governing life in classrooms were dominated by the language of and an interest in production, well-adjusted economic functioning, and bureaucratic skills. In this process the underlying reasons for reform in a modern industrial society slowly changed from active concern for valuative consensus to a recognized need for economic functionalism.[18] But this could only occur if the prior period, with its search for a standardized national character built in large part through the characteristics of schools, had been both perceived and accepted as successful. Thus it was that the institutional outlines of schools, the relatively standardized day-to-day forms of interaction, provided the mechanisms by which a normative consensus could be "taught." And within these broad outlines, these behavioral regularities of the institution if you will, an ideological set of commonsense rules for curriculum selection and organizing school experience based on efficiency, economic functionalism, and bureaucratic exigencies took hold. The valuative consensus became the deep structure, the first hidden curriculum, which encased the normative economic one. Once the hidden curriculum became hidden, when a uniform and standardized learning context became established and when social selection and control were taken as given in schooling, only then could attention be paid to the needs of the individual or other more "ethereal" concerns.[19]

Thus it was that a core of commonsense meanings combining normative consensus and economic adjustment was built into the very structure of formal education. This is not to say that there have been no significant educational movements toward, say, education for self-development. Rather, it would appear that behind preferential choices about individual needs there is a more powerful set of expectations surrounding schooling that provides the constitutive structure of school experience. As a number of economists have recently noted, the most economically important "latent function" of school life seems to be the selection and generation of personality attributes and normative meanings that enable one to have supposed chance at economic rewards.[20] Since the school is the only major institution that stands between the family and the labor market, it is not odd that, both historically and currently, certain social meanings that have differential benefits are distributed in schools. But what are these particular social meanings? It is these questions to which we shall now turn.

Ideology and the Curriculum in Use

The larger concerns with the relationship between ideology and school knowledge, between meaning and control, of the prior section tend to be altogether too vague unless they can be seen as active forces in the activity of schoolpeople and students as they go about their particular lives in the classroom. As investigators of the hidden curriculum and others have noted, the concrete modes by which knowledge is distributed in classrooms and the commonsense practices of teachers and students can illuminate the connection between school life and the structures of ideology, power, and economic resources, of which schools are a part.[21]

Just as there is a social distribution of cultural capital in society, so, too, is there a social distribution of knowledge within classrooms. For example, different "kinds" of students get different kinds of knowledge, as Nell Keddie so well documents in her study of the knowledge teachers have of their students and the curricular knowledge then made available to the students.[22] While the differential distribution of classroom knowledge does exist and is intimately linked to the process of social labeling that occurs in schools,[23] it is less important to this analysis than what might be called the "deep structure" of school experience. What underlying meanings are negotiated and transmitted in schools behind the actual formal "stuff" of curriculum content? What happens when knowledge is filtered through teachers? Through what categories of normality and deviance is knowledge filtered? What is the *basic and organizing framework* of normative and conceptual knowledge that students actually get? In short, what is the curriculum in use? Only by seeing the deeper structure does it become obvious that social norms, institutions, and ideological rules are ongoingly sustained by the day-to-day interaction of commonsense actors as they go about their normal practices.[24] This is especially true in classrooms. Social definitions about school knowledge, definitions that are both dialectically related to and rest within the larger context of the surrounding social and economic institutions, are maintained and re-created by the commonsense practices of teaching and evaluation in classrooms.[25]

We shall focus on kindergarten here because it occupies a critical moment in the process by which students become competent in the rules, norms, values, and dispositions "necessary" to function within institutional life as it now exists. Learning the role of student is a complex activity, one that takes time and requires continual interaction with institutional expectations. By focusing on both how this occurs and the content of the dispositions that are both overtly and covertly part of kindergarten knowledge, it is possible to illuminate the background knowledge children use as organizing principles for much of the rest of their school career.

In short, the social definitions internalized during initial school life provide the constitutive rules for later life in classrooms. Thus, what is construed as work or play, "school knowledge" or merely "my knowledge," or normality or deviance are the elements that require observation. As we shall see, the use of praise, rules governing access to materials, control of both time and emotion—all make significant contributions to teaching social meanings in school. But as we shall also see it is the meanings attached to the category of work that most clearly illuminate the possible place of schools in the complex nexus of economic and social institutions that surround us all.

Kindergarten experience serves as a foundation for the years of schooling to follow. Children who have attended kindergarten tend to demonstrate a general superiority in achievement in the elementary grades over children who have not attended kindergarten. Attempts to determine exactly which teaching techniques and learning experiences contribute most directly to the "intellectual and emotional growth" of kindergarten children have, however, produced inconclusive results. Kindergarten training appears to exert its most powerful and lasting influence on the attitudes and the behavior of children by acclimating them to a classroom environment. The children are introduced to their roles as elementary school pupils, and it is the understanding and mastery of this *role* that makes for the greater success of kindergarten-trained children in elementary school.

Socialization in kindergarten classrooms includes the learning of norms and definitions of social interactions. It is the continuous development of a working definition of the situation by the participants. In order to function adequately in a social situation, those involved must reach a common understanding of the meanings, limitations, and potential the setting affords for their interaction. During the first few weeks of the school year, the children and the teacher forge a common definition of the situation out of repeated interaction in the classroom. When one common set of social meanings is accepted, classroom activities proceed smoothly. Most often these common meanings remain relatively stable unless the flow of events in the setting ceases to be orderly.

Socialization is not, however, a one-way process.[26] To some extent, the children in a classroom socialize the teacher as well as becoming socialized themselves, but children and teacher do not have an equal influence in determining the working definition of the situation. On the first day of school in a kindergarten classroom, the teacher has a more highly organized set of commonsense rules than the children do. Since the teacher also holds most of the power to control events and resources in the classroom, it is his or her set of meanings that is dominant. This does not mean that teachers are free to define the classroom situation in any way they choose. As we saw earlier in this presentation, the school is a well-established institution, and it may be that neither the teacher nor the children can perceive more than marginal ways to deviate to any significant degree from the commonsense rules and expectations that set the school apart from any other institution.

The negotiation of meanings in a kindergarten classroom is a critical phase in the socialization of the children. The meanings of classroom objects and events are not intrinsic to them, but are formed through social interaction. As with other aspects of the definition of the situation, these meanings may shift initially. At some point, however, they become stable, and they are not likely to be renegotiated unless the orderly flow of events in the classroom is disrupted.

The meanings of objects and events become clear to the children as they participate in the social setting. The *use* of materials, the nature of authority, the quality of personal relationships, the spontaneous remarks, as well as other aspects of daily classroom life, contribute to the children's growing awareness of their roles in the classroom and their understanding of the social setting. Therefore, to understand the social reality of schooling, it is necessary to study it in actual classroom settings. Each concept, role, and object is a social creation bound to the situation in which it is produced. The meanings of classroom interaction cannot be assumed; they must be discovered. The abstraction of these meanings and the generalizations and insights drawn from them may apply to other contexts, but the researcher's initial descriptions, understandings, and interpretations require that social phenomena be encountered where they are produced, that is, in the classroom.[27]

By observing and interviewing the participants in one particular public school kindergarten classroom it was established that the social meanings of events and materials became fixed remarkably early in the school year.[28] As with most classroom settings, the socialization of the children took overt priority during the opening weeks of school. The four most important skills the teacher expected the children to learn during those opening weeks were to share, to listen, to put things away, and to follow the classroom routine. It was her statement of her goals for the children's early school experiences that constituted the definition of socialized behavior in the classroom.

The children had no part in organizing the classroom materials and had little effect on the course of daily events. The teacher made no special effort to make the children comfortable in the room or to reduce their uncertainty about the schedule of activities. Rather than mediating intrusive aspects of the environment, she chose to require that the children accommodate themselves to the materials as presented. When the noise from another class in the hallway distracted the children, for example, the teacher called for their attention, but she did not close the door. Similarly, the individual cubbies where the children kept their crayons, smocks, and tennis shoes were not labeled although the children had considerable difficulty remembering which cubby was theirs. Despite the many instances of lost crayons and crying children, the teacher refused to permit the student teacher to label the cubbies. She told the student teacher that the children must learn to remember their assigned cubbies because "that is their job." When one girl forgot where her cubby was on the day after they had been assigned, the teacher pointed her out to the class as an example of a "girl who was not listening yesterday."

The objects in the classroom were attractively displayed in an apparent invitation to the class to interact with them. Most of the materials were placed on the floor or on shelves within easy reach of the children. Opportunities to interact with materials in the classroom were, however, severely circumscribed. The teacher's organization of time in the classroom contradicted the apparent availability of materials in the physical setting. During most of the kindergarten session, the children were not permitted to handle objects. The materials, then, were organized so that the children learned restraint; they learned to handle things within easy reach only when permitted to do so by the teacher. The children were "punished" for touching things when the time was not right and praised for the moments when they were capable of restraint. For example, the teacher praised the children for prompt obedience when they quickly stopped bouncing basketballs after being told to do so in the gym, but made no mention of their ball-handling skills.

The teacher made it clear to the children that good kindergarteners were quiet and cooperative. One morning a child brought two large stuffed dolls to school and put them in her assigned seat. During the first period of large group instruction, the teacher referred to them saying, "Raggedy Ann and Raggedy Andy are such good helpers! They haven't said a thing all morning."

As part of learning to exhibit socialized behavior, the children learned to tolerate ambiguity and discomfort in the classroom and to accept a considerable degree of arbitrariness in their school activities. They were required to adjust their emotional responses to conform to those considered appropriate by the teacher. They learned to respond to her personally and to the manner in which she organized the classroom environment.

After some two weeks of kindergarten experience, the children had established a category system for defining and organizing their social reality in the classroom, but interview responses indicated that the activities in the classroom did not have intrinsic meanings. The children assigned meanings depending upon the context in which each was carried on. The teacher presented the classroom materials either as a part of instruction, or, more overtly, she discussed and demonstrated their uses to the class. This is a critical point. The use of a particular object, that is, the manner in which we are predisposed to act toward it, constitutes its meaning for us. In defining the meanings of the things in the classroom, then, a teacher defines the nature of the relationships between the children and the materials with contextual meanings bound to the classroom environment.

When asked about classroom objects, the children responded with remarkable agreement and uniformity. The children divided the materials into two categories: things to work with and things to play with. No child organized any material in violation to what seemed to be their guiding principle. Those materials which the children used at the direction of the teacher were work materials. They included books, paper, paste, crayons, glue, and other materials traditionally associated with school tasks. No child chose to use these materials during "play" time early in the school year. The materials which the children chose during free time were labeled play materials or toys. They included, among other things, games, small manipulatives, the playhouse, dolls, and the wagon. The meaning of classroom materials, then, is derived from the nature of the activity in which they are used, and the separate categories for work and play emerge as powerful organizers of classroom reality early in the school year.

Both the teacher and the children considered work activities more important than play activities. Information which the children said they learned in school was what the teacher had told them during activities they considered "work." Play activities were permitted only if time allowed and the child had finished the assigned work activities. Observation data revealed that the category of work had several well-defined parameters that sharply separated it from the category of play. First, work includes any and all teacher-directed activities; only free-time activities were called "play" activities by the children. Activities such as coloring, drawing, waiting in line, listening to stories, watching movies, cleaning up, and singing were called "work." To work, then, is to do what one is *told* to do, no matter what the nature of the activity involved. Second, all work activities, and only work activities, were compulsory. For example, children were required to draw pictures about specific topics on numerous occasions. During singing the teacher often interrupted to encourage and exhort the children who were not singing or who were singing too softly. Any choices permitted during work periods were circumscribed to fit the limits of accepted uniform procedure.

During an Indian dance, for example, the kindergarten teacher allowed the "sleeping" children to snore if they wanted. After a trip to the fire station all of the children were required to draw a picture, but each child was permitted to choose whatever part of the tour he liked best as the subject of his picture. (Of course it is also true that each child was required to illustrate his favorite part of the trip.) When introducing another art project, the teacher said, "Today you will make a cowboy horse. You can make your horse any color you want, black or gray or brown." At another time she announced with great emphasis that the children could choose three colors for the flowers they were making from cupcake liners. The children gasped with excitement and applauded. These choices did not change the fact that the children were required to use the same materials in the same manner during work periods. If anything, the nature of the choices emphasizes the general principle. Not only was every work activity required, but every child had to start at the designated time. The entire class worked on all assigned tasks simultaneously. Further, all of the children were required to complete the assigned tasks during the designated work period. In a typical incident that occurred on the second day of school, many children complained that they either could not or did not want to finish a lengthy art project. The teacher said that everyone must finish. One child asked if she could finish "next time," but the teacher replied, "You must finish now."

In addition to requiring that all the children do the same thing at the same time, work activities also involved the children with the same materials. During work periods the same materials were presented to the entire class simultaneously. All of the children were expected to use work materials in the same way. Even seemingly inconsequential procedures had to be followed by every child. For example, after large-group instruction on the second day of school, the teacher told the children, "Get a piece of paper and your crayons, and go back to your seats." One child, who got her crayons first, was reminded to get her paper first.

The products or skills which the children exhibited at the completion of a period of work were also supposed to be similar or identical. The teacher demonstrated most art projects to the entire class before the children got their materials. The children then tried to produce a product as similar to the one the teacher had made as possible. Only those pieces of artwork that most closely resembled the product the teacher used for demonstration were saved and displayed in the classroom.

Work periods, as defined by the children, then, involved every child simultaneously in the same directed activity with the same materials to the same ends. The point of work activities was to *do* them, not necessarily to do them well. By the second day of school, many children hastily finished their assigned tasks in order to join their friends playing with toys. During music, for example, the teacher exhorted the children to sing loudly. Neither tunefulness, rhythm, nor purity of tone and mood were mentioned to the children, or expected of them. It was enthusiastic and lusty participation that was required. Similarly, the teacher accepted any child's art project upon which sufficient time had been spent. The assigned tasks were compulsory and identical, and, in accepting all finished products, the teacher often accepted poor or shoddy work. The acceptance of such work nullified the notion of excellence as an evaluative category. Diligence, perseverence, obedience, and participation—behaviors of the children, not characteristics of their work—were rewarded. In this way the notion of excellence became separated from the concept of successful or acceptable work and was replaced by the criteria of adequate participation.

The children interviewed in September, and again in October, used the categories of work and play to create and describe their social reality. Their responses indicated that the first few weeks of school were an important time for learning about the nature of work in the classroom. In September no child said "work" when asked what children do in kindergarten. In October half of these interviewed responded with the word "work." All of the children talked more about working and less about playing in October than they had in September. The teacher was pleased with the progress of the class during the first weeks of school and repeatedly referred to the children as "my good workers."

The teacher often justified her presentation of work activities in the classroom in terms of the preparation of the children for elementary school and for adulthood. For example, she believed that work activities should be compulsory because the children needed practice following directions without exercising options as preparation for the reality of adult work. The children were expected to view kindergarten as a year of preparation for the first grade. In stressing the importance of coloring neatly or putting pictures in the proper sequence, the teacher spoke of the necessity of having these skills in first grade and how difficult it would be the following year for children who were inattentive in kindergarten. The children were relatively powerless to influence the flow of daily events, and obedience was valued more highly than ingenuity. Again, this atmosphere was seen as an important bridge between home and future work situations. The teacher expected the children to adjust to the classroom setting and to tolerate whatever level of discomfort that adjustment included.

Thus, as part of initiation into the kindergarten community, young children also receive their first initiation into the social dimension of the world of work. The content of specific lessons is relatively less important than the experience of being a worker. Personal attributes of obedience, enthusiasm, adaptability, and perseverance are more highly valued than academic competence. Unquestioning acceptance of authority and the vicissitudes of life in institutional settings are among the first lessons learned in kindergarten. It is in the progressive acceptance as natural, as the world "tout court," of meanings of important and unimportant knowledge, of work and play, of normality and deviance, that these lessons reside.

Beyond A Rhetorical Humanism

As the late Italian social theorist Antonio Gramsci argued, the control of the knowledge-preserving and producing sectors of a society becomes a critical factor in enhancing the ideological dominance of one group of people or class over less powerful groups of people or classes.[29] If this is so, the role of the school in selecting, preserving, and passing on conceptions of competence, ideological norms and values, and often only certain social groups' "knowledge"—all of which are embedded within both the overt and hidden curricula in schools—is of no small moment.

At least two aspects of school life serve rather interesting distributive social and economic functions. As the growing literature on the hidden curriculum and the historical and empirical evidence provided here seek to demonstrate, the forms of interaction in school life may serve as mechanisms for communicating normative and dispositional meanings to students. Yet, the body of school knowledge itself—what is included and excluded, what is important and what is unimportant—also often serves an ideological purpose.

As one of this paper's authors has demonstrated in an earlier analysis, much of the formal content of curricular knowledge is dominated by a consensus ideology. Conflict, either intellectual or normative, is seen as a negative attribute in social life.[30] Thus, there is a peculiar kind of redundancy in school knowledge. Both the everyday experience and the curricular knowledge itself display messages of normative and cognitive consensus. The deep structure of school life, the basic and organizing framework of commonsense rules that is negotiated, internalized, and ultimately seems to give meaning to our experiences in educational institutions, appears to be closely linked to the normative and communicative structures of industrial life.[31] How could it be otherwise?

Perhaps we can expect little more from school experience than what has been portrayed here, given the distribution of resources in the United States and given the wishes of a major segment of the citizenry. Nor can one dismiss the hypothesis that schools actually do work. In an odd way they may succeed in reproducing a population that is roughly equivalent to the economic and social stratification in society. Thus, when one asks of schools, "Where is their humaneness?" perhaps the answers may be more difficult to grapple with than the questioner expects.

For example, one could interpret this presentation as being a statement against a particular community's commitment to education or as a negative statement about particular kinds of teachers who are "less able than they might be." This would, however, be inaccurate. The city in question is educationally oriented. It spends a sizable proportion of its resources on schooling and feels that it deserves its reputation as having one of the best school systems in the area, if not the nation.

Just as important, we should be careful not to view this kind of teacher as poorly trained, unsuccessful, or uncaring. Exactly the opposite is often the case. The classroom teacher who was observed is, in fact, perceived as a competent teacher by administrators, colleagues, and parents. Given this, the teacher's activities must be understood not merely in terms of the patterns of social interaction that dominate classrooms, but in terms of the wider patterning of social and economic relationships in the social structure of which he or she and the school itself are a part.[32]

When teachers distribute normative interpretations of, say, work and play like the ones we have documented historically and currently here, one must ask, "To what problems are these viable solutions for the teacher?"[33] "What is the commonsense interpretive framework of teachers and to what set of ideological presuppositions does it respond?" In this way we can situate classroom knowledge and activity within the larger framework of structural relationships which, either through teacher and parent expectations, the classroom material environment, the focus of important problems, or the relationship between schools and, say, the economic sector of a society, often determine what goes on in classrooms.

This work alone will not confirm the fact that schools seem to act latently to enhance an already unequal and stratified social order. It does, however, confirm a number of recent analyses that point out how schools, through their distribution of a number of social and ideological categories, contribute to the promotion of a rather static framework of institutions.[34] Thus, our argument should not be seen as a statement against an individual school or any particular group of teachers. Rather, it suggests that educators need to see teachers as "encapsulated" within a social and economic context that by necessity often produces the problems teachers are confronted with and the material limitations on their responses. This very "external" context provides substantial legitimation for the allocation of teachers' time and energies[35] and for the kinds of cultural capital embodied in the school itself.

If this is the case, as we strongly suggest it is, the questions asked should go beyond the humanistic level (without losing their humanistic and emancipatory intent) to a more relational approach. While educators continue to ask what is wrong in schools and what can be done (Can our problems be "solved" with more humanistic teachers, more openness, better content, and so on?), it is of immense importance that we begin to take seriously these questions: "In whose interest do schools often function today?" "What is the relation between the distribution of cultural capital and economic capital?" "Can we deal with the political and economic realities of creating institutions that enhance meaning and lessen control?"

Rachel Sharp and Anthony Green summarize this concern about a rhetorical humanism rather well:

. . .[We] want to stress that a humanist concern for the child necessitates a greater awareness of the limits within which teacher autonomy can operate, and to pose the questions, "What interests do schools serve, those of the parents and children, or those of the teachers and headmaster?" and "What wider interests are served by the school?", and, possibly more importantly, "How do we conceptualize 'interests' in social reality?" Therefore instead of seeing the classroom as a social system and as such insulated from wider structural processes, we suggest that the teacher who has developed an understanding of his [or her] location in the wider process may well be in a better position to understand where and how it is possible to alter that situation. The educator who is of necessity a moralist must preoccupy himself with the social and [economic] preconditions for the achievement of his ideals. Rather than affirming the separation of politics and education, as is done within commonsense liberal assumptions, the authors assume all education to be in its implications a political process.[36]

Thus, to isolate school experience from the complex totality of which it is a constitutive part is to be a bit too limited in one's analysis. In fact, the study of the relationship between ideology and school knowledge is especially important for understanding the larger social collectivity of which we are all a part. It enables us to begin to see how a society reproduces itself, how it perpetuates its conditions of existence through the selection and transmission of certain kinds of cultural capital upon which a complex yet unequal industrial society depends, and how it maintains cohesion among its classes and individuals by propagating ideologies that ultimately sanction existing institutional arrangements that can cause unnecessary stratification and inequality in the first place.[37] Can we afford not to understand these things?

Notes

1. C. Silberman, *Crisis in the Classroom* (New York: Random House, 1970).

2. H. Gintis and S. Bowles, "The Contradictions of Liberal Educational Reform," in *Work, Technology, and Education*, ed. W. Feinberg and H. Rosemont, Jr. (Urbana: University of Illinois Press, 1975), p. 109.

3. That this is not merely an "intellectual" interest, but embodies social and ideological commitments, is examined in greater depth in M. W. Apple, "The

Adequacy of Systems Management Procedures in Education," in *Regaining Educational Leadership,* ed. R. H. Smith (New York: John Wiley, 1975).

4. M. F. D. Young, "Knowledge and Control," in *Knowledge and Control,* ed. id. (London: Collier-Macmillan, 1971).

5. J. Kennett, "The Sociology of Pierre Bourdieu," *Educational Review* 25 (June 1973): 238.

6. On the necessity of seeing institutions relationally, see B. Ollman, *Al enation: Marx's Conception of Man in Capitalist Society* (New York: Cambridge University Press, 1971).

7. D. Kallos, "Educational Phenomena and Educational Research," Report from the Institute of Education, University of Lund, Lund, Sweden, p. 7.

8. D. Warwick, "Ideologies, Integration and Conflicts of Meaning," in *Educability, Schools and Ideology,* ed. M. Flude and J. Ahier (London: Halstead Press, 1974), p. 94. See also M. W. Apple, "Curriculum as Ideological Selection," *Comparative Education Review* 20 (June 1976).

9. B. Williamson, "Continuities and Discontinuities in the Sociology of Education," in *Educability,* ed. Flude and Ahier, pp. 10–11.

10. Ibid.

11. B. Franklin, "The Curriculum Field and the Problem of Social Control, 1918—1938: A Study in Critical Theory" (Unpublished dissertation, University of Wisconsin, Madison, 1974), pp. 2–3.

12. Ibid., pp. 4–5. It should be noted here that scientific management itself was not necessarily a neutral technology for creating more efficient institutions. It was developed as a mechanism for the further division and control of labor. This is provocatively portrayed in H. Braverman, *Labor and Monopoly Capital: The Degradation of Work in the Twentieth Century* (New York: Monthly Review Press, 1975).

13. Ibid.

14. Ibid., p. 317.

15. W. Feinberg, *Reason and Rhetoric: The Intellectual Foundations of Twentieth Century Liberal Educational Policy* (New York: John Wiley, 1975).

16. P. Jackson, *Life in Classrooms* (New York: Holt, Rinehart & Winston, 1968).

17. E. Vallance, "Hiding the Hidden Curriculum," *Curriculum Theory Network* 4 (Fall 1973–74): 15.

18. Ibid.

19. Ibid., pp. 18–19.

20. Gintis and Bowles, "Contradictions of Liberal Educational Reform," p. 133. These normative meanings and personality attributes are distributed unequally to different "types" of students, often by social class or occupational expectation as well. Not all students get the same dispositional elements; nor are the same meanings attached to them by the distributor of cultural capital. See ibid., p. 136.

21. See, for example, M. W. Apple, "Ivan Illich and Deschooling Society: The Politics of Slogan Systems," in *Social Forces and Schooling,* ed. Nobuo Shimahara and Adam Scrupski (New York: David McKay, 1975), pp. 337–60; M. F. D. Young, "An Approach to the Study of Curricula as Socially Organized Knowledge," in *Knowledge and Control,* ed. id., pp. 19–46.

22. N. Keddie, "Classroom Knowledge," in *Knowledge and Control,* ed. Young, pp. 133–60.

23. M. W. Apple, "Common Sense Categories and Curriculum Thought," in *Schools in Search of Meaning,* ed. J. B. Macdonald and E. Zaret (Washington, D.C.: Association for Supervision and Curriculum Development, 1975), pp. 116–48.

24. This, of course, is a fundamental tenet of ethnomethodological studies as well. See P. McHugh, *Defining the Situation* (Indianapolis, Ind.: Bobbs-Merrill Co., 1968); *Ethnomethodology,* ed. R. Turner (Baltimore: Penguin Books, 1974); A. Cicourel, *Cognitive Sociology* (New York: Free Press, 1974).

25. For further explication of this point, see B. Bernstein, "On the Classification and Framing of Educational Knowledge," in *Knowledge and Control,* ed. Young, pp. 47–69.

26. R. MacKay, "Conceptions of Children and Models of Socialization," in *Recent Sociology. No. 5: Childhood and Socialization,* ed. H. P. Dreitzel (New York: Macmillan, 1973).

27. An excellent treatment of this "ethnographic" tradition can be found in P. E. D. Robinson, "An Ethnography of Classrooms," *Contemporary Research in the Sociology of Education,* ed. J. Eggleston (London: Methuen & Co., 1974), pp. 251–66.

28. For a more complete discussion of this research project, see N. R. King, "The Hidden Curriculum and the Socialization of Kindergarten Children," unpublished dissertation, University of Wisconsin, Madison, 1976).

29. T. R. Bates, "Gramsci and the Theory of Hegemony," *Journal of the History of Ideas* 36 (April–June 1975): 360.

30. M. W. Apple, "The Hidden Curriculum and the Nature of Conflict," *Interchange* 2:4 (1971): 29–40.

31. Habermas' arguments about patterns of communicative competence in advanced industrial "orders" are quite interesting as interpretive schemata here. See, for example, J. Habermas, "Towards a Theory of Communicative Competence," in *Recent Sociology. No. 2: Patterns of Communicative Behavior,* ed. H. P. Dreitzel (New York: Macmillan, 1970), pp. 115–48; T. Schroyer, *The Critique of Domination* (New York: George Braziller, 1973).

32. R. Sharp and A. Green, *Education and Social Control: A Study in Progressive Primary Education* (Boston: Routledge & Kegan Paul, 1975).

33. Ibid., p. 13.

34. Ibid., pp. 110–12. See also the provocative analysis found in B. Bernstein, *Class, Codes, and Control.* Vol. III: *Towards a Theory of Educational Transmissions* (Boston: Routledge & Kegan Paul, 1975).

35. Sharp and Green, *Education and Social Control,* p. 116.

36. Ibid., p. x.

37. Ibid., p. 221.

5

Social Education in the Classroom:
The Dynamics of the Hidden Curriculum

Henry Giroux and Anthony Penna

The belief that schooling can be defined as the sum of its official course offerings is a naive one. Yet such an implicit belief served as the theme of the social studies curriculum development reform movement of the 1960s and early 1970s. Developers believed that if they changed the curriculum of the nation's schools, the school's ills would be remedied.[1] In recent years, however, numerous reasons have been offered to explain the seeming inability of the reform movement to penetrate the traditional patterns of instruction in the schools. Inadequate teacher preparation and curriculum materials that overestimated the perceived capabilities of students represent the more familiar, albeit uncritical, explanations offered by educators. Now some of them lend uncritical support for the "back-to-basics" movement in social studies education, assuming once again that new curriculum materials will provide an answer to the question of how to bring about change in social studies education. Attend to the cognitive needs and capabilities of students, they argue, and the failures of the recent reform movement will be overcome.[2]

Unfortunately, such recommendations are based heavily on structural-functional educational models of curriculum theory,[3] which fail to perceive the purpose of social education beyond its limited explicit instructional outcomes. Further, there is a failure to recognize the complex, intimate relationship between the institution of the school and the nation's

Reprinted, by permission, from *Theory and Research in Social Education* 7:1 (Spring 1979): 21–42.

economic and political institutions. Once the relationship between school-ing and the larger society is recognized, questions about the nature and meaning of the schooling experience can be viewed from a theoretical per-spective capable of illuminating the often-ignored relationship between school knowledge and social control. By viewing schools within the context of the larger society, social studies developers can begin to focus on the tacit teaching that goes on in schools and help to uncover the ideological mes-sages embedded in both the content of the formal curriculum and the social relations of the classroom encounter.

It is only recently that some educators have begun to raise questions that point to the need for a thorough study of the interconnections between ideology, instruction, and curriculum.[4] For instance, Michael Apple argues that we need to:

... examine critically not just "how a student acquires more knowledge" (the domi-nant question in our efficiency-minded field) but "why and how particular aspects of the collective culture are presented in school as objective, factual knowledge." How concretely may official knowledge represent ideological configurations of the dominant interests in a society? How do schools legitimate these limited and partial standards of knowing as unquestioned truths? These questions must be asked of at least three areas of school life: (1) How the basic day-to-day regularities of schools contribute to students learning these ideologies; (2) how the specific forms of curric-ular knowledge reflect these configurations; and (3) how these ideologies are reflected in the fundamental perspectives educators themselves employ to order, guide, and give meaning to their own activity.[5]

If educators such as Apple, Bourdieu, and Bernstein are correct, and we think they are, then social studies developers will have to build their peda-gogical models upon a theoretical framework which situates schools within a sociopolitical context. As such, the main assertion of this paper is that if social studies developers seek to change classroom life through various in-tervention strategies, then they will have to comprehend the school as an agent of socialization. Furthermore, they will have to identify those struc-tural properties at the core of the schooling process that link it to comparable properties in the work place and other sociopolitical spheres. In brief, they will have to approach their task systemically rather than in the traditional fragmented fashion, which assumes incorrectly that the classroom can be-come a vehicle for helping each student to develop his or her full potential as a critical thinker and responsible participant in the democratic process by changing only the content and methodology of the school's official social studies curricula.

We believe that a major task for social studies educators is to identify those social processes that work against the ethical and political purpose of schooling in a democratic society and construct new elements that provide the underpinning for new social studies programs. Initially, developers will have to understand the contradictions between the official curriculum, namely the explicit cognitive and affective goals of formal instruction, and the "hidden curriculum,"[6] namely the unstated norms, values, and beliefs that are transmitted to students through the underlying structure of meaning in both the formal content as well as the social relations of school and classroom life. Most important, they will have to recognize the function of a hidden curriculum and its capacity for undermining the goals of social education.

Social studies developers will have to shift their attention from a technical, ahistorical view of schooling to a sociopolitical perspective which focuses on the relationship between schooling and the idea of justice. The goals of social education should be redefined and understood as an extension of ethics directed toward "the arena of excellence and responsibility whereby acting together, men [and women] can become truly free."[7] Thus, social studies developers will have to answer anew the question, What is learned in school? Fortunately, a few educators writing out of a number of different theoretical traditions have already taken up the challenge.

Traditions in Educational Theory

Three different traditions in educational theory have helped to illuminate the socializing role of schools and the meaning and structure of the hidden curriculum. They are (1) a structural-functional view of schooling, (2) a phenomenological view characteristic of the "new" sociology of education, and (3) a radical critical view, often associated with the neo-Marxist analysis of educational theory and practice. Each of these views shares distinctly different theoretical assumptions concerning the meaning of knowledge, classroom social relationships, and the political and cultural nature of schooling. While we have based our analysis of the hidden curriculum on assumptions and insights drawn from all three traditions, we believe that the structural-functional and phenomenological approaches suffer from serious deficiencies. The neo-Marxist position, it seems to us, provides the most insightful and comprehensive model for a more progressive approach to understanding the nature of schooling and developing an emancipatory program for social education. Before examining the specific contributions that these three traditions have made to the notion of the hidden curriculum and the socializing role of schools, a general overview of some of their basic assumptions will be provided.

The structural-functionalist approach has as one of its primary interests how social norms and values are transmitted within the context of the schools. Relying primarily upon a positivist sociological model, this approach has highlighted how schools socialize students to accept unquestionably a set of beliefs, rules, and dispositions as fundamental to the functioning of the larger society. For the structural-functionalists, the school provides a valuable service in training students to uphold commitments and to learn skills required by society.[8] The value of this approach is threefold: (1) it makes clear that schools do not exist in precious isolation, removed from the interests of the larger society; (2) it spells out specific norms and structural properties of the hidden curriculum; and (3) it raises questions about the specifically historical character of meaning and social control in schools.[9]

While insightful in many respects, the structural-functional model is marred by a number of theoretical shortcomings which characterize its basic assumptions. Rejecting the notion that growth develops from conflict, it stresses consensus and stability rather than movement. As a result, it downplays the notions of social conflict and competing socioeconomic interests. Moreover, it represents an apolitical posture that sees as unproblematic the basic beliefs, values, and structural socioeconomic arrangements characteristic of American society.[10] Consequently, the structural-functionalist position defines students in reductionist-behavioral terms as products of socialization. By defining students as passive recipients, conflict is explained mainly as a function of faulty socialization, the causes of which usually lie in institutions outside of the classroom or school or in the individual as deviant. As such, in the structural-functional view, the school appears to exist happily beyond the imperatives and influence of class and power. Similarly, knowledge is appreciated for its instrumental market value. Finally, in the structural-functional model, students accept social conformity and lose the ability to make meaning for themselves.

The social-phenomenological approach to educational theory, often called the new sociology, moves far beyond the structural-functionalist position in its approach to the study of schooling. The new sociology focuses critically on a number of assumptions about classroom interactions and social encounters. For the new sociologists, any valid theory of socialization has to be seen as "a theory of the construction of social reality, if not of a particular historical social order."[11] They posit a model of socialization in which meaning is made interactively. That is, meaning is "given" by situations but also created by students as they interact in classrooms. Moreover, the social construction of meaning by both teachers and students raises anew questions about the objective nature of knowledge itself. For the new sociologists, the principles governing the organization, distribution, and evaluation of knowledge are not absolute and objective; instead, they are sociohistorical constructs forged by active human beings creating rather than simply existing in the world.

In this approach, the view of students as actors with a fixed identity is replaced by a more dynamic model of student behavior. The new sociologists focus on the participation of students in defining and redefining their worlds. Thus the focus of classroom studies with the rise of the new sociology has shifted from an exclusive emphasis on institutional behavior to a focus on students' interactions with language, social relations, and categories of meaning. The proponents of the new sociology have provided a new dimension to the study of the relationship between socialization and the school curriculum.[12] The new sociology raises to a new level of discussion the relationship between the distribution of power and knowledge. It requires social studies curriculum developers to make problematic many of the truisms that characterized the selection, organization, and distribution of knowledge and pedagogical styles inherent in curriculum development. In one sense, the new sociology has stripped the school curriculum of its innocence.

But the new sociology is not without flaws—flaws that undermine its ability to resolve the very problems it identified. The most thoughtful critique lodged against the new sociology is that it represents a form of subjective idealism.[13] Allegedly, at its core the new sociology lacks an adequate theory of social change and consciousness. While it helps educators to uncover the ways in which knowledge is defined and imposed, it fails to provide criteria for measuring the value of different forms of classroom knowledge. By endorsing the value and relevance of students' intentionality, the new sociology has succumbed to a notion of cultural relativity. It lacks a theoretical construct to explain the role ideology plays in the construction of knowledge by students. It fails to account for the fact that the way students perceive the external world does not always correspond to the actual structure and content of that world. Subjective perceptions are dialectically related to the social world and do not simply "mirror" it. To ignore this, as the new sociology proponents have, is to fall prey to a distorted subjectivism. Sharp and Green have captured this position cogently.

The social world is more than the mere constellations of meaning. Although we can accept that the knowing subject acts in the world on the basis of his understanding, that there is always a subjective factor which enters into knowledge of the world, it does not follow from this that the world possesses the character which the knowing subject bestows upon it, that the objects which we know in the social world are mere subjective creations capable of being differently constituted in an infinite variety of ways. The phenomenologist appears to be putting forward what we could argue is an extreme form of subjective idealism. Where the external objective world is merely a constitution of the creative consciousness, the subject-object dualism disappears in the triumph of the constituting subject.[14]

In the final analysis, the new sociology fails in spite of its desire for radical change and fundamental egalitarianism. Its failure lies in its inability to illuminate how social and political structures function to mask reality and promote ideological hegemony.[15] Thus, this position not only fails to explain how different varieties of classroom meanings, knowledge, and experiences arise, it also fails to explain how they are able to sustain themselves. By focusing exclusively on the microlevel of schooling, on studies of classroom interaction, the new sociology falls short of illustrating how sociopolitical arrangements influence and constrain individual and collective efforts to construct knowledge and meaning. These arrangements probably play an important role in influencing the very texture of classroom life.

A third position is a neo-Marxist approach to socialization and social change. While this position is not without its own flaws, its value lies in being able to move beyond the apolitical view of the functionalist position as well as the subjective idealism of the new sociology. At the core of the neo-Marxist approach is a recognition of the relationship between economic and cultural reproduction. Moreover, inherent in this perspective is an intersection of theory, ideology, and social practice. Schools are viewed in this approach as agents of ideological control which function to reproduce and to maintain dominant beliefs, values, and norms. This is not meant to suggest that schools are merely factories that process students and "mirror" the interests of the larger society; such a perspective is clearly mechanistic and reductionist.[16] The neo-Marxist position points out that schools in corresponding ways are linked to the principles and processes governing the work place. The cutting edge of this perspective is its insistence on connecting macro forces in the larger society to microanalysis such as classroom studies.

The neo-Marxist approach, more clearly than the other two approaches identified in this chapter, illuminates how social reproduction of knowledge is related to the notion of false consciousness. While stressing the importance of a student's subjective role in constituting meaning for himself, neo-Marxists are equally concerned with the way in which social and economic conditions constrain and distort social construction of meaning, particularly as mediated through the hidden curriculum. Not only do classroom studies have to be linked to the study of the larger society, they have to be connected to a notion of justice, one that is capable of articulating how certain unjust social structures can be identified and replaced.

School Knowledge and Classroom Relations

While the neo-Marxist perspective provides an important focus on the ideological nature of the process of schooling and the larger social order, it has done little to explicate in specific terms the kinds of knowledge and classroom social relationships that have been used to reproduce the reified consciousness that maintains the cultural and economic interests of a stratified society. This is where the structural-functionalists and new sociology adherents have made valuable contributions to the study of curriculum and social education. By drawing on the insights within a new Marxist framework, we can begin to answer the fundamental question of what is learned in schools.

In response to this question, Robert Dreeben points out that the student learns more than simply instructional knowledge and skills and that the traditional view of schooling as being "primarily cognitive in nature is at best only partially tenable."[17] Stephen Arons reinforces this view by calling school "a social environment from which a child may learn much more than what is in the formal curriculum."[18] Implicit in this analysis of the school and classroom as a socializing agent is an important pedagogical premise. The premise is that any curriculum designed to introduce positive changes in classrooms will fail unless such a proposal is rooted in an understanding of those sociopolitical forces that strongly influence the very texture of day-to-day classroom pedagogical practices.

Since it is not entirely clear to social studies educators that schools are indeed sociopolitical institutions, a case must first be made to validate the position that schools are inextricably linked to other social agencies and institutions within American society. Ralph Tyler highlights the social function of schools by pointing out that all educational philosophies are essentially an outgrowth of one of two possible theoretical perspectives.[19] He claims that a statement of educational philosophy can be built upon one of the following questions: "Should the schools develop young people to fit into present society as it is, or does the school have a revolutionary mission to develop young people who will seek to improve the society?"[20]

Tyler's point about educational philosophy is important for a number of reasons. First, it reinforces the notion that schools have a sociopolitical function and cannot exist independently of the society in which they operate. Second, it suggests that underlying every educational program designed to intervene in the structure of the schools there lies a theoretical frame of reference. Paulo Freire, the Brazilian educator, argues both points in his claim that:

There is no such thing as a neutral educational process. Education either functions as an instrument which is used to facilitate the integration of the younger generation into the logic of the present system and bring about conformity to it, or it becomes the "practice of freedom"—the means by which men and women deal critically and creatively with reality and discover how to participate in the transformation of their world.[21]

Whether they realize it or not, social studies educators work in the service of one of the two positions outlined by Tyler and Freire.

An examination of schooling and its sociological ties to the family and the work place can illuminate the social and political functions of schools.

While a number of sociologists convincingly point out that schools no longer assume the role of a surrogate family, they do perform a socializing function that the social structure of the family cannot satisfy. For instance, comparing the functions of the family to those of the school, Robert Dreeben argues that the structural properties of the family, while satisfying specific affective needs of children, cannot adequately socialize them to function in the adult world.[22] According to him, schooling demands the formation of social relationships that are more time bounded, more diverse, less dependent, and less emotive than those of the family. Unlike the family, schools separate performance from emotional expression and perform what is considered their most explicit purpose: "Imparting the skills, information, and beliefs each child will eventually need as an adult member of society."[23]

He argues that schools do more than provide instruction. They provide norms, or principles of conduct, which are learned through the varied social experiences in schools that influence students' lives. Though Dreeben ignores the political nature of these social experiences, he does mention four important norms that students learn: independence, achievement, universalism, and specificity.

Worth noting is Dreeben's failure to mention in specific ideological terms the cultural values that support and give meaning to these norms. Two examples will suffice. Independence is defined as "handling tasks with which under different circumstances, one can rightfully expect the help of others."[24] Achievement is defined so as to assure pupils of the gratification of "winning and losing" and, while not stated by Dreeben, justifies extrinsic rewards and the notion that someone must always come in last.

That students learn more than cognitive skills is illuminated further in Bernstein's analysis, which brings into sharp focus some of the features of the political nature of schooling. His analysis argues that students learn values and norms that would produce "good" industrial workers. Students internalize values that stress a respect for authority, punctuality, cleanliness, docility, and conformity. What the students learn from the formally sanctioned content of the curriculum is much less important than what they learn from the ideological assumptions embedded in the school's three message systems: the system of curriculum; the system of classroom pedagogical styles; and the system of evaluation.[25] In describing what students learn from the school's hidden curriculum, Stanley Aronowitz provides a capsule view of the socializing processes that operate within these "message" systems:

Indeed, the child learns in school. . . . The child learns that the teacher is the authoritative person in the classroom, but that she is subordinate to a principal. Thus the structure of society can be learned through understanding the hierarchy of power within the structure of the school. Similarly, the working-class child learns its role in society. On the one side, school impresses students as a whole with their powerlessness since they are without the knowledge required to become citizens and workers. On the other, the hierarchy of occupations and classes is reproduced by the hierarchy of grade levels and tracks within grades. Promotion to successive grades is the reward for having mastered the approved political and social behavior as well as the prescribed "cognitive" material. But within grades, particularly in large urban schools, further distinctions among students are made on the basis of imputed intelligence and that in turn is determined by the probable ability of children to succeed in terms of standards set by the educational system.[26]

Writers such as Dreeben and Aronowitz have helped to make it clear that the school functions as an agency of socialization within a network of larger institutions. Yet, with few exceptions, the political role of the school and how that role affects educational objectives, methods, content, and organizational structures has not been adequately illuminated by social studies educators.[27]

While commenting on the consequences of ignoring the political nature of education, Jerome Bruner candidly indicates that educators can no longer strike a fictional posture of neutrality and objectivity.

A theory of instruction is a political theory in the power sense that it derives from consensus concerning the distribution of power within the society—who shall be educated and to fulfill what roles? In the very same sense, pedagogical theory must surely derive from a conception of economics, for where there is a division of labor within the society and an exchange of goods and services for wealth and prestige, then how people are educated and in what number and with what constraints on the use of resources are all relevant issues. The psychologist or educator who formulates pedagogical theory without regard to the political, economic, and social setting of the educational process courts triviality and merits being ignored in the community and in the classroom.[28]

As mentioned previously, a serious approach to social studies educational change would have to begin with an examination of the contradictions that exist between the school's hidden curriculum and official curriculum. Any approach to social studies curriculum development that ignores the existence of the hidden curriculum runs the risk of not only being incomplete but also insignificant. For the heart of the school's function is not to be found simply in the daily dispensing of information by teachers but also "in the social relations of the educational encounter."[29]

School Curriculum Organization

But before any study of classroom social relations is put forth, it must be made clear that the *content* of what is taught in social studies classes plays a vital role in the political socialization of students. For instance, studies by

Apple, Anyon, and Popkewitz[30] have pointed out that what counts as "objective" knowledge in social studies textbooks in fact often represents a one-sided and theoretically distorted view of the subject under study. Knowledge is often accepted as truth legitimizing a specific view of the world that is either questionable or patently false. The selection, organization, and distribution of social studies knowledge is hidden from the realm of ideology.[31] In addition to its overt and covert messages, the way knowledge is selected and organized represents a priori assumptions by the educator about its value and legitimacy. In the final analysis, these are ideological considerations that structure the students' perception of the world. If the fragile ideological nature of these considerations is not made clear to students, then they will learn more about social conformity than critical inquiry. To break through the "hidden curriculum" of knowledge, social studies educators must help students understand that knowledge is not only variable and linked to human interest but also must be examined in regards to its claims to validity. Popkewitz has succinctly focused in on this issue for social studies educators with his claim.

Constructing curriculum requires that educators give attention to the social disciplines as a human product whose meanings are transmitted in social processes. Instruction should give serious attention to the conflicting views of the world these crafts generate, the social location and the social contexts of inquiry. To plan for children's study of ideas, educators are compelled to inquire into the nature and character of the discourse found in history, sociology, or anthropology. What problems does each deal with? What modes of thought exist? What are its paradigmatic tasks? What limitations are placed on the knowledge of their findings? Instruction should be concerned with the different perspectives of phenomena that are within each discipline and how these men and women come to know what they know.[32]

Moreover, it follows that equal weight must be given in any analysis of the hidden curriculum to the organizational structures that influence and govern teacher-student interactions within the classroom. For these suggest an ideological character that is no less compelling than curriculum content in the socialization process at work in the classroom encounter. Though distinctly apolitical in nature, Philip Jackson's work represents one important attempt to analyze the social processes that give shape to another dimension of the hidden curriculum.[33] Unlike the official curriculum, with its stated cognitive and affective objectives, the hidden curriculum in this case is rooted in those organizational aspects of classroom life which are not commonly perceived by either students or teachers. According to Jackson, elements of the hidden curriculum are shaped by three key analytical concepts: crowds, praise, and power.

In short, working in classrooms means learning to live in crowds. Coupled with the prevailing values of the educational system, this has profound implications for the social education established in the schools. Equally significant is the fact that schools are evaluative settings, and what a student learns is not only how to be evaluated but how to evaluate himself and others as well. Finally, schools are marked by a basic, concrete division between the powerful (teachers) and the powerless (students). As Jackson points out, what this means "in three major ways, then—as members of crowds, as potential recipients of praise or reproof, and as pawns of institutional authorities—students are confronted with aspects of reality that at least during their childhood years are relatively confined to the hours spent in the classroom."[34]

In more specific terms, especially those that highlight student-teacher interactions, Jackson's analysis of the hidden curriculum proves to be particularly instructive. Learning to live in crowds affects students in a number of important ways. Students have to learn constantly to wait to use resources, with the ultimate outcome being that they learn to postpone or give up desires. In spite of the constant interruptions in the classroom, students have to learn to be quiet. Though students work in groups with other people whom they eventually get to know, they have to learn how to be isolated in a crowd. For Jackson, the quintessential virtue learned by students under these conditions is patience (that is, not a patience rooted in mediated restraint but one that is rooted in an unwarranted submission to authority). "They must also, to some extent, learn to suffer in silence. They are expected to bear with equanimity, in other words, the continued delay, denial, and interruption of their personal wishes and desires."[35]

Praise and power in the classroom are inextricably connected to one another. While students may find themselves in a position occasionally in which they can evaluate each other, the unquestioned source of praise and reproof is the teacher. Though the administration of positive and negative sanctions is the teacher's most visible symbol of power, the real significance of his or her role lies in the network of social relationships and values that are reproduced with the use of that authority. The nature of the hidden curriculum is nowhere more clearly revealed than in the system of evaluation. The potential effect of evaluation comes into sharp focus where one recognizes that what is taught and evaluated in the classroom is both academic and nonacademic, and includes in the latter institutional adjustment and specific personal qualities.

In fact, some notable studies have been made that support the above hypothesis; Bowles and Gintis, after reviewing a number of studies that link personality traits, attitudes, and behavioral attributes to school grades, reached the following conclusions:

Students are rewarded for exhibiting discipline, subordinacy, intellectually as opposed to emotionally oriented behavior, and hard work independent from intrinsic task motivation. Moreover, these traits are rewarded independently of any effect of "proper demeanor" on scholastic achievement."[36]

In addition, they point out that students who are rated high in citizenship (that is, conformity to the social order of the school), also rated "significantly below average on measures of creativity and mental flexibility."[37] Viewed from the student's perspective, the classroom becomes a miniature work place in which time, space, content, and structure are fixed by others. Rewards are extrinsic, and all social interaction between teachers and students is mediated by hierarchically organized structures. The underlying message learned in this context points less to schools helping students to think critically about the world in which they live than it does to schools acting as agents of social control.

Teachers obviously play a vital role in maintaining the structure of schools and transmitting the values needed to support the larger social order.[38] Lortie's study of teachers indicates that they generally are unable to offset the conservative pedagogical influences accepted by them during their precollege and college schooling. He also claims that "recruitment resources foster a conservative outlook among entrants . . . they appeal strongly to young people who are favorably disposed toward the existing system of schools."[39] Lortie's study also found that one of the most severe shortcomings of teachers was their subjective, idiosyncratic approach to teaching. Lacking a thought-out theoretical framework from which to develop a methodology and content, teachers lacked significant criteria to shape, guide, or evaluate their own work. But more importantly, they pass their distrust of theory on to their students and help in perpetuating intellectual passivity.

As mentioned before, at the heart of the social educational encounter is a hidden curriculum whose values shape and influence practically every aspect of the student's educational experience. But this should not suggest that the hidden curriculum is so powerful that there is little hope for educational reform. Instead, the hidden curriculum should be seen not as an *impassable* boundary but as *providing* a possible direction for focusing educational change. For instance, while social studies developers alone cannot eliminate the hidden curriculum, they can identify its organizational structure and the political assumptions upon which it rests. By doing so, they can develop a pedagogy, curriculum materials, and classroom structural properties that offset the most undemocratic features of the traditional hidden curriculum. In doing so, a first but significant step will be made to help teachers and students reach beyond the classroom experience and tentatively move toward changing those institutional arrangements.

Democratic Conditions and Collective Action

Before changes in social education and in social studies development can be undertaken, however, social studies educators will have to develop very specific classroom processes designed to promote values and beliefs that encourage democratic, critical modes of student-teacher participation and interaction. That the traditional hidden curriculum of schooling is inimical to the stated aims of the official curriculum is a fact that no longer escapes astute social analysis.[40] Instead of preparing students to enter the society with skills that will allow them to reflect critically upon and intervene in the world in order to change it, schools act as conservative forces that, for the most part, socialize students to conform to the status quo. The structure, organization, and content of contemporary schooling serve to equip students with the personality requisites desired in the bureaucratically structured, hierarchically organized work force. As Philip Jackson has pointed out:

So far as their power structure is concerned, classrooms are not too dissimilar from factories and offices, those ubiquitous organizations in which so much of our adult life is spent. Thus, schools might really be called a preparation for life but not in the usual sense in which educators employ that term.[41]

The remaining section of this paper will identify an alternative set of values and classroom social processes. In our view, these alternatives represent a basis for formulating a collectivist and democratic social education, stripped of egoistic individualism and alienating social relationships. These values and processes should be used by social studies educators in developing a content and pedagogy which link theory and practice and restore to students and teachers an awareness of the social and personal importance of active participation and critical thinking. While the values will be enumerated at the outset, the classroom processes will be illuminated through an analysis of the specific features that in our judgment should characterize social education.

The values and social processes which provide the theoretical underpinning for social education include developing in students a respect for moral commitment, group solidarity, and social responsibility. In addition, a nonauthoritarian individualism should be fostered, one that maintains a balance with group cooperation and social awareness. Every effort should be made to give students an awareness of the necessity of developing choices of their own and to act on those choices with an understanding of situational constraints. The educational process itself will be open to examination in relation to its links to the larger society.

Students should experience social studies as an apprenticeship in the milieu of social action, or as Freire has stated, students should be taught the practice of thinking about practice.[42] One way of doing this is to view and evaluate each learning experience, whenever possible, with respect to its connections with the larger social-economic totality. Moreover, it is important that students not only think about both the content and practice of critical communication but recognize as well the importance of translating the outcome of these experiences into concrete action. For example, it is folly in our view to engage students in topics of political and social inequality in the classroom and in the larger political world and to ignore the realities and pernicious effects of economic and income inequality on the quality of life of substantial numbers of people in schools, communities, and nations. Even when linkage to the larger reality is made, a failure to address and to implement the practical will not provide students with the learning implied in Freire's appeal. In other words, it is important that social studies educators provide students with the opportunity to grasp the dynamic dialectic between critical consciousness and social action. There is a need then to integrate critical awareness, social processes, and social practice in such a way that what is made clear to students is not simply how the forces of social control work but also how they can be overcome. Students should be able to recognize the truth value of Marx's eleventh thesis on Feuerbach ". . . the philosophers have only interpreted the world in various ways; the point is, to change it."[43]

Many liberal social studies educators accept these values and social processes and attempt to develop content-based curricula that translates them into practice. But, in effect, liberals strip these values and social processes of their radical content by situating them within the framework of social adjustment rather than social and political emancipation. The liberal philosophic stance with its emphasis on progress through social meliora-tion, the value of meritocracy and the professional expert, and the viability of a mass education system dedicated *to serving* the needs of the industrial order fails to penetrate and utilize the radical cutting edge of the values and social processes we support. Elizabeth Cagan captures the contradiction between liberal thought and radical values and social practices in her comment:

While liberal reformers intend to use education to promote equality, community, and humanistic social interaction, they do not confront those aspects of the schools which pull in the opposite direction. Their blindness to these contradictions may stem from their class position: as middle-class reformers they are unwilling to advo-cate the kind of egalitarianism which is necessary for a true human community. Re-forms in pedagogical technique have been instituted, but the . . . [hidden curriculum] . . . remain[s] in effect. This hidden curriculum promotes competitiveness, individ-ualism, and authoritarianism.[44]

The social processes of most classrooms militate against students devel-oping a sense of community. As in the larger societal order, competition and individual striving are at the core of American schooling. In ideological terms, collectivity and social solidarity represent powerful structural threats

to the ethos of capitalism. This ethos is built not only upon the atomization
and division of labor but the fragmentation of consciousness and social
relationships.[45] Whatever virtues about collectivity that are brought to the
public's attention exist solely in form and not in substance. Both in and out
of schools, self-interest represents the criterion for acting on and entering
into social relationships. The structure of schooling reproduces the ethos of
privatization and the moral posture of selfishness at almost every level of the
formal and hidden curricula. Whether gently supporting the philosophy of
"do your own thing" or maintaining pedagogical structures which undermine collective action, the message coming from most classrooms is one
that enshrines the self at the expense of the group. The hidden message is
one that supports alienation.[46]

The classroom scenario that fosters this unbridled notion of individualism
is a familiar one. Students traditionally sit in rows staring at the back of
each others' heads and at the teacher who faces them in symbolic, authoritarian fashion or else in a large semicircle with teacher and student space
rigidly proscribed. Events in the classroom are governed by a rigid time
schedule imposed by a system of bells and reinforced by cues from teachers
while the class is in session. Instruction and, hopefully, some formal learning usually begin and end because it is the correct predetermined time, not
because a cognitive process has been stimulated into action.

Implementation

A number of social processes help to undermine the authoritarian effects
of the hidden curriculum in the classroom. Our terminology will be familiar
to all social studies developers; liberals among them will espouse the
immediate instructional goals, but only reconstructionists will accept the
long-range implications of these processes for life in classrooms, schools,
and larger social-political institutions.

The pedagogical foundation for democratic processes in the classroom
can be established by eliminating the pernicious practice of "tracking"
students. This tradition in schools of grouping students according to "abilities" and perceived performance is of dubious instructional value. The
justification for this practice is based on traditional genetic theories which
have been systematically refuted on intellectual and ethical grounds.[47] A
more heterogeneous class provides a better opportunity for flexibility to be
manifested. For instance, in the heterogeneous class setting, students who
qualitatively perform faster than other students could be given the opportunity to function as peers acting as individual or group leaders for other
students. In such a situation, students can act collectively in the process of
learning and teaching. As such, knowledge becomes the vehicle for dialogue
and analysis as well as the basis for new classroom social relationships.

Moreover, not only are more progressive social relationships developed in this context, but traditional notions of learning and achievement are now made problematic. It must be stressed that social education should be based on a notion of achievement that is at odds with traditional genetic theories of intelligence, which serve as the theoretical base to support tracking.

With the elimination of tracking, power is further diffused in a classroom so individuals in both peer and group-leadership roles are able to assume leadership positions formerly reserved for the teacher alone. In other words, with the breakdown of rigid, hierarchical roles and rules, which Basil Bernstein has called strong framing, both students and teachers can explore democratic relationships rarely developed in the traditional classroom.[48] These new relationships will also allow teachers to set the groundwork for breaking down the cellular structure exposed by Dan Lortie's study. The cellular structure refers to the failure of teachers to mutually adapt their task and actions. Most teachers do not share pedagogical strategies; and, thus, they lack any cohesiveness in their professional interpersonal relationships.[49] By sharing their power and roles, teachers will be in a better position to break through the provincialism and narrow socialization that prevents them from sharing and examining their theory and practice of pedagogy with both students and colleagues.

Another important change that such courses should perpetuate centers around the issue of authority and grades. Extrinsic rewards should be minimized whenever possible, and students should be given the opportunity to experience roles that will enable them to direct the learning process independently of the behavior usually associated with an emphasis on grades as rewards. Social relationships in the traditional classroom are based upon power relations inextricably linked to the teacher's allotment and distribution of grades. Grades become in many cases the ultimate discipline instruments by which the teacher imposes his or her desired values, behavior patterns, and beliefs upon students.[50] Dialogical grading eliminates this pernicious practice since it allows students to gain some control over the distribution of grades and thereby weakens the traditional correspondence between grades and authority. We refer to such grading as dialogical because it involves a dialogue between students and teachers over the criteria, function, and consequences of the system of evaluation. The use of the term is in fact an extension of Freire's emphasis on the role of dialogue in clarifying and democratizing social relationships.[51]

While opportunities for dialogue with teachers and peers should be encouraged, they are not conducive to large group settings. In small groups, students should evaluate and test the logic in each other's work. The importance of group work to social education rests on a number of crucial assumptions. Group work represents one of the most effective ways to demystify the traditional, manipulative role of the teacher; moreover, it provides students with social contexts that stress social responsibility and group solidarity.

Group interaction provides students with the experiences that they need in order to realize that they can learn from one another. Only by diffusing authority along horizontal lines will students be able to share and appreciate the importance of learning collectively. Crucial to such a process is the element of dialogue. Through group dialogue, the norms of cooperation and sociability offset the traditional hidden curriculum's emphasis on competition and excessive individualism. In addition, the process of group instruction provides students with the opportunity for experiencing, rather than simply hearing about, the dynamics of participatory democracy.

In short, developing an awareness that is nurtured in a shared task to democratize classroom relationships is imperative for students if they are to overcome the lack of community reminiscent of the traditional classroom and the larger social order. The group encounter provides the social basis for the development of such a consciousness. Under such conditions, social relations of education marked by dominance, subordination, and an uncritical respect for authority can be effectively minimized.

Social relations marked by reciprocity and communality are not the only by-products of the group component. Another important feature centers around giving students the opportunity to serve an apprenticeship in teaching. By evaluating each other's work, acting as peer leaders, participating in and leading discussions, students learn that teaching is not based on intuitive and imitative pedagogical approaches. Instead, by establishing a close working relationship with teachers and peers, students are given the chance to understand that an analytical, codified body of experience is the central element in any pedagogy. This helps both students and teachers to recognize that behind any pedagogy are values, beliefs, and assumptions informed by a particular world view. Most students see teaching in terms of individual personalities rather than the result of a thought-out set of socially constructed pedagogical axioms.[52] By using this course of action, both students and teachers are provided with a "particular" framework for teaching that highlights the theoretical underpinnings of classroom pedagogy.

The concept of time in schools restricts the development of healthy social and intellectual relationships among students and teachers. Reminiscent of life in factories with its production schedules and hierarchical work relationships, the daily routine of most classrooms acts as a brake upon participation and democratic processes. Modified self-pacing is a classroom process that is more compatible with the view that aptitude is the amount of time required by the students to develop a critical comprehension and resolution of the task under study.

It is imperative that students be given the opportunity to work alone and in groups at a comfortable learning pace so as to be able to develop quickly a learning style that enables them to move beyond the fragmented and atheoretical pedagogies that now characterize American education.[53] The flexible use of a mode of self-paced learning could modify these practices.

Self-pacing is important for other reasons. The delay and denial characteristic of most conventional classrooms can be offset by freeing teachers and students to respond to each other almost immediately. Students need not wait to get feedback and communication about their work. This militates against students giving up or postponing their desire to learn or to share and analyze what they have learned with other students. Modified self-pacing allows students to work alone or with other students at a comfortable pace within reasonable bounds mutually agreed upon by teachers and students. Under this format, the clock ceases to shape the pace and character of the class, and the tyranny of a rigid time schedule gives way to a schedule governed by reciprocal exchanges. Moreover, since students have a measure of control over their work, grades, and time, this eliminates pitting students against one another and reinforces the notion that learning is essentially a shared phenomenon.

In political terms, the self-pacing and peer-leader features inveigh against the myth of considering the teacher as the indispensable expert, alone qualified to define and distribute knowledge.[54] Moreover, with the use of peers and modified self-pacing, democratic classroom relationships are developed and the one-dimensionality of traditional classroom social relationships gives way to the possibility of infinitely richer classroom social encounters. These classroom social encounters are reciprocally humanizing and are mediated through an emancipatory conceptual framework.

The peer-leader and self-paced features represent two social processes that significantly offset some of the organizational and structural properties of the traditional classroom. In most traditional classrooms, students work in an isolated and independent fashion. This is usually rationalized by educators on the grounds that it fosters independence. In part, this is true, but it fosters a type of independence that precludes the development of social relationships among age peers and adults that promote opportunities to share and work in an interdependent fashion. Moreover, its function appears to be more ideological than rational and represents a strong pedagogical component in upholding the division of labor characteristic of the larger society. In any case, the traditional notion of independence does not strike a balance between developing one's specific talents and sharing tasks with other students. The self-paced and peer features smoothly reconcile this contradiction. Students not only are given ample opportunity to explore their talents and interests at a pace they can control, they also can share their interests with other people. They get help both from the classroom leaders and from their peers.

Conclusion

This paper provides the groundwork for a new thrust in the task of identifying the dynamics and ideological assumptions underlying specific patterns of socialization in social studies classrooms. By identifying the social processes of classroom and school life which make these patterns operative and highlighting the normative nature of social studies knowledge, it attempts to clarify the dichotomy between the goals of social studies developers and the process of schooling. In our judgment, the recognition of this dichotomy between the official and hidden curriculum will compel social studies educators to develop a new theoretical perspective about the dynamics of educational change, one that penetrates the functional relationships that exist between the institutions of the schools, the work place and the political world. In so doing, they will begin to uncover those social processes in all sociopolitical institutions including the classroom that militate against the creation of a democratic, social education. Further enumeration and elucidation of those processes as well as the search for interconnections among them will become the necessary prerequisites for educators planning to intervene into the educational process.

For the message is a clear one. Social studies educators will run the risk of repeated failure unless they develop a structural foundation that will counter the social processes and values of the hidden curriculum. If social solidarity, individual growth, and dedication to social action are to emerge from social education, the hidden curriculum will have to be either eliminated or minimized as much as possible. There is little room in social education for tracking and social sorting, hierarchical social relationships, the correspondence between evaluation and power, and the fragmented and isolated interpersonal dynamics of the classroom encounter, all of which characterize the hidden curriculum. These classroom processes will have to be replaced by democratic social processes and values that take into consideration the reciprocal interaction of goals, pedagogy, content, and structure.

The above task will not be an easy one; the changes to be made will be difficult and often frustrating but nonetheless necessary. Educational reformers can no longer operate within the limited confines of traditional educational theory and practice. It should be clear that social education is normative and political in essence and at its best can be both emancipatory and reflective. By stepping outside the traditional parameters of educational theory and practice, we can view schooling as inextricably linked to a web of larger socioeconomic and political arrangements. And by analyzing the nature of the relationship between schools and the dominant society in political and normative terms, we can counter a hidden curriculum defined through the ideology of traditional classroom social processes. If social education is in Kant's words to be used to educate students for a better society, social studies educators will even have to go further than democratizing their schools and classrooms. They will have to do more than help develop changes in student consciousness; they will have to help implement the rationale for reconstructing a new social order whose institutional arrangements, in the final analysis, will provide the basis for a truly humanizing education.

Notes

1. C. E. Silberman, *Crisis in the Classroom: The Remaking of American Education* (New York: Random House, 1970); J. Spring, *The Sorting Machine: National Educational Policy Since 1945* (New York: David McKay, 1976), pp. 93–39.

2. G. Lyons, "The Higher Illiteracy," *Harper's* 253:1516 (September 1976): 33–40; B. Brodinsky, "Back to the Basics: The Movement and Its Meanings," *Phi Delta Kappan* 58:7 (March 1977): 522–27.

3. W. F. Pinar, "Notes on the Curriculum Field 1978," *American Educational Research Journal* 7:8 (September 1978): 5–12.

4. P. Bourdieu and J. C. Passeron, *Reproductions in Education, Society and Culture* (London: Sage Publications, 1977); B. Bernstein, *Class, Codes and Control* (London: Collier-Macmillan, 1976).

5. M. Apple, "Curriculum as Ideological Selection," *Comparative Educational Review* 20 (June 1975): 210–11.

6. R. Dreeben, *On What Is Learned in Schools* (Reading, Mass.: Addison-Wesley, 1968); P. Jackson, *Life in Classrooms* (New York: Holt, Rinehart & Winston, 1968); N. Overly, ed., *The Unstudied Curriculum* (Washington, D.C.: Association for Supervision and Curriculum Development, 1970); M. Apple, "The Hidden Curriculum and the Nature of Conflict," *Interchange* 2:4 (1971); M. Apple and N. King, "What Do Schools Teach?" in *Humanistic Education*, ed. R. H. Weller (Berkeley: McCutchan, 1977), pp. 29–63.

7. P. Stern and J. Yarbrough, "Hannah Arendt," *American Scholar* 47:3 (Summer 1978): 380.

8. T. Parsons, "The School Class as a Social System: Some of Its Functions in American Society," *Harvard Educational Review* 29:4 (Fall 1959): 297–318; R. Dreeben, "The Contribution of Schooling to the Learning of Norms," *Socialization and Schools* (Cambridge: Harvard University Press, 1968).

9. M. Apple, "Some Aspects of the Relationships Between Economics and Cultural Reproduction" (Paper presented at Kent State Invitational Conference on Curriculum Theory, November 11, 1977), p. 29.

10. J. Karabel and A. H. Halsey, eds., *Power and Ideology in Education* (New York: Oxford University Press, 1972).

11. J. O'Neill, "Embodiment and Child Development: A Phenomenological Approach," in *Childhood and Socialization*, ed. H. P. Dreitzel (New York: Macmillan, 1973), p. 65.

12. M. F. D. Young, ed., *Knowledge and Control* (London: Collier-Macmillan,

1976); N. Keddie, ed., *The Myth of Cultural Deprivation* (Baltimore: Penguin Books, 1973); C. Jenks, ed., *Rationality, Education and the Social Organization of Knowledge* (London: Routledge & Kegan Paul, 1977); J. Eggleston, *The Sociology of the School Curriculum* (London: Routledge & Kegan Paul, 1977).

13. R. Sharp and A. Green, *Educational and Social Control* (London: Routledge & Kegan Paul, 1975); M. Sarup, *Marxism and Education* (London: Routledge & Kegan Paul, 1978).

14. Sharp and Green, *Educational and Social Control*, p. 21.

15. A. Gramsci, *Selections from the Prison Notebooks*, ed. and trans. Q. Hoare and G. Smith (New York: International Publishers, 1971); H. Entwhistle, "Antonio Gramsci and the School as Hegemonic," *Educational Theory* 28:1 (Winter 1978): 23–33.

16. R. LaBrecque, "The Correspondence Theory," *Educational Theory* 28:3 (Summer 1978): 194–201.

17. Dreeben, *On What Is Learned*, p. 24.

18. S. Arons, "The Separation of School and State: Pierce Reconsidered," *Harvard Educational Review* 46 (February 1976): 98.

19. R. Tyler, *Basic Principles of Curriculum and Instruction* (Chicago: University of Chicago Press, 1949).

20. Ibid., p. 35. Traditionalists like Tyler raise the question only to ignore it as a focus for investigation.

21. P. Freire, *Pedagogy of the Oppressed* (New York: Seabury Press, 1973), p. 15.

22. Dreeben, *On What Is Learned*.

23. Ibid., p. 13.

24. Ibid., p. 66.

25. Bernstein, *Class, Codes and Control*.

26. S. Aronowitz, *False Promises: The Shaping of American Working Class Consciousness* (New York: McGraw-Hill, 1973), p. 75.

27. M. Apple, "The Hidden Curriculum"; H. Giroux and A. Penna, "Social Relations in the Classroom: The Dialectic of the Hidden Curriculum," *Edcentric* 40:41 (Spring-Summer 1977): 39–47.

28. J. Bruner, *The Relevance of Education* (New York: W. W. Norton & Co., 1973), p. 115.

29. S. Bowles and H. Gintis, *Schooling in Capitalist America: Educational Reform and the Contradictions of Economic Life* (New York: Basic Books, 1976).

30. Apple, "The Hidden Curriculum"; J. Anyon, "Elementary Social Studies Textbooks and Legitimating Knowledge," *Theory and Research in Social Education* 6:3 (September 1978): 40–54; T. Popkewitz, "The Latent Values of the Discipline-Centered Curriculum in Social Education," *Theory and Research in Social Education* 5 (April 1977): 41–60.

31. Apple, "The Hidden Curriculum"; Popkewitz, "Latent Values."

32. Popkewitz, "Latent Values," p. 58.

33. Jackson, *Life in Classrooms*.

34. Ibid., p. 16.

35. Ibid., p. 18.

36. Bowles and Gintis, *Schooling in Capitalist America*, p. 40.

37. Ibid., p. 41.

38. N. Keddie, "Classroom Knowledge," in *Knowledge and Control*, ed. M. F. D. Young (London: Collier-Macmillan, 1971).

39. D. Lortie, *Schoolteacher: A Sociological Study* (Chicago: University of Chicago Press, 1975), p. 54.

40. I. Illich, "After Deschooling, What?" in *After Deschooling What?*, ed. A. Gartner, C. Greer, and F. Reisman (New York: Holt, Rinehart & Winston, 1973); R. Bernstein, *The Restructuring of Social and Political Theory* (Philadelphia: University of Pennsylvania Press, 1976).

41. Jackson, *Life in Classrooms*, p. 33.

42. P. Freire, *Pedagogy in Process* (New York: Seabury Press, 1978).

43. K. Marx, "Theses on Feuerbach," in *The German Ideology*, ed. C. J. Arthur (New York: International Publishers, 1972), p. 123.

44. E. Cagan, "Individualism, Collectivism and Radical Educational Reform" *Harvard Educational Review* 48:2 (May 1978): 227–66.

45. H. Braverman, *Labor and Monopoly Capital* (New York: Monthly Review Press, 1974); S. Ewen, *Captains of Consciousness* (New York: McGraw-Hill, 1976).

46. P. Slater, *The Pursuit of Loneliness* (Boston: Beacon Press, 1970); Cagan, "Individualism, Collectivism."

47. N. Daniels, "The Smart White Man's Burden," *Harper's* 247 (October 1973); B. Berger, "A New Interpretation of the I.Q. Controversy," *The Public Interest* 50 (Winter 1978): 29–48; J. B. Biggs, "Genetics and Education: Alternative to Jensenism," *Educational Researcher* 7 (April 1978): 11–17.

48. Bernstein, *Class, Codes and Control*, pp. 88–89.

49. Lortie, *Schoolteacher: A Sociological Study*.

50. Bowles and Gintis, *Schooling in Capitalist America*.

51. Freire, *Pedagory of the Oppressed*.

52. Lortie, *Schoolteacher: A Sociological Study*.

53. S. Aronowitz, "Mass Culture and the Eclipse of Reason: The Implications for Pedagogy," *College English* 38:8 (April 1977): 768–74.

54. I. Illich, *Deschooling Society* (New York: Harper & Row, 1971).

6

What Should We Do with a Hidden Curriculum When We Find One?

Jane Martin

At the end of a very interesting article, "Hiding the Hidden Curriculum," Elizabeth Vallance raises the question of what to do with the hidden curriculum now that we have found it. We can embrace it wholeheartedly, she says, or we can attempt to expunge it altogether, or we can do something between these two extremes. Vallance leaves the question open and I have no intention of closing it here; indeed, I am not sure it is one that can or should be closed. I would, however, like to explore some of the things that can be done with a hidden curriculum once it is found and some of the pitfalls of doing those things. But first we need to get clearer than we now are on the nature of the beast.

Misleading Labels

Most of the labels we use when talking about hidden curriculum are either singularly unilluminating or highly misleading. To call hidden curriculum "covert" or "latent," as people often do, does no harm, but neither does it promote our understanding. To call hidden curriculum "what schooling does to people," "by-products of schooling," or "nonacademic outcomes of schooling" would seem to promote our understanding but in fact leads us astray.[1] For these last three labels, and others, too, make

Reprinted from *Curriculum Inquiry* 6: 2 (1976): 135–51. Copyright © 1976 by The Ontario Institute for Studies in Education. Reprinted by permission of John Wiley & Sons, Inc.

it seem as if hidden curriculum is necessarily tied to schools and schooling when it is not. Much of our education—and I am talking now of formal education and not simply of the informal education which enters into all aspects of our lives—much of this education has always taken place outside of schools. In an earlier day, apprenticeships to craftsmen prevailed. Presently there are internships in hospitals, management training programs in industry, fieldwork placements in social agencies; there are private music lessons, group karate lessons, swimming programs at the Y; there are summer camps, Cub Scouts, basic training in the armed forces. I see no reason whatsoever to suppose that schools have a hidden curriculum but that formal educational programs in nonschool settings do not. Labels such as "by-products of schooling" or "what schooling does to people" do no harm if we realize that they refer to one particular class of hidden curricula, namely, the hidden curricula of schools. We must not, however, let them dominate our thinking lest they blind us to the hidden curricula lurking in other habitats.

These labels mislead in another way, too, for they give the impression that everything an educational setting does to people belongs to its hidden curriculum. But while hidden curriculum is not necessarily tied to schools and schooling, it is always and everywhere tied to learning. Both schools and nonschool educational settings do lots of things to people—they have all sorts of by-products. It needs to be stressed, therefore, that only *some* of the things done by a given educational setting constitute its hidden curriculum. Some hospitals because of their location create traffic jams, some swimming programs because of their pools cause earaches, and some schools because of their expenditures produce rising tax rates, but these results or outcomes do not belong to the hidden curriculum of the educational setting in question. They do not because although they happen, they are not *learned*.

Implicit in hidden curriculum talk, moreover, is a contrast between hidden curriculum and what for want of a better name I will call *curriculum proper*—that thing, difficult as it is to define, about which philosophers and educational theorists have long debated and which curriculum specialists have long tried to plan and develop. The contrast is between what it is openly intended that students learn and what, although not openly intended, they do, in fact, learn. Indeed, one important thrust of the critique of contemporary schooling mounted by those who have been called radical school reformers is that curriculum proper is failing while hidden curriculum thrives:[2] students do not learn to read, they do not learn math or science or any of the other subjects and skills endorsed by all parties to the educational enterprise; what they do learn is to be docile and obedient, to value competition over cooperation, to stifle their creative impulses, and to believe in what Ivan Illich calls the "Myth of Unending Consumption."[3] Thus, some results or outcomes of school or of nonschool educational settings are not constituents of a hidden curriculum because they are not states that individuals have attained through learning: what I will henceforth call *learning states*. Other results are not because they are openly intended learning states, hidden from neither teacher nor student. In a school which openly acknowledges the goal that students learn to speak French and provides courses to that end, the ability to speak French, if achieved, although a learning state, is not part of its hidden curriculum.

I do not mean to suggest that knowledge of French could never be part of a hidden curriculum. It is tempting to conceive of the contrast with curriculum proper implicit in hidden curriculum talk as one between academic and nonacademic learning states in the manner of one of the labels listed above, but this is a mistake. Curriculum proper can and often does quite directly and openly aim at what is normally taken to be nonacademic learning, be it of moral values, religious attitudes, political preferences, or vocational skills. We are so used to thinking of the academic dimension of curriculum proper that we forget this. And just as a curriculum proper can be nonacademic, so a hidden curriculum can consist of what normally would be considered academic learning, be it learning of addition facts, scientific theories, or French. To be sure, the hidden curriculum of contemporary public schooling discovered to date is what most of us would call nonacademic. But it does not follow from this discovery that a hidden curriculum *could* not consist of academic learning states. A hidden curriculum, like a curriculum proper, has subject matter, but just as there is no particular subject matter which must be present in or absent from every curriculum proper, so there is none which must or cannot belong to every hidden curriculum.

In sum, a hidden curriculum consists of some of the outcomes or by-products of schools or of nonschool settings, particularly those states which are learned yet are not openly intended. There is no special subject matter which always and everywhere characterizes hidden curriculum, although, of course, a hidden curriculum must have *some* subject matter. It should perhaps be stressed that this neutrality with respect to subject matter means not only that the learning states of a hidden curriculum can be academic as well as nonacademic; it means that the subject matter can be significant as well as trivial, worthwhile as well as worthless.

Actually, when one speaks of learning states one is usually speaking of two things at once: some *state* a learner is in (for example, a state of knowing or believing or being interested or being cautious), and something which may be called the *object* of that state—provided "object" is construed broadly enough to include not just physical objects but such things as the theory of relativity, *David Copperfield*, the free enterprise system, and love. Thus, a learning state is not 2 + 3 = 5, but believing or remembering that

$2 + 3 = 5$; it is not the free enterprise system as such, but being committed to or, perhaps, being adamantly opposed to the system.[4] When I said just now that there is no special subject matter necessarily associated with hidden curriculum, I meant that the learning states which constitute a hidden curriculum are not limited to one sort of object. But they are not limited to one sort of state either. The learning states of a hidden curriculum can be states which we think of as character traits—for example, docility or conformity. They can also be cognitive states such as believing or knowing, states of readiness or of skill, emotional states, attitudinal states, or some combination of those other sorts of states.[5]

The Hidden Curriculum

Those who describe the hidden curriculum of contemporary schooling talk of the hidden curriculum as if there is and can be only one, as if hidden curriculum is everywhere the same. But of course it is not. A hidden curriculum is always *of* some setting, and there is no reason to suppose that different settings will have identical hidden curricula. Actually, a hidden curriculum is not only of some setting but is *at* some time; therefore, we cannot even assume that a single setting will have identical hidden curricula at different times. Settings change, and as they do some learning states may become extinct as new ones emerge.

It is sometimes said that learning states must occur systematically if they are to belong to a hidden curriculum.[6] I am not sure what this means. True, they must *be* results of the setting. However, the learning states of a hidden curriculum need not be systematic in the sense that they are mass products—learning states for all or even most learners in that setting. If John is the only one of his classmates who comes to appreciate good art as a result of the teacher's putting Picasso prints on the classroom walls—the teacher in this instance wanting to make the room more attractive and having no thought of learning states—this learning state of John's belongs to the hidden curriculum of his school, at least for him. A hidden curriculum, like a curriculum proper, is of some setting, *at* some time, and *for* some learner.

In view of this relativity to context, talk of *the* hidden curriculum is normally elliptical. Those who speak in this way usually have a particular setting in mind—often, but not always, public schooling in the United States—and they have a particular time, usually the present, in mind. From the standpoint of the learner, moreover, the hidden curriculum is an abstraction, for it is neither the set of learning states attained by anyone in particular nor the set attained by all the learners in a given setting. Idiosyncratic learning states are overlooked when a portrait of the hidden curriculum is painted, and rightly so, for the hidden curriculum of a setting consists not in all the learning states therein attained, but rather in the dominant ones. An account of *the* hidden curriculum of a setting, like an account of *the* history of an era, is selective. Attention is directed to common themes running through the learning states, presumably themes of some importance. Learning states which seem insignificant or that do not fit readily into the general pattern will be shunned, even though they are in fact produced by the setting.

The learning states of the hidden curriculum of a setting do, then, occur systematically in the sense that idiosyncratic states are ignored. But what is considered idiosyncratic will depend on one's interest. Learning states which are legitimately ignored when the hidden curriculum of some setting is the focus of attention may require attention when the hidden curriculum for some learner is at issue. Suppose what is unlikely, namely, that Mary is the only person in her school in the last twenty years who has come to believe as an unintended result of her schooling that women cannot be doctors. This idiosyncratic learning state is rightly ignored by those trying to determine the hidden curriculum of *Mary's school.* But those trying to discover the hidden curriculum of that school *for Mary* would be remiss if they did not take it seriously, since it might well play a very significant role in Mary's life.

I want to emphasize here, because I think it too often forgotten, that our interest can be in hidden curricula for learners as well as of settings. And just as the hidden curriculum of a setting is an abstraction from the standpoint of learners, so the hidden curriculum for a learner is an abstraction from the standpoint of settings. The hidden curriculum for Mary cuts across settings, so that to discover it we must look not simply at Mary's schooling, but at the other settings having hidden curricula in which Mary is a participant—or perhaps is simply an unwilling victim. Once again, the hidden curriculum is a selection from among the relevant learning states; it is a set of learning states thought to be dominant for Mary.

Finding a Hidden Curriculum

A hidden curriculum is not something one just finds; one must go hunting for it. Since a hidden curriculum is a set of learning states, ultimately one must find out what is learned as a result of the practices, procedures, rules, relationships, structures, and physical characteristics which constitute a given setting. But one can begin by spotting learning states and making sure they can be traced back to the setting, or by examining aspects of the setting and discovering what learning states they produce. Motivations for the search can, of course, vary. Some investigators may simply want to know what is learned in school, others will want to make their teaching methods more efficient, and still others will be intent on revealing connections between education and the larger social order. But whatever the motivation may be, a full-blown theory of curriculum cannot afford to neglect the hunt for hidden curricula, for the quarry plays a central role in the education of each one of us.

One consequence of the relativity of hidden curriculum to setting, time, and learner is that investigative work on it is never done. New settings with their own hidden curricula are forever being created and old ones are forever changing. Information gathered yesterday on the hidden curriculum of a given setting may not accurately portray that setting's hidden curriculum today. Thus, the scope of the search for hidden curricula needs to be extended beyond schools to nonschool settings, and at the same time the searchers must continually retrace their steps.

Even if hidden curricula did not change over time, there would be reason to revisit the old haunts, for the information gathered at any time is never the whole story. Regardless of setting or time, what we find when we investigate hidden curricula is a function of what we look for and what we look at. The literature describing the hidden curriculum of public schooling in the United States published in the mid to late 1960s provides an interesting case in point. It draws our attention to learning states having class and racial overtones, but it overlooks those having sexist implications.[7] Yet no one who has seen the film *High School* or read even a sampling of the articles in *And Jill Came Tumbling After* can doubt that public schooling in the 1960s included a wide range of sexist practices and that its hidden curriculum included sexist beliefs, attitudes, and values.[8] If sexist learning states were not found it is not because they did not exist, but because they were not seen or—if they were seen—because they were not recognized for what they were.

A description of the hidden curriculum of public schooling of the 1960s, or for that matter of the 1970s, written today would most likely draw our attention to its sexist component. But who knows what other components it might overlook! Christian doctrine? Heterosexual bias? Speciesism? The search for hidden curricula needs to retrace its steps, then, because even if a hidden curriculum does not change over time, *we* change. Our interests shift, our knowledge of the world is enlarged, our consciousness is raised, and we therefore come to see and care about things in a hidden curriculum we did not care about, indeed perhaps could not see, before.

One way to determine if we have overlooked important parts of a hidden curriculum is to examine the different aspects or elements of the relevant setting or settings to see what learning states they produce. In other words, look beyond learning states to sources.[9] Thanks to a variety of inquiries, many of which Vallance cites in her article, we have an idea of some of the sources of important elements of hidden curricula of schools. Vallance mentions, for example, the social structure of the classroom, the teacher's exercise of authority, the rules governing the relationship between teacher and student.[10] Standard learning activities are also sources. Who can forget

Jules Henry's description of a classroom game of spelling baseball or John Holt's account of twenty questions?[11] In a somewhat different vein, Joanne Bronars has drawn our attention to dissecting frogs and catching insects.[12] Another source of hidden curricula is the teacher's use of language.[13] And, of course, there are textbooks and audio-visual aids, furnishings and architecture, disciplinary measures, timetables, tracking systems, and curricular priorities.

The problem in looking to sources is that it is not clear that a list of sources of the learning states which constitute hidden curricula will have an end, for as new practices, procedures, environments, and the like are introduced into educational settings, they become potential generators of hidden curricula. Can anyone doubt that the new classification of students as learning-disabled and the practices which accompany it are generating a hidden curriculum, or rather elements of one? As pocket calculators begin to be used in math and science classes, will they not generate hidden learning states? Just as there are no limits on the subject matter of the learning outcomes which can constitute a hidden curriculum, I think we must conclude that there are none on the elements or aspects of educational settings which can be sources of those states.

There is, of course, a good reason for looking to sources and for recognizing that when limits are placed on the sorts of things within a setting which can generate elements of hidden curricula, they are arbitrary. If our concern is not simply to discover hidden curricula but to do something about them, we must find out which elements or aspects of a given setting help bring about which components of that setting's hidden curriculum. For if we do not know the sources of the learning states belonging to a hidden curriculum, we must either let that hidden curriculum be or do away with the whole setting. But some hidden curricula or parts thereof quite clearly ought not to be left as they are; and on the other hand, if we do away with whole settings, we may be doing away with practices, procedures, physical environments, and the like which on balance generate desirable learning outcomes.

Rational intervention requires that we know sources. It requires also that we return to the scene of our interventions to make sure we have not done more harm than good. There is no guarantee that, when we change an educational setting so as to do away with a portion of its hidden curriculum we find abhorrent, we will succeed; indeed, if we are not careful, the changes we make can generate the very learning states we are trying to banish or, for that matter, ones even more unsavory. The learning-disabilities movement purports to be trying to end the practice of labeling students because of the hidden curriculum resulting from it, but one wonders if the movement is not in fact promoting the very learning states it claims to reject.[14]

Once we recognize that any aspect of an educational setting can have learning states which are not openly intended, that changes in settings can produce such states, that the learning states produced by a setting may be different for every learner, and that new learners constantly enter educational settings, then I think we must acknowledge that for any given setting hidden curricula cannot be avoided. We can get rid of a particular hidden curriculum of a setting, but in principle we cannot avoid some hidden curriculum or other unless we abolish the setting itself. I stress this point because educators often suppose that if their reforms are put into practice we will never again have to worry about hidden curricula. As the documentary film *Infants School* unwittingly testifies, this is a terrible mistake, for the most enlightened practices can carry with them an undesirable hidden curriculum.[15] In many ways, the British infants school of the film is a model of school reform, yet if one looks closely one sees traditional sex roles and stereotypes being transmitted. Those of us concerned with educational settings cannot rest on our laurels. It is impossible to do away with all hidden curricula; hence, for any given setting, we must always be on our guard.

Two Kinds of Hiddenness

That *some* hidden curriculum or other for any given setting is inevitable ought not to be taken as grounds for maintaining the status quo in education.

To say that some hidden curriculum or other is inevitable for any given setting is not to say that a hidden curriculum consisting in learning states we take to be undesirable is inevitable. We need to guard against replacing an objectionable hidden curriculum with a worse one, but although there is always the possibility of our ending up with a worse one, there is no necessity at work here. And there is always the possibility that we will end up with a better one.

I realize that an important part of the message of Illich's *Deschooling Society* is that the hidden curriculum of contemporary public schooling cannot be changed—at least not for the better—by changes in the setting. Hence the need for deschooling. Illich has been attacked on this score by critics speaking from very different points on the educational spectrum. It is all too easy, however, to do less than justice to his claim. He is surely not saying that *none* of the hidden learning states produced by contemporary public schooling can be banished or that *no* changes for the better can be produced by changes in the setting. His view of the hidden curriculum of public schooling is highly selective, and his claim about the resistance of public schooling to reform that makes a real difference must be understood as holding only for the learning outcomes with which he is concerned. Exactly what these are and whether he is right about them is a topic for another occasion. But whether or not he is right, there is certainly nothing in his remarks which shows reform of hidden curricula to be *in general* impossible. His claim applies only to school settings, and he is the first to point out that nonschool settings also have hidden curricula.[16] Some of these latter might be as resistant to real reform as he says schools are, but there is no reason to suppose that all would be.

The inevitability thesis is not a counsel for inaction. Yet inaction is, in fact, one viable alternative when we find a hidden curriculum and wonder what we ought to do with it. I [have] indicated that we may be forced to let a hidden curriculum be when we find it because we do not know its exact sources. It should be clear, however, that even if we know its sources, we can nonetheless choose not to abolish or even alter them in any way. It may be wondered, however, if a hidden curriculum, once it is found, *can* be left as is. Once we find a hidden curriculum doesn't it stop being hidden, hence being a hidden curriculum?

Our discussion has for too long avoided the question of the hiddenness of the learning states belonging to a hidden curriculum. Suppose a sociologist studies a school or school system and finds elements of its hidden curriculum. Is that hidden curriculum, simply by virtue of being known to the sociologist, no longer a *hidden* curriculum? Surely not. Being hidden, like being north of, is a relation; just as Boston is north of Miami but not north of Montreal, so something can be hidden from one person or group but not from another. When we speak of something as hidden, moreover, we usually have some context in mind in relation to which we make our judgments of hiddenness. In the game hide and seek, a player is hidden just so long as the one who is "it" has not found him or her; that others know where the player is has no bearing on the player's hiddenness from the standpoint of the game; and when the player is found, that others do not know where the player is also has no bearing on the player's hiddenness.

Education is no game, but nonetheless a hidden curriculum is in this respect like a hidden player in hide and seek. Once the learners in a setting are aware of the learning states they are acquiring or are supposed to acquire, these learning outcomes no longer belong to the hidden curriculum of that setting. Indeed, once learning states are openly acknowledged so that the learners can readily become aware of them even if they do not, the learning states can no longer be considered hidden. Until learning states are acknowledged or the learners are aware of them, however, they remain hidden even if sociologists, bureaucrats, and teachers are all aware of them. Thus, a hidden curriculum can be found yet remain hidden, for finding is one thing and telling is another.

There are, in effect, two kinds of hiddenness, and an account of hidden curriculum needs to come to terms with both. Something can be hidden in the sense in which a cure for cancer is hidden or in the sense in which a penny in the game hide the penny is hidden. Both academicians who investigate the hidden curriculum of public schooling today and radical school reformers who decry it vacillate on this issue. Some make it sound as if a hidden curriculum is hidden by someone or some group in the manner of the penny in the children's game. Others seem to assume that the learning states of a hidden curriculum have not been hidden by anyone— they just happen to be unknown to us, much as the cure for cancer is unknown to us at the present time.

Whether we are trying to explain why the hidden curriculum of a given setting is what it is or [how] to change a hidden curriculum, we need to take into account this basic ambiguity in the notion of hidden curriculum. For any set of hidden learning states which interests us, we must try to settle the question of intent. It makes no sense to explain a hidden curriculum by means of a conspiracy theory, as some of those writers who point out that the hidden curriculum of public schooling in the United States serves capitalism do, and at the same time describe its learning states as the unintended by-products of schooling. Nor does it make sense simply to tinker with school practices and procedures in order to do away with a given hidden curriculum if it is really the product of intent.

Some readers would doubtless prefer that I characterize hidden curriculum solely in terms of unintended learning states. To introduce intention muddies the waters, they will say. Yet I do not think we have any choice here. It is not only that those writers most concerned with hidden curricula move back and forth between the two kinds of hiddenness. The relevant research on intent has not all been done. We may assume that all the elements of the hidden curricula discovered to date are unintended, but we certainly do not know for sure that they are. A characterization that accommodates the descriptions of hidden curricula we now have is surely to be preferred over one which may require us when the evidence is in to reject some on the grounds that the learning states they describe were intended although we did not realize it.

Earlier I characterized hidden curriculum in terms of learning states which are not openly intended. The point of that negative formulation was to accommodate the two kinds of hiddenness. That characterization did not, however, take into account the learner's point of view. Although a learning state of a setting is not openly intended, a learner can be aware of it, in which case it will not belong to the hidden curriculum of that setting for that learner. Thus, my earlier characterization must be amended. A hidden curriculum consists of those learning states of a setting which are either unintended or intended but not openly acknowledged to the learners in the setting unless the learners are aware of them.

Out of the Frying Pan

What then can we do with a hidden curriculum once we have found it? This depends, of course, on who "we" are. Assuming we are the educators in a setting and have found both hidden curriculum and sources, there are a number of alternatives open to us.

1. We can do nothing; we can leave the setting alone rather than try to change it, in which case the relevant learning states become foreseen by us, whereas previously they were not, but they do not otherwise change; in particular, the hidden curriculum remains hidden. This may seem to be the alternative of despair, but that is not necessarily the case, for there may be some hidden curricula, or elements thereof, with respect to which we are neutral—we do not positively value them but we do not consider them undesirable either. In relation to such learning states, doing nothing is a reasonable alternative.

2. We can change our practices, procedures, environments, rules, and the like in an effort to root out those learning states we consider undesirable. The radical school-reform movement known as open education has tried to do just this. It has opposed tracking, grading, and examinations, changed the physical environment of classrooms, introduced new learning activities and educational materials, and tried to alter both teacher-pupil and pupil-pupil relationships in order to avoid the hidden curriculum of contemporary public schooling. The free-school movement, while varying in its details from open education, can be understood in this same light.

3. Instead of changing a setting, we can simply abolish it. This, of course, is the alternative those in the deschooling movement recommend. I say "simply" abolish, but for some educational settings, notably the public school systems of modern industrial societies, abolition is not a simple matter. Abolition of a setting does, however, guarantee abolition of that setting's hidden curriculum, but not of all hidden curricula like it.

4. It is always possible that we will want to embrace rather than abolish the hidden curriculum we find. There are many today who applaud the learning states of neatness and competitiveness, docility and obedience to authority attributed to the hidden curriculum of our public schools.[17] They actually have two alternatives: (a) they can openly acknowledge these learning states, thereby shifting them from hidden curriculum to curriculum proper, or (b) they can intend these learning states but not openly, in which case they remain part of the hidden curriculum.[18]

What *should* we do with a hidden curriculum when we find it? The significance of the question is a function of the quality of the hidden curriculum we find. If a hidden curriculum is harmless, what we do with it will not matter very much. It is when the one we find is not harmless—when it instills beliefs, attitudes, values, or patterns of behavior which are undesirable—that our question takes on urgency. And it becomes more urgent the more undesirable the learning states are. There can be no doubt that when the hidden curriculum we find contains harmful learning states, we must try to root them out. But this is sometimes easier said than done. A teacher can stop using the game of spelling baseball as a learning activity, but this will be but a small step toward rooting out learning states such as competitiveness, self-hatred, and hostility toward one's peers. Attitudes and traits such as these seldom have a single, easily isolated source; indeed, those which are most offensive, because very basic, are likely to be products of a complex set of interrelated and entrenched practices and structures. To give up or modify one of these may well accomplish very little.

Large-scale changes, perhaps even total destruction, of a setting may be necessary if a hidden curriculum or some central part thereof is to be abolished. And this, of course, is what the radical school-reform movement in all its variations has been about.[19] The hidden curriculum of contemporary public schooling in the United States has been held to be abhorrent— and rightly so. Drastic changes have been seen—again rightly in my view— as the only hope if its highly undesirable and very deep-seated learning outcomes are to be banished. This is not the place to catalog or assess those proposals, though they need to be assessed in a way they have not yet been. I do, however, want to draw attention to a problem which confronts anyone who tries to change drastically or abolish altogether an educational setting in order to do away with its hidden curriculum—a problem too many radical school reformers have ignored.

Some changes in educational settings involve the deliberate placing of the learners of that setting in other settings so as to break down the barriers between the setting and the "real" world, meanwhile enhancing learning. Thus, for example, schools are encouraged to put students in nonschool settings where they will learn through being apprenticed to master craftsmen and women, through working at a job, through helping others do their jobs, or, perhaps, simply through watching and observing. Other changes in educational settings involve restricting its function so as to reduce its power over its participants. It has been proposed, for example, that schools be limited to giving basic skill training.[20] In this case, even if participants in the setting are not deliberately placed in other settings, the likelihood of their drifting into them is great. And of course there is the total abolition of a setting, in which case the participants may simply be abandoned to other settings. In all three sorts of reform, the risk is real that those on the receiving end of the offending learning states will be taken out of the frying pan only to be sent or allowed to leap into the fire.

It is not just formal educational settings which have hidden curricula. Any setting can have one and most do. When I argued initially that hidden curricula can exist in nonschool settings, I limited the discussion to formal educational settings such as teaching hospitals, private piano lessons, and basic training in the armed services. But learning states occur in settings which are not usually considered educational at all. At IBM and Bell Telephone, at one's local gas station and city hall, workers learn more than their jobs; attitudes, values, and patterns of behavior are as much the product of these settings as of formal educational ones. It seems not only legitimate, therefore, but theoretically important that we recognize explicitly that hidden curricula can be found anywhere learning states are found. IBM and Bell Telephone are not exempt; neither are one's neighborhood streets, one's church, or the national book club one joins. And what is important to remember is that there is no good reason at all to suppose that the hidden curricula of these and kindred settings are significantly better than the one which is the target of school reforms.

Radical school reformers have been called romantics—this label, needless to say, having derogatory connotations. The source of their romanticism is seen as lying in their view of the child as by nature a happy, curious, creative, and good being who is ruined by school. Perhaps some radical school reformers do romanticize the child, but in general this is a caricature of their position. If the reformers are romantics it is not in their beliefs about human nature, but in their beliefs about the world outside schools. It is as if they bracket their critique of contemporary society when they begin to theorize about education. I am sure that they are as aware as anyone of the sorry state of the outside world. Indeed, they were probably aware of the sorry state of *it* long before they perceived the sorry state of schools. But they forget it in their excitement upon discovering the hidden curriculum of contemporary public schooling. Make the outside world, not the schools, the dominant educational setting, they say, and all will be well—as if the world out there were a benign setting, one in which there either are no hidden curricula or in which only worthwhile ones thrive.[21]

A mistake we all tend to make—except perhaps when we are thinking of our own children—is to concentrate on the hidden curriculum *of* a given setting when what matters is the hidden curriculum *for* a given individual or group. To do away with the complex network of practices and structures, which in a given setting produce highly undesirable learning outcomes— assuming this is possible, and to some extent I think it is—may leave the learning states *for someone* unchanged. This may be so because our very reforms send a person, or allow the person to drift, into settings having hidden curricula similar to the one we have been trying to abolish. Or it may be so because the learning states in question were all along the result of more than one setting. Settings can combine to produce learning states. And they surely do. The learning states of docility and conformity, competitiveness and unending consumption, which are said to belong to the hidden curriculum of public schooling in the United States today, are certainly not the products of that schooling alone. Who can doubt that family, church, community organizations, place of work, and the media have all combined to produce them?

The problem I spoke of is really two problems, both hinging on the obvious point that different settings can but need not have significantly different hidden curricula. The one problem is that some educational reforms designed to rid us of undesirable hidden curricula can be self-defeating, because they substitute for the old setting new ones producing essentially the same learning states. The other problem is that the reform of a given educational setting may simply not be enough to do the job if other settings having the same old hidden curriculum survive. It has been pointed out that radical school reform can only succeed if it goes hand in hand with radical societal reform.[22] That this is so becomes especially clear once we shift our attention from the hidden curriculum of schooling to the hidden curriculum for those being schooled. For it is not just that wide-scale basic reform of public schooling—that is, reform of the whole system as opposed to small units within or alongside it—may not be possible without concomitant societal reform. Supposing it to be possible, it is not at all obvious that the hidden curriculum for those being schooled will be materially improved if the other dominant educational settings in their lives remain the same.

Knowledge Can Be Power

I am not as optimistic as some about the prospects of radical societal reform. But whether one takes these prospects to be good or not, there are two courses of action open to us when we find a hidden curriculum we abhor which we still need to consider. One is part and parcel of many radical school-reform programs. The other is not.

Radical school reformers do not all take learners out of the frying pan and, with no thought of the fire outside, send them to get burned. Both those who advocate open classrooms and those in the free-school movement try to provide their learners with insulation so that the fire, even if it singes, will not burn. They do this by advocating practices and structures which have a dual function: they are intended to do away with the hidden curriculum of public schooling and at the same time to substitute for the attitudes and values of that hidden curriculum ones considered to be admirable. Thus, competition is to be replaced by cooperation while conformity is to be replaced by creativity and initiative. The attitudes and values espoused by radical school reformers are openly acknowledged by some and embraced not so openly by others. But be they part of the curriculum proper of radical school reform or of its hidden curriculum, they are expected to take hold not just while the learner is in school and until graduation, but in nonschool settings too and for life. If any policy can successfully protect learners from the hidden curricula of the larger unreconstructed society, surely the policy of fostering learning states in conflict with those fostered by the larger society can.

It should be noted that some radical school reformers deplore this aspect of the reform movement. In their view, schools should get out of the business of forming attitudes and values altogether.[23] It is not clear, however, that schools *can* get out of the business. Even schools whose functions are pared away and minimized through reform will have hidden curricula, hidden curricula which may or may not themselves be minimal so far as attitudes and values are concerned. I am afraid that those who condemn the hidden curriculum of public schooling today, yet want to preserve schools in some form or other without substituting better values and attitudes for the ones to be abolished, are being unrealistic. The question they should be asking of those who try to insulate learners from the fires outside is not whether the schools should do the insulating, but whether schools alone can do it. If the larger society remains as it is, will schools be allowed to foster values and attitudes counter to those of surrounding institutions? And, if so, will these values and attitudes "take"; will they really provide the needed protection?

I do not know the answer to these questions, but I am pessimistic enough to want to consider one more thing that can be done with a hidden curriculum when we find it, something which, although independent of the course of action just described, is compatible with it and indeed could be used to buttress it. When we find a hidden curriculum, we can show it to those destined to be its recipients. Consciousness raising, if you will, with a view to counteracting the hidden curricula of settings we are not now in a position to change or abolish. Not that consciousness raising is any guarantee that a person will not succumb to a hidden curriculum. But still, one is in a better position to resist if one knows what is going on. Resistance to what one does not know is difficult, if not impossible.

The raising to consciousness of hidden curricula can proceed in many different ways. It can take place in informal rap sessions or formal seminars and can be aimed at those in a setting, those about to enter it, or those who once were in it. But whatever form it takes, it will consist in transforming the learning states of the hidden curriculum of a setting into the subject matter of a person's curriculum proper. I do not mean by this that the hidden curricula we find abhorrent are to be openly embraced. Quite the contrary. The point of raising a hidden curriculum to consciousness is not to *foster* but to *prevent* the acquisition of the learning states belonging to it. The method of prevention is to make these learning states themselves the objects of new and very different learning states.

Most of us never stop to think that the settings we enter have hidden curricula, let alone what those hidden curricula might be. A program of consciousness raising would aim at such simple yet not at all obvious learning states as realizing that a given setting has a hidden curriculum, knowing what that hidden curriculum is, knowing which practices of the setting are responsible for the various learning states of its hidden curriculum, and understanding the significance of these learning states for one's own life and for the larger society. It would aim not only at making the hidden curriculum of a setting an object of a cognitive state such as these, but of skill states, too—for example, being able to spot a hidden curriculum, being able to recognize heretofore undiscovered sources, and knowing how to avoid the learning outcomes one does not want to acquire.

Having knowledge and skill concerning hidden curricula can be a form of self-defense against the onslaught of unasked-for learning states. But consciousness raising, as I understand it, aims at the acquisition of attitudes and values too. Certainly consciousness raising in the women's movement is not thought to be successful if a woman in coming to know the facts about sexist practices in modern society also comes to approve of them. Knowledge of hidden curricula will not provide a defense against them if those subject to hidden curricula do not *want* to resist.

To do its job, consciousness raising with respect to hidden curricula must tend to attitudes and values and feelings while imparting knowledge and skill. In this respect, it resembles the program of those who want to substitute cooperativeness for competitiveness and creativity for conformity. But if it, too, is in the business of forming attitudes and values, there is a difference; for in consciousness raising the attitudes and values acquired are, or at least are supposed to be, the result of a direct confrontation between learner and hidden curriculum. To see it is to despise it, to want to resist it, perhaps even to want to go out in the world and try to change it. The attitudes and values honored by radical school reformers have perhaps been chosen by them because of their own confrontation with a hidden curriculum, but the students who are to acquire them do not do so as a result of such confrontation.

The consciousness raising I am suggesting would seem to require a knowledge of the hidden curricula of nonschool settings which is not now available. Am I not then proposing a course of action for which we are not ready, one which would require an investment of funds and scholarly energy which is not likely to be forthcoming? Again, we must look to consciousness raising in the women's movement for our model. It has generated knowledge even while relying on it, for much if not all of the important research on women being done now is surely a direct result of it. I would expect the consciousness raising I am recommending to have a similar effect on our knowledge: that it would generate research into hidden curricula, research which in turn produced new subject matter for it. Thus, although knowledge of hidden curricula in nonschool settings is surely needed, consciousness raising can begin with the little we have, in the expectation that we will soon have more.

Lest there be any doubt, we do have some with which to begin—if nothing else, our own experiences in these settings. We may, however, have more knowledge now than we realize. Our knowledge of the hidden curricula of schools comes primarily from two sources: from those who have worked in schools and those who have done research on schools. To discover the hidden curricula of other institutions we must turn to those who study them: to medical sociologists and to sociologists of family, church, science, sports, and business. We must turn also to those who have taken or given management training courses at Gulf and those who have worked the switchboard at the telephone company. Perceptive practitioners are not the monopoly of schools. Hospitals, businesses, even city halls have their James Herndons and John Holts who see and record hidden curricula for us.

Who should conduct this consciousness raising? Insofar as schools send their students into nonschool settings to learn, one would hope that they would do their own consciousness raising: that medical schools would do it for prospective interns, social work schools for students doing fieldwork, education schools for practice teachers, and high schools for those sent out to learn on the job. One would hope that schools trying to abolish their own hidden curriculum while keeping students within their walls would conduct consciousness-raising sessions about the hidden curricula in the larger society, too. Schools that did this would, in effect, become centers for the critique of social institutions. I believe strongly that schools should serve this function, but perhaps only an optimist would think they could or would serve it as long as they remain public and society remains the way it is. Schools are not the only possible forum for consciousness raising with respect to hidden curricula, however. Victims of a given hidden curriculum can do it for themselves as women have done and blacks have done.

As I have said, there is no guarantee that consciousness raising will insulate us successfully against learning states we do not want and should not acquire. Certainly we must not view it as a substitute for institutional and societal reform. Yet, as the women's movement has shown, knowledge about what has happened or is happening to one can have powerful effects. I would not count on a single individual whose consciousness had been raised in private, so to speak, to withstand the hidden curriculum of a setting in which he or she is put. But when knowledge is shared and there is strong peer support, consciousness raising may be the best weapon individuals who are subject to hidden curricula have.

Notes

1. I have taken these labels from E. Vallance, "Hiding the Hidden Curriculum: An Interpretation of the Language of Justification in Nineteenth-Century Educational Reform," *Curriculum Theory Network* 4: 1 (1973/74): 6.

2. See, for example, B. Gross and R. Gross, eds., *Radical School Reform* (New York: Simon & Schuster, 1969).

3. I. Illich, *Deschooling Society* (New York: Harper & Row, 1971).

4. It is possible that some states of an individual have no object—for example, a generalized state of despair. Normally, however, the states that constitute learning states will have objects, albeit very complex ones at times. Thus, although the state of being competitive may seem to have no object, an individual will in fact be competitive with respect to certain situations or types of situations, and those would constitute the object of the state.

5. It will be noted that I have characterized hidden curriculum as what happens (and curriculum proper as what is intended to happen), rather than as statements about what happens (or is intended to happen). Should the reader prefer the linguistic level—that is, a characterization of hidden curriculum as a set of statements about learning states rather as the learning states themselves—the present account can readily be translated into it.

6. Vallance suggests as much in "Hiding the Hidden Curriculum," p. 7.

7. See, for example, J. Henry, *Culture Against Man* (New York: Random House, 1963); J. Herndon, *The Way It Spozed to Be* (New York: Simon & Schuster, 1968); J. Kozol, *Death at an Early Age* (Boston: Houghton Mifflin Co., 1967).

8. J. Stacy, S. Bereaud, and J. Daniels, eds., *And Jill Came Tumbling After: Sexism in American Education* (New York: Dell, 1974).

9. As I have characterized hidden curriculum, the sources of the learning states of a hidden curriculum do not themselves belong to that curriculum. Should the reader prefer a broader characterization, one that includes the practices that produce the relevant learning states, the necessary adjustments in my formulation of the problem of finding hidden curricula can readily be made.

10. Vallance, "Hiding the Hidden Curriculum," pp. 6–7.

11. Henry, *Culture Against Man*; J. Holt, *How Children Fail* (New York: Dell, 1964).

12. J. Bronars, "Tampering with Nature in Elementary School Science," in *Readings in the Philosophy of Education: A Study of Curriculum*, ed. J. R. Martin (Boston: Allyn & Bacon, 1970).

13. N. Gayer, "On Making Morality Operational," in *Readings in the Philosophy of Education*, ed. Martin.

14. P. Schrag and D. Divoky, *The Myth of the Hyperactive Child* (New York: Pantheon Books, 1975).

15. "Infants School," by L. Weber, is distributed by Education Development Center, Newton, Massachusetts.

16. Illich, *Deschooling Society,* p. 48.

17. W. Pursell, *A Conservative Alternative School: The A+ School in Cupertino* (Bloomington, Ind.: Phi Delta Kappa, 1976).

18. It should be noted that learning outcomes intended by us could all along have been intended by others, for example, by those who hired us.

19. For purposes of this discussion I take the radical school-reform movement to include not just open-classroom advocates, free-school proponents, and those wanting to decentralize the control of schools, but also deschoolers and those who advocate minimal schooling.

20. See, for example, C. Bereiter, *Must We Educate?* (Englewood Cliffs, N.J.: Prentice-Hall, 1973); M. B. Katz, *Class, Bureaucracy and Schools: The Illusion of Educational Change in America* (New York: Praeger, 1971).

21. I do not mean to suggest that all radical school reformers romanticize the world outside the schools. Illich does not. Nor does A. Graubard, *Free the Children* (New York: Random House, 1972).

22. For example, see Graubard, *Free the Children.*

23. See, for example, Bereiter, *Must We Educate?*; and Katz, *Class, Bureaucracy.*

Section II

Applications of The Concept

7

Social Class and the
Hidden Curriculum of Work

Jean Anyon

Scholars in political economy and the sociology of knowledge have recently argued that public schools in complex industrial societies like our own make available different types of educational experience and curriculum knowledge to students in different social classes. Bowles and Gintis,[1] for example, have argued that students in different social-class backgrounds are rewarded for classroom behaviors that correspond to personality traits allegedly rewarded in the different occupational strata—the working classes for docility and obedience, the managerial classes for initiative and personal assertiveness. Basil Bernstein, Pierre Bourdieu, and Michael W. Apple,[2] focusing on school knowledge, have argued that knowledge and skills leading to social power and regard (medical, legal, managerial) are made available to the advantaged social groups but are withheld from the working classes, to whom a more "practical" curriculum is offered (manual skills, clerical knowledge). While there has been considerable argumentation of these points regarding education in England, France, and North America, there has been little or no attempt to investigate these ideas empirically in elementary or secondary schools and classrooms in this country.[3]

This article offers tentative empirical support (and qualification) of the above arguments by providing illustrative examples of differences in student *work* in classrooms in contrasting social class communities. The examples were gathered as part of an ethnographical study of curricular, pedagogical, and pupil evaluation practices in five elementary schools. The

Reprinted, by permission, from *Journal of Education* 162: 1 (Winter 1980): 67–92.

article attempts a theoretical contribution as well and assesses student work in the light of a theoretical approach to social-class analysis. The organization is as follows: the methodology of the ethnographical study is briefly described; a theoretical approach to the definition of social class is offered; income and other characteristics of the parents in each school are provided, and examples from the study that illustrate work tasks and interaction in each school are presented; then the concepts used to define social class are applied to the examples in order to assess the theoretical meaning of classroom events. It will be suggested that there is a "hidden curriculum" in schoolwork that has profound implications for the theory—and consequence—of everyday activity in education.

Methodology

The methods used to gather data were classroom observation; interviews of students, teachers, principals, and district administrative staff; and assessment of curriculum and other materials in each classroom and school. All classroom events to be discussed here involve the fifth grade in each school. Except for that school where only one fifth-grade teacher could be observed, all the fifth-grade teachers (that is, two or three) were observed as the children moved from subject to subject. In all schools the art, music, and gym teachers were also observed and interviewed. All teachers in the study were described as "good" or "excellent" by their principals. All except one new teacher had taught for more than four years. The fifth grade in each school was observed by the investigator for ten three-hour periods between September 15, 1978, and June 20, 1979.

Before providing the occupations, incomes, and other relevant social characteristics of the parents of the children in each school, I will offer a theoretical approach to defining social class.

Social Class

One's occupation and income level contribute significantly to one's social class, but they do not define it. Rather, social class is a series of relationships. A person's social class is defined here by the way that person relates to the process in society by which goods, services, and culture are produced.[4] One relates to several aspects of the production process primarily through one's work. One has a relationship to the system of ownership, to other people (at work and in society), and to the content and process of one's own productive activity. One's relationship to all three of these aspects of production determines one's social class; that is, all three relationships are necessary, and none is sufficient for determining a person's relation to the process of production in society.

Ownership Relations

In a capitalist society, a person has a relation to the system of private ownership of capital. Capital is usually thought of as being derived from physical property. In this sense capital is property that is used to produce profit, interest, or rent in sufficient quantity so that the result can be used to produce more profit, interest, or rent—that is, more capital. Physical capital may be derived from money, stocks, machines, land, or the labor of workers (whose labor, for instance, may produce products that are sold by others for profit). Capital, however, can also be symbolic. It can be the socially legitimated knowledge of how the production process works, its financial, managerial, technical, or other "secrets." Symbolic capital can also be socially legitimated skills—cognitive (for example, analytical), linguistic, or technical skills that provide the ability to, say, produce the dominant scientific, artistic, and other culture or to manage the systems of industrial and cultural production. Skillful application of symbolic capital may yield social and cultural power and perhaps physical capital as well.

The ownership relation that is definitive for social class is one's relation to physical capital. The first such relationship is that of capitalist. To be a member of the capitalist class in the present-day United States, one must participate in the ownership of the apparatus of production in society. The number of such persons is relatively small; while one person in ten owns some stock, for example, a mere 1.6 percent of the population owns 82.2 percent of *all* stock, and the wealthiest one-fifth owns almost all the rest.[5]

At the opposite pole of this relationship is the worker. To be in the United States working class, a person will not ordinarily own physical capital; on the contrary, his or her work will be wage or salaried labor that is either a *source* of profit (that is, capital) to others or that makes it possible for others to *realize* profit. Examples of the latter are white-collar clerical workers in industry and distribution (office and sales) as well as the wage and salaried workers in the institutions of social and economic legitimation and service (in state education and welfare institutions).[6] According to the criteria to be developed here, the number of persons who presently comprise the working class in the United States is between 50 percent and 60 percent of the population.[7]

In between the defining relationship of capitalist and worker are the middle classes, whose relationship to the process of production is less clear and whose relationship may indeed exhibit contradictory characteristics. For example, social service employees have a somewhat contradictory relationship to the process of production because, although their income may be at middle-class levels, some characteristics of their work are working class (they may have very little control over their work). Analogously, there are persons at the upper income end of the middle class, such as upper-middle-class professionals, who may own quantities of stocks and will therefore share characteristics of the capitalist class. As the next criterion to be discussed makes clear, however, to be a member of the present-day capitalist class in the United States, one must also participate in the social *control* of this capital.

Relationships Between People

The second relationship that contributes to one's social class is the relation one has to authority and control at work and in society.[8] One characteristic of most working-class jobs is that there is no built-in mechanism by which the worker can control the content, process, or speed of work. Legitimate decision making is vested in personnel supervisors, in middle or upper management, or—as in an increasing number of white-collar working-class (and most middle-class) jobs—by bureaucratic rule and regulation. For upper-middle-class professional groups there is an increased amount of autonomy regarding work. Moreover, in middle- and upper-middle-class positions there is an increasing chance that one's work will also involve supervising the work of others. A capitalist is defined within these relations of control in an enterprise by having a position that participates in the direct control of the entire enterprise. Capitalists do not directly control workers in physical production and do not directly control ideas in the sphere of cultural production. However, more crucial to control, capitalists make the decisions over how resources are used (that is, where money is invested) and how profit is allocated.

Relations Between People and Their Work

The third criterion that contributes to a person's social class is the relationship between that person and his or her own productive activity—the type of activity that constitutes his or her work. A working-class job is often characterized by work that is routine and mechanical and that is a small, fragmented part of a larger process with which workers are not usually acquainted. These working-class jobs are usually blue-collar, manual labor. A few skilled jobs such as plumbing and printing are not mechanical, however, and an increasing number of working-class jobs are *white*-collar. These white-collar jobs, such as clerical work, may involve work that necessitates a measure of planning and decision making, but one still has no built-in control over the content. The work of some middle- and most upper-middle-class managerial and professional groups is likely to involve the need for conceptualization and creativity, with many professional jobs demanding one's full creative capacities. Finally, the work that characterizes the capitalist position is that this work is almost entirely a matter of conceptualization (planning and laying out) that has as its object management and control of the enterprise.

One's social class, then, is a result of the relationships one has, largely through one's work, to physical capital and its power, to other people at work and in society, and to one's own productive activity. Social class is a lived, developing process. It is not an abstract category, and it is not a fixed, inherited position (although one's family background is, of course, important). Social class is perceived as a complex of social relations that one develops as one grows up—as one acquires and develops certain bodies of knowledge, skills, abilities, and traits, and as one has contact and opportunity in the world.[9] In sum, social class describes relationships that we as adults have developed, may attempt to maintain, and in which we participate every working day. These relationships in a real sense define our material ties to the world. An important concern here is whether these relationships are developing in children in schools within particular social-class contexts.

The Sample of Schools

With the above discussion as a theoretical backdrop, the social-class designation of each of the five schools will be identified, and the income, occupation, and other relevant available social characteristics of the students and their parents will be described. The first three schools are in a medium-sized city district in northern New Jersey, and the other two are in a nearby New Jersey suburb.

The first two schools I will call *working-class schools*. Most of the parents have blue-collar jobs. Less than a third of the fathers are skilled, while the majority are in unskilled or semiskilled jobs. During the period of the study (1978–1979), approximately 15 percent of the fathers were unemployed. The large majority (85 percent) of the families are white. The following occupations are typical: platform, storeroom, and stockroom workers; foundrymen, pipe welders, and boilermakers; semiskilled and unskilled assembly-line operatives; gas station attendants, auto mechanics, maintenance workers, and security guards. Less than 30 percent of the women work, some part-time and some full-time, on assembly lines, in storerooms and stockrooms, as waitresses, barmaids, or sales clerks. Of the fifth-grade parents, none of the wives of the skilled workers had jobs. Approximately 15 percent of the families in each school are at or below the federal "poverty" level;[10] most of the rest of the family incomes are at or below $12,000, except some of the skilled workers whose incomes are higher. The incomes of the majority of the families in these two schools (at or below $12,000) are typical of 38.6 percent of the families in the United States.[11]

The third school is called the *middle-class school*, although because of neighborhood residence patterns, the population is a mixture of several social classes. The parents' occupations can be divided into three groups: a small group of blue-collar "rich," who are skilled, well-paid workers such as printers, carpenters, plumbers, and construction workers. The second group is composed of parents in working-class and middle-class white-collar jobs: women in office jobs, technicians, supervisors in industry, and parents employed by the city (such as firemen, policemen, and several of the school's teachers). The third group is composed of occupations such as personnel directors in local firms, accountants, "middle management," and a few small capitalists (owners of shops in the area). The children of several local doctors attend this school. Most family incomes are between $13,000 and $25,000, with a few higher. This income range is typical of 38.9 percent of the families in the United States.[12]

The fourth school has a parent population that is at the upper income level of the upper middle class and is predominantly professional. This school will be called the *affluent professional school.* Typical jobs are: cardiologist, interior designer, corporate lawyer or engineer, executive in advertising or television. There are some families who are not as affluent as the majority (the family of the superintendent of the district's schools, and the one or two families in which the fathers are skilled workers). In addition, a few of the families are more affluent than the majority and can be classified in the capitalist class (a partner in a prestigious Wall Street stock brokerage firm). Approximately 90 percent of the children in this school are white. Most family incomes are between $40,000 and $80,000. This income span represents approximately 7 percent of the families in the United States.[13]

In the fifth school the majority of the families belong to the capitalist class. This school will be called the *executive elite school* because most of the fathers are top executives (for example, presidents and vice-presidents) in major United States-based multinational corporations—for example, ATT, RCA, City Bank, American Express, U.S. Steel. A sizable group of fathers are top executives in financial firms in Wall Street. There are also a number of fathers who list their occupations as "general counsel" to a particular corporation, and these corporations are also among the large multinationals. Many of the mothers do volunteer work in the Junior League, Junior Fortnightly, or other service groups; some are intricately involved in town politics; and some are themselves in well-paid occupations. There are no minority children in the school. Almost all the family incomes are over $100,000, with some in the $500,000 range. The incomes in this school represent less than 1 percent of the families in the United States.[14]

Since each of the five schools is only one instance of elementary education in a particular social class context, I will not generalize beyond the sample. However, the examples of schoolwork which follow will suggest characteristics of education in each social setting that appear to have theoretical and social significance and to be worth investigation in a larger number of schools.

Social Class and Schoolwork

There are obvious similarities among United States schools and classrooms. There are school and classroom rules, teachers who ask questions and attempt to exercise control and who give work and homework. There are textbooks and tests. All of these were found in the five schools. Indeed, there were other curricular similarities as well: all schools and fifth grades used the same math book and series (*Mathematics Around Us,* Scott Foresman, 1978); all fifth grades had at least one boxed set of an individualized reading program available in the room (although the variety and amounts of teaching materials in the classrooms increased as the social class of the school population increased); and, all fifth-grade language arts curricula included aspects of grammar, punctuation, and capitalization.[15]

This section provides examples of work and work-related activities in each school that bear on the categories used to define social class. Thus, examples will be provided concerning students' relation to capital (for example, as manifest in any symbolic capital that might be acquired through schoolwork); students' relation to persons and types of authority regarding schoolwork; and students' relation to their own productive activity. The section first offers the investigator's interpretation of what school-work *is* for children in each setting and then presents events and interactions that illustrate that assessment.

The Working-Class Schools

In the two working-class schools, work is following the steps of a procedure. The procedure is usually mechanical, involving rote behavior and very little decision making or choice. The teachers rarely explain why the work is being assigned, how it might connect to other assignments, or what the idea is that lies behind the procedure or gives it coherence and perhaps meaning or significance. Available textbooks are not always used, and the teachers often prepare their own dittos or put work examples on the board. Most of the rules regarding work are designations of what the children are to do; the rules are steps to follow. These steps are told to the children by the teachers and are often written on the board. The children are usually told to copy the steps as notes. These notes are to be studied. Work is often evaluated not according to whether it is right or wrong but according to whether the children followed the right steps.

The following examples illustrate these points. In math, when two-digit division was introduced, the teacher in one school gave a four-minute lecture on what the terms are called (which number is the divisor, dividend, quotient, and remainder). The children were told to copy these names in their notebooks. Then the teacher told them the steps to follow to do the problems, saying, "This is how you do them." The teacher listed the steps on the board, and they appeared several days later as a chart hung in the middle of the front wall: "Divide, Multiply, Subtract, Bring Down." The children often did examples of two-digit division. When the teacher went over the examples with them, he told them what the procedure was for each problem, rarely asking them to conceptualize or explain it themselves: "Three into twenty-two is seven; do your subtraction and one is left over." During the week that two-digit division was introduced (or at any other time), the investigator did not observe any discussion of the idea of grouping involved in division, any use of manipulables, or any attempt to relate two-digit division to any other mathematical process. Nor was there any attempt to relate the steps to an actual or possible thought process of the children. The observer did not hear the terms *dividend, quotient,* and so on, used again. The math teacher in the other working-class school followed similar procedures regarding two-digit division and at one point her class seemed confused. She said, "You're confusing yourselves. You're tensing up. Remember, when you do this, it's the same steps over and over again—and that's the way division always is." Several weeks later, after a test, a group of her children "still didn't get it," and she made no attempt to explain the concept of dividing things into groups or to give them manipulables for their own investigation. Rather, she went over the steps with them again and told them that they "needed more practice."

In other areas of math, work is also carrying out often unexplained fragmented procedures. For example, one of the teachers led the children through a series of steps to make a 1-inch grid on their paper *without* telling them that they were making a 1-inch grid or that it would be used to study scale. She said, "Take your ruler. Put it across the top. Make a mark at every number. Then move your ruler down to the bottom. No, put it across the bottom. Now make a mark on top of every number. Now draw a line from . . ." At this point a girl said that she had a faster way to do it and the teacher said, "No, you don't; you don't even know what I'm making yet. Do it this way, or it's wrong." After they had made the lines up and down and across, the teacher told them she wanted them to make a figure by connecting some dots and to measure that, using the scale of 1 inch equals 1 mile. Then they were to cut it out. She said, "Don't cut until I check it."

In both working-class schools, work in language arts is mechanics of punctuation (commas, periods, question marks, exclamation points), capitalization, and the four kinds of sentences. One teacher explained to me, "Simple punctuation is all they'll ever use." Regarding punctuation, either a teacher or a ditto stated the rules for where, for example, to put commas. The investigator heard no classroom discussion of the aural context of punctuation (which, of course, is what gives each mark its meaning). Nor did the investigator hear any statement or inference that placing a punctuation mark could be a decision-making process, depending, for example, on one's intended meaning. Rather, the children were told to follow the rules. Language arts did not involve creative writing. There were several writing assignments throughout the year, but in each instance the children were given a ditto, and they wrote answers to questions on the sheet. For example, they wrote their "autobiography" by answering such questions as "Where were you born?" "What is your favorite animal?" on a sheet entitled "All About Me."

In one of the working-class schools, the class had a science period several times a week. On the three occasions observed, the children were not called upon to set up experiments or to give explanations for facts or concepts. Rather, on each occasion the teacher told them in his own words what the book said. The children copied the teacher's sentences from the board. Each day that preceded the day they were to do a science experiment, the teacher told them to copy the directions from the book for the procedure they would carry out the next day and to study the list at home that night. The day after each experiment, the teacher went over what they had "found" (they did the experiments as a class, and each was actually a class demonstration led by the teacher). Then the teacher wrote what they "found" on the board, and the children copied that in their notebooks. Once or twice a year there are science projects. The project is chosen and assigned by the teacher from a box of 3-by-5-inch cards. On the card the teacher has written the question to be answered, the books to use, and how much to write. Explaining the cards to the observer, the teacher said, "It tells them exactly what to do, or they couldn't do it."

Social studies in the working-class schools is also largely mechanical, rote work that was given little explanation or connection to larger contexts. In one school, for example, although there was a book available, social studies work was to copy the teacher's notes from the board. Several times a week for a period of several months the children copied these notes. The fifth grades in the district were to study United States history. The teacher used a booklet she had purchased called "The Fabulous Fifty States." Each day she put information from the booklet in outline form on the board and the children copied it. The type of information did not vary: the name of the state, its abbreviation, state capital, nickname of the state, its main products, main business, and a "Fabulous Fact" ("Idaho grew twenty-seven billion potatoes in one year. That's enough potatoes for each man, woman, and . . ."). As the children finished copying the sentences, the teacher erased them and wrote more. Children would occasionally go to the front to pull down the wall map in order to locate the states they were copying, and the teacher did not dissuade them. But the observer never saw her refer to the map; nor did the observer ever hear her make other than perfunctory remarks concerning the information the children were copying. Occasionally the children colored in a ditto and cut it out to make a stand-up figure (representing, for example, a man roping a cow in the Southwest). These were referred to by the teacher as their social studies "projects."

Rote behavior was often called for in classroom work. When going over math and language art skills sheets, for example, as the teacher asked for the answer to each problem, he fired the questions rapidly, staccato, and the scene reminded the observer of a sergeant drilling recruits: above all, the questions demanded that you stay at attention: "The next one? What do I put here? . . . Here? Give us the next." Or "How many commas in this sentence? Where do I put them . . . The next one?"

The four fifth-grade teachers observed in the working-class schools attempted to control classroom time and space by making decisions without consulting the children and without explaining the basis for their decisions. The teacher's control thus often seemed capricious. Teachers, for instance, very often ignored the bells to switch classes—deciding among themselves to keep the children after the period was officially over to continue with the work or for disciplinary reasons or so they (the teachers) could stand in the hall and talk. There were no clocks in the rooms in either school, and the children often asked, "What period is this?" "When do we go to gym?" The children had no access to materials. These were handed out by teachers and closely guarded. Things in the room "belonged" to the teacher: "Bob, bring me my garbage can." The teachers continually gave the children orders. Only three times did the investigator hear a teacher in either working-class school preface a directive with an unsarcastic "please," or "let's" or "would you." Instead, the teachers said, "Shut up," "Shut your mouth," "Open your books," "Throw your gum away—if you want to rot your teeth, do it on your own time." Teachers made every effort to control the movement of the children, and often shouted, "Why are you out of your seat??!!" If the children got permission to leave the room, they had to take a written pass with the date and time.

The control that the teachers have is less than they would like. It is a result of constant struggle with the children. The children continually resist the teachers' orders and the work itself. They do not directly challenge the teacher's authority or legitimacy, but they make indirect attempts to sabotage and resist the flow of assignments:

Teacher:	I will put some problems on the board. You are to divide.
Child:	We got to divide?
Teacher:	Yes.
Several children:	(Groan) Not again. Mr. B., we done this yesterday.
Child:	Do we put the date?
Teacher:	Yes. I hope we remember we work in silence. You're supposed to do it on white paper. I'll explain it later.
Child:	Somebody broke my pencil. (Crash—a child falls out of his chair.)

| Child: | (repeats) Mr. B., somebody broke my *pencil!* |
| Child: | Are we going to be here all morning? |

(Teacher comes to the observer, shakes his head and grimaces, then smiles.)

The children are successful enough in their struggle against work that there are long periods where they are not asked to *do* any work but just to sit and be quiet.[16] Very often the work that the teachers assign is "easy," that is, not demanding and thus receives less resistance. Sometimes a compromise is reached where, although the teachers insist that the children continue to work, there is a constant murmur of talk. The children will be doing arithmetic examples, copying social studies notes, or doing punctuation or other dittos, and all the while there is muted but spirited conversation— about somebody's broken arm, an after-school disturbance the day before, and so on. Sometimes the teachers themselves join in the conversation because, as one teacher explained to me, "It's a relief from the routine."

Middle-Class School

In the middle-class school, work is getting the right answer. If one accumulates enough right answers, one gets a good grade. One must follow the directions in order to get the right answers, but the directions often call for some figuring, some choice, some decision making. For example, the children must often figure out by themselves what the directions ask them to do and how to get the answer: what do you do first, second, and perhaps third? Answers are usually found in books or by listening to the teacher. Answers are usually words, sentences, numbers, or facts and dates; one writes them on paper, and one should be neat. Answers must be given in the right order, and one cannot make them up.

The following activities are illustrative. Math involves some choice: one may do two-digit division the long way or the short way, and there are some math problems that can be done "in your head." When the teacher explains how to do two-digit division, there is recognition that a cognitive process is involved; she gives several ways and says, "I want to make sure you understand what you're doing—so you get it right"; and, when they go over the homework, she asks the *children* to tell how they did the problem and what answer they got.

In social studies the daily work is to read the assigned pages in the textbook and to answer the teacher's questions. The questions are almost always designed to check on whether the students have read the assignment and understood it: who did so-and-so; what happened after that; when did it happen, where, and sometimes, why did it happen? The answers are in the book and in one's understanding of the book; the teacher's hints when one doesn't know the answers are to "read it again" or to look at the picture or at the rest of the paragraph. One is to search for the answer in the "context," in what is given.

Language arts is "simple grammar, what they need for everyday life."
The language arts teacher says, "They should learn to speak properly, to
write business letters and thank-you letters, and to understand what nouns
and verbs and simple subjects are." Here, as well, actual work is to choose
the right answers, to understand what is given. The teacher often says,
"Please read the next sentence and then I'll question you about it." One
teacher said in some exasperation to a boy who was fooling around in class,
"If you don't know the answers to the questions I ask, then you can't stay in
this *class!* [pause] You *never* know the answers to the questions I ask, and
it's not fair to me—and certainly not to you!"

Most lessons are based on the textbook. This does not involve a critical
perspective on what is given there. For example, a critical perspective in
social studies is perceived as dangerous by these teachers because it may lead
to controversial topics; the parents might complain. The children, however,
are often curious, especially in social studies. Their questions are tolerated
and usually answered perfunctorily. But after a few minutes the teacher will
say, "All right, we're not going any farther. Please open your social studies
workbook." While the teachers spend a lot of time explaining and expanding on what the textbooks say, there is little attempt to analyze how or why
things happen, or to give thought to how pieces of a culture, or, say, a
system of numbers or elements of a language fit together or can be analyzed.
What has happened in the past and what exists now may not be equitable or
fair, but (shrug) that is the way things are and one does not confront such
matters in school. For example, in social studies after a child is called on to
read a passage about the pilgrims, the teacher summarizes the paragraph
and then says, "So you can see how strict they were about everything." A
child asks, "Why?" "Well, because they felt that if you weren't busy you'd
get into trouble." Another child asks, "Is it true that they burned women at
the stake?" The teacher says, "Yes, if a woman did anything strange, they
hanged them. [sic] What would a woman do, do you think, to make them
burn them?" [sic] See if you can come up with better answers than my other
[social studies] class." Several children offer suggestions, to which the
teacher nods but does not comment. Then she says, "Okay, good," and calls
on the next child to read.

Work tasks do not usually request creativity. Serious attention is rarely
given in school work on *how* the children develop or express their own
feelings and ideas, either linguistically or in graphic form. On the occasions
when creativity or self-expression is requested, it is peripheral to the main
activity or it is "enrichment" or "for fun." During a lesson on what similes
are, for example, the teacher explains what they are, puts several on the
board, gives some other examples herself, and then asks the children if they
can "make some up." She calls on three children who give similes, two of
which are actually in the book they have open before them. The teacher

does not comment on this and then asks several others to choose similes from the list of phrases in the book. Several do so correctly, and she says, "Oh good! You're picking them out! See how good we are?" Their homework is to pick out the rest of the similes from the list.

Creativity is not often requested in social studies and science projects, either. Social studies projects, for example, are given with directions to "find information on your topic" and write it up. The children are not supposed to copy but to "put it in your own words." Although a number of the projects subsequently went beyond the teacher's direction to find information and had quite expressive covers and inside illustrations, the teacher's evaluative comments had to do with the amount of information, whether they had "copied," and if their work was neat.

The style of control of the three fifth-grade teachers observed in this school varied from somewhat easygoing to strict, but in contrast to the working-class schools, the teachers' decisions were usually based on external rules and regulations—for example, on criteria that were known or available to the children. Thus, the teachers always honor the bells for changing classes, and they usually evaluate children's work by what is in the textbooks and answer booklets.

There is little excitement in schoolwork for the children, and the assignments are perceived as having little to do with their interests and feelings. As one child said, what you do is "store facts up in your head like cold storage—until you need it later for a test or your job." Thus, doing well is important because there are thought to be *other* likely rewards: a good job or college.[17]

Affluent Professional School

In the affluent professional school, work is creative activity carried out independently. The students are continually asked to express and apply ideas and concepts. Work involves individual thought and expressiveness, expansion and illustration of ideas, and choice of appropriate method and material. (The class is not considered an open classroom, and the principal explained that because of the large number of discipline problems in the fifth grade this year they did not departmentalize. The teacher who agreed to take part in the study said she is "more structured" this year than she usually is.) The products of work in this class are often written stories, editorials and essays, or representations of ideas in mural, graph, or craft form. The products of work should not be like everybody else's and should show individuality. They should exhibit good design, and (this is important) they must also fit empirical reality. Moreover, one's work should attempt to interpret or "make sense" of reality. The relatively few rules to be followed regarding work are usually criteria for, or limits on, individual activity. One's product is usually evaluated for the quality of its expression and for the apropriateness of its conception to the task. In many cases, one's own satisfaction with the product is an important criterion for its evaluation. When right answers are called for, as in commercial materials like SRA (Science Research Associates) and math, it is important that the children decide on an answer as a result of thinking about the idea involved in what they're being asked to do. Teacher's hints are to "think about it some more."

The following activities are illustrative. The class takes home a sheet requesting each child's parents to fill in the number of cars they have, the number of television sets, refrigerators, games, or rooms in the house, and so on. Each child is to figure the average number of a type of possession owned by the fifth grade. Each child must compile the "data" from all the sheets. A calculator is available in the classroom to do the mechanics of finding the average. Some children decide to send sheets to the fourth-grade families for comparison. Their work should be "verified" by a classmate before it is handed in.

Each child and his or her family has made a geoboard. The teacher asks the class to get their geoboards from the side cabinet, to take a handful of rubber bands, and then to listen to what she would like them to do. She says, "I would like you to design a figure and then find the perimeter and area. When you have it, check with your neighbor. After you've done that, please transfer it to graph paper and tomorrow I'll ask you to make up a question about it for someone. When you hand it in, please let me know whose it is and who verified it. Then I have something else for you to do that's really fun. [pause] Find the average number of chocolate chips in three cookies. I'll give you three cookies, and you'll have to *eat* your way through, I'm afraid!" Then she goes around the room and gives help, suggestions, praise, and admonitions that they are getting noisy. They work sitting, or standing up at their desks, at benches in the back, or on the floor. A child hands the teacher his paper and she comments, "I'm not accepting this paper. Do a better design." To another child she says, "That's fantastic! But you'll never find the area. Why don't you draw a figure inside [the big one] and subtract to get the area?"

The school district requires the fifth grade to study ancient civilization (in particular, Egypt, Athens, and Sumer). In this classroom, the emphasis is on illustrating and re-creating the culture of the people of ancient times. The following are typical activities: The children made an 8mm film on Egypt, which one of the parents edited. A girl in the class wrote the script, and the class acted it out. They put the sound on themselves. They read stories of those days. They wrote essays and stories depicting the lives of the people and the societal and occupational divisions. They chose from a list of projects, all of which involved graphic representations of ideas: for example, "Make a mural depicting the division of labor in Egyptian society."

Each child wrote and exchanged a letter in hieroglyphics with a fifth

grader in another class, and they also exchanged stories they wrote in cunei-
form. They made a scroll and singed the edges so it looked authentic. They
each chose an occupation and made an Egyptian plaque representing that
occupation, simulating the appropriate Egyptian design. They carved their
design on a cylinder of wax, pressed the wax into clay, and then baked the
clay. Although one girl did not choose an occupation but carved instead a
series of gods and slaves, the teacher said, "That's all right, Amber, it's beautiful." As they were working the teacher said, "Don't cut into your clay until
you're satisfied with your design."

Social studies also involves almost daily presentation by the children of
some event from the news. The teacher's questions ask the children to expand what they say, to give more details, and to be more specific. Occasionally she adds some remarks to help them see connections between events.

The emphasis on expressing and illustrating ideas in social studies is accompanied in language arts by an emphasis on creative writing. Each child
wrote a rhebus story for a first grader whom they had interviewed to see what
kind of story the child liked best. They wrote editorials on pending decisions
by the school board and radio plays, some of which were read over the school
intercom from the office and one of which was performed in the auditorium.
There is no language arts textbook because, the teacher said, "The principal
wants us to be creative." There is not much grammar, but there is punctuation. One morning when the observer arrived, the class was doing a punctuation ditto. The teacher later apologized for using the ditto. "It's just for
review," she said. "I don't teach punctuation that way. We use their language." The ditto had three unambiguous rules for where to put commas in
a sentence. As the teacher was going around to help the children with the
ditto, she repeated several times, "Where you put commas depends on how
you say the sentence; it depends on the situation and what you want to say."
Several weeks later the observer saw another punctuation activity. The
teacher had printed a five-paragraph story on an oak tag and then cut it into
phrases. She read the whole story to the class from the book, then passed out
the phrases. The group had to decide how the phrases could best be put together again. (They arranged the phrases on the floor.) The point was not
to replicate the story, although that was not irrelevant, but to "decide what
you think the best way is." Punctuation marks on cardboard pieces were then
handed out, and the children discussed and then decided what mark was best
at each place they thought one was needed. At the end of each paragraph the
teacher asked, "Are you satisfied with the way the paragraphs are now? Read
it to yourself and see how it sounds." Then she read the original story again,
and they compared the two.

Describing her goals in science to the investigator, the teacher said, "We
use ESS (Elementary Science Study). It's very good because it gives a hands-
on experience—so they can make *sense* out of it. It doesn't matter whether it

[what they find] is right or wrong. I bring them together and there's value in discussing their ideas."

The products of work in this class are often highly valued by the children and the teacher. In fact, this was the only school in which the investigator was not allowed to take original pieces of the children's work for her files. If the work was small enough, however, and was on paper, the investigator could duplicate it on the copying machine in the office.

The teacher's attempt to control the class involves constant negotiation. She does not give direct orders unless she is angry because the children have been too noisy. Normally, she tries to get them to foresee the consequences of their actions and to decide accordingly. For example, lining them up to go see a play written by the sixth graders, she says, "I presume you're lined up by someone with whom you want to sit. I hope you're lined up by someone you won't get in trouble with." The following two dialogues illustrate the process of negotiation between student and teacher.

Teacher:	Tom, you're behind in your SRA this marking period.
Tom:	So what!
Teacher:	Well, last time you had a hard time catching up.
Tom:	But I have my [music] lesson at 10:00.
Teacher:	Well, that doesn't mean you're going to sit here for twenty minutes.
Tom:	Twenty minutes! OK. (He goes to pick out an SRA booklet and chooses one, puts it back, then takes another, and brings it to her.)
Teacher:	OK, this is the one you want, right?
Tom:	Yes.
Teacher:	OK, I'll put tomorrow's date on it so you can take it home tonight or finish it tomorrow if you want.
Teacher:	(to a child who is wandering around during reading) Kevin, why don't you do *Reading for Concepts*?
Kevin:	No, I don't like *Reading for Concepts*.
Teacher:	Well, what are you going to do?
Kevin:	(pause) I'm going to work on my DAR. (The DAR has sponsored an essay competition on "Life in the American Colonies.")

One of the few rules governing the children's movement is that no more than three children may be out of the room at once. There is a school rule that anyone can go to the library at any time to get a book. In the fifth grade I observed, they sign their name on the chalkboard and leave. There are no passes. Finally, the children have a fair amount of officially sanctioned say over what happens in the class. For example, they often negotiate what work is to be done. If the teacher wants to move on to the next subject, but the children say they are not ready, they want to work on their present projects some more, she very often lets them do it.

Executive Elite School

In the executive elite school, work is developing one's analytical intellectual powers. Children are continually asked to reason through a problem, to produce intellectual products that are both logically sound and of top academic quality. A primary goal of thought is to conceptualize rules by which elements may fit together in systems and then to apply these rules in solving a problem. Schoolwork helps one to achieve, to excel, to prepare for life.

The following are illustrative. The math teacher teaches area and perimeter by having the children derive formulas for each. First she helps them, through discussion at the board, to arrive at $A = W \times L$ as a formula (not *the* formula) for area. After discussing several, she says, "Can anyone make up a formula for perimeter? Can you figure that out yourselves? [pause] Knowing what we know, can we think of a formula?" She works out three children's suggestions at the board, saying to two, "Yes, that's a good one," and then asks the class if they can think of any more. No one volunteers. To prod them, she says, "If you use rules and good reasoning, you get many ways. Chris, can you think up a formula?"

She discusses two-digit division with the children as a decision-making process. Presenting a new type of problem to them, she asks, "What's the *first* decision you'd make if presented with this kind of example? What is the first thing you'd *think*? Craig?" Craig says, "To find my first partial quotient." She responds, "Yes, that would be your first decision. How would you do that?" Craig explains, and then the teacher says, "OK, we'll see how that works for you." The class tries his way. Subsequently, she comments on the merits and shortcomings of several other children's decisions. Later, she tells the investigator that her goals in math are to develop their reasoning and mathematical thinking and that, unfortunately, "there's no *time* for manipulables."

While right answers are important in math, they are not "given" by the book or by the teacher but may be challenged by the children. Going over some problems in late September the teacher says, "Raise your hand if you do not agree." A child says, "I don't agree with sixty-four." The teacher responds, "OK, there's a question about sixty-four. [to class] Please check it. Owen, they're disagreeing with you. Kristen, they're checking yours." The teacher emphasized this repeatedly during September and October with statements like "Don't be afraid to say you disagree. In the last [math] class, somebody disagreed, and they were right. Before you disagree, check yours, and if you still think we're wrong, then we'll check it out." By Thanksgiving, the children did not often speak in terms of right and wrong math problems but of whether they agreed with the answer that had been given.

There are complicated math mimeos with many word problems. Whenever they go over the examples, they discuss how each child has set up the problem. The children must explain it precisely. On one occasion the teacher said, "I'm more—just as interested in *how* you set up the problem as in what answer you find. If you set up a problem in a good way, the answer is *easy* to find."

Social studies work is most often reading and discussion of concepts and independent research. There are only occasional artistic, expressive, or illustrative projects. Ancient Athens and Sumer are, rather, societies to analyze. The following questions are typical of those that guide the children's independent research. "What mistakes did Pericles make after the war?" "What mistakes did the citizens of Athens make?" "What are the elements of a civilization?" "How did Greece build an economic empire?" "Compare the way Athens chose its leaders with the way we choose ours." Occasionally the children are asked to make up sample questions for their social studies tests. On an occasion when the investigator was present, the social studies teacher rejected a child's question by saying, "That's just fact. If I asked you that question on a test, you'd complain it was just memory! Good questions ask for concepts."

In social studies—but also in reading, science, and health—the teachers initiate classroom discussions of current social issues and problems. These discussions occurred on every one of the investigator's visits, and a teacher told me, "These children's opinions are important—it's important that they learn to reason things through." The classroom discussions always struck the observer as quite realistic and analytical, dealing with concrete social issues like the following: "Why do workers strike?" "Is that right or wrong?" "Why do we have inflation, and what can be done to stop it?" "Why do companies put chemicals in food when the natural ingredients are available?" and so on. Usually the children did not have to be prodded to give their opinions. In fact, their statements and the interchanges between them struck the observer as quite sophisticated conceptually and verbally, and well-informed. Occasionally the teachers would prod with statements such as, "Even if you don't know [the answers], if you think logically about it, you can figure it out." And "I'm asking you [these] questions to help you think this through."

Language arts emphasizes language as a complex system, one that should be mastered. The children are asked to diagram sentences of complex grammatical construction, to memorize irregular verb conjugations (he lay, he has lain, and so on . . .), and to use the proper participles, conjunctions, and interjections in their speech. The teacher (the same one who teaches social studies) told them, "It is not enough to get these right on tests; you must use what you learn [in grammar classes] in your written and oral work. I will grade you on that."

Most writing assignments are either research reports and essays for social studies or experiment analyses and write-ups for science. There is only an occasional story or other "creative writing" assignment. On the occasion observed by the investigator (the writing of a Halloween story), the points the teacher stressed in preparing the children to write involved the structural aspects of a story rather than the expression of feelings or other ideas. The teacher showed them a filmstrip, "The Seven Parts of a Story," and lectured them on plot development, mood setting, character development, consistency, and the use of a logical or appropriate ending. The stories they subsequently wrote were, in fact, well-structured, but many were also personal and expressive. The teacher's evaluative comments, however, did not refer to the expressiveness or artistry but were all directed toward whether they had "developed" the story well.

Language arts work also involved a large amount of practice in presentation of the self and in managing situations where the child was expected to be in charge. For example, there was a series of assignments in which each child had to be a "student teacher." The child had to plan a lesson in grammar, outlining, punctuation, or other language arts topic and explain the concept to the class. Each child was to prepare a worksheet or game and a homework assignment as well. After each presentation, the teacher and other children gave a critical appraisal of the "student teacher's" performance. Their criteria were: whether the student spoke clearly, whether the lesson was interesting, whether the student made any mistakes, and whether he or she kept control of the class. On an occasion when a child did not maintain control, the teacher said, "When you're up there, you have authority and you have to use it. I'll back you up."

The teacher of math and science explained to the observer that she likes the ESS program because "the children can manipulate variables. They generate hypotheses and devise experiments to solve the problem. Then they have to explain what they found."

The executive elite school is the only school where bells do not demarcate the periods of time. The two fifth-grade teachers were very strict about changing classes on schedule, however, as specific plans for each session had been made. The teachers attempted to keep tight control over the children during lessons, and the children were sometimes flippant, boisterous, and occasionally rude. However, the children may be brought into line by reminding them that "It is up to you." "You must control yourself," "you are responsible for your work," you must "set your priorities." One teacher told a child, "You are the only driver of your car—and only you can regulate your speed." A new teacher complained to the observer that she had thought "these children" would have more control.

While strict attention to the lesson at hand is required, the teachers make relatively little attempt to regulate the movement of the children at other

times. For example, except for the kindergartners the children in this school
do not have to wait for the bell to ring in the morning; they may go to their
classroom when they arrive at school. Fifth graders often came early to read,
to finish work, or to catch up. After the first two months of school, the fifth-
grade teachers did not line the children up to change classes or to go to gym,
and so on, but, when the children were ready and quiet, they were told they
could go—sometimes without the teachers.

In the classroom, the children could get materials when they needed them
and took what they needed from closets and from the teacher's desk. They
were in charge of the office at lunchtime. During class they did not have to
sign out or ask permission to leave the room; they just got up and left. Because of the pressure to get work done, however, they did not leave the room
very often. The teachers were very polite to the children, and the investigator
heard no sarcasm, no nasty remarks, and few direct orders. The teachers never
called the children "honey" or "dear" but always called them by name. The
teachers were expected to be available before school, after school, and for part
of their lunchtime to provide extra help if needed.

Discussion and Conclusion

One could attempt to identify physical, educational, cultural, and interpersonal characteristics of the environment of each school that might contribute to an empirical explanation of the events and interactions. For
example, the investigator could introduce evidence to show that the following *increased* as the social class of the community increased (with the most
marked differences occurring between the two districts): increased variety
and abundance of teaching materials in the classroom; increased time reported spent by the teachers on preparation; higher social-class background
and more prestigious educational institutions attended by teachers and administrators; more stringent board of education requirements regarding
teaching methods; more frequent and demanding administrative evaluation
of teachers; increased teacher support services such as in-service workshops;
increased parent expenditure for school equipment over and above district
or government funding; higher expectations of student ability on the part of
parents, teachers, and administrators; higher expectations and demands
regarding student achievement on the part of teachers, parents, and administrators; more positive attitudes on the part of the teachers as to the probable
occupational futures of the children; an increase in the children's acceptance
of classroom assignments; increased intersubjectivity between students and
teachers; and increased cultural congruence between school and community.

All of these—and other—factors may contribute to the character and
scope of classroom events. However, what is of primary concern here is not
the immediate causes of classroom activity (although these are in themselves

quite important). Rather, the concern is to reflect on the deeper social meaning, the wider theoretical significance, of what happens in each social setting. In an attempt to assess the theoretical meaning of the differences among the schools, the work tasks and milieu in each will be discussed in light of the concepts used to define social class.

What potential relationships to the system of ownership of symbolic and physical capital, to authority and control, and to their own productive activity are being developed in children in each school? What economically relevant knowledge, skills, and predispositions are being transmitted in each classroom, and for what future relationship to the system of production are they appropriate? It is of course true that a student's future relationship to the process of production in society is determined by the combined effects of circumstances beyond elementary schooling. However, by examining elementary school activity in its social-class context in the light of our theoretical perspective on social class, we can see certain potential relationships already developing. Moreover, in this structure of developing relationships lies theoretical—and social—significance.

The working-class children are developing a potential *conflict* relationship with capital. Their present schoolwork is appropriate preparation for future wage labor that is mechanical and routine. Such work, insofar as it denies the human capacities for creativity and planning, is degrading; moreover, when performed in industry, such work is a source of profit to others. This situation produces industrial conflict over wages, working conditions, and control. However, the children in the working-class schools are not learning to be docile and obedient in the face of present or future degrading conditions or financial exploitation. They are developing abilities and skills of resistance. These methods are highly similar to the "slowdown," subtle sabotage, and other modes of indirect resistance carried out by adult workers in the shop, on the department store sales floor, and in some offices.[18] As these types of resistance develop in school, they are highly constrained and limited in their ultimate effectiveness. Just as the children's resistance prevents them from learning socially legitimated knowledge and skills in school and is therefore ultimately debilitating, so is this type of resistance ultimately debilitating in industry. Such resistance in industry does not succeed in producing—nor is it intended to produce—fundamental changes in the relationships of exploitation or control. Thus, the methods of resistance that the working-class children are developing in school are only temporarily and *potentially* liberating.

In the middle-class school the children are developing somewhat different potential relationships to capital, authority, and work. In this school the work tasks and relationships are appropriate for a future relation to capital that is *bureaucratic*. Their schoolwork is appropriate for white-collar working-class and middle-class jobs in the supportive institutions of United States society. In these jobs one does the paperwork, the technical work, the sales and the social service in the private and state bureaucracies. Such work does not usually demand that one be creative, and one is not often rewarded for critical analysis of the system. One is rewarded, rather, for knowing the answers to the questions one is asked, for knowing where or how to find the answers, and for knowing which form, regulation, technique, or procedure is correct. While such work does not usually satisfy human needs for engagement and self-expression, one's salary can be exchanged for objects or activities that attempt to meet these needs.

In the affluent professional school the children are developing a potential relationship to capital that is instrumental and expressive and involves substantial negotiation. In their schooling these children are acquiring *symbolic capital*: they are being given the opportunity to develop skills of linguistic, artistic, and scientific expression and creative elaboration of ideas into concrete form. These skills are those needed to produce, for example, culture (for example, artistic, intellectual, and scientific ideas and other "products"). Their schooling is developing in these children skills necessary to become society's successful artists, intellectuals, legal, scientific, and technical experts and other professionals. The developing relation of the children in this school to their work is creative and relatively autonomous. Although they do not have control over which ideas they develop or express, the creative act in itself affirms and utilizes the human potential for conceptualization and design that is in many cases valued as intrinsically satisfying.

Professional persons in the cultural institutions of society (in, say, academe, publishing, the nonprint media, the arts, and the legal and state bureaucracies) are in an expressive relationship to the system of ownership in society because the ideas and other products of their work are often an important means by which material relationships of society are given ideological (for example, artistic, intellectual, legal, and scientific) expression. Through the system of laws, for example, the ownership relations of private property are elaborated and legitimated in legal form; through individualistic and meritocratic theories in psychology and sociology, these individualistic economic relations are provided scientific "rationality" and "sense." The relationship to physical capital of those in society who create what counts as the dominant culture or ideology also involves substantial negotiation. The producers of symbolic capital often do not control the socially available physical capital nor the cultural uses to which it is put. They must therefore negotiate for money for their own projects. However, skillful application of one's cultural capital may ultimately lead to social (for example, state) power and to financial reward.

The executive elite school gives its children something that none of the other schools does: knowledge of and practice in manipulating the socially legitimated tools of analysis of systems. The children are given the opportunity to learn and to utilize the intellectually and socially prestigious grammatical, mathematical, and other vocabularies and rules by which elements are arranged. They are given the opportunity to use these skills in the analysis of society and in control situations. Such knowledge and skills are a most important kind of *symbolic capital*. They are necessary for control of a production system. The developing relationship of the children in this school to their work affirms and develops in them the human capacities for analysis and planning and helps to prepare them for work in society that would demand these skills. Their schooling is helping them to develop the abilities necessary for ownership and control of physical capital and the means of production in society.

The foregoing analysis of differences in schoolwork in contrasting social class contexts suggests the following conclusion: the "hidden curriculum" of schoolwork is tacit preparation for relating to the process of production in a particular way. Differing curricular, pedagogical, and pupil evaluation practices emphasize different cognitive and behavioral skills in each social setting and thus contribute to the development in the children of certain potential relationships to physical and symbolic capital, to authority, and to the process of work. School experience, in the sample of schools discussed here, differed qualitatively by social class. These differences may not only contribute to the development in the children in each social class of certain types of economically significant relationships and not others but would thereby help to *reproduce* this system of relations in society. In the contribution to the reproduction of unequal social relations lies a theoretical meaning and social consequence of classroom practice.

The identification of different emphases in classrooms in a sample of contrasting social class contexts implies that further research should be conducted in a large number of schools to investigate the types of work tasks and interactions in each to see if they differ in the ways discussed here and to see if similar potential relationships are uncovered. Such research could have as a product the further elucidation of complex but not readily apparent connections between everyday activity in schools and classrooms and the unequal structure of economic relationships in which we work and live.

Notes

1. S. Bowles and H. Gintis, *Schooling in Capitalist America: Educational Reform and the Contradictions of Economic Life* (New York: Basic Books, 1976).

2. B. Bernstein, *Class, Codes and Control, Vol. 3. Towards a Theory of Educational Transmission*, 2d ed. (London: Routledge & Kegan Paul, 1977); P. Bourdieu and J. Passeron, *Reproduction in Education, Society and Culture* (Beverly Hills, Calif.: Sage, 1977); M. W. Apple, *Ideology and Curriculum* (Boston: Routledge & Kegan Paul, 1979).

3. But see, in a related vein, M. W. Apple and N. King, "What Do Schools Teach?" *Curriculum Inquiry* 6 (1977): 341–58; R. C. Rist, *The Urban School: A Factory for Failure* (Cambridge, Mass.: MIT Press, 1973).

4. The definition of social class delineated here is my own, but it relies heavily on my interpretation of the work of E. O. Wright, *Class, Crisis and the State* (London: New Left Books, 1978); Bourdieu and Passeron, *Reproduction in Education*; and R. Williams, *Marxism and Literature* (New York: Oxford University Press, 1977).

5. New York Stock Exchange, *Census* (New York: New York Stock Exchange, 1975); J. D. Smith and S. Franklin, "The Concentration of Personal Wealth, 1922–1969," *American Economic Review* 64 (1974): 162–67; J. R. Lampman, "The Share of Top Wealth Holders in National Wealth, 1922–1956," A Study of the National Bureau of Economic Research (New Jersey: Princeton University Press, 1962).

6. For discussion of schools as agencies of social and economic legitimation, see L. Althusser, *Lenin and Philosophy and Other Essays*, trans. B. Brewster (New York: Monthly Review Press, 1971); J. Anyon, "Elementary Social Studies Textbooks and Legitimating Knowledge," *Theory and Research in Social Education* 6 (1978): 40–55; J. Anyon, "Ideology and United States History Textbooks," *Harvard Educational Review* 49 (1979): 361–86.

7. Wright, *Class, Crisis and State*; H. Braverman, *Labor and Monopoly Capital: The Degradation of Work in the Twentieth Century* (New York: Monthly Review Press, 1974); A. Levison, *The Working Class Majority* (New York: Penguin Books, 1974).

8. While relationships of control in society will not be discussed here, it can be said that they roughly parallel the relationships of control in the work place, which will be the focus of this discussion. That is, working-class and many middle-class persons have less control than members of the upper-middle and capitalist classes do, not only over conditions and processes of their work but over their nonwork lives as well. In addition, it is true that persons from the middle and capitalist classes, rather than workers, are most often those who fill the positions of state and other power in United States society.

9. Occupations may change their relation to the means of production over time—as the expenditure and ownership of capital changes, as technology, skills, and the social relations of work change. For example, some jobs that were middle-class, managerial positions in 1900 and necessitated conceptual laying out and planning are now working class and increasingly mechanical, for example, quality control in industry, clerical work, and computer programming. See H. Braverman, *Labor and Monopoly Capital*.

10. The U.S. Bureau of the Census defines *poverty* for a nonfarm family of four as a yearly income of $6,191 a year or less. U.S. Bureau of the Census, *Statistical Abstract of the United States: 1978* (Washington, D.C.: U.S. Government Printing Office. 1978), p. 465, table 754.

11. U.S. Bureau of the Census, "Money Income in 1977 of Families and Persons in the United States," *Current Population Reports* Series P-60, no. 118 (Washington, D.C.: U.S. Government Printing Office, 1979), p. 2, table A.

12. Ibid.

13. This figure is an estimate. According to the Bureau of the Census, only 2.6 percent of families in the United States have money income of $50,000 or over. U.S.

Bureau of the Census, *Current Population Reports* Series P-60. For figures on income at these higher levels, see Smith and Franklin, "The Concentration of Personal Wealth, 1922–1969."

14. Smith and Franklin, "Concentration of Personal Wealth."

15. For other similarities alleged to characterize United States classrooms and schools but which will not be discussed here, see R. Dreeben, *On What Is Learned in School* (Reading, Mass.: Addison-Wesley, 1968); P. Jackson, *Life in Classrooms* (New York: Holt, Rinehart & Winston, 1968); and S. Sarasan, *The Culture of School and the Problem of Change* (Boston: Allyn & Bacon, 1971).

16. Indeed, strikingly little teaching occurred in either of the working-class schools, and this naturally curtailed the amount that the children learned. Incidentally, it increased the amount of time that had to be spent by the researcher to collect data on teaching style and interaction.

17. A dominant feeling, expressed directly and indirectly by teachers in this school, was boredom with their work. They did, however, in contrast to the working-class schools, almost always carry out lessons during class times.

18. See, for example, discussions in A. Levison, *The Working-Class Majority* (New York: Penguin Books, 1974); S. Aronowitz, "Marx, Braverman, and the Logic of Capital," *The Insurgent Sociologist* 8 (1978): 126–46; and S. Benson, "The Clerking Sisterhood: Rationalization and the Work Culture of Saleswomen in American Department Stores, 1890–1960," *Radical America* 12 (1978): 41–55.

8

Curriculum and Consciousness

Maxine Greene

Curriculum, from the learner's standpoint, ordinarily represents little more than an arrangement of subjects, a structure of socially prescribed knowledge, or a complex system of meanings which may or may not fall within his grasp. Rarely does it signify possibility for him as an existing person, mainly concerned with making sense of his own life-world. Rarely does it promise occasions for ordering the materials of that world, for imposing "configurations"[1] by means of experiences and perspectives made available for personally conducted cognitive action. Sartre says that "knowing is a moment of *praxis*," opening into "what has not yet been."[2] Preoccupied with priorities, purposes, programs of "intended learning"[3] and intended (or unintended) manipulation, we pay too little attention to the individual in quest of his own future, bent on surpassing what is merely "given," on breaking through the everyday. We are still too prone to dichotomize: to think of "disciplines" or "public traditions" or "accumulated wisdom" or "common culture" (individualization despite) as objectively existent, external to the knower—there to be discovered, mastered, learned.

Quite aware that this may evoke Dewey's argument in *The Child and the Curriculum*, aware of how times have changed since 1902, I have gone in search of contemporary analogies to shed light on what I mean. ("Solution comes," Dewey wrote, "only by getting away from the meaning of terms that is already fixed upon and coming to see the conditions from

Reprinted, by permission, from *Teachers College Record* 73: 2 (December 1971): 253–69.

another point of view, and hence in a fresh light.")[4] My other point of view
is that of literary criticism, or more properly philosophy of criticism, which
attempts to explicate the modes of explanation, description, interpretation,
and evaluation involved in particular critical approaches. There is presently
an emerging philosophic controversy between two such approaches, one
associated with England and the United States, the other with the Continent,
primarily France and Switzerland; and it is in the differences in orientation
that I have found some clues.

These differences are, it will be evident, closely connected to those separating what is known as analytic or language philosophy from existentialism
and phenomenology. The dominant tendency in British and American
literary criticism has been to conceive literary works as objects or artifacts,
best understood in relative isolation from the writer's personal biography and
undistorted by associations brought to the work from the reader's own daily
life. The new critics on the Continent have been called "critics of
consciousness."[5] They are breaking with the notion that a literary work can
be dealt with objectively, divorced from experience. In fact, they treat each work
as a manifestation of an individual writer's experience, a gradual growth of
consciousness into expression. This is in sharp contrast to such a view as
T. S. Eliot's emphasizing the autonomy and the "impersonality" of literary
art. "We can only say," he wrote in an introduction to *The Sacred Wood*,
"that a poem, in some sense, has its own life; that its parts form something
quite different from a body of neatly ordered biographical data; that the
feeling, or emotion, or vision resulting from the poem is something different
from the feeling or emotion or vision in the mind of the poet."[6] Those who
take this approach or an approach to a work of art as "a self-enclosed isolated
structure"[7] are likely to prescribe that purely aesthetic values are to be found
in literature, the values associated with "significant form"[8] or, at most, with
the contemplation of an "intrinsically interesting possible."[9] M. H. Abrams
has called this an "austere dedication to the poem *per se*,"[10] for all the
enlightening analysis and explication it has produced. "But it threatens
also to commit us," he wrote, "to the concept of a poem as a language game,
or as a floating Laputa, insulated from life and essential human concerns
in a way that accords poorly with our experience in reading a great work of
literature."

For the critic of consciousness, literature is viewed as a genesis, a conscious
effort on the part of an individual artist to understand his own experience
by framing it in language. The reader who encounters the work must re-
create it in terms of *his* consciousness. In order to penetrate it, to experience
it existentially and empathetically, he must try to place himself within the
"interior space"[11] of the writer's mind as it is slowly revealed in the course of
his work. Clearly, the reader requires a variety of cues if he is to situate
himself in this way; and these are ostensibly provided by the expressions and

attitudes he finds in the book, devices which he must accept as orientations and indications—"norms," perhaps, to govern his re-creation. *His* subjectivity is the substance of the literary object; but, if he is to perceive the identity emerging through the enactments of the book, he must subordinate his own personality as he brackets out his everyday, "natural" world.[12] His objective in doing so, however, is not to analyze or explicate or evaluate; it is to extract the experience made manifest by means of the work. Sartre says this more concretely:

> Reading seems, in fact, to be the synthesis of perception and creation. . . . The object is essential because it is strictly transcendent, because it imposes its own structures, and because one must wait for it and observe it; but the subject is also essential because it is required not only to disclose the object (that is, to make *there be* an object) but also that this object might *be* (that is, to produce it). In a word, the reader is conscious of disclosing in creating, of creating by disclosing. . . . If he is inattentive, tired, stupid, or thoughtless most of the relations will escape him. He will never manage to "catch on" to the object (in the sense in which we see that fire "catches" or "doesn't catch"). He will draw some phrases out of the shadow, but they will appear as random strokes. If he is at his best, he will project beyond the words a synthetic form, each phrase of which will be no more than a partial function: the "theme," the "subject," or the "meaning."[13]

There must be, he is suggesting, continual reconstructions if a work of literature is to become meaningful. The structures involved are generated over a period of time, depending upon the perceptiveness and attentiveness of the reader. The reader, however, does not simply regenerate what the artist intended. His imagination can move him beyond the artist's traces, "to project beyond the words a synthetic form," to constitute a new totality. The autonomy of the art object is sacrificed in this orientation; the reader, conscious of lending his own life to the book, discovers deeper and more complex levels than the level of "significant form." (Sartre says, for instance, that "Raskolnikov's waiting is *my* waiting, which I lend him. Without this impatience of the reader he would remain only a collection of signs. His hatred of the police magistrate who questions him is my hatred which has been solicited and wheedled out of me by signs, and the police magistrate himself would not exist without the hatred I have for him via Raskolnikov.")[14]

Disclosure, Reconstruction, Generation

The reader, using his imagination, must move within his own subjectivity and break with the commonsense world he normally takes for granted. If he could not suspend his ordinary ways of perceiving, if he could not allow for the possibility that the horizons of daily life are not inalterable, he would not be able to engage with literature at all. As Dewey put it: "There is work done on the part of the percipient as there is on the part of the artist. The one who is too lazy, idle, or indurated in convention to perform this work will not see or hear. His 'appreciation' will be a mixture of scraps of learning with conformity to norms of conventional admiration and with a confused, even if genuine, emotional excitation."[15] The "work" with which we are here concerned is one of disclosure, reconstruction, generation. It is a work which culminates in a bringing something into being by the reader—in a "going beyond" what he has been.[16]

Although I am going to claim that learning, to be meaningful, must involve such a "going beyond," I am not going to claim that it must also be in the imaginative mode. Nor am I going to assert that, in order to surpass the "given," the individual is required to move into and remain within a sealed subjectivity. What I find suggestive in the criticism of consciousness is the stress on the gradual disclosure of structures by the reader. The process is, as I have said, governed by certain cues or norms perceived in the course of reading. These demand, if they are to be perceived, what Jean Piaget has called a "continual 'decentering' without which [the individual subject] cannot become free from his intellectual egocentricity."[17]

The difference between Piaget and those interested in consciousness is, of course, considerable. For one thing, he counts himself among those who prefer not to characterize the subject in terms of its "lived experience." For another thing, he says categorically that "the 'lived' can only have a very minor role in the construction of cognitive structures, for these do not belong to the subject's *consciousness* but to his operational *behavior,* which is something quite different."[18] I am not convinced that they are as different as he conceives them to be. Moreover, I think his differentiation between the "individual subject" and what he calls "the epistemic subject, that cognitive nucleus which is common to all subjects at the same level,"[19] is useful and may well shed light on the problem of curriculum, viewed from the vantage point of consciousness. Piaget is aware that his stress on the "epistemic subject" looks as if he were subsuming the individual under some impersonal abstraction,[20] but his discussion is not far removed from those of Sartre and the critics of consciousness, particularly when they talk of the subject entering into a process of generating structures whose being (like the structures Piaget has in mind) consists in their "coming to be."

Merleau-Ponty, as concerned as Piaget with the achievement of rationality, believes that there is a primary reality which must be taken into account if the growth of "intellectual consciousness" is to be understood. This primary reality is a perceived life-world; and the structures of the "perceptual consciousness"[21] through which the child first comes in contact with his environment underlie all the higher-level structures which develop later in his life. In the prereflective, infantile stage of life he is obviously incapable of generating cognitive structures. The stage is characterized by what

Merleau-Ponty calls "egocentrism" because the "me" is part of an anony-
mous collectivity, unaware of itself, capable of living "as easily in others as
it does in itself."[22] Nevertheless, even then, before meanings and configurations are imposed, there is an original world, a natural and social world in
which the child is involved corporeally and affectively. Perceiving that
world, he effects certain relations within his experience. He organizes and
"informs" it before he is capable of logical and predicative thought. This
means for Merleau-Ponty that consciousness exists primordially—the
ground of all knowledge and rationality.

The growing child assimilates a language system and becomes habituated to using language as "an open system of expression" which is capable
of expressing "an indeterminate number of cognitions or ideas to come."[23]
His acts of naming and expression take place, however, around a core of
primary meaning found in "the silence of primary consciousness." This
silence may be understood as the fundamental awareness of being present
in the world. It resembles what Paulo Freire calls "background awareness"[24]
of an existential situation, a situation actually lived before the codifications
which make new perceptions possible. Talking about the effort to help
peasants perceive their own reality differently (to enable them, in other
words, to learn), Freire says they must somehow make explicit their "real
consciousness" of their worlds, or what they experienced while living
through situations they later learn to codify.

The point is that the world is constituted for the child (by means of the
behavior called perception) prior to the "construction of cognitive structures." This does not imply that he lives his life primarily in that world. He
moves outward into diverse realms of experience in his search for meaning.
When he confronts and engages with the apparently independent structures
associated with rationality, the so-called cognitive structures, it is likely
that he does so as an "epistemic subject," bracketing out for the time his
subjectivity, even his presence to himself.[25] But the awareness remains in
the background; the original perceptual reality continues as the ground of
rationality, the base from which the leap to the theoretical is taken.

Merleau-Ponty, recognizing that psychologists treat consciousness as
"an object to be studied," writes that it is simply not accessible to mere factual observation:

The psychologist always tends to make consciousness into just such an object of
observation. But all the factual truths to which psychology has access can be applied
to the concrete subject only after a philosophical correction. Psychology, like physics
and the other sciences of nature, uses the method of induction, which starts from facts
and then assembles them. But it is very evident that this induction will remain blind
if we do not know in some other way, and indeed from the inside of consciousness
itself, what this induction is dealing with.[26]

Induction must be combined "with the reflective knowledge that we can obtain from ourselves as conscious objects." This is not a recommendation that the individual engage in introspection. Consciousness, being intentional, throws itself outward *towards* the world. It is always consciousness *of* something—a phenomenon, another person, an object in the world. Reflecting upon himself as a conscious object, the individual—the learner, perhaps—reflects upon his relation to the world, his manner of comporting himself with respect to it, the changing perspectives through which the world presents itself to him. Merleau-Ponty talks about the need continually to rediscover "my actual presence to myself, the fact of my consciousness which is in the last resort what the word and the concept of consciousness mean."[27] This means remaining in contact with one's own perceptions, one's own experiences, and striving to constitute their meanings. It means achieving a state of what Schutz calls "wide-awakeness . . . a plane of consciousness of highest tension originating in an attitude of full attention to life and its requirements."[28] Like Sartre, Schutz emphasizes the importance of attentiveness for arriving at new perceptions, for carrying out cognitive projects. All this seems to me to be highly suggestive for a conception of a learner who is "open to the world,"[29] eager, indeed *condemned* to give meaning to it— and, in the process of doing so, re-creating or generating the materials of a curriculum in terms of his own consciousness.

Some Alternative Views

There are, of course, alternative views of consequence for education today. R. S. Peters, agreeing with his philosophic precursors that consciousness is the hallmark of mind and always "related in its different modes to objects," asserts that the "objects of consciousness are first and foremost objects in a public world that are marked out and differentiated by a public language into which the individual is initiated."[30] (It should be said that Peters is, *par excellence*, the exponent of an "objective" or "analytic" approach to curriculum, closely related to the objective approach to literary criticism.) He grants that the individual "represents a unique and unrepeatable viewpoint on this public world"; but his primary stress is placed upon the way in which the learning of language is linked to the discovery of that separately existing world of "objects in space and time." Consciousness, for Peters, cannot be explained except in connection with the demarcations of the public world which meaning makes possible. It becomes contingent upon initiation into public traditions, into (it turns out) the academic disciplines. Since such an initiation is required if modes of consciousness are to be effectively differentiated, the mind must finally be understood as a "product" of such initiation. The individual must be enabled to achieve a state of mind characterized by "a mastery of and care for the worthwhile things that have been transmitted, which are viewed in some kind of cognitive perspective."[31]

Philip H. Phenix argues similarly that "the curriculum should consist entirely of knowledge which comes from the disciplines, for the reason that the disciplines reveal knowledge in its teachable forms."[32] He, however, pays more heed to what he calls "the experience of reflective self-consciousness,"[33] which he associates specifically with "concrete existence in direct personal encounter."[34] The meanings arising out of such encounter are expressed, for him, in existential philosophy, religion, psychology, and certain dimensions of imaginative literature. They are, thus, to be considered as one of the six "realms of meaning" through mastery of which man is enabled to achieve self-transcendence. Self-transcendence, for Phenix, involves a duality which enables the learner to feel himself to be agent and knower, and at once to identify with what he comes to know. Self-transcendence is the ground of meaning; but it culminates in the engendering of a range of "essential meanings," the achievement of a hierarchy in which all fundamental patterns of meaning are related and through which human existence can be fulfilled. The inner life of generic man is clearly encompassed by this scheme; but what is excluded, I believe, is what has been called the "subjectivity of the actor," the *individual* actor ineluctably present to himself. What is excluded is the feeling of separateness, of strangeness when such a person is confronted with the articulated curriculum intended to counteract meaninglessness.

Schutz writes:

When a stranger comes to the town, he has to learn to orientate in it and to know it. Nothing is self-explanatory for him and he has to ask an expert . . . to learn how to get from one point to another. He may, of course, refer to a map of the town, but even to use the map successfully he must know the meaning of the signs on the map, the exact point within the town where he stands and its correlative on the map, and at least one more point in order correctly to relate the signs on the map to the real objects in the city.[35]

The prestructured curriculum resembles such a map; the learner, the stranger just arrived in town. For the cartographer, the town is an "object of his science," a science which has developed standards of operation and rules for the correct drawing of maps. In the case of the curriculum-maker, the public tradition or the natural order of things is "the object" of his design activities. Here too there are standards of operation: the subject matter organized into disciplines must be communicable; it must be appropriate to whatever are conceived as educational aims. Phenix has written that education should be understood as "a guided recapitulation of the processes of inquiry which gave rise to the fruitful bodies of organized knowledge comprising the disciplines."[36] Using the metaphor of the map, we might say that this is like asking a newcomer in search of direction to recapitulate the complex processes by which the cartographer made his map. The map may represent a fairly complete charting of the town; and it may ultimately be extremely useful for the individual to be able to take a cartographer's perspective. When that individual first arrives, however, his peculiar plight ought not to be overlooked: his "background awareness" of being alive in an unstable world; his reasons for consulting the map; the interests he is pursuing as he attempts to orient himself when he can no longer proceed by rule of thumb. He himself may recognize that he will have to come to understand the signs on the map if he is to make use of it. Certainly he will have to decipher the relationship between those signs and "real objects in the city." But his initial concern will be conditioned by the "objects" he wants to bring into visibility, by the landmarks he needs to identify if he is to proceed on his way.

Learning—A Mode of Orientation

Turning from newcomer to learner (contemporary learner, in our particular world), I am suggesting that his focal concern is with ordering the materials of his own life-world when dislocations occur, when what was once familiar abruptly appears strange. This may come about on an occasion when "future shock" is experienced, as it so frequently is today. Anyone who has lived through a campus disruption, a teachers' strike, a guerilla theatre production, a sit-in (or a be-in, or a feel-in) knows full well what Alvin Toffler means when he writes about the acceleration of change. "We no longer 'feel' life as men did in the past," he says. "And this is the ultimate difference, the distinction that separates the truly contemporary man from all others. For this acceleration lies behind the impermanence—the transience—that penetrates and tinctures our consciousness, radically affecting the way we relate to other people, to things, to the entire universe of ideas, art and values."[37] Obviously, this does not happen in everyone's life; but it is far more likely to occur than ever before in history, if it is indeed the case that change has speeded up and that forces are being released which we have not yet learned to control. My point is that the contemporary learner is more likely than his predecessors to experience moments of strangeness, moments when the recipes he has inherited for the solution of typical problems no longer seem to work. If Merleau-Ponty is right and the search for rationality is indeed grounded in a primary or perceptual consciousness, the individual may be fundamentally aware that the structures of "reality" are contingent upon the perspective taken and that most achieved orders are therefore precarious.

The stage sets are always likely to collapse.[38] Someone is always likely to ask unexpectedly, as in Pinter's *The Dumb Waiter*, "Who cleans up after we're gone?"[39] Someone is equally likely to cry out, "You seem to have no

conception of where we stand! You won't find the answer written down for
you in the bowl of a compass—I can tell you that."[40] Disorder, in other
words, is continually breaking in; meaninglessness is recurrently overcoming
landscapes which once were demarcated, meaningful. It is at moments like
these that the individual reaches out to reconstitute meaning, to close the
gaps, to make sense once again. It is at moments like these that he will be
moved to pore over maps, to disclose or generate structures of knowledge
which may provide him unifying perspectives and thus enable him to restore
order once again. His learning, I am saying, is a mode of orientation—or
reorientation—in a place suddenly become unfamiliar. And "place" is a
metaphor, in this context, for a domain of consciousness, intending, forever
thrusting outward, "open to the world." The curriculum, the structures of
knowledge, must be presented to such a consciousness as possibility. Like
the work of literature in Sartre's viewing, it requires a subject if it is to be
disclosed; it can only *be* disclosed if the learner, himself engaged in generating the structures, lends the curriculum his life. If the curriculum, on the
other hand, is seen as external to the search for meaning, it becomes an alien
and an alienating edifice, a kind of "Crystal Palace" of ideas.[41]

There is, then, a kind of resemblance between the ways in which a learner
confronts socially prescribed knowledge and the ways in which a stranger
looks at a map when he is trying to determine where he is in relation to
where he wants to go. In Kafka's novel, *Amerika,* I find a peculiarly suggestive description of the predicament of someone who is at once a stranger and
a potential learner (although, it eventually turns out, he never succeeds in
being taught). He is Karl Rossmann, who has been "packed off to America"
by his parents and who likes to stand on a balcony at his Uncle Jacob's house
in New York and look down on the busy street:

From morning to evening and far into the dreaming night that street was a channel
for the constant stream of traffic which, seen from above, looked like an inextricable
confusion, forever newly improvised, of foreshortened human figures and the roofs
of all kinds of vehicles, sending into the upper air another confusion, more riotous
and complicated, of noises, dusts and smells, all of it enveloped and penetrated by a
flood of light which the multitudinous objects in the street scattered, carried off and
again busily brought back, with an effect as palpable to the dazzled eye as if a glass
roof stretched over the street were being violently smashed into fragments at every
moment.[42]

Karl's uncle tells him that the indulgence of idly gazing at the busy life of the
city might be permissible if Karl were traveling for pleasure; "but for one
who intended to remain in the States it was sheer ruination." He is going to
have to make judgments which will shape his future life; he will have, in effect, to be reborn. This being so, it is not enough for him to treat the unfamiliar landscape as something to admire and wonder at (as if it were a cubist

construction or a kaleidoscope). Karl's habitual interpretations (learned far away in Prague) do not suffice to clarify what he sees. If he is to learn, he must identify what is questionable, try to break through what is obscure. Action is required of him, not mere gazing; praxis, not mere reverie.

If he is to undertake action, however, he must do so against the background of his original perceptions, with a clear sense of being present to himself. He must do so, too, against the background of his European experience, of the experience of rejection, of being "packed off" for reasons never quite understood. Only with that sort of awareness will he be capable of the attentiveness and commitment needed to engage with the world and make it meaningful. Only with the ability to be reflective about what he is doing will he be brave enough to incorporate his past into the present, to link the present to a future. All this will demand a conscious appropriation of new perspectives on his experience and continual reordering of that experience as new horizons of the "Amerika" become visible, as new problems arise. The point is that Karl Rossmann, an immigrant in an already structured and charted world, must be conscious enough of himself to strive towards rationality; only if he achieves rationality will he avoid humiliations and survive.

As Kafka tells it, he never does attain that rationality; and so he is continually manipulated by forces without and within. He never learns, for example, that there can be no justice if there is no good will, even though he repeatedly and sometimes eloquently asks for justice from the authorities—always to no avail. The ship captains and pursers, the businessmen, the head waiters and porters all function according to official codes of discipline which are beyond his comprehension. He has been plunged into a public world with its own intricate prescriptions, idiosyncratic structures, and hierarchies; but he has no way of appropriating it or of constituting meanings. Throughout most of the novel, he clings to his symbolic box (with the photograph of his parents, the memorabilia of childhood and home). The box may be egocentrism; it may signify his incapacity to embark upon the "decentering" required if he is to begin generating for himself the structures of what surrounds.

In his case (and, I would say, in the case of many other people) the "decentering" that is necessary is not solely a cognitive affair, as Piaget insists it is. Merleau-Ponty speaks of a "lived decentering,"[43] exemplified by a child's learning "to relativise the notions of the youngest and the eldest" (to learn, for example, to become the eldest in relation to the newborn child) or by his learning to think in terms of reciprocity. This happens, as it would have to happen to Karl, through actions undertaken within the "vital order," not merely through intellectual categorization. It does not exclude the possibility that a phenomenon analogous to Piaget's "epistemic subject" emerges, although there appears to be no reason (except, perhaps, from the viewpoint of empirical psychology) for separating it off from the "individual subject." (In fact, the apparent difference between Piaget and those who talk of "lived experience" may turn upon a definition of "consciousness." Piaget, as has been noted,[44] distinguishes between "consciousness" and "operational behavior," as if consciousness did *not* involve a turning outward to things, a continuing reflection upon situationality, a generation of cognitive structures.) In any case, every individual who consciously seeks out meaning is involved in asking questions which demand essentially epistemic responses.[45] These responses, even if incomplete, are knowledge claims; and, as more and more questions are asked, there is an increasing "sedimentation" of meanings which result from the interpretation of past experiences looked at from the vantage point of the present. Meanings do not inhere in the experiences that emerge; they have to be constituted, and they can only be constituted through cognitive action.

Returning to Karl Rossmann and his inability to take such action, I have been suggesting that he *cannot* make his own "primary consciousness" background so long as he clings to his box; nor can he actively interpret his past experience. He cannot (to stretch Piaget's point somewhat) become or will himself to be an "epistemic subject." He is, as Freire puts it, submerged in a "dense, enveloping reality or a tormenting blind alley" and will be unless he can "perceive it as an objective-problematic situation."[46] Only then will he be able to intervene in his own reality with attentiveness, with awareness—to act upon his situation and make sense.

It would help if the looming structures which are so incomprehensible to Karl were somehow rendered cognitively available to him. Karl might then (with the help of a teacher willing to engage in dialogue with him, to help him pose his problems) reach out to question in terms of what he feels is thematically relevant or "worth questioning."[47] Because the stock of knowledge he carries with him does not suffice for a definition of situations in which porters manhandle him and women degrade him, in which he is penalized for every spontaneous action, he cannot easily refer to previous situations for clues. In order to cope with this, he needs to single out a single relevant element at first (from all the elements in what is happening) to transmute into a theme for his "knowing consciousness." There is the cruel treatment meted out to him, for example, by the Head Porter who feels it his duty "to attend to things that other people neglect." (He adds that, since he is in charge of all the doors of the hotel [including the "doorless exits"], he is "in a sense placed over everyone," and everyone has to obey him absolutely. If it were not for his repairing the omissions of the Head Waiter in the name of the hotel management, he believes, "such a great organization would be unthinkable.")[48] The porter's violence against Karl might well become the relevant element, the origin of a theme.

Making Connections

"What makes the theme to be a theme," Schutz writes, "is determined by motivationally relevant interest-situations and spheres of problems. The theme which thus has become relevant has now, however, become a problem to which a solution, practical, theoretical, or emotional, must be given."[49] The problem for Karl, like relevant problems facing any individual, is connected with and a consequence of a great number of other perplexities, other dislocations in his life. If he had not been so badly exploited by authority figures in time past, if he were not so childishly given to blind trust in adults, if he were not so likely to follow impulse at inappropriate moments, he would never have been assaulted by the Head Porter. At this point, however, once the specific problem (the assault) has been determined to be thematically relevant for him, it can be detached from the motivational context out of which it derived. The meshwork of related perplexities remains, however, as an outer horizon waiting to be explored or questioned when necessary. The thematically relevant element can then be made interesting in its own right and worth questioning. In the foreground, as it were, the focus of concern, it can be defined against the background of the total situation. The situation is not in any sense obliterated or forgotten. It is *there,* at the fringe of Karl's attention while the focal problem is being solved; but it is, to an extent, "bracketed out." With this bracketing out and this foreground focusing, Karl may be for the first time in a condition of wide-awakeness, ready to pay active attention to what has become so questionable and so troubling, ready to take the kind of action which will move him ahead into a future as it gives him perspective on his past.

The action he might take involves more than what is understood as problem-solving. He has, after all, had some rudimentary knowledge of the Head Porter's role, a knowledge conditioned by certain typifications effected in the prepredicative days of early childhood. At that point in time, he did not articulate his experience in terms of sense data or even in terms of individual figures standing out against a background. He saw typical structures according to particular zones of relevancy. This means that he probably saw his father, or the man who was father, not only as bearded face next to his mother, not only as large figure in the doorway, but as overbearing, threatening, incomprehensible authority who was "placed over everyone" and had the right to inflict pain. Enabled, years later, to confront something thematically relevant, the boy may be solicited to recognize his present knowledge of the porter as the sediment of previous mental processes.[50] The knowledge of the porter, therefore, has a history beginning in primordial perceptions; and the boy may succeed in moving back from what is seemingly "given" through the diverse mental processes which constituted the porter over time. Doing so, he will be exploring both the inner and outer horizons of the problem, making connections within the field of his consciousness, interpreting his own past as it bears on his present, reflecting upon his own knowing.

And that is not all. Having made such connections between the relevant theme and other dimensions of his experience, he may be ready to solve his problem; he may even feel that the problem is solved. This, however, puts him into position to move out of his own inner time (in which all acts are somehow continuous and bound together) into the intersubjective world where he can function as an epistemic subject. Having engaged in a reflexive consideration of the activity of his own consciousness, he can now shift his attention back to the life-world, which had been rendered so unrecognizable by the Head Porter's assault. Here too, meanings must be constituted; the "great organization" must be understood, so that Karl can orient himself once again in the everyday. Bracketing out his subjectivity for the time, he may find many ways of engaging as a theoretical inquirer with the problem of authority in hotels and the multiple socioeconomic problems connected with that. He will voluntarily become, when inquiring in this way, a partial self, an inquirer deliberately acting a role in a community of inquirers. I am suggesting that he could not do so as effectively or as authentically if he had not first synthesized the materials within his inner time, constituted meaning in his world.

The analogy to the curriculum question, I hope, is clear. Treating Karl as a potential learner, I have considered the hotels and the other structured organizations in his world as analogous to the structures of prescribed knowledge—or to the curriculum. I have suggested that the individual, in our case the student, will only be in a position to learn when he is committed to act upon his world. If he is content to admire it or simply accept it as given, if he is incapable of breaking with egocentrism, he will remain alienated from himself and his own possibilities; he will wander lost and victimized upon the road; he will be unable to learn. He may be conditioned; he may be trained. He may even have some rote memory of certain elements of the curriculum; but no matter how well devised is that curriculum, no matter how well adapted to the stages of his growth, learning (as disclosure, as generating structures, as engendering meanings, as achieving mastery) will not occur.

At once, I have tried to say that unease and disorder are increasingly endemic in contemporary life, and that more and more persons are finding the recipes they habitually use inadequate for sense-making in a changing world. This puts them, more and more frequently, in the position of strangers or immigrants trying to orient themselves in an unfamiliar town. The desire, indeed the *need*, for orientation is equivalent to the desire to

constitute meanings, all sorts of meanings, in the many dimensions of existence. But this desire, I have suggested, is not satisfied by the authoritative
confrontation of student with knowledge structures (no matter how "teachable" the forms in which the knowledge is revealed). It is surely not satisfied
when the instructional situation is conceived to be, as G. K. Plochmann has
written, one in which the teacher is endeavoring "with respect to his subject
matter, to bring the understanding of the learner in equality with his own
understanding."[51] Described in that fashion, with "learner" conceived ge-
nerically and the "system" to be taught conceived as preexistent and objectively real, the instructional situation seems to me to be one that alienates
because of the way it ignores both existential predicament and primordial
consciousness. Like the approach to literary criticism Abrams describes, the
view appears to commit us to a concept of curriculum "as a floating Laputa,
insulated from life and essential human concerns. . . ."[52]

The cries of "irrelevance" are still too audible for us to content ourselves
with this. So are the complaints about depersonalization, processing, and
compulsory socialization into a corporate, inhuman world. Michael Novak,
expressing some of this, writes that what our institutions "decide is real is
enforced as real." He calls parents, teachers, and psychiatrists (like policemen
and soldiers) "the enforcers of reality"; then he goes on to say:

When a young person is being initiated into society, existing norms determine what
is to be considered real and what is to be annihilated by silence and disregard. The
good, docile student accepts the norms; the recalcitrant student may lack the intelligence—or have too much; may lack maturity—or insist upon being his own man.[53]

I have responses like this in mind when I consult the phenomenologists for
an approach to curriculum in the present day. For one thing, they remind
us of what it means for an individual to be present to himself; for another,
they suggest to us the origins of significant quests for meaning, origins
which ought to be held in mind by those willing to enable students to be
themselves.

If the existence of a primordial consciousness is taken seriously, it will be
recognized that awareness begins perspectively, that our experience is always
incomplete. It is true that we have what Merleau-Ponty calls a "prejudice"
in favor of a world of solid, determinate objects, quite independent of our
perceptions. Consciousness does, however, have the capacity to return to the
precognitive, the primordial, by "bracketing out" objects as customarily
seen. The individual can release himself into his own inner time and rediscover the ways in which objects arise, the ways in which experience develops.
In discussing the possibility of Karl Rossmann exploring his own past, I
have tried to show what this sort of interior journey can mean. Not only may
it result in the effecting of new syntheses within experience; it may result in

an awareness of the process of knowing, of believing, of perceiving. It may even result in an understanding of the ways in which meanings have been sedimented in an individual's own personal history. I can think of no more potent mode of combatting those conceived to be "enforcers of the real," including the curriculum designers.

But then there opens up the possibility of presenting curriculum in such a way that it does not impose or enforce. If the student is enabled to recognize that reason and order may represent the culminating step in his constitution of a world, if he can be enabled to see that what Schutz calls the attainment of a "reciprocity of perspectives"[54] signifies the achievement of rationality, he may realize what it is to generate the structures of the disciplines on his own initiative, against his own "background awareness." Moreover, he may realize that he is projecting beyond his present horizons each time he shifts his attention and takes another perspective on his world. "To say there exists rationality," writes Merleau-Ponty, "is to say that perspectives blend, perceptions confirm each other, a meaning emerges."[55] He points out that we witness at every moment "the miracles of related experiences, and yet nobody knows better than we do how this miracle is worked, for we are ourselves this network of relationships." Curriculum can offer the possibility for students to be the makers of such networks. The problem for their teachers is to stimulate an awareness of the questionable, to aid in the identification of the thematically relevant, to beckon beyond the everyday.

I am a psychological and historical structure, and have received, with existence, a manner of existence, a style. All my actions and thoughts stand in a relationship to this structure, and even a philosopher's thought is merely a way of making explicit his hold on the world, and what he is. The fact remains that I am free, not in spite of, or on the hither side of these motivations, but by means of them. For this significant life, this certain significance of nature and history which I am, does not limit my access to the world, but on the contrary is my means of entering into communication with it. It is by being unrestrictedly and unreservedly what I am at present that I have a chance of moving forward; it is by living my time that I am able to understand other times, by plunging into the present and the world by taking on deliberately what I am fortuitously, by willing what I will and doing what I do, that I can go further.[56]

To plunge in; to choose; to disclose; to move; this is the road, it seems to me, to mastery.

Notes

1. M. Merleau-Ponty, *The Primacy of Perception*, ed. J. M. Edie (Evanston, Ill.: Northwestern University Press, 1964), p. 99.

2. J. Sartre, *Search for a Method* (New York: Alfred A. Knopf, 1963), p. 92.

3. R. W. Crary, *Humanizing the School: Curriculum Development and Theory* (New York: Alfred A. Knopf, 1969), p. 13.

4. J. Dewey, "The Child and the Curriculum," in *Dewey on Education*, ed. M. S. Dworkin (New York: Teachers College Bureau of Publications, 1959), p. 91.

5. S. Lawall, *Critics of Consciousness* (Cambridge: Harvard University Press, 1968).

6. T. S. Eliot, *The Sacred Wood* (New York: Barnes & Noble University Paperbacks, 1960), p. x.

7. D. Walsh, "The Cognitive Content of Art," in *Aesthetics*, ed. F. J. Coleman (New York: McGraw-Hill, 1968), p. 297.

8. C. Bell, *Art* (London: Chatto & Windus, 1914).

9. Walsh, "Content of Art."

10. M. H. Abrams, "Belief and the Suspension of Belief," in *Literature and Belief*, ed. id. (New York: Columbia University Press, 1957), p. 9.

11. M. Blanchot, *L'Espace littéraire* (Paris: Gallimard, 1955).

12. See, for example, A. Schutz, "Some Leading Concepts of Phenomenology," in *Collected Papers I*, ed. M. Natanson (The Hague: Martinus Nijhoff, 1967), pp. 104–05.

13. J. Sartre, *Literature and Existentialism*, 3rd ed. (New York: Citadel Press, 1965), p. 43.

14. Ibid., p. 45.

15. J. Dewey, *Art as Experience* (New York: Minton, Balch & Company, 1934), p. 54.

16. Sartre, *Search for a Method*, p. 91.

17. J. Piaget, *Structuralism* (New York: Basic Books, 1970), p. 139.

18. Ibid., p. 68.

19. Ibid., p. 139.

20. Ibid.

21. M. Merleau-Ponty, *Phenomenology of Perception* (London: Routledge & Kegan Paul, 1962).

22. Merleau-Ponty, *Primacy of Perception*, p. 119.

23. Ibid., p. 99.

24. P. Freire, *Pedagogy of the Oppressed* (New York: Herder & Herder, 1970), p. 108.

25. Schutz, "On Multiple Realities," p. 248.

26. Merleau-Ponty, *Primacy of Perception*, p. 58.

27. Merleau-Ponty, *Phenomenology of Perception*, p. xvii.

28. Schutz, "On Multiple Realities."

29. Merleau-Ponty, *Phenomenology of Perception*, p. xv.

30. R. S. Peters, *Ethics and Education* (London: George Allen & Unwin, 1966), p. 50.

31. R. S. Peters, *Ethics and Education* (Glenview, Ill.: Scott, Foresman & Co., 1967), p. 12.

32. P. H. Phenix, "The Uses of the Disciplines as Curriculum Content," in *Theory of Knowledge and Problems of Education*, ed. D. Vandenberg (Urbana: University of Illinois Press, 1969), p. 195.

33. P. H. Phenix, *Realms of Meaning* (New York: McGraw-Hill, 1964), p. 25.

34. Ibid.

35. Schutz, "Problem of Rationality in the Social World," in *Collected Papers* II, ed. Natanson (The Hague: Martinus Nijhoff, 1967), p. 66.

36. Phenix, "Disciplines as Curriculum Content," p. 195.

37. A. Toffler, *Future Shock* (New York: Random House, 1970), p. 18.

38. A. Camus, *The Myth of Sisyphus* (New York: Alfred A. Knopf, 1955), p. 72.

39. H. Pinter, *The Dumb Waiter* (New York: Grove Press, 1961), p. 103.

40. T. Stoppard, *Rosencrantz and Guildenstern Are Dead* (New York: Grove Press, 1967), pp. 58–59.

41. Compare F. Dostoevsky, *Notes from Underground,* in *The Short Novels of Dostoevsky* (New York: Dial Press, 1945). "You believe in a palace of crystal that can never be destroyed . . . a palace at which one will not be able to put out one's tongue or make a long nose on the sly." p. 152.

42. F. Kafka, *Amerika* (Garden City, N.Y.: Doubleday Anchor Books, 1946), p. 38.

43. Merleau-Ponty, *Primacy of Perception,* p. 110.

44. Piaget, *Structuralism.*

45. R. M. Zaner, *The Way of Phenomenology* (New York: Pegasus Books, 1970), p. 27.

46. Freire, *Pedagogy of the Oppressed,* p. 100.

47. Schutz, "The Life-World," in *Collected Papers* III, ed. Natanson, p. 125.

48. Kafka, *Amerika,* p. 201.

49. Schutz, "The Life-World," p. 124.

50. Schutz, "Leading Concepts of Phenomenology," p. 111.

51. G. K. Plochmann, "On the Organic Logic of Teaching and Learning," in *Theory of Knowledge,* ed. Vandenberg, p. 244.

52. Compare footnote 10.

53. M. Novak, *The Experience of Nothingness* (New York: Harper & Row, 1970), p. 94.

54. Schutz, "Symbols, Reality, and Society," *Collected Papers* I, ed. Natanson, p. 315.

55. Merleau-Ponty, *Phenomenology of Perception,* p. xix.

56. Ibid., pp. 455–56.

9

Frame Factors

Ulf Lundgren

Frame Factors: The First Approximation

If we take the actual teaching as a starting point, we can make a first as-sumption, namely, that the transactions in the teaching situation are con-strained and governed by various political and bureaucratic decisions. Thus, we have to make a distinction between factors that are constraining the pro-cess and factors that are governing it. The term *frame* will be used to refer only to the constraints on the teaching situation. The concept of frame has been used both by Dahllöf[1] and by Bernstein.[2] Although their theoretical contexts were different, I shall here expand the definition of this concept us-ing Dahllöf's and Bernstein's works as point of reference.

In Bernstein's terminology, frame refers to the options available as to the curriculum content. But in a broader sense, the number of options as to the form of transaction, the methods (instructional and otherwise), and the time that may be devoted to a certain subject (or content unit) during a definable period (for example, a school year) could also be regarded as limited, or "framed."[3]

Dahllöf uses the concept of frame more broadly, in relation to decisions that are outside the teacher's and student's control. This usage thus links the macro- and the microlevel of analysis.[4] It should be remembered, however, that the concept of frame as used by Dahllöf was developed in order to cope with the special problem of ability grouping.

In a study by Lundgren,[5] Dahllöf's earlier findings concerning ability

Reprinted from *Model of Analysis Pedagogical Process* (Lund, Sweden: LWK Gleerup, 1977), pp. 24–38. Reprinted with permission of the author.

grouping were tested. His conceptual framework was also expanded, and the elaborated model is illustrated in Figure 9-1. The model relates frame factors, steering group, and the nature of the teaching process, as well as indicating the concepts used to describe both frame factors and the teaching process. In the following pages we shall explain the three main demands of this model and describe an empirical study[6] that tested it. The results of this study pinpointed some important shortcomings in the model, which will then be discussed.

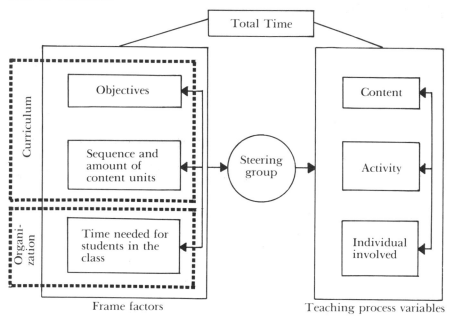

Figure 9-1

Model of the relationship between frame factors, steering group, and teaching process variables.[7]

As can be seen in Figure 9-1, the model includes three types of frame factors, all of which are interrelated. The first refers to the goals or objectives of teaching and may vary from generally expressed to clearly stated goals of behavior. The second factor refers to the sequence of content units within which these various educational goals may be achieved. This factor varies in relation to the structure of the content taught. The third factor is the time needed by a student to master the content and, hence, achieve the goals. For each student, the time needed is a consequence of the subject that is taught and how this subject is transformed in the teaching situation. Therefore, the time needed will always be an expression of both learning capacity and the structure of the educational system in relation to the student's experiences. Hence, the model is not restricted to the microlevel, for it can also be used as a description for the curriculum-planning process (that is, at the macrolevel).

The total time available to the teacher can be classified in three ways:

1. The time is sufficient to satisfy the relations between the frame factors.
2. The time is more than is needed.
3. The time is not sufficient.

In the last instance the time will act as a frame factor. In that event the teacher must make various decisions in relation to the frames. Since the total time cannot be prolonged, the teacher must place a priority on certain goals or students or both.

In this sense the creation of a steering group can be interpreted as a solution the teacher can follow when the time is not sufficient. As a criterion for judging when he can finish one section of the syllabus and begin another, the teacher uses the progress of a particular group of students. But at the same time, it is obvious that access to time is not the only explanation for the differentiation by the teacher of students and groups of students. The governing rules of the teaching situation demand such differentiation in the form of achievement scores or grades. Thus, differentiation cannot be explained by the frame system alone; the evaluation system (including rules for control, that is, evaluation procedures and so on) must also be taken into account.[8]

The decisions the teacher takes are also dependent on the curriculum and class organization (ability grouping, class size, and so forth), as well as the teacher's perception of these factors. While the effects of the constraints will be most visible when time is not sufficient, subjective interpretation of these constraints will also determine how time is used. Of course, some may always interpret the time as insufficient because they hold teaching goals that are too ambitious to fulfill. This interpretation is also a consequence of the rules and obligations that the teacher must fulfill. If she is obliged to describe the outcomes of her teaching in terms of student grades, she will then be forced to make a differentiated interpretation of the frame factors (goals, content, and available time). Thus, the combination of an evaluation system according to which the teacher has to make differentiation between students will always cause a situation in which the time available is not sufficient for some groups of students to achieve the goals. Thus, my second assumption will be that if there are evaluation criteria governing teaching in such a way that the teacher is obliged to present qualitative descriptions of student outcomes, then the time available for subgroups of students will not be sufficient to reach the goals set for other subgroups. These two basic assumptions may seem fairly truistic, but they are necessary in order to classify different groups of factors governing, controlling, and constraining the teaching process. In this way, the assumption of a steering group can now be further explained.

In the model in Figure 9-1, three concepts were used as teaching-process variables: content, activity, and person involved. Using these concepts as a starting point, we conducted an empirical study in which this model was tested.[9] The study was carried out on students in the Swedish high school grade 11 (ages seventeen to eighteen). Two types of data were collected: survey data (the extensive study) and in-depth data (the intensive study). The survey data were collected from a panel study on teaching in forty-six classes in the natural science and social science streams. Five subjects were studied: English, civics, history, mathematics, and Swedish. Questionnaires were sent to the teachers on four separate occasions during the school year. In each questionnaire the teachers were asked to describe how they had actually conducted their classes during the intervening periods and what they had really planned to do. They also answered questions about the teaching methods used, the decisions they made when they had to change their plans, their perceptions of teaching, and the problems they experienced. On three occasions the students were also questioned about their behavior in class, their attitudes towards their teachers, their subjects and their homework, and the reason for their choice of subjects. The in-depth study covered eight classes, which were observed a total of fifty-seven times. The unit of analysis was the pedagogical move.[10] In all, a little over 11,000 moves were classified, according to the Bellack system, the VICS-system[11] and Bales's category system.[12]

In the survey study, the textbook was used as a frame of reference. The first step was to analyze the content of the textbooks in relation to the syllabus so that different classes using different textbooks could be compared. Next, the responses of the teachers were used to build up a description of their teaching as it had been conducted and as it had been planned. The third step was to compare the teaching process in different classes. To do this, we assumed that students between the tenth and twenty-fifth percentiles in general intellectual ability formed the steering groups so that classes could be divided into three categories: those in which the steering group had a high-average ability, those with a low-average level, and those in between.

Classes with high-ability steering groups and low-ability steering groups were found to follow the planned teaching better than those with a middle-ability group. The interpretation of this was that the teachers of these classes can either follow their plans or can revise them at an early stage and then follow them through. Teachers in the average-level classes that were unable to get through the units originally planned were forced to make a series of decisions: to lower the goals, leave out parts of the syllabus, or let students lag behind.

The fourth step was to analyze the decisions made by the teachers when the pace of the teaching could not be maintained and when different groups of students could not master a certain unit satisfactorily. Up to that point, parts of the first model could be empirically proved, and the assumed relationship held true.

In the in-depth study, data were analyzed in two stages. In the first stage, the relationship between the ability level of the steering group and the relative frequency of various verbal utterances was determined. A markedly significant relationship was obtained, and it was found that the relationship formed a consistent pattern irrespective of the coding system used. When the steering group was made up of students with a high level of general ability, the degree of subject-relevant utterances increased, as did behavioral sequences typical of a traditional style of teaching: the question-answer pattern increased, there was less disruptive behavior, the amount of disciplining decreased, the number of predictable answers increased, the teaching climate became more positive, and the behavior of the teacher more indirect.

In the second stage of the in-depth study, the steering group was redefined. The assumption was that teaching is not directed towards individuals but towards groups of students. The teacher's perceptual grouping of the students was determined and then analyzed in relation to the classroom behavior of the various groups in order to delineate the pattern of student roles.[13]

Although this empirical study verified the assumptions the model in Figure 9-1 made, it went no further in developing the conceptual framework. The basic relationship between frame factors and the teaching process has been established, but it is also necessary to explain how these relationships are formed and the way in which they affect the teaching process. The limitations of the model can now be clarified with the following points:

1. The frame concept and the concept of curriculum should be separated because the curriculum articulated in the syllabus, textbooks, and teaching materials governs rather than constrains the process. But governing factors are similar to constraining factors in that they are both determined at decision-making levels above the teaching process.

2. In making a distinction between governing and constraining factors, the nature of the governing process must be described in relation to the teaching process, that is, curriculum determines the classroom language. While the constraining factors structure the classroom language, the governing factors (curriculum) determine the content of this language.

3. The distinctions between frames and curriculum are not sufficient to explain the structure of the teaching process. The legislative system regulating the teachers' duties must also be taken into consideration (the marking system, the examination system, and so on).

4. The model should be related to a general theory of education and its function in society.

The final point is the most essential. The internal functions and effects of education cannot be explained without relating them to a basic theory of education and society. This theory must, then, be built on an explanatory model that specifies the determinants of the teaching process.

External and Internal Functions of Teaching

Educational researchers cannot be expected to develop a complete social theory, but on the other hand it is evident that educational research should be based upon the conclusions of the more comprehensive social theories. Although the statements may seem truistic, they have rarely been reflected in research. With the possible exception of central European countries, contemporary educational research is mainly empirical in nature and is heavily influenced by positivistic philosophy. The "narrow view of science,"[14] which conceives science as descriptive, value-free, and nomothetic, is presented as a basis for pedagogical inquiry in standard textbooks on research strategies.[15] According to these sources, research is an "objective" enterprise, and objectivity is in its turn defined with reference to a set of acceptable methods. This concentration upon research methodology can be regarded as the result of long chains of transformations between problems and methods leading to a reification of the problems by perceiving them as purely methodological. One basic assumption is that there exists an objective observational language separated from the theoretical language and that translations between these languages can be performed through the use of a set of translation rules. The consequence of this assumption has been a concentration upon methodology. Science and, thereby, objectivity have been defined in terms of methodology.

In educational research the aim of researchers has been to establish laws through descriptions which have been correlational, experimental, or even quasi-experimental in nature. Also evident in educational research as a further consequence of this basic assumption is the belief that "objective" interpretation can only be achieved through the use of strict rules for the formulation and verification of hypotheses. These rules have been based essentially upon the idea that educational phenomena can be expressed quantitatively.

To summarize: the scientific ideas and perspectives within the main tradition of educational research have been expressed in terms of acceptable research strategies or methods, which then obviously influence the kind of problems that may be studied. One consequence of this scientific perspective, in our view, has been the lack of adequate conceptualizations of pedagogical phenomena that link explanations of economic, social, and cultural change in the society to explanations of the nature of the educational processes.

A concrete illustration of the consequences of this research tradition can be seen in the type of teaching research that has been done. With some few exceptions, this has been based on the view of teaching contained in the curriculum, that is, that teaching leads to the learning of the stated goals.

An educational system operates according to an explicit or implicit definition of its role in society. Clearly, education has external effects in the society, and the assumption is that the inner functions of schooling can be derived from the external functions. From another perspective, the general purpose of all pedagogical processes is to inculcate the value system of the society. There are, of course, different ideas about what the external functions of education are and about the value systems, knowledge, and experiences that should be included. There are also different ideas about the actual correspondence of the internal and external functions. However, many of these ideas are ideological and do not reflect the real relationship between education's internal and external functions.

An empirical educational theory must then be based on data concerning the educational process as it exists in reality and not on analyses of what researchers think these processes ought to be.[16] Such a theory thus constitutes a heuristic device for classroom research by serving as an indicator of important processes occurring in the classroom. The purpose of research should be to examine the various forms in which these processes are manifested. These will be determined by frame factors, in the sense that they define certain allowable "outer limits" seen as necessary for the fulfillment of that process. But the frame factors themselves can, in turn, be derived from the political, economic, and social structure of the society. This is also a consequence of the fact that pedagogical processes are artificial[17] *but not arbitrary and subjective.* The school is an institution that promotes learning in terms of postulated knowledge, skills, attitudes, and values. Legislation and rules prescribe the form of this institution, while the available resources in terms of personnel, teaching aids, and composition of students determine how the actual teaching corresponds to the formal goals and regulations. Curricula, regulations, personnel, and teaching aids as well as available time and the composition and size of classes are the most visible frames and forces constraining and governing the teaching process. These frames are translations of the external functions of education to internal frames, but they cannot of course explain the whole process.

Education has several other functions that are not expressed in any curricula.[18] Abrahamsson[19] and Cohen,[20] for instance, have pointed out the following external functions of schooling: reproduction of labor and absorption of labor; social control and selection and individual welfare. Although these factors have not been thoroughly analyzed, they can be used as concrete examples of various functions of education.

The learning of the content of the curriculum within the constraints given by the frame factors is of course not the only type of learning that occurs in classrooms. If research is restricted only to the narrow learning perspective, neglecting the external functions of education, the relationship between frame factors and the teaching process will appear to be fairly random. Obviously, the teaching process is determined and constrained not only by the formal frames but also by many external factors inherent in the cultural context. Many of these external influences operate outside the consciousness of the acting individuals.

This is, of course, neither dramatic nor new in itself. However, existing educational research has been directed towards analyses of the teaching process in terms of the learning of the curriculum content. But in the real teaching situation, the learning of school subjects may actually function as a more general socialization process that bears little relationship to the theories of learning and development formulated on the basis of experimental situations.[21]

We can also illustrate these statements from another point of view. Traditional research on teaching has aimed at the acquisition of knowledge in order to improve the teacher's competency. This has resulted in two research goals—to discover the types of teaching behavior related to student achievement and to isolate those behaviors that it is possible to manipulate. The results obtained have consequently been interpreted in relation to teacher education.[22] Two points must be clarified here. First, although the behavior of the teacher in the classroom is the main source of learning, the teacher is her- or himself part of a wider context. By disregarding this context, researchers have been unable to identify those factors that could be manipulated in order to bring about changes in the teaching process. Second, the link between teacher behavior and teacher education is a complex one, as teachers' colleges operate in the same social context as do the schools. Hence, a knowledge of the social context is also necessary to bring about changes in teacher education.

Up to this point I have discussed, albeit broadly, the concept of frame in relation to the educational and scientific perspective in which it must be understood. This was done in order to establish a starting point. Furthermore, the first model (Fig. 9-1) has been developed and expanded with the aid of an empirical study. While this study was shown to confirm some of the basic assumptions and relationships in the model, it also illustrated the need for an expansion of the model. Consequently, a distinction was made between the concept of frame and the concept of curriculum, and successively we have shown the need for another distinction between frames, curriculum, and the formal obligations of teachers.

The definition of frame used up to this point includes any factor that limits the teaching process. However, this definition is rather broad and should be supplemented by a stipulative definition: *frame factors are those factors which are determined outside the teaching process*. Hence, frames are outside the control of the teachers and students.

The next step will thus be to distinguish between three systems that constrain, govern, and regulate the teaching process. From here on, the term *frame system* will be used instead of frame factors. Hence, the three systems are:

the goal system
the frame system
the formal rule system.

The goal system includes the concrete consequences of a specific curriculum, that is, the syllabus, recommendations for teaching, teaching materials, textbooks, and so on. The frame system includes everything that constrains the teaching process that is determined outside teaching. This would include physical equipment such as rooms, organizational arrangements such as size of school and class, ability grouping, time available for teaching, and so forth. The formal rule system includes regulations of a legislative nature concerning the duties of the teacher such as marking systems and rules concerning the employment of teachers such as the required number of lessons per week and demands of competency.

These three groups of systems are linked to three main concepts:

curriculum
the administrative apparatus
school laws and school legislation.

It is usual in the teaching situation that these factors cannot be influenced by either the teacher or the students. The only way of influencing them is through the political process. In turn, then, the curriculum, the administrative apparatus, and the laws of the school can be analyzed and related to the economic, social, and political structure of the society. The relationship between these concepts would thus be:

$\longrightarrow$ curriculum $\longrightarrow$ goal system $\longrightarrow$
$\longrightarrow$ administrative apparatus $\longrightarrow$ frame system $\longrightarrow$
$\longrightarrow$ judicial apparatus $\longrightarrow$ formal rule system $\longrightarrow$

Figure 9-2
School-society model

In the first model the concepts used were not particularly well defined, mainly because their pedagogical and psychological relevance were mixed. I have discussed only the pedagogical relevance of the concepts. This can lead to a conceptual paradigm in which the teaching process is looked upon as more or less mechanically determined by the structure of society. A purely pedagogical explanation of the educational process, even if it does take into account the social context, is as limited in its usefulness as a purely psychological explanation. This "joining" of a psychological conceptual structure and a pedagogical conceptual structure to explain educational processes is the central idea of the theory being developed here.

The main argument is that to explain any educational process, we must have a conceptual apparatus that relates the economic and social structure of society to the teaching process. This means that we must have concepts on different levels of analyses that can be related to each other using empirical references. But such a conceptual apparatus would constitute only one of two necessary parts of an explanation.

We can use an example to make this more concrete. Both the formulation of a curriculum and its manifestation in a goal system are determined by the particular cultural context. The curriculum will also express the structure of social and economic power in the society. The student's interpretation of the meaning of the teaching process is interpreted by him in relation to the social context in which he lives. His access to the content of the goal system is dependent upon the psychological prerequisites of the student. These prerequisites are not determined by nature alone but are also expressions of the economic, social, and political structure.

To return to the question of ability grouping, it is clear that this must be linked to both a pedagogical analysis of the functions of education and the manner in which these functions are transformed into the frames and curriculum. This idea is the key to our later analysis of educational research.

If we return to our first model (Fig. 9-1), we can now summarize our discussion as follows:

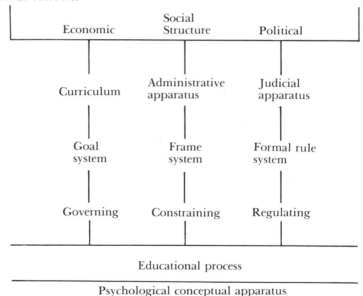

Figure 9-3
Advanced frame model

Notes

1. U. Dahllöf, *Ability Grouping, Content Validity and Curriculum Process Analysis* (Goteborg: Reports from the Institute of Education, University of

Goteborg, 1969); U. Dahllöf, *Ability Grouping, Content Validity and Curriculum Process Analysis* (New York: Teachers College Press, Columbia University, 1971).

2. B. Bernstein, "On the Classification and Framing of Educational Knowledge," in *Knowledge and Control: New Directions for the Sociology of Education,* ed. M. F. D. Young (London: Collier-Macmillan, 1971), pp. 47–69; B. Bernstein, "Class and Pedagogics: Visible and Invisible," *Educational Studies* 1 (1975): 23–41.

3. U. Dahllöf, *Skoldifferentiering Och Undervisningsforlopp* (Stockholm: Almqvist & Wiksell, 1967); Dahllöf, *Ability Grouping* (1969); Dahllöf, *Ability Grouping* (1971); Dahllöf, "Trends in Process-Related Research at Different Problem Levels in Educational Sciences," *Scandinavian Journal of Educational Research* 19: 55–77; D. Kallos and U. P. Lundgren, *En Diskussion av Forutsattningar Och Riktlinger For Forsoksverskamhet Med Individanpassad Universitetsundervisning* (Stockholm: Universitetskanslersambetet, 1972); D. Kallos and U. P. Lundgren, "Evaleuring av Universitetsundervisning Som Pedagogiskt Vetenskapligt Problem," in *Utvardering av Universitet (Evaluation of Universities),* ed. D. Kallos (Kopenhamn: Nordiska Radet, Nordisk Utredningsserie, 1974), pp. 47–57; U. P. Lundgren, *Frame Factors and the Teaching Process: A Contribution to Curriculum Theory and Theory of Teaching* (Stockholm: Almqvist & Wiksell, 1972); U. P. Lundgren, *Pedagogical Frames and the Teaching Process: A Report from an Empirical Curriculum Project* (Paper read at the annual meeting of the American Educational Research Association in New Orleans, 1973, Goteborg: Institute of Education, University of Goteborg).

4. See, for example, Dahllöf, *Skoldifferentiering*; Dahllöff, *Ability Grouping* (1969); Dahllöf, "Trends in Process-Related Research"; U. Dahllöf and U. P. Lundgren, "Macro and Micro Approaches Combined for Curriculum Process Analysis: A Swedish Educational Field Project" (mimeographed 1970); U. Dahllöf, U. P. Lungren, M. Sioo, "Reform Implementation Studies as a Basis for Curriculum Theory," *Curriculum Theory Network Monographs Supplement* (1971), pp. 99–117.

5. Lundgren, *Frame Factors*; Lundgren, *Pedagogical Frames.*

6. Lundgren, *Frame Factors.*

7. Ibid., p. 43.

8. G. Arfwedson, *Vad Kan Larare Gora? Ett Makroperspektiv Pa Lararnas Arbetssituation* (Stockholm: Pedagogiska Institutionen, Lararhogskolan i Stockholm, Fakta Och Debatt, 1976).

9. Lundgren, *Frame Factors.*

10. See, for example, A. A. Bellack et al., *The Language of the Classroom* (New York: Teachers College Press, Columbia University, 1966).

11. E. Amidon and E. Hunter, *Improving Teaching: The Analysis of Verbal Interaction* (New York: Holt, Rinehart & Winston, 1967).

12. R. F. Bales, *Interaction Process Analysis* (Reading, Mass.: Addison-Wesley, 1950).

13. See also U. P. Lundgren, "Pedagogical Roles in the Classroom," in *Contemporary Research in the Sociology of Education,* ed. J. Eggleston (London: Methuen Press, 1974), pp. 200–14.

14. H. B. Dunkel, "Wanted: New Paradigms and a Normative Base for Research," in *Philosophical Redirection of Education Research,* ed. L. G. Thomas (Chicago: University of Chicago Press, 1972), pp. 77–93.

15. N. F. Kerlinger, *Foundations of Behavioral Research,* 2d ed. (London: Holt,

Rinehart & Winston, 1973); R. M. W. Travers, *An Introduction to Educational Research*, 3d ed. (New York: Macmillan, 1970).

16. R. G. Paulston, *Conflicting Theories of Social and Educational Change: A Typological Review* (Pittsburgh: University Center for International Studies, University of Pittsburgh, 1976), p. 44.

17. See, for example, D. B. Gowin, "Is Educational Research Distinctive?" in Thomas, *Philosophical Redirection of Educational Research*.

18. See, for example, E. Altvater and F. Huisken, *Materialen zur Politischen Okonomie der Ausbildungssektors* (Erlangen: Politladen, 1971); P. Bourdieu and J. C. Passeron, *La Reproduction: Elemente pour une Theorie du Systeme d'Enseigement* (Paris: Edition de Minuit, 1970).

19. B. Abrahamsson, "Utbuildning och Samhalle: Nagra problemomraden," *Skolan som Arbetsplats* (Stockholm: Utbildningsdepartementet, Statens Offentliga Utredningar, 1974), pp. 291–338.

20. Y. A. Cohen, "Schools and Civilizational States," in *The Social Sciences and the Comparative Study of the Educational System*, ed. J. F. Tischer (Scranton, Pennsylvania: International Textbook Co., 1970).

21. See, for example, N. Keddie, "Classroom Knowledge," in *Knowledge and Control*, ed. M. F. D. Young (London: Collier-Macmillan, 1971).

22. See, for example, N. L. Gage, *Teacher Effectiveness and Teacher Education* (Palo Alto, Calif.: Pacific Books, 1972).

10

Mass Culture and the Rise of the New Illiteracy:
Implications for Reading

Henry Giroux

Secure yourselves Knowledge, you who are frozen!
You who are starving, grab hold of the book: It's a Weapon.
You must take over the leadership.
—Brecht

In this era of capitalism, Americans appear to be faced with a major paradox about the relationship between technology, culture, and emancipation. On the one hand, the increasing development of science and technology provides the possibility of freeing humans from dehumanizing and backbreaking labor. In turn, this freedom offers humanity new opportunities for the development of, and access to, a culture that promotes a more critical and qualitatively discriminatory sensibility in all modes of communication and experience. On the other hand, the development of technology and science, constructed according to the laws of capitalist rationality, has ushered in forms of domination and control that appear to thwart rather than to extend the possibilities of human emancipation.[1]

It is within the parameters of this paradox that an examination of the value and function of reading in a multimedia society can be analyzed. The necessity for such a perspective rests with the intricate, though often overlooked, linkages that exist between the various modes of communication and the existing sociopolitical forces that dominate this society. To speak of

Reprinted, by permission, from *Interchange* 10: 4 (1979-1980): 89–98. © 1980, The Ontario Institute for Studies in Education.

one without the other represents not only a conceptual problem but a political failing as well. In broad general terms, this means that any understanding of the relationship between the electronic media and the print
culture becomes muddled unless such a relationship is situated within the
specific social and historical context in which it is found. To place one's
analysis in such a context is to oppose mainstream social theorists who have
failed to study the dynamics of the print and visual modes of communication within the larger critical concepts of history, mass culture, and ideology.[2] Their failure to do so is, in fact, indicative of the more serious ideological failure to recognize the changing dialectical qualities and functions
that both electronic media and print culture have had historically and continue to have today.[3] Historically, the relationship between changes in society and changes in communication has been dictated less by the nature of
the developing technology of communication than by the dominant ideology and existing social formations of the given society. For instance, in
contrast to the United States today, reading aloud and in public was commonplace during the late Middle Ages, as it is in contemporary China today. Similarly, unlike most countries in the West, there are no copyright
laws in Cuba because the government believes that books should be used to
diffuse culture and not be used for commercial purposes.[4] This indicates
that the interaction between social and technical changes is a complex one
in which the shape and use of a mode of communication is determined by
forces other than those of the existing technology. In addition, there are
profound questions lurking behind the varied functions that print and
visual modes of communication have in different social and historical contexts. Who controls the different modes of communication, and in whose
interests do they operate? More succinctly put, do the modes of communication operate in the interest of oppression or liberation? Unfortunately,
these are questions that mainstream social theorists have chosen to ignore.[5]
One way of approaching these questions is through what I have termed the
dialectic of use and potential in technology.

Underlying the dialectic of oppression and liberation that is inherent in
all forms of communication is the fundamental distinction between the
use that is made of a particular mode of communication, such as television,
and the potential use it may have in a given society. To focus on the contradiction between use and potential represents one viable way of analyzing
the changing relationship between visual and print cultures in this society.
Not to do so is to fall prey to either a brand of technological fatalism or a
brand of technological utopianism.[6] In both cases, technology is abstracted
from its sociohistorical roots, removed from the imperatives of class and
power, and defined within the conceptual straitjacket of technological
determinism.

A more critical approach would attempt to lay bare "some of the concrete and complex linkages between cultural creation and distribution and economic and social forms."[7] This requires that we redefine culture in political terms, and look at the way visual and print cultures operate as mechanisms of social and cultural reproduction. But the concept of social and cultural reproduction must first be explained before we can analyze its mechanisms in detail. The notion of reproduction clarifies the relationship between culture and society so as to suggest the subordinacy of culture to the dominant society. This is an important point for two reasons. First, mainstream anthropologists have traditionally depoliticized the notion of culture by making it synonymous with "a peoples' way of life."[8] Consequently, they have made it difficult to study the important relationship between society and culture, particularly the relationship between ideology and social control. Second, the locus of domination in the advanced industrial countries has undergone a significant change, and we need a politicized notion of culture to examine that change. A more fruitful analysis than that of mainstream social scientists can be found in the work of the late Italian social theorist, Antonio Gramsci, as well as in the more recent work of the Frankfurt School and their followers.[9]

Cultural Hegemony

From the perspective of Gramsci and others, the locus of domination in the advanced industrial countries of the West has shifted from a reliance upon force (police, army, and so on) to the use of a cultural apparatus which promotes consensus through the reproduction and distribution of dominant systems of beliefs and attitudes. Gramsci called this form of control ideological hegemony, a form of control that not only manipulates consciousness but also saturates the daily routines and practices that guide everyday behavior. The Frankfurt School carried this analysis much further and pointed to the increasing development of technology to reproduce the dominant culture and maintain existing socioeconomic arrangements. More recently, the work of Pierre Bourdieu and Basil Bernstein has demonstrated that the dominant society not only distributes materials and goods but also reproduces and distributes cultural capital—that is, those systems of meanings, taste, dispositions, attitudes, and norms that are directly and indirectly defined by the dominant society as socially legitimate.[10] From this perspective, the reproduction of a society is intimately tied to the production and distribution of its cultural messages. As such, the cultural apparatus for reproducing the dominant culture and communicating it to the public becomes an important political issue. In effect, culture is now viewed not only as an ideological expression of the dominant society but also refers to the form and structure of the technology that communicates the messages that "lay the psychological and moral foundations for the economic and political system."[11]

As an ideological expression of the dominant society, the dominant culture is deeply tied to the ethos of consumerism and positivism. As the culture became industrialized in the early part of the twentieth century, it reached into new forms of communication to spread its message. The production of goods was not paralleled by the evergrowing reproduction of consciousness. Moreover, as twentieth-century capitalism gave rise to mass advertising and its attendant gospel of unending consumerism, all spheres of social existence were now informed, though far from entirely controlled, by the newly charged rationality of advanced industrial capitalism. Mass marketing, for example, drastically changed the realms of work and leisure and, as Stuart Ewen has pointed out, set the stage for control over daily life.

During the 1920s the stage was set by which the expanding diversity of corporate organization might do cultural battle with a population which was in need of, and demanding, social change. The stage was in the theatre of daily life, and it was within the intimacies of that reality—productive, cultural, social, psychological— that a corporate pièce-de-théâtre was being scripted.[12]

While industrialized culture was radically transforming daily life, scientific management was altering traditional patterns of work. Craft production gave way to a fragmented work process in which conception was separated from both the execution and experience of work. One result was a work process that reduced labor to a series of preordained and lifeless gestures.[13]

Accompanying these changes in the work place and the realm of leisure was a form of technocratic legitimation based on a positivist view of science and technology. This form of rationality defined itself through the alleged unalterable and productive effects that the developing forces of technology and science were having on the foundations of twentieth-century progress. Whereas progress in the United States in the eighteenth and nineteenth centuries was linked to the development of moral self-improvement and self-discipline in the interest of building a better society, progress in the twentieth century was stripped of its concern with improving the human condition and became dedicated to material and technical growth.[14] What was once considered humanly possible, an issue involving values and human ends, was now reduced to what was technically possible. The application of scientific methodology to new forms of technology appeared as a social force generated by its own laws, laws governed by a rationality that appeared to exist above and beyond human control.

As a mode of legitimation, this form of technocratic rationality has become the prevailing cultural hegemony. As the prevailing consciousness, it celebrates the continued enlargement of the comforts of life and the productivity of labor through increasing submission of the public to laws that govern the technical mastery of both human beings and nature. The price for increased productivity is the continued refinement and administration of not simply the forces of production but the constitutive nature of consciousness itself.

The Culture Industry

Hans Enzensberger has claimed that the electronic media, operating in the service of this technocratic rationality, has become the major force in what he calls the industrialization of the mind.[15] He points out that the mind industry transcends particularistic discussion of the print and visual cultures. He writes that "Hardly anyone seems to be aware of the phenomenon as a whole: the industrialization of the human mind. This is a process which cannot be understood by a mere examination of its machinery."[16] Moreover,

The mind industry's main business and concern is not to sell its product, it is to 'sell' the existing order. To perpetuate the pattern of man's domination by man, no matter who runs the society, and by whatever means. Its main task is to expand and train our consciousness—in order to exploit it.[17]

More recent critics have gone much further than Enzensberger and claim that the mass culture industry at the present time in the United States represents an assault on the capacity of human beings to even think in critical terms or, for that matter, to engage in meaningful social discourse.[18] Aronowitz refers to this phenomenon as the "new illiteracy" and claims that not only critical thinking but the substance of democracy itself is at stake. He speaks eloquently to this issue:

The new situation raises the issue of the competence of people to effectively communicate ideational content. The issue is the capacity for conceptual thought itself. . . . Since critical thinking is the fundamental precondition for an autonomous and self-motivated public or citizenry, its decline would threaten the future of democratic social, cultural, and political forms.[19]

These critics view visual culture in particular as playing a significant and important role in reducing collective thought and imagination to strictly technical dimensions. Yet none of these critics supports the Orwellian nightmare of a monolithic consciousness industry that runs without contradictions or resistance. Such a position is vulgar and overly deterministic. Moreover, it fails to acknowledge that the electronic media, as well as print culture, are not causal agents as much as mediating forces in the reproduction of consciousness.[20] The technology of the consciousness industry cannot *produce* culture; it can only reproduce and distribute it. Concomitantly, the consciousness industry is not the only agency of socialization. In other words, mass culture in its various forms generates contradictions as well as consensus, though not with equal weight. In both objective and subjective terms, the technology of the mass culture industry creates pockets of resistance fueled by its own contradictions. For instance, it constantly generates expectations and needs that it cannot ultimately satisfy, yet it contains within its technology the possibility of real communication among people—that is, people could become transmitters as well as receivers of information.

Print versus Visual

The important question that remains is whether a distinction should be made between print and visual cultures regarding their possibilities as forces for liberation or domination at this moment in history. For [the following] reasons, I think the answer is a resounding yes.

It is fairly obvious that each culture has its own center of gravity, providing a different experience as well as a different form of access to knowledge. But it is not so obvious what this means when analyzed in sociopolitical terms. For example, in ideal-essence terms, print and visual cultures should complement each other, but at the present historical juncture, they don't. The visual culture, particularly television, is the most dominant form of communication because its technology offers much greater possibilities for manipulation and social control. This becomes particularly apparent when it is compared to the technology of reading.

While it is true that, historically, reading created a class-specific audience because of the technical and critical skills needed to use it, the same cannot be said of the visual culture, which has all but eliminated any reliance upon a class-specific audience to use its technology or to understand its messages. To put it another way, the visual culture has eliminated the need for any specific public to use the kind of critical and discriminating skills that are necessary to approach a mode of communication. The very notion of "mass culture" suggests not only the importance of quantity but also the reduction of thought and experience to the level of mere spectatorship. The disease in this case is powerlessness, and the cure is a form of manufactured escapism. Of course, the print culture lends itself to the manipulation of consciousness as well, and in an important sense all modes of communication can be manipulatory. The real question is how possible it is to turn everyone into a manipulator of the technology of mass communication. A number of critics have pointed out that the development of print culture helped to produce a mass bourgeois public sphere that nurtured the discussion of current events, newspapers, and books.[21] This is a crucial point, because the technology of the print media necessitates a form of rationality that contains room for critical thinking and analysis. For instance, print culture is a medium that demands attentiveness. It is not as obtrusive as the visual culture; it lacks the "tactile" qualities of the latter. As a result, one has to approach it with intentionality; this form of intentionality becomes clear when we consider that the written word is governed by the logic of conciseness, clarity, and cogency. It has to be that way, at least in principle, because the printed word "freezes" information. When reading, one has more time to stop and reflect on what has been written. It is possible with the written word to assess more rigorously the validity and truth value of an argument. The form of print technology itself retains a check on the overly blatant manipulation of the written message. In other words, there is a tension in print technology between its form and content. The critical eye that reading ideally demands puts a check on the manipulation of the message.

There are other considerations regarding print technology that make it emancipatory at the present time. It is inexpensive to produce and consume. Consequently, through the plethora of books, newspapers, and magazines that flood the market, one has access to a great number of views and positions on any subject. The American left has been accused of relying too heavily upon print technology.[22] The critique is revealing not because it belies a certain amount of elitism on the part of the left, but because it indicates that reading technology provides a greater opportunity for transmitting one's views than any other form of communication. The left simply does not have access to the visual culture. Television, radio, and film production are centrally controlled by the ruling interests. Moreover, these modes of communication are much too important to the corporate interests to be democratized. The visual media are presently the demagogue of one-way communication. And part of the reason for this lies in their power to influence people, a characteristic as endemic to their technology as it is to the social relations that determine their one-sided use. The power of that influence can, in part, be measured by the following figures: ". . . that 96 percent of American households own at least one television, that the average television is on over six hours a day, and that ten percent of American households own at least three televisions."[23]

Theodore Adorno has written that "whoever speaks of culture speaks about administration as well, whether this is his intention or not."[24] Aronowitz illuminates Adorno's remarks by claiming that *visual culture* is industrializing the mind by colonizing the realm of leisure.[25] Again, it is worth pointing out that such a position does not overlook the dialectical interplay between the visual culture and the public at large. People respond to visual culture with different attitudes and needs. The issue is that the visual culture has grown so large and is so centralized, penetrating the "private space" of individuals to such a degree that, in many cases, it reduces cognition and human experience to a mere shadow of technique and the consumer culture.

The visual culture is presently accessible only as a one-way mode of communication. In addition, as a motor force in shaping experience, it has some powerful advantages over print culture. The visual culture, especially television, is situated in "tactile" stimuli such as imagery and sound which, in different combinations and forms, closely simulate face-to-face reality. The power of the visual culture to monopolize thought patterns derives not only from the messages and myths it distributes (a topic too well known to be discussed here) but from the techniques that it uses.

The dominant technique that characterizes the visual culture has its roots in the division of labor that it emulates in the larger society. Fragmentation and immediacy of information are the order of the day. Rapid camera work and sharp editing create the immediate effect of appealing to the emotions while, at the same time, short-circuiting critical reflection.[26] Since it is impossible for the viewer, unless he has a videotape machine, to slow down or reobserve the rapid diffusion of images, he has little opportunity to distance himself from the context of the visual production and reflect on its meaning. Furthermore, the images are not only presented with machine-gun speed; they usually lack a particular unity, as in news presentations, or they lack a larger context—that is, they are unfocalized. In this context, the "image" subsumes reality, and the "fact" becomes the arbiter of the truth. The French situationists refer to the enshrinement of the image as the "spectacle." As Norman Fruchter describes it:

The spectacle is the continuously produced and therefore continuously evolving pseudo-reality, predominantly visual, which each individual encounters, inhabits, and accepts as public and official reality, thereby denying as much as possible the daily private reality of exploration, suffering, and inauthenticity he or she experiences.[27]

The enshrinement of the image, the spectacle, finds some of its manifestations in the star system, the identification of the aesthetic with "entertainment," and the glorification of sensational and violent themes. Between the glut of stylistic and overdramatized images of reality, the visual media, especially television, soothe the public with their display of "objectivity" and their concern with the "facts." The objectivity of the visual media appears guaranteed in the brute presence of the camera, with its ability either to focus immediately on a given event or to capture every gesture and movement in its dramatic rendering of reality. Fredric Jameson describes this position well when he writes:

We are made secure in the illusion that the camera is witnessing everything exactly as it happened and that what it sees is all there is. The camera is absolute presence and absolute truth; thus, the aesthetic of representation collapses the density of the historical event, and flattens it back into fiction.[28]

Amidst the fragmentation of images and the overflow of information, the intrusion of the "fact" appears like a reliable trustworthy tool to sort out the confusion and uncertainty. As Gitlin points out in his analysis of television and the culture of positivism:

Television contributes powerfully to a fetishism of facts. . . . Since history is bewildering, complex, and outside popular control, the raw muscular fact takes on an inordinate importance. . . . The facts themselves seem to explain, to reassure, or to alarm, all in a managed way. Facts demand attention, they get into the stream of discussion, they seem legitimate and trustworthy, they guide—and all along they seem to be leaving the choice to the consumer, the audience.[29]

While the visual media are not the only force in promoting social and cultural reproduction, they may be the most powerful. Aronowitz points to studies that suggest a growing tendency among students to view things literally rather than conceptually; these studies have also pointed to the growing inability of students to think dialectically, to see things in a wider context, or to make connections between seemingly unrelated objects or events. He and others have also complained about students being tied to the "factuality" of the world and appearing to have a great deal of difficulty in using concepts which may controvert appearances.[30]

The response of some critics to the developing power and sophistication of the visual media has been to celebrate the virtues of the electronic media in general while, at the same time, calling for a moratorium on reading and print.[31] These critics point to the virtues and possibilities in two-way communication inherent in the electronic media, and suggest that the age of print is a dying cultural relic. They also point out that the visual culture is not going to go away, and they urge their readers to grapple with it. This is a noble but misguided position. The electronic media are in the hands of the corporate trust, and it would take a redistribution of power and wealth to place them at the public's disposal.[32] This is an important task, but it must be preceded by a change in the collective consciousness and accompanied by the development of an ongoing political struggle. Moreover, it underestimates the power of the visual media to define the use of their own technology. In other words, even with the growing accessibility of such means of electronic communication as cameras, video systems, as well as non-visual electronic media such as CB radios, the public views these modes of communication as important only for leisure activities.[33]

Redefinition of Literacy

If the visual culture within the context of the present society threatens self-reflection and critical thought, we are going to have to redefine our notions of literacy and rely heavily upon the print culture to teach people the rudiments of critical thinking and social action. The point here is that we must move beyond the positivistic notion of literacy that characterizes the social sciences today.[34] Instead of formulating literacy in terms of the mastery of techniques, we must broaden its meaning to include the ability to read critically, both within and outside one's experiences, and with conceptual power. This means that literacy would enable people to decode critically their personal and social worlds and thereby further their ability to challenge the myths and beliefs that structure their perceptions and experiences. Literacy, as Freire never tires of telling us, must be linked to a theory of knowledge, one that is consistent with an emancipatory political perspective and one that gives the fullest expression to illuminating the power of social relationships in the act of knowing. This is crucial because it suggests not only that one should learn how to read messages critically but also that critical analysis can only take place when knowledge serves as a subject of investigation, as a mediating force between people.[35]

In other words, true literacy involves dialogue and social relationships free from top-to-bottom authoritarian structures. At the present historical juncture, reading provides the opportunity for the development of progressive approaches to literacy as both a mode of critical consciousness and a fundamental springboard for social action. Print culture is accessible and cheap, and its materials can be produced and manufactured by the public. Reading in groups, as well as reading alone, affords the "private" space and distance that the electronic and visual cultures seldom provide. Print technology contains the immediate promise of turning people into social agents who can manipulate and use the book, newspaper, and other forms of print communication to their own advantage. It contains the promise of emancipation. Moreover, print culture allows for the development of methods of conceptualization and social organization that might eliminate the present role of the electronic and the visual media as an oppressive force. This is the concept that gives Brecht's exhortation—"You who are starving, grab hold of the book: It's a weapon. . . ."[36]—more urgency today than it did when he wrote it over three decades ago.

Notes

1. H. Marcuse, *One Dimensional Man* (Boston: Beacon Press, 1964); M. Horkheimer, *Eclipse of Reason* (New York: Seabury Press, 1974); D. F. Noble, *America by Design* (New York: Alfred A. Knopf, 1977); S. Aronowitz, *False Promises* (New York: McGraw-Hill, 1973).

2. J. W. Freiberg, "Critical Social Theory in the American Conjuncture," in *Critical Sociology*, ed. id. (New York: Irvington Press, 1979), pp. 1–21.

3. T. Gitlin, "Media Sociology," *Theory and Society* 6 (1978): 205–53.

4. M. Hoyles, "The History and Politics of Literacy," in *The Politics of Literacy*, ed. id. (London: Writers & Readers Publishing Cooperative, 1977), pp. 14–32.

5. Gitlin, "Media Sociology," p. 205; S. Aronowitz, "Mass Culture and the Eclipse of Reason," *College English* 38: 8 (April 1977): 768.

6. Technological utopianism finds its most popular expression in M. McLuhan, *Understanding Media* (New York: Signet Books, 1963); technological fatalism is captured flawlessly in J. Ellul, *The Technological Society* (New York: Alfred A. Knopf, 1965). A critique of both of these positions can be found in H. A. Giroux, "The Politics of Technology, Culture, and Alienation," *Left Curve* 6 (Summer–Fall 1976): 32–42.

7. M. W. Apple, "Television and Cultural Reproduction," *Journal of Aesthetic Education* 12 (October 1979): 109.

8. C. Lasch, *Haven in a Heartless World* (New York: Basic Books, 1977), pp. 93–94; H. P. Dreitzel, "On the Political Meaning of Culture," in *Beyond the Crisis,* ed. N. Birnbaum (New York: Oxford University Press, 1977), pp. 83–138.

9. A. Gramsci, *Prison Notebooks* (New York: International Publishers, 1971). An excellent representative sampling of Frankfurt School writers can be found in A. Arato and E. Gebhardt, cds., *The Essential Frankfurt School Reader* (New York: Urizon Books, 1978).

10. P. Bourdieu and J. C. Passeron, *Reproduction in Education, Society and Culture* (London: Sage Publications, 1977); B. Bernstein, *Class, Codes, and Control, Vol. 3: Towards a Theory of Educational Transmissions* (London and Boston: Routledge & Kegan Paul, 1975).

11. H. P. Dreitzel, "On the Political Meaning of Culture," in *Beyond the Crisis,* ed. Birnbaum.

12. S. Ewen, *Captains of Consciousness* (New York: McGraw-Hill, 1976).

13. H. Braverman, *Labor and Monopoly Capital* (New York: Monthly Review Press, 1974); Ewen, *Captains of Consciousness,* p. 195.

14. T. McCarthy, *The Critical Theory of Jurgen Habermas* (Cambridge, Mass.: MIT Press, 1978), p. 37.

15. H. M. Enzensberger, *The Consciousness Industry* (New York: Seabury Press, 1974).

16. Ibid., p. 5.

17. Ibid., p. 16.

18. One critic claims that American society is characterized by a "falling rate of intelligence, one that represents a tendency rather than an iron law. Intellectual obsolescence annihilates memory and history so as to spur stagnating demand and production. The result is memoryless repetition—a social amnesia." In R. Jacoby, "A Falling Rate of Intelligence," *Telos* 27 (Spring 1976): 144.

19. Aronowitz, "Mass Culture," pp. 761, 770.

20. See D. Ben-Horin, "Television Without Tears," *Socialist Review* 35 (September–October): 7–35.

21. A. Gouldner, *The Dialectic of Ideology and Technology* (New York: Seabury Press, 1976).

22. Enzensberger, *Consciousness Industry,* pp. 94–128.

23. T. Gitlin, "Spotlights and Shadows: Television and the Culture of Politics," *College English* 38: 8 (April 1977): 791.

24. T. Adorno, "Television and Patterns of Mass Culture," in *Mass Culture: The Popular Arts in America,* ed. B. Rosenberg and D. Manning White (New York: Free Press of Glencoe, 1957), p. 93.

25. Aronowitz, *False Promises,* pp. 50–134.

26. Adorno, "Television and Patterns of Mass Culture," p. 484.

27. N. Fruchter, "Movement Propaganda and the Culture of the Spectacle," *Liberation* (May 1971): 4–17.

28. F. Jameson, "Class and Allegory in Contemporary Mass Culture: *Dog Day Afternoon* as a Political Film," *College English* 38: 8 (April 1977): 848.

29. Gitlin, "Spotlights and Shadows," p. 791.

30. Aronowitz, "Mass Culture and the Eclipse of Reason," p. 770. Also see D. Lazere, "Literacy and Political Consciousness: A Critique of Left Critiques," *Radical Teacher* 8 (May 1975): 20–21.

31. J. MacDonald, "Reading in an Electronic Age," in *Social Perspectives in Reading*, ed. id. (Delaware: International Reading Association, 1973), pp. 24–27; Also Enzensberg, *Consciousness Industry*, pp. 95–128.

32. Gitlin, "Media Sociology," pp. 205–53.

33. O. Negt, "Mass Media: Tools of Domination or Instruments of Liberation," *New German Critique* 14 (Spring 1978): 70.

34. Examples of this tendency have been critiqued in N. Elasser and V. P. John-Steiner, "An Interactionist Approach to Advancing Literacy," *Harvard Educational Review* 43: 3 (1977): 355–69. Representative examples of positivist approaches to literacy in reading can be found in R. C. Calfee and P. A. Drum, "Learning to Read: Theory, Research, and Practice," *Curriculum Theory* 8: 3 (Fall 1978): 183–250.

35. H. A. Giroux, "Beyond the Limits of Radical Educational Reform: Towards a Critical Theory of Education," *Journal of Curriculum Theorizing* 2:1 (1980).

36. B. Brecht, "In Praise of Learning," in *Politics of Literacy*, ed. Hoyes, p. 78.

11

Woman's Place in Man's Life Cycle

Carol Gilligan

In the second act of *The Cherry Orchard*, Lopahin, the young merchant, describes his life of hard work and success. Failing to convince Madame Ranevskaya to cut down the cherry orchard to save her estate, he will go on, in the next act, to buy it himself. He is the self-made man, who, in purchasing "the estate where grandfather and father were slaves," seeks to eradicate the "awkward, unhappy life" of the past, replacing the cherry orchard with summer cottages where coming generations "will see a new life" (Act III). Elaborating this developmental vision, he describes the image of man that underlies and supports this activity: "At times when I can't go to sleep, I think: Lord, thou gavest us immense forests, unbounded fields and the widest horizons, and living in the midst of them we should indeed be giants." At which point, Madama Ranevskaya interrupts him, saying, "You feel the need for giants—They are good only in fairy tales, anywhere else they only frighten us" (Act II).

Conceptions of the life cycle represent attempts to order and make coherent the unfolding experiences and perceptions, the changing wishes and realities of everyday life. But the truth of such conceptions depends in part on the position of the observer. The brief excerpt from Chekhov's play suggests that when the observer is a woman, the truth may be of a different sort.[1] This discrepancy in judgment between men and women is the center of my consideration.

This essay traces the extent to which psychological theories of human development, theories that have informed both educational philosophy and

Reprinted, by permission, from *Harvard Educational Review* 49: 4 (November 1979): 431–46. Copyright © 1979 by President and Fellows of Harvard College.

classroom practice, have enshrined a view of human life similar to Lopahin's while dismissing the ironic commentary in which Chekhov embeds this view. The specific issue I address is that of sex differences, and my focus is on the observation and assessment of sex differences by life-cycle theorists. In talking about sex differences, however, I risk the criticism which such generalization invariably invites. As Virginia Woolf said, when embarking on a similar endeavor: "When a subject is highly controversial—and any question about sex is that—one cannot hope to tell the truth. One can only show how one came to hold whatever opinion one does hold."[2]

At a time when efforts are being made to eradicate discrimination between the sexes in the search for equality and justice, the differences between the sexes are being rediscovered in the social sciences. This discovery occurs when theories formerly considered to be sexually neutral in their scientific objectivity are found instead to reflect a consistent observational and evaluative bias. Then the presumed neutrality of science, like that of language itself, gives way to the recognition that the categories of knowledge are human constructions. The fascination with point of view and the corresponding recognition of the relativity of truth that has informed the fiction of the twentieth century begin to infuse our scientific understanding as well when we begin to notice how accustomed we have become to seeing life through men's eyes.

A recent discovery of this sort pertains to the apparently innocent classic by Strunk and White, *The Elements of Style*. The Supreme Court ruling on the subject of discrimination in classroom texts led one teacher of English to notice that the elementary rules of English usage were being taught through examples which counterposed the birth of Napoleon, the writings of Coleridge, and statements such as, "He was an interesting talker, a man who had traveled all over the world and lived in half a dozen countries" with "Well, Susan, this is a fine mess you are in" or, less drastically, "He saw a woman, accompanied by two children, walking slowly down the road."[3]

Psychological theorists have fallen as innocently as Strunk and White into the same observational bias. Implicitly adopting the male life as the norm, they have tried to fashion women out of a masculine cloth. It all goes back, of course, to Adam and Eve, a story which shows, among other things, that if you make a woman out of a man you are bound to get into trouble. In the life cycle, as in the Garden of Eden, it is the woman who has been the deviant.

The penchant of developmental theorists to project a masculine image, and one that appears frightening to women, goes back at least to Freud, who built his theory of psychosexual development around the experiences of the male child that culminate in the Oedipus complex.[4] In the 1920s, Freud struggled to resolve the contradictions posed for his theory by the different configuration of female sexuality and the different dynamics of the young girl's early family relationships. After trying to fit women into his masculine conception, seeing them as envying that which they missed, he came instead to acknowledge, in the strength and persistence of women's pre-Oedipal attachments to their mothers, a developmental difference. However, he considered this difference in women's development to be responsible for what he saw as women's developmental failure.

Deprived by nature of the impetus for a clear-cut Oedipal resolution, women's superego, the heir to the Oedipus complex, consequently was compromised. It was never, Freud observed, "so inexorable, so impersonal, so independent of its emotional origins as we require it to be in men."[5] From this observation of difference, "that for women the level of what is ethically normal is different from what it is in men," Freud concluded that "women have less sense of justice than men, that they are less ready to submit to the great exigencies of life, that they are more often influenced in their judgments by feelings of affection and hostility."[6]

Chodorow addresses this evaluative bias in the assessment of sex differences in her attempt to account for "the reproduction within each generation of certain general and nearly universal differences that characterize masculine and feminine personality and roles."[7] Writing from a psychoanalytic perspective, she attributes these continuing differences between the sexes not to anatomy but rather to "the fact that women, universally, are largely responsible for early child care and for (at least) later female socialization."[8] Because this early social environment differs for and is experienced differently by male and female children, basic sex differences recur in personality development. As a result, "in any given society, feminine personality comes to define itself in relation and connection to other people more than masculine personality does. (In psychoanalytic terms, women are less individuated than men; they have more flexible ego boundaries.)"[9]

In her analysis, Chodorow relies primarily on Stoller's research on the development of gender identity and gender-identity disturbances. Stoller's work indicates that male and female identity, the unchanging core of personality formation, is "with rare exception firmly and irreversibly established for both sexes by the time a child is around three."[10] Given that for both sexes the primary caretaker in the first three years of life is typically female, the interpersonal dynamics of gender identity formation are different for boys and girls. Female identity formation takes place in a context of ongoing relationship as "mothers tend to experience their daughters as more like, and continuous with, themselves. Correspondingly, girls tend to remain part of the dyadic primary mother-child relationship itself. This means that a girl continues to experience herself as involved in issues of merging and separation, and in an attachment characterized by primary identification and the fusion of identification and object choice."[11]

In contrast, "mothers experience their sons as a male opposite" and, as a

result, "boys are more likely to have been pushed out of the preoedipal relationship and to have had to curtail their primary love and sense of empathic
tie with their mother."[12] Consequently, boys' development entails a "more
emphatic individuation and a more defensive firming of ego boundaries."
For boys, but not for girls, "issues of differentiation have become intertwined
with sexual issues."[13]

Thus Chodorow refutes the masculine bias of psychoanalytic theory,
claiming that the existence of sex differences in the early experiences of individuation and relationship "does not mean that women have 'weaker ego
boundaries' than men or are more prone to psychosis."[14] What it means instead is that "the earliest mode of individuation, the primary construction
of the ego and its inner object-world, the earliest conflicts and the earliest
unconscious definitions of self, the earliest threats to individuation, and the
earliest anxieties which call up defenses, all differ for boys and girls because
of differences in the character of the early mother-child relationship for
each."[15] Because of these differences, "girls emerge from this period with a
basis for 'empathy' built into their primary definition of self in a way that
boys do not."[16] Chodorow thus replaces Freud's negative and derivative description of female psychology with a more positive and direct account of
her own:

Girls emerge with a stronger basis for experiencing another's needs and feelings as
one's own (or of thinking that one is so experiencing another's needs and feelings).
Furthermore, girls do not define themselves in terms of the denial of preoedipal relational modes to the same extent as do boys. Therefore, regression to these modes tends
not to feel as much a basic threat to their ego. From very early, then, because they are
parented by a person of the same gender . . . girls come to experience themselves as
less differentiated than boys, as more continuous with and related to the external
object-world, and as differently oriented to their inner object-world as well."[17]

Consequently, "issues of dependency, in particular, are handled and experienced differently by men and women."[18] For boys and men, separation
and individuation are critically tied to gender identity since separation from
the mother is essential for the development of masculinity. "For girls and
women, by contrast, issues of femininity or feminine identity are not problematic in the same way";[19] they do not depend on the achievement of separation from the mother or on the progress of individuation. Since, in
Chodorow's analysis, masculinity is defined through separation while femininity is defined through attachment, male gender identity will be threatened
by intimacy while female gender identity will be threatened by individuation. Thus males will tend to have difficulty with relationships while females
will tend to have problems with separation. The quality of embeddedness in
social interaction and personal relationships that characterizes women's
lives in contrast to men's, however, becomes not only a descriptive difference

but also a developmental liability when the milestones of childhood and adolescent development are described by markers of increasing separation. Then women's failure to separate becomes by definition a failure to develop.

The sex differences in personality formation that Chodorow delineates in her analysis of early childhood relationships as well as the bias she points out in the evaluation of these differences, reappear in the middle childhood years in the studies of children's games. Children's games have been considered by Mead and Piaget as the crucible of social development during the school years.[20] In games children learn to take the role of the other and come to see themselves through another's eyes. In games they learn respect for rules and come to understand the ways rules can be made and changed.

Lever, considering the peer group to be the agent of socialization during the elementary school years and play to be a major activity of socialization at that time, set out to discover whether there were sex differences in the games that children play.[21] Studying 181 fifth-grade, white, middle-class, Connecticut children, ages ten and eleven, she observed the organization and structure of their playtime activities. She watched the children as they played during the school recess, lunch, and in physical education class, and, in addition, kept diaries of their accounts as to how they spent their out-of-school time.

From this study, Lever reports the following sex differences: boys play more out of doors than girls do; boys more often play in large and age-heterogeneous groups; they play competitive games more often than girls do; and their games last longer than girls' games.[22] The last is in some ways the most interesting finding. Boys' games appeared to last longer not only because they required a higher level of skill and were thus less likely to become boring, but also because when disputes arose in the course of a game, the boys were able to resolve the disputes more effectively than the girls: "During the course of this study, boys were seen quarrelling all the time, but not once was a game terminated because of a quarrel and no game was interrupted for more than seven minutes. In the gravest debates, the final word was always to 'repeat the play,' generally followed by a chorus of 'cheater's proof.' "[23] In fact, it seemed that the boys enjoyed the legal debates as much as they did the game itself, and even marginal players of lesser size or skill participated equally in these recurrent squabbles. In contrast, the eruption of disputes among girls tended to end the game.

Thus Lever extends and corroborates the observations reported by Piaget[24] in his naturalistic study of the rules of the game, where he found boys becoming increasingly fascinated with the legal elaboration of rules and the development of fair procedures for adjudicating conflicts, a fascination that, he noted, did not hold for girls. Girls, Piaget observed, had a more "pragmatic" attitude toward rules, "regarding a rule as good as long as the game repaid it."[25] As a result, he considered girls to be more tolerant in their attitudes toward rules, more willing to make exceptions, and more easily reconciled to innovations. However, and presumably as a result, he concluded that the legal sense which he considered essential to moral development "is far less developed in little girls than in boys."[26]

This same bias that led Piaget to equate male development with child development also colors Lever's work. The assumption that shapes her discussion of results is that the male model is the better one. It seems, in any case, more adaptive since as Lever points out it fits the requirements Riesman describes for success in modern corporate life.[27] In contrast, the sensitivity and care for the feelings of others that girls develop through their primarily dyadic play relationships have little market value and can even impede professional success. Lever clearly implies that, given the realities of adult life, if a girl does not want to be dependent on men, she will have to learn to play like a boy.

Since Piaget argues that children learn the respect for rules necessary for moral development by playing rule-bound games, and Kohlberg adds that these lessons are most effectively learned through the opportunities for role-taking that arise in the course of resolving disputes, the moral lessons inherent in girls' play appear to be fewer than for boys.[28] Traditional girls' games like jump rope and hopscotch are turn-taking games where competition is indirect in that one person's success does not necessarily signify another's failure. Consequently, disputes requiring adjudication are less likely to occur. In fact, most of the girls whom Lever interviewed claimed that when a quarrel broke out, they ended the game. Rather than elaborating a system of rules for resolving disputes, girls directed their efforts instead toward sustaining affective ties.

Lever concludes that from the games they play boys learn both independence and the organization skills necessary for coordinating the activities of large and diverse groups of people. By participating in controlled and socially approved competitive situations, they learn to deal with competition in a relatively forthright manner—to play with their enemies and compete with their friends, all in accordance with the rules of the game. In contrast, girls' play tends to occur in smaller, more intimate groups, often the best-friend dyad, and in private places. This play replicates the social pattern of primary human relationships in that its organization is more cooperative and points less toward learning to take the role of the generalized other than it does toward the development of the empathy and sensitivity necessary for taking the role of the particular other.

Chodorow's analysis of sex differences in personality formation in early childhood is thus extended by Lever's observations of sex differences in the play activities of middle childhood. Together these accounts suggest that boys and girls arrive at puberty with a different interpersonal orientation and a different range of social experiences. While Sullivan,[29] tracing the sequence of male development, posits the experience of a close same-sex friendship in preadolescence as necessary for the subsequent integration of sexuality and intimacy, no corresponding account is available to describe girls' development at this critical juncture. Instead, since adolescence is considered a crucial time for separation and individuation, the period of "the second individuation process,"[30] it has been in adolescence that female development has appeared most divergent and thus most problematic.

"Puberty," Freud said, "which brings about so great an accession of libido in boys, is marked in girls by a fresh wave of repression,"[31] necessary for the transformation of the young girls' "masculine sexuality" into the "specifically feminine" sexuality of her adulthood. Freud posits this transformation on the girl's acknowledgement and acceptance of "the fact of her castration." In his account puberty brings for girls a new awareness of "the wound to her narcissism" and leads her to develop, "like a scar, a sense of inferiority."[32] Since adolescence is, in Erikson's expansion of Freud's psychoanalytic account, the time when the ego takes on an identity which confirms the individual in relation to society, the girl arrives at this juncture in development either psychologically at risk or with a different agenda.

The problem that female adolescence presents for psychologists of human development is apparent in Erikson's account. Erikson charts eight stages of psychosocial development in which adolescence is the fifth.[33] The task of this stage is to forge a coherent sense of self, to verify an identity that can span the discontinuity of puberty and make possible the adult capacity to love and to work. The preparation for the successful resolution of the adolescent identity crisis is delineated in Erikson's description of the preceding four stages. If in infancy the initial crisis of trust versus mistrust generates enough hope to sustain the child through the arduous life cycle that lies ahead, the task at hand clearly becomes one of individuation. Erikson's second stage centers on the crisis of autonomy versus shame and doubt, the walking child's emerging sense of separateness and agency. From there, development goes on to the crisis of initiative versus guilt, successful resolution of which represents a further move in the direction of autonomy. Next, following the inevitable disappointment of the magical wishes of the Oedipal period, the child realizes with respect to his parents that to bear them he must first join them and learn to do what they do so well. Thus in the middle childhood years, development comes to hinge on the crisis of industry versus inferiority, as the demonstration of competence becomes critical to the child's developing self-esteem. This is the time when children strive to learn and master the technology of their culture in order to recognize themselves and be recognized as capable of becoming adults. Next comes adolescence, the celebration of the autonomous, initiating, industrious self through the forging of an identity based on an ideology that can support and justify adult commitments. But about whom is Erikson talking?

Once again it turns out to be the male child—the coming generation of men like George Bernard Shaw, William James, Martin Luther, and Mahatma Gandhi—who provide Erikson with his most vivid illustrations. For the woman, Erikson says, the sequence is a bit different.[34] She holds her identity in abeyance as she prepares to attract the man by whose name she will be known, by whose status she will be defined, the man who will rescue her from emptiness and loneliness by filling "the inner space."[35] While for men, identity precedes intimacy and generativity in the optimal cycle of human separation and attachment, for women these tasks seem instead to be fused. Intimacy precedes, or rather goes along with, identity as the female comes to know herself as she is known, through her relationships with others.

Two things are essential to note at this point. The first is that, despite Erikson's observation of sex differences, his chart of life-cycle stages remains unchanged: identity continues to precede intimacy as the male diagonal continues to define his life-cycle conception. The second is that in the male life cycle there is little preparation for the intimacy of the first adult stage. Only the initial stage of trust versus mistrust suggests the type of mutuality that Erikson means by intimacy and generativity and Freud by genitality: The rest is separateness, with the result that development itself comes to be identified with separation and attachments appear as developmental impediments, as we have repeatedly found to be the case in the assessment of women.

Erikson's description of male identity as forged in relation to the world and of female identity as awakened in a relationship of intimacy with another person, however controversial, is hardly new. In Bettelheim's discussion of fairy tales in *The Uses of Enchantment*[36] an identical portrayal appears. While Bettelheim argues, in refutation of those critics who see in fairy tales a sexist literature, that opposite models exist and could readily be found, nevertheless the ones upon which he focuses his discussion of adolescence conform to the pattern we have begun to observe.

The dynamics of male adolescence are illustrated archetypically by the conflict between father and son in "The Three Languages."[37] Here a son, considered hopelessly stupid by his father, is given one last chance at education and sent for a year to study with a famous master. But when he returns, all he has learned is "what the dogs bark."[38] After two further attempts of this sort, the father gives up in disgust and orders his servants to take the child into the forest and kill him. The servants, however, those perpetual rescuers of disowned and abandoned children, take pity on the child and decide simply to leave him in the forest. From there, his wanderings take him to a land beset by furious dogs whose barking permits nobody to rest and who periodically devour one of the inhabitants. Now it turns out that our hero has learned just the right thing: he can talk with the dogs and is able to quiet them, thus restoring peace to the land. The other knowledge he acquires serves him equally well, and he emerges triumphant from his adolescent confrontation with his father, a giant of the life-cycle conception.

In contrast, the dynamics of female adolescence are depicted through the telling of a very different story. In the world of the fairy tale, the girl's first bleeding is followed by a period of intense passivity in which nothing seems to be happening. Yet in the deep sleep of Snow White and Sleeping Beauty, Bettelheim sees that inner concentration which he considers to be the necessary counterpart to the activity of adventure. The adolescent heroines awaken from their sleep not to conquer the world but to marry the prince. Their feminine identity is inwardly and interpersonally defined. As in Erikson's observation, for women, identity and intimacy are more intricately conjoined. The sex differences depicted in the world of the fairy tales, like the fantasy of the woman warrior in Maxine Hong Kingston's[39] recent autobiographical novel (which in turn echoes the old stories of Troilus and Cressida and Tancred and Chlorinda) indicate repeatedly that active adventure is a male activity, and if women are to embark on such endeavors, they must at least dress like men.

These observations about sex difference support the conclusion reached by McClelland that "sex role turns out to be one of the most important determinants of human behavior. Psychologists have found sex differences in their studies from the moment they started doing empirical research."[40] But since it is difficult to say "different" without saying "better" or "worse," and since there is a tendency to construct a single scale of measurement, and since that scale has been derived and standardized on the basis of men's observations and interpretations of research data predominantly or exclusively drawn from studies of males, psychologists have tended, in McClelland's words, "to regard male behavior as the 'norm' and female behavior as some kind of deviation from that norm."[41] Thus when women do not conform to the standards of psychological expectation, the conclusion has generally been that something is wrong with the woman.

What Horner found to be wrong with women was the anxiety they showed about competitive achievement.[42] From the beginning, research on human motivation using the Thematic Apperception Test (TAT) was plagued by evidence of sex differences which appeared to confuse and complicate data analysis. The TAT presents for interpretation an ambiguous cue—a picture about which a story is to be written or a brief story stem to be completed. Such stories in reflecting projective imagination are considered to reveal the ways in which people construe what they perceive—that is, the concepts and interpretations they bring to their experience and thus presumably the kind of sense that they make of their lives. Prior to Horner's work, it was clear that women made a different kind of sense than men of situations of competitive achievement, that in some way they saw the situation differently or the situation aroused in them some different response.

On the basis of his studies of men, McClelland had divided the concept of achievement motivation into what appeared to be its two logical components, a motive to approach success ("hope success") and a motive to avoid failure ("fear failure").[43] When Horner began to analyze the problematic projective data on female achievement motivation, she identified as a third category the unlikely motivation to avoid success ("fear success").[44] Women appeared to have a problem with competitive achievement, and that problem seemed, in Horner's interpretation, to emanate from a perceived conflict between femininity and success, the dilemma of the female adolescent who struggles to integrate her feminine aspirations and the identifications of her early childhood with the more masculine competence she has acquired at school. Thus Horner reports, "When success is likely or possible, threatened by the negative consequences they expect to follow success, young women become anxious and their positive achievement strivings become thwarted."[45] She concludes that this fear exists because, for most women, the anticipation of success in competitive achievement activity, especially against men, produced anticipation of certain negative consequences, for example, threat of social rejection and loss of femininity.

It is, however, possible to view such conflicts about success in a different light. Sassen, on the basis of her reanalysis of the data presented in Horner's thesis, suggests that the conflicts expressed by the women might instead indicate "a heightened perception of the 'other side' of competitive success, that is, the great emotional costs of success achieved through competition, or an understanding which, while confused, indicates an awareness that something is rotten in the state in which success is defined as having better grades than everyone else."[46] Sassen points out that Horner found success anxiety to be present in women only when achievement was directly competitive, that is, where one person's success was at the expense of another's failure.

From Horner's examples of fear of success, it is impossible to differentiate between neurotic or realistic anxiety about the consequences of achievement, the questioning of conventional definitions of success, or the discovery of personal goals other than conventional success. The construction of the problem posed by success as a problem of identity and ideology that appears in Horner's illustrations, if taken at face value rather than assumed to be derivative, suggests Erikson's distinction between a conventional and neohumanist identity, or, in cognitive terms, the distinction between conventional and postconventional thought.[47]

In his elaboration of the identity crisis, Erikson discusses the life of George Bernard Shaw to illustrate the young person's sense of being co-opted prematurely by success in a career he cannot wholeheartedly endorse. Shaw at seventy, reflecting upon his life, describes his crisis at the age of twenty as one caused not by lack of success or the absence of recognition, but by too much of both:

I made good in spite of myself, and found, to my dismay, that Business, instead of expelling me as the worthless imposter I was, was fastening upon me with no intention of letting me go. Behold me, therefore, in my twentieth year, with a business training, in an occupation which I detested as cordially as any sane person lets himself detest anything he cannot escape from. In March, 1876, I broke loose.[48]

At which point Shaw settled down to study and to write as he pleased. Hardly interpreted as evidence of developmental difficulty, of neurotic anxiety about achievement and competition, Shaw's refusal suggested to Erikson, "the extraordinary workings of an extraordinary personality coming to the fore."[49]

We might on these grounds begin to ask not why women have conflicts about succeeding but why men show such readiness to adopt and celebrate a rather narrow vision of success. Remembering Piaget's observation, corroborated by Lever, that boys in their games are concerned more with rules while girls are more concerned with relationships, often at the expense of the game itself; remembering also that, in Chodorow's analysis, men's social orientation is positional and women's orientation is personal, we begin to understand why, when Anne becomes John in Horner's tale of competitive success and the stories are written by men, fear of success tends to disappear. John is considered by other men to have played by the rules and won. He has the *right* to feel good about his success. Confirmed in his sense of his own identity as separate from those who, compared to him, are less competent, his positional sense of self is affirmed. For Anne, it is possible that the position she could obtain by being at the top of her medical school class may not, in fact, be what she wants.

"It is obvious," Virginia Woolf said, "that the values of women differ very often from the values which have been made by the other sex."[50] Yet, she adds, it is the masculine values that prevail. As a result, women come to question the "normality" of their feelings and to alter their judgments in deference to the opinion of others. In the nineteenth-century novels written by women, Woolf sees at work "a mind slightly pulled from the straight, altering its clear vision in the anger and confusion of deference to external authority."[51] The same deference that Woolf identifies in nineteenth-century fiction can be seen as well in the judgments of twentieth-century women. Women's reluctance to make moral judgments, the difficulty they experience in finding or speaking publicly in their own voice, emerge repeatedly in the form of qualification and self-doubt, in intimations of a divided judgment, a public and private assessment which are fundamentally at odds.[52]

Yet the deference and confusion that Woolf criticizes in women derive from the values she sees as their strength. Women's deference is rooted not only in their social circumstances but also in the substance of their moral concern. Sensitivity to the needs of others and the assumption of responsibility for taking care lead women to attend to voices other than their own and to include in their judgment other points of view. Women's moral weakness, manifest in an apparent diffusion and confusion of judgment, is thus inseparable from women's moral strength, an overriding concern with relationships and responsibilities. The reluctance to judge can itself be indicative of the same care and concern for others that infuses the psychology of women's development and is responsible for what is characteristically seen as problematic in its nature.

Thus women not only define themselves in a context of human relationship but also judge themselves in terms of their ability to care. Woman's place in man's life cycle has been that of nurturer, caretaker, and helpmate, the weaver of those networks of relationships on which she in turn relies. While women have thus taken care of men, however, men have in their theories of psychological development tended either to assume or devalue that care. The focus on individuation and individual achievement that has dominated the description of child and adolescent development has recently been extended to the depiction of adult development as well. Levinson in his study, *The Seasons of a Man's Life*,[53] elaborates a view of adult development in which relationships are portrayed as a means to an end of individual achievement and success. In the critical relationships of early adulthood, the "Mentor" and the "Special Woman" are defined by the role they play in facilitating the man's realization of his "Dream." Along similar lines Vaillant, in his study of men,[54] considers altruism a defense, characteristic of mature ego functioning and associated with successful "adaptation to life," but conceived as derivative rather than primary in contrast to Chodorow's analysis, in which empathy is considered "built-in" to the woman's primary definition of self.

The discovery now being celebrated by men in mid-life of the importance of intimacy, relationships, and care is something that women have known from the beginning. However, because that knowledge has been considered "intuitive" or "instinctive," a function of anatomy coupled with destiny, psychologists have neglected to describe its development. In my research, I have found that women's moral development centers on the elaboration of that knowledge. Women's moral development thus delineates a critical line of psychological development whose importance for both sexes becomes apparent in the intergenerational framework of a life-cycle perspective. While the subject of moral development provides the final illustration of the reiterative pattern in the observation and assessment of sex differences in the literature on human development, it also indicates more particularly why the nature and significance of women's development has for so long been obscured and considered shrouded in mystery.

The criticism that Freud makes of women's sense of justice, seeing it as compromised in its refusal of blind impartiality, reappears not only in the work of Piaget[55] but also in that of Kohlberg.[56] While girls are an aside in Piaget's account of *The Moral Judgment of the Child,*[57] an odd curiosity to whom he devotes four brief entries in an index that omits "boys" altogether because "the child" is assumed to be male, in Kohlberg's research on moral development, females simply do not exist. Kohlberg's six stages that describe the development of moral judgment from childhood to adulthood were derived empirically from a longitudinal study of eighty-four boys from the United States. While Kohlberg[58] claims universality for his stage sequence and considers his conception of justice as fairness to have been naturalistically derived, those groups not included in his original sample rarely reach his higher stages.[59] Prominent among those found to be deficient in moral development when measured by Kohlberg's scale are women, whose judgments on his scale seemed to exemplify the third stage in his six-stage sequence. At this stage morality is conceived in terms of relationships, and goodness is equated with helping and pleasing others. This concept of goodness was considered by Kohlberg and Kramer to be functional in the lives of mature women insofar as those lives took place in the home and thus were relationally bound.[60] Only if women were to go out of the house to enter the arena of male activity would they realize the inadequacy of their Stage Three perspective and progress like men toward higher stages where morality is societally or universally defined in accordance with a conception of justice as fairness.

In this version of human development, however, a particular conception of maturity is assumed, based on the study of men's lives and reflecting the importance of individuation in their development. When one begins instead with women and derives developmental constructs from their lives, then a different conception of development emerges, the expansion and elaboration of which can also be traced through stages that comprise a developmental sequence. In Loevinger's test for measuring ego development that was drawn from studies of females,[61] fifteen of the thirty-six sentence stems to complete begin with the subject of human relationships (for example, "Raising a family. . . . ; If my mother. . . . ; Being with other people. . . . ; When I am with a man. . . . ; When a child won't join in group activities. . . .").[62] Thus ego development is described and measured by Loevinger through conception of relationships as well as by the concept of identity that measures the progress of individuation.

Research on moral judgment has shown that when the categories of women's thinking are examined in detail[63] the outline of a moral conception different from that described by Freud, Piaget, or Kohlberg begins to emerge and to inform a different description of moral development. In this conception, the moral problem is seen to arise from conflicting responsibilities rather than from competing rights and to require for its resolution a mode of thinking that is contextual and inductive rather than formal and abstract.

This conception of morality as fundamentally concerned with the capacity for understanding and care also develops through a structural progression of increasing differentiation and integration. This progression witnesses the shift from an egocentric through a societal to the universal moral perspective that Kohlberg described in his research on men, but it does so in different terms. The shift in women's judgment from an egocentric to a conventional to a principled ethical understanding is articulated through their use of a distinct moral language, in which the terms "selfishness" and "responsibility" define the moral problem as one of care. Moral development then consists of the progressive reconstruction of this understanding toward a more adequate conception of care.

The concern with caring centers moral development around the progressive differentiation and integration that characterize the evolution of the understanding of relationships just as the conception of fairness delineates the progressive differentiation and balancing of individual rights. Within the responsibility orientation, the infliction of hurt is the center of moral concern and is considered immoral whether or not it can otherwise be construed as fair or unfair. The reiterative use of the language of selfishness and responsibility to define the moral problem as a problem of care sets women apart from the men whom Kohlberg studied and from whose thinking he derived his six stages. This different construction of the moral problem by women may be seen as the critical reason for their failure to develop within the constraints of Kohlberg's system.

Regarding all constructions of responsibility as evidence of a conventional moral understanding, Kohlberg defines the highest stages of moral development as deriving from a reflective understanding of human rights. That the morality of rights differs from the morality of responsibility in its emphasis on separation rather than attachment, in its consideration of the individual rather than the relationship as primary, is illustrated by two quotations that exemplify these different orientations. The first comes from a twenty-five-year-old man who participated in Kohlberg's longitudinal study. The quotation itself is cited by Kohlberg to illustrate the principled conception of morality that he scores as "integrated [Stage] Five judgment, possibly moving to Stage Six."

[What does the word morality mean to you?] Nobody in the world knows the answer. I think it is recognizing the right of the individual, the rights of other individuals, not interfering with those rights. Act as fairly as you would have them treat you. I think it is basically to preserve the human being's right to existence. I think that is the most important. Secondly, the human being's right to do as he pleases, again without interfering with somebody else's rights.

[How have your views on morality changed since the last interview?] I think I am more aware of an individual's rights now. I used to be looking at it strictly from my point of view, just for me. Now I think I am more aware of what the individual has a right to.[64]

"Clearly," Kohlberg states,

these responses represent attainment of the third level of moral theory. Moving to a perspective outside of that of his society, he identifies morality with justice (fairness, rights, the Golden Rule), with recognition of the rights of others as these are defined, naturally or intrinsically. The human's right to do as he pleases without interfering with somebody else's rights is a formula defining rights prior to social legislation and opinion which defines what society may expect rather than being defined by it.[65]

The second quotation comes from my interview with a woman, also twenty-five years old and at the time of the interview a third-year student at Harvard Law School. She described her conception of morality as follows:

[Is there really some correct solution to moral problems or is everybody's opinion equally right?] No., I don't think everybody's opinion is equally right. I think that in some situations . . . there may be opinions that are equally valid and one could conscientiously adopt one of several courses of action. But there are other situations which I think there are right and wrong answers, that sort of inhere in the nature of existence, of all individuals here who need to live with each other to live. We need to depend on each other and hopefully it is not only a physical need but a need of fulfillment in ourselves, that a person's life is enriched by cooperating with other people and striving to live in harmony with everybody else, and to that end, there are right and wrong, there are things which promote that end and that move away from it, and in that way, it is possible to choose in certain cases among different courses of action, that obviously promote or harm that goal.

[Is there a time in the past when you would have thought about these things differently?] Oh, yah. I think that I went through a time when I thought that things were pretty relative, that I can't tell you what to do and you can't tell me what to do, because you've got your conscience and I've got mine. . . .

[When was that?] When I was in high school. I guess that it just sort of dawned on me that my own ideas changed and because my own judgments changed, I felt I couldn't judge another person's judgment. . . . but now I think even when it is only the person himself who is going to be affected, I say it is wrong to the extent it doesn't cohere with what I know about human nature and what I know about you, and just from what I think is true about the operation of the universe, I could say I think you are making a mistake.

[What led you to change, do you think?] Just seeing more of life, just recognizing that there are an awful lot of things that are common among people . . . there are certain things that you come to learn promote a better life and better relationships and more personal fulfillment than other things that in general tend to do the opposite and the things that promote these things, you would call morally right.

These responses also represent a reflective reconstruction of morality

following a period of relativistic questioning and doubt, but the reconstruction of moral understanding is based not on the primacy and universality of individual rights, but rather on what she herself describes as a "very
strong sense of being responsible to the world." Within this construction,
the moral dilemma changes from how to exercise one's rights without interfering with the rights of others to how "to lead a moral life which includes obligations to myself and my family and people in general." The
problem then becomes one of limiting responsibilities without abandoning
moral concern. When asked to describe herself, this woman says that she
values

having other people that I am tied to and also having people that I am responsible
to. I have a very strong sense of being responsible to the world, that I can't just live
for my enjoyment, but just the fact of being in the world gives me an obligation to
do what I can to make the world a better place to live in, no matter how small a scale
that may be on.

Thus while Kohlberg's subject worries about people interfering with one
another's rights, this woman worries about "the possibility of omission, of
your not helping others when you could help them."

The issue this law student raises is addressed by Loevinger's fifth "autonomous" stage of ego development. The terms of its resolution lie in achieving partial autonomy from an excessive sense of responsibility by recognizing that other people have responsibility for their own destiny.[66] The
autonomous stage in Loevinger's account witnesses a relinquishing of moral
dichotomies and their replacement with "a feeling for the complexity and
multifaceted character of real people and real situations."[67]

Whereas the rights conception of morality that informs Kohlberg's
principled level (Stages Five and Six) is geared to arriving at an objectively
fair or just resolution to the moral dilemmas to which "all rational men can
agree," the responsibility conception focuses instead on the limitations of
any particular resolution and describes the conflicts that remain. This limi-
tation of moral judgment and choice is described by a woman in her thirties
when she says that her guiding principle in making moral decisions has to
do with "responsibility and caring about yourself and others, not just a principle that once you take hold of, you settle [the moral problem]. The principle put into practice is still going to leave you with conflict."

Given the substance and orientation of these women's judgments, it becomes clear why a morality of rights and noninterference may appear to
women as frightening in its potential justification of indifference and un-
concern. At the same time, however, it also becomes clear why, from a male
perspective, women's judgments appear inconclusive and diffuse, given
their insistent contextual relativism. Women's moral judgments thus eluci-

date the pattern that we have observed in the differences between the sexes, but provide an alternative conception of maturity by which these differences can be developmentally considered. The psychology of women that has consistently been described as distinctive in its greater orientation toward relationships of interdependence implies a more contextual mode of judgment and a different moral understanding. Given the differences in women's conceptions of self and morality, it is not surprising that women bring to the life cycle a different point of view and that they order human experience in terms of different priorities.

The myth of Demeter and Persephone, which McClelland cites as exemplifying the feminine attitude toward power, was associated with the Eleusinian Mysteries celebrated in ancient Greece for over two thousand years.[68] As told in the Homeric *Hymn to Demeter*,[69] the story of Persephone indicates the strengths of "interdependence, building up resources and giving"[70] that McClelland found in his research on power motivation to characterize the mature feminine style. Although, McClelland says, "it is fashionable to conclude that no one knows what went on in the Mysteries, it is known that they were probably the most important religious ceremonies, even partly on the historical record, which were organized by and for women, especially at the onset before men by means of the cult of Dionysius began to take them over."[71] Thus McClelland regards the myth as "a special presentation of feminine psychology."[72] It is, as well, a life-cycle story par excellence.

Persephone, the daughter of Demeter, while out playing in the meadows with her girl friends, sees a beautiful narcissus which she runs to pick. As she does so, the earth opens and she is snatched away by Pluto, who takes her to his underworld kingdom. Demeter, goddess of the earth, so mourns the loss of her daughter that she refuses to allow anything to grow. The crops that sustain life on earth shrivel and dry up, killing men and animals alike, until Zeus takes pity on man's suffering and persuades his brother to return Persephone to her mother. But before she leaves, Persephone eats some pomegranate seeds which insures that she will spend six months of every year in the underworld.

The elusive mystery of women's development lies in its recognition of the continuing importance of attachment in the human life cycle. Woman's place in man's life cycle has been to protect that recognition while the developmental litany intones the celebration of separation, autonomy, individuation, and natural rights. The myth of Persephone speaks directly to the distortion in this view by reminding us that narcissism leads to death, that the fertility of the earth is in some mysterious way tied to the continuation of the mother-daughter relationship, and that the life cycle itself arises from an alternation between the world of women and that of men. My intention in this essay has been to suggest that only when life-cycle theorists equally divide their attention and begin to live with women as they have lived with men will their vision encompass the experience of both sexes and their theories become correspondingly more fertile.

Notes

1. A. Chekhov, *The Cherry Orchard*, trans. Stark Young (New York: Modern Library, 1956). Originally published, 1904.

2. V. Woolf, *A Room of One's Own* (New York: Harcourt, Brace & World, 1929), p. 4.

3. W. Strunk and E. B. White, *The Elements of Style* (New York: Macmillan, 1959), pp. 3–8.

4. S. Freud, "Three Essays on Sexuality," in *The Standard Edition of the Complete Psychological Works of Sigmund Freud*, vol. 7, ed. J. Strachey (London: Hogarth Press, 1961). Originally published, 1905.

5. S. Freud, "Some Psychical Consequences of the Anatomical Distinction Between the Sexes," in *The Standard Edition of the Complete Psychological Works of Sigmund Freud*, vol. 19, ed. J. Strachey (London: Hogarth Press, 1961). Originally published, 1925, p. 257.

6. Ibid., pp. 257–58.

7. N. Chodorow, "Family Structure and Feminine Personality," in *Women, Culture and Society*, ed. M. Rosaldo and L. Lamphere (Stanford, Calif.: Stanford University Press, 1974), p. 43.

8. Ibid., p. 43.

9. Ibid., p. 44.

10. N. Chodorow, *The Reproduction of Mothering* (Berkeley: University of California Press, 1978), p. 150.

11. Ibid., p. 166.

12. Ibid.

13. Ibid., p. 167.

14. Ibid.

15. Ibid.

16. Ibid.

17. Ibid.

18. Chodorow, "Family Structure and Feminine Personality," p. 44.

19. Ibid.

20. G. H. Mead, *Mind, Self and Society* (Chicago: University of Chicago Press, 1934); J. Piaget, *The Moral Judgment of the Child* (New York: Free Press, 1965). Originally published, 1932.

21. J. Lever, "Sex Differences in the Games Children Play," *Social Problems* (1976): 23, 478–87.

22. Ibid.

23. Ibid., p. 482.

24. Piaget, *Moral Judgment of the Child*.

25. Ibid., p. 83.

26. Ibid., p. 77.

27. D. Riesman, *The Lonely Crowd* (New Haven, Conn.: Yale University Press, 1961).

28. L. Kohlberg, "From Is to Ought: How to Commit the Naturalistic Fallacy and Get Away with It in the Study of Moral Development," in *Cognitive Development and Epistemology,* ed. T. Mischel (New York: Academic Press, 1971).

29. H. S. Sullivan, *The Interpersonal Theory of Psychiatry* (New York: W. W. Norton & Co., 1953).

30. P. Blos, "The Second Individuation Process of Adolescence," in *The Psychoanalytic Study of the Child,* vol. 22, ed. A. Freud (New York: International Universities Press, 1967).

31. Freud, "Three Essays on Sexuality," p. 220.

32. Freud, "Distinction Between the Sexes," p. 253.

33. E. Erikson, *Childhood and Society* (New York: W. W. Norton & Co., 1950).

34. E. Erikson, *Identity: Youth and Crisis* (New York: W. W. Norton & Co., 1968).

35. Ibid.

36. B. Bettelheim, *The Uses of Enchantment* (New York: Alfred A. Knopf, 1976).

37. Ibid.

38. Ibid., p. 97.

39. M. H. Kingston, *The Woman Warrior* (New York: Vintage Books, 1977).

40. D. McClelland, *Power: The Inner Experience* (New York: Irvington Publishers, 1975), p. 81.

41. Ibid.

42. M. Horner, "Toward an Understanding of Achievement-Related Conflicts in Women," *Journal of Social Issues* 28: 2 (1972): 157–74.

43. D. McClelland, *The Achieving Society* (New York: Van Nostrand, 1961).

44. Horner, "Achievement-Related Conflicts in Women."

45. Ibid., p. 171.

46. G. Sassen, "Success Anxiety in Women: A Constructivist Theory of Its Sources and Its Significance," *Harvard Educational Review* 50 (1980): 13–25.

47. J. Loevinger and R. Wessler, *The Meaning and Measurement of Ego Development* (San Francisco: Jossey-Bass, 1970); B. Inhelder and J. Piaget, *The Growth of Logical Thinking from Childhood to Adolescence* (New York: Basic Books, 1958); Kohlberg, "From Is to Ought"; W. Perry, *Forms of Intellectual and Ethical Development in the College Years* (New York: Holt, Rinehart & Winston, 1968).

48. Erikson, *Identity: Youth and Crisis,* p. 144.

49. Ibid.

50. Woolf, *A Room of One's Own,* p. 76.

51. Ibid., p. 77.

52. C. Gilligan, "In a Different Voice: Women's Conceptions of the Self and of Morality," *Harvard Educational Review* 47 (1977): 481–517.

53. D. Levinson, *The Seasons of a Man's Life* (New York: Alfred A. Knopf, 1978).

54. G. Vaillant, *Adaptation to Life* (Boston: Little, Brown, 1977).

55. Piaget, *Moral Judgment of the Child.*

56. L. Kohlberg, "The Development of Modes of Thinking and Choices in Years 10 to 16" (Ph. D. dissertation, University of Chicago, 1958).

57. Piaget, *Moral Judgment of the Child.*

58. L. Kohlberg, *Continuities and Discontinuities in Childhood and Adult Moral Development Revisited* (Unpublished manuscript, Harvard University, 1973).

59. C. P. Edwards, "Societal Complexity and Moral Development: A Kenyan

Study," *Ethos* 3 (1975): 505–27; Gilligan, "In a Different Voice."

60. L. Kohlberg and R. Kramer, "Continuities and Discontinuities in Childhood and Adult Moral Development," *Human Development* 12 (1969): 93–120.

61. Loevinger and Wessler, *Measurement of Ego Development.*

62. Ibid., p. 141.

63. Gilligan, "In a Different Voice."

64. Kohlberg, *Childhood and Adult Moral Development Revisited,* p. 29.

65. Ibid., pp. 29–30.

66. Loevinger and Wessler, *Measurement of Ego Development.*

67. Ibid., p. 6.

68. McClelland, *Power: The Inner Experience,* p. 96.

69. *The Homeric Hymn,* trans. C. Boer (Chicago: Swallow Press, 1971).

70. McClelland, *Power: The Inner Experience,* p. 96.

71. Ibid.

72. Ibid.

12

IQ in the United States Class Structure

Samuel Bowles and Herbert Gintis

Introduction

The 1960s and early 1970s have witnessed a sustained political assault against economic inequality in the United States. Blacks, women, welfare recipients, and young rank-and-file workers have brought the issue of inequality into the streets, forced it onto the front pages, and thrown it into the legislature and the courts. The dominant response of the privileged has been concern, tempered by a hardy optimism that social programs could be devised to reduce inequality, alleviate social distress, and bring the nation back from the brink of chaos. This optimism has been at once a reflection of and rooted in a pervasive body of liberal social thought, as codified in modern mainstream economics and sociology. At the core of this conventional wisdom in the social sciences is the conviction that in the advanced capitalist system of the United States significant progress toward equality of economic opportunity can be achieved through a combination of enlightened persuasion and social reforms, particularly in the sphere of education and vocational training.

The disappointing results of the War on Poverty, the apparent lack of impact of compensatory education, and in a larger sense the persistence of poverty and racism in the United States have dented the optimism of the liberal social scientist and the liberal policymaker alike. The massive and well-documented failure of the social reformers of the 1960s invited a conservative reaction, most notably in the resurgence of the genetic interpretation of IQ.

Reprinted, by permission of the authors, from *Social Policy* 3 (November/December 1972, January/February 1973): 65–96.

Sensing the opportunity afforded by the liberal debacle, Arthur Jensen began his celebrated article on the heritability of IQ with "Compensatory education has been tried, and apparently it has failed." In the debate that has ensued, an interpretation of the role of IQ in the class structure has been elaborated: the poor are poor because they are intellectually incompetent; their incompetence is particularly intractable because it is rooted in the genetic structure inherited from their poor and also intellectually deficient parents.[1] An explanation of the intergenerational reproduction of the class structure is thus found in the heritability of IQ. The idea is not new: an earlier wave of genetic interpretations of economic and ethnic inequality followed in the wake of the purportedly egalitarian but largely unsuccessful educational reforms of the Progressive Era.[2]

The revival of the debate on the genetic interpretation of economic inequality is thus firmly rooted in the fundamental social struggles of the past decade. Yet the debate has been curiously superficial. "The most important . . . that we can know about a man," says Louis Wirth, "is what he takes for granted, and the elemental and important facts about a society are those that are seldom debated and generally regarded as settled."[3] This essay questions the undisputed assumption underlying both sides of the recently revised IQ controversy: that IQ is of basic importance to economic success.

Amid a hundred-page statistical barrage relating to the genetic and environmental components of intelligence, the initiator of the most recent exchange saw fit to devote only three sparse and ambiguous pages to this issue.[4] Later advocates of the "genetic school" have considered this "elemental fact," if anything, less necessary of support.[5] Nor has their choice of battleground proved injudicious: to our knowledge not one of their environmentalist critics has taken the economic importance of IQ any less for granted.[6]

This review inspires one highly perplexing question: Why have American social scientists so consistently refused to question the actual role of intelligence in occupational success and income determination, in spite of the fact that the empirical data necessary for such an endeavor are well known?

Our findings, based for the most part on widely available published data, document the fact that IQ is not an important cause of economic success: nor is the inheritance of IQ the reason why rich kids grow up to be rich and poor kids tend to stay poor. The intense debate on the heritability of IQ is thus largely irrelevant to an understanding of poverty, wealth, and inequality of opportunity in the United States.

These results give rise to a host of novel questions—novel in the sense that they would never be asked were the importance of IQ "taken for granted." We shall deal with some of these in succeeding sections of this essay. First, if the social function of IQ distinctions is not status attainment or transmission, what is their function? We shall argue that the emphasis on intelligence as the basis for economic success serves to legitimate an authoritarian, hierarchical, stratified, and unequal economic system of production, and to reconcile the individual to his or her objective position within this system. Legitimation is enhanced merely when people believe in the intrinsic importance of IQ. This belief is facilitated by the strong associations among all the economically desirable attributes—social class, education, cognitive skills, occupational status, and income—and is integrated into a pervasive ideological perspective. Second, if IQ is not a major determinant of social class structure, what is? What are the criteria for admission to a particular social stratum, and what are the sources of intergenerational status transmission? We shall argue that access to an occupational status is contingent upon a pattern of noncognitive personality traits (motivation, orientation to authority, discipline, internalization of work norms), as well as a complex of personal attributes including sex, race, age, and educational credentials through which the individual aids in legitimating and stabilizing the structure of authority in the modern enterprise itself. Thus, primarily because of the central economic role of the school system, the generation of adequate cognitive skills becomes a spin-off, a by-product of a stratification mechanism grounded in the supply, demand, production, and certification of these noncognitive personal attributes.

Finally we shall comment on the implications of our perspective on the stratification process for political action and social change.

The IQ Controversy

The argument that differences in genetic endowments are of central and increasing importance in the stratification systems of advanced technological societies has been advanced, in similar forms, by a number of contemporary researchers.[7] At the heart of this argument lies the venerable thesis that IQ as measured by tests such as the Stanford-Binet is largely inherited via genetic transmission, rather than molded through environmental influences.[8]

This thesis bears a short elucidation. That IQ is highly heritable is merely to say that individuals with similar genes will exhibit similar IQs independent of differences in the social environments they might experience during their mental development. The main support of the genetic school is several studies of individuals with precisely the same genes (identical twins) raised in different environments (that is, separated at birth and reared in families with different social statuses). Their IQs tend to be fairly similar.[9] In addition, there are studies of individuals with no common genes (unrelated individuals) raised in the same environment (for example, the same family) as well as studies of individuals with varying genetic similarities (for example, fraternal twins, siblings, fathers and sons, aunts and nieces) and varying environments (for example, siblings raised apart, cousins raised in their respective homes). The difference in IQs for these groups is roughly conformable to the genetic inheritance model suggested by the identical twin and unrelated individual studies.[10]

As Eysenck suggests, while geneticists will quibble over the exact magnitude of heritability of IQ, nearly all will agree that heritability exists and is significant.[11] Environmentalists, while emphasizing the paucity and unrepresentativeness of the data, have presented rather weak evidence for their own position and have made little dent in the genetic position.[12] Unable to attack the central proposition of the genetic school, environmentalists have emphasized that it bears no important social implications. They have claimed that, although raised in the context of the economic and educational deprivation of blacks in the United States, the genetic theory says nothing about the "necessary" degree of racial inequality or the limits of compensatory education. First, environmentalists deny that there is any evidence that the IQ difference between blacks and whites (amounting to about fifteen IQ points) is genetic in origin,[13] and, second, they deny that any estimate of heritability tells us much about the capacity of "enriched environments" to lessen IQ differentials, either within or between racial groups.[14]

But the environmentalists' defense strategy has been costly. First, plausible, if not logical, inference now lies on the side of the genetic school, and it is up to environmentalists to "put up or shut up" as to feasible environment enrichment programs. Second, in their egalitarian zeal vis-à-vis racial differences, the environmentalists have sacrificed the modern liberal interpretation of social stratification. The modern liberal approach is to attribute social class differences to "unequal opportunity." That is, while the criteria for economic success are objective and achievement-orientated, the failures and successes of parents are passed on to their children via distinct learning and cultural environments. Thus the achievement of a more equal society merely requires that all youth be afforded the educational and other social conditions of the best and most successful.[15] But by focusing on the environmental differences *between* races, they implicitly accept that intelligence differences among whites of differing social class backgrounds are rooted in differences in genetic endowments. Indeed the genetic school's data come precisely from observed differences in the IQ of whites across socioeconomic levels! The fundamental tenet of modern liberal social policy—that "progressive social welfare measures" can gradually reduce and eliminate social class differences, cultures of poverty and affluence, and inequalities of opportunity—seems to be undercut. Thus the "classical liberal" attitude,[16] which emphasizes that social classes sort themselves out on the basis of innate individual capacity to cope successfully in the social environment, and hence tend to reproduce themselves from generation to generation, is restored.[17]

The vigor of reaction in face of Jensen's argument indicates the liberals' agreement that IQ is a basic social determinant (at least ideally) of occupational status and intergenerational mobility. In Jensen's words, "psychologists' concept of the intelligence demands of an occupation . . . is very much like the general public's concept of the prestige or social standing of an occupation, and both are closely related to an independent measure of . . . occupational status."[18] Jensen continues, quoting O. D. Duncan: " . . . intelligence . . . is not essentially different from that of achievement or status in the occupational sphere . . . what we now *mean* by intelligence is something like the probability of acceptable performance (given the opportunity) in occupations varying in social status."[19] Moreover, Jensen argues that the purported trend toward intelligence being an increasing requirement for occupational status will continue.[20] This emphasis on the role of intelligence in explaining social stratification is set even more clearly by Carl Bereiter in the same issue of the *Harvard Educational Review*: "The prospect is of a meritocratic caste system, based . . . on the natural consequences of inherited differences in intellectual potential . . . It would tend to persist even though everyone at all levels of the hierarchy considered it a bad thing."[21] Something like death and taxes.

Jensen et al. cannot be accused of employing an overly complicated social theory. Jensen's reason for the "inevitable" association of status and intelligence is that society "rewards talent and merit," and Herrnstein adds that society recognizes "the importance and scarcity of intellectual ability."[22] Moreover, the association of intelligence and social class is due to the "screening process,"[23] via education and occupation, whereby each generation is further refined into social strata on the basis of IQ. Finally, adds Herrnstein, "new gains of wealth . . . will increase the IQ gap between upper and lower classes, making the social ladder even steeper for those left at the bottom."[24] Herrnstein celebrates the genetic school's crowning achievement by turning liberal social policy directly against itself, noting that the heritability of intelligence, and hence the increasing pervasiveness of social stratification, will increase the more "progressive" of our social policies: "the growth of a virtually hereditary meritocracy will arise out of the successful realization of contemporary political and social goals . . . as the environment becomes more favorable for the development of intelligence, its heritability will increase . . ."[25] Similarly, the more we break down discriminatory and a-scriptive criteria for hiring, the stronger will become the link between IQ and occupational success, and the development of modern technology can only quicken the process.[26]

Few will be surprised that such statements are made by the "conservative" genetic school. But why, amid a spirited liberal counterattack in which the minutest details of the genetic hypothesis are contested and scathingly criticized, is the validity of the genetic school's description of the social function of intelligence blandly accepted? The widespread agreement among participants in the debate that IQ is an important determinant of economic success can hardly be explained by compelling empirical evidence adduced in support of the position. Quite the contrary. As we will show in the next section, the available data point strongly to the unimportance of IQ in getting ahead economically. We shall then argue that the actual function of IQ testing and its associated ideology is that of legitimating the stratification system, rather than generating it. The treatment of IQ in many strands of liberal sociology and economics merely reflects its actual function in social life: the legitimation and rationalization of the existing social relations of production.

The Importance of IQ

The most immediate support for the IQ theory of social stratification—which we will call IQism—flows from the strong association of IQ and economic success. This is illustrated in Table 12.1, which exhibits the probability of achieving any particular decile in the economic success distribution for an individual whose adult IQ lies in a specified decile.[27]

The data, most of which were collected by the United States Census Current Population Survey in 1962, refer to "non-Negro" males, aged twenty-five to thirty-four, from non-farm backgrounds in the experienced labor force. We have chosen this population because it represents the dominant labor force and the group into which minority groups and women would have to integrate to realize the liberal ideal of equal opportunity, and hence to whose statistical associations these groups would become subject. The data relating to childhood IQ and adult IQ are from a 1966 survey of veterans by the National Opinion Research Center and the California Guidance Study.[28] The quality of the data preclude any claims to absolute precision in our estimation. Yet our main propositions remain supported, even making allowance for substantive degrees of error. We must emphasize, however, that the validity of our basic propositions does not depend on our particular data set. While we believe our data base to be the most representative and careful construction from available sources, we have checked our results against several other data bases, including Jencks, Hauser, Lutterman, and Sewell; Conlisk, Griliches and Mason; and Duncan and Featherman.[29] When corrections are made for measurement error and restriction of range (see Bowles and Jencks),[30] statistical analysis of each of these data bases strongly supports all of our major propositions.

The interpretation of Table 12-1 is straightforward. The entries in the table are calculated directly from the simple correlation coefficient between our variables, adult IQ, and economic success. In addition to reporting the correlation coefficient in terms of the differing probability of economic success for people at various positions in the distribution of IQs, we cannot stress

Table 12-1

Probability of attainment of different levels of economic success for individuals of differing levels of adult IQ by deciles.

Adult IQ by deciles

		x 10	9	8	7	6	5	4	3	2	1
	y 10	30.9	19.8	14.4	10.9	8.2	6.1	4.4	3.0	1.7	0.6
	9	19.2	16.9	14.5	12.4	10.5	8.7	7.0	5.4	3.6	1.7
	8	13.8	14.5	13.7	12.6	11.4	10.1	8.7	7.1	5.3	2.8
	7	10.3	12.4	12.6	12.3	11.7	11.0	10.0	8.7	7.0	4.1
	6	7.7	10.4	11.4	11.7	11.8	11.5	11.0	10.1	8.7	5.7
	5	5.7	8.7	10.1	11.0	11.5	11.8	11.7	11.4	10.4	7.7
	4	4.1	7.0	8.7	10.0	11.0	11.7	12.3	12.6	12.4	10.3
	3	2.8	5.3	7.1	8.7	10.1	11.4	12.6	13.7	14.5	13.8
	2	1.7	3.6	5.4	7.0	8.7	10.5	12.4	14.5	16.9	19.2
	1	0.6	1.7	3.0	4.4	6.1	8.2	10.9	14.4	19.8	30.9

(leftmost label: Economic success by deciles)

Table 12-1 corresponds to a correlation of efficient $r = 0.52$.
Examples of use: For an individual in the 85th percentile in adult IQ ($x = 9$), the probability of attaining between the 20th and 30th percentiles in economic success is 5.3 percent (the entry in column 9, row 3).

too strongly that while the correlation coefficients in this and later tables are estimated from the indicated data, the entries in the table represent nothing more than a simple translation of their correlations, using assumptions that—though virtually universally employed in this kind of research—substantially simplify the complexity of the actual data. Now, turning to the table, we can see, for example, that a correlation between these two variables of 0.52 implies that an individual whose adult IQ lies in the top 10 percent of the population has a probability of 30.9 percent of ending up in the top tenth of the population in economic success, and a probability of 0.6 percent of ending up in the bottom tenth. Since an individual chosen at random will have a probability of 10 percent of ending up in any decile of economic success, we can conclude that being in the top decile in IQ renders an individual (white male) 3.09 times as likely to be in the top economic success decile, and 0.06 times as likely to end up in the bottom, as would be predicted by chance. Each of the remaining entries in Table 12-1 can be interpreted correspondingly.

Yet Tables 12-2 and 12-3, which exhibit the corresponding probabilities of economic success given number of years of schooling and level of socioeconomic background,[31] show that this statistical support is surely misleading; even stronger associations appear between years of schooling and economic success, as well as between social background and economic suc-

Table 12-2

Probability of attainment of different levels of economic success for individuals of differing levels of education, by deciles.

Years of schooling by deciles

		x 10	9	8	7	6	5	4	3	2	1
	y										
	10	37.6	22.3	24.6	9.8	6.6	4.3	2.6	1.4	0.6	0.1
	9	20.9	19.5	16.2	13.1	10.3	7.9	5.7	3.8	2.1	0.6
	8	13.5	16.1	15.3	13.8	12.0	10.1	8.0	5.9	3.7	1.4
	7	9.1	13.0	13.8	13.6	12.8	11.6	10.0	8.0	5.6	2.5
	6	6.1	10.2	12.0	12.8	12.9	12.5	11.6	10.1	7.8	4.0
	5	4.0	7.8	10.1	11.6	12.5	12.9	12.8	12.0	10.2	6.1
	4	2.5	5.6	8.0	10.0	11.6	12.8	13.6	13.8	13.0	9.1
	3	1.4	5.7	5.9	8.0	10.1	12.0	13.8	15.3	16.1	13.5
	2	0.6	2.1	3.8	5.7	7.9	10.3	13.1	16.2	19.5	20.9
	1	0.1	0.6	1.4	2.6	4.3	6.6	9.8	14.6	22.3	37.6

Economic success by deciles (left axis label)

Table 12-2 corresponds to a correlation of efficient $r = 0.63$.
Examples of use: For an individual in the 85th percentile in education ($x = 9$), the probability of attaining between the 20th and 30th percentiles in economic success ($y = 3$) is 3.7 percent (the entry in column 9, row 3).

cess. For example, being in the top decile in years of schooling renders an individual 3.76 times as likely to be at the top of the economic heap, and 0.1 times as likely to be at the bottom, while the corresponding ratios are 3.26 and 0.04 for social background. It is thus quite possible to draw from aggregate statistics, equally cogently, both an "educational attainment theory" of social stratification and a "socioeconomic background" theory. Clearly there are logical errors in all such facile inferences.

Of course, the IQ proponent will argue that there is no real problem here: the association of social class background and economic success follows the importance of IQ to economic success, and the fact that individuals of higher class background have higher IQ. Similarly, one may argue that the association of education and economic success follows from the fact that education simply picks out and develops the talents of intelligent individuals. The problem is that equally cogent arguments can be given for the primacy of either education or social class, and the corresponding subordinateness of the others. The above figures are equally compatible with all three interpretations.

In this section we shall show that all three factors (IQ, social class background, and education) contribute independently to economic success, but that IQ is by far the least important. Specifically we will demonstrate the truth of the following three propositions, which constitute the empirical basis of our thesis concerning the unimportance of IQ in generating the class structure.

First, although higher IQs and economic success tend to go together, higher IQs are not an important cause of economic success. The statistical association between adult IQ and economic success, while substantial, derives largely from the common association of both of these variables with social class background and level of schooling. Thus to appraise the economic importance of IQ, we must focus attention on family and school.

Second, although higher levels of schooling and economic success likewise tend to go together, the intellectual abilities developed or certified in school make little causal contribution to getting ahead economically. Thus only a minor portion of the substantial statistical association between schooling and economic success can be accounted for by the schools' role in producing or screening cognitive skills. The predominant economic function of schools must therefore involve the accreditation of individuals, as well as the production and selection of personality traits and other personal attributes rewarded by the economic system. Our third proposition asserts a parallel result with respect to the effect of social class background.

Third, the fact that economic success tends to run in the family arises almost completely independently from any genetic inheritance of IQ. Thus, while one's economic status tends to resemble that of one's parents, only a minor portion of this association can be attributed to social class differences in childhood IQ, and a virtually negligible portion to social class differences in genetic endowments, even accepting the Jensen estimates of heritability. Thus a perfect equalization of IQs across social classes would reduce the intergenerational transmission of economic status by a negligible amount. We conclude that a family's position in the class structure is reproduced primarily by mechanisms operating independently of the inheritance, production, and certification of intellectual skills.

Our statistical technique for the demonstration of these propositions will be that of linear regression analysis. This technique allows us to derive numerical estimates of the independent contribution of each of the separate but correlated influences (social class background, childhood IQ, years of schooling, adult IQ) on economic success, by answering the question: what is the magnitude of the association between any one of these influences among individuals who are equal on some or all the others? Equivalently it answers the question: what are the probabilities of attaining particular deciles in economic success among individuals who are in the same decile in some or all of the above influences but one, and in varying deciles in this one variable alone?

The IQ argument is based on the assumption that social background and education are related to economic success because they are associated with higher adult cognitive skills. Table 12-4 shows this to be essentially incorrect. This table, by exhibiting the relation between adult IQ and economic success among individuals with the same social class background and level of schooling, shows that the IQ economic success association exhibited in

Table 12-3

Probability of attainment of different levels of economic success for individuals of differing levels of social class background.

Social class background by deciles

		x 10	9	8	7	6	5	4	3	2	1
	y 10	32.6	20.4	14.5	10.7	7.8	5.7	3.9	2.5	1.4	0.4
	9	19.7	17.5	14.9	12.6	10.5	8.5	6.7	5.0	3.2	1.3
	8	13.8	14.9	14.1	12.9	11.6	10.1	8.6	6.9	4.9	2.4
	7	10.0	12.5	12.9	12.6	12.0	11.1	10.0	8.5	6.7	3.7
	6	7.3	10.4	11.5	12.0	12.0	11.7	11.1	10.1	8.5	5.3
	5	5.3	8.5	10.1	11.1	11.7	12.0	12.0	11.5	10.4	7.3
	4	3.7	6.7	8.5	10.0	11.1	12.0	12.6	12.9	12.5	10.0
	3	2.4	4.9	6.9	8.6	10.1	11.6	12.9	14.1	14.9	13.8
	2	1.3	3.2	5.0	6.7	8.5	10.5	12.6	14.9	17.5	19.7
	1	0.4	1.4	2.5	3.9	5.7	7.8	10.7	14.5	20.4	32.6

Economic success by deciles (left vertical axis label)

Table 12-3 corresponds to a correlation of efficient $r = 0.55$.
Examples of use: For an individual in the 85th percentile in social class ($x = 9$), the probability of attaining between the 20th and 30th percentile in economic success ($y = 3$) is 4.9 percent (the entry in column 9, row 3).

Table 12-1 is largely a by-product of these more basic social influences. That is, for a given level of social background and schooling, differences in adult IQ add very little to our ability to predict eventual economic success. Thus, for example, an individual with an average number of years of schooling and an average socioeconomic family background, but with a level of cognitive skill to place him in the top decile of the IQ distribution, has a probability of 14.1 percent of attaining the highest economic success decile. This figure may be compared with 10 percent, the analogous probability for an individual with average levels of IQ as well as schooling and social background. Our first proposition—that the relation between IQ and economic success is not causal, but rather operates largely through the effects of the correlated variables, years of schooling and social class background—is thus strongly supported.[32] We are thus led to focus directly on the role of social class background and schooling in promoting economic success.

Turning first to schooling, the argument of the IQ proponents is that the strong association between level of schooling and economic success exhibited in Table 12-2 is due to the fact that economic success depends on cognitive capacities, and schooling both selects individuals with high intellectual ability for further training and then develops this ability into concrete adult cognitive skills. Table 12-5 shows this view to be false. This table exhibits the effect of schooling on chances for economic success, for individuals who have the same adult IQ. Comparing Table 12-5 with Table 12-2, we see that cognitive differences account for a negligible part of schooling's influence on economic success: individuals with similar levels of adult IQ but

Table 12-4

Differential probabilities of attaining economic success for individuals of equal levels of education and social class background, but differing levels of adult IQ.

Adult IQ by deciles

Economic success by deciles

y \ x	10	9	8	7	6	5	4	3	2	1
10	14.1	12.3	11.4	10.7	10.1	9.6	9.0	8.5	7.8	6.6
9	12.4	11.4	10.9	10.5	10.2	9.8	9.5	9.1	8.6	7.7
8	11.4	10.9	10.6	10.4	10.2	9.9	9.7	9.4	9.1	8.4
7	10.7	10.5	10.4	10.3	10.1	10.0	9.9	9.7	9.5	9.0
6	10.1	10.2	10.2	10.1	10.1	10.1	10.0	9.9	9.8	9.5
5	9.5	9.8	9.9	10.0	10.1	10.1	10.1	10.2	10.2	10.1
4	9.0	9.5	9.7	9.9	10.0	10.1	10.3	10.4	10.5	10.7
3	8.4	9.1	9.4	9.7	9.9	10.2	10.4	10.6	10.9	11.4
2	7.7	8.6	9.1	9.5	9.8	10.2	10.5	10.9	11.4	12.4
1	6.6	7.8	8.5	9.0	9.6	10.1	10.7	11.4	12.3	14.1

Table 12-4 corresponds to a standardized regression coefficient $\beta = 0.13$. Example of use: Suppose two individuals have the same levels of education and social class background, but one is in the 85th percentile in adult IQ ($x = 9$), while the other is in the 15th decile in adult IQ ($x = 2$). Then the first individual is $10.9/9.1 = 1.2$ times as likely as the second to attain the 8th decile in economic success (column 9, row 8, divided by column 2, row 8).

Table 12-5

Differential probabilities of attaining economic success for individuals of equal adult IQ but differing levels of education.

Years of schooling by deciles

Economic success by deciles

y \ x	10	9	8	7	6	5	4	3	2	1
10	33.2	20.6	14.6	10.6	7.7	5.5	3.8	2.4	1.3	0.4
9	19.9	17.8	15.1	12.7	10.5	8.5	6.6	4.8	3.1	1.2
8	13.8	15.0	14.2	13.0	11.6	10.1	8.5	6.8	4.8	2.3
7	9.9	12.6	13.0	12.7	12.1	11.2	10.0	8.5	6.6	3.5
6	7.2	10.4	11.6	12.1	12.1	11.8	11.2	10.1	8.4	5.1
5	5.1	8.4	10.1	11.2	11.8	12.1	12.1	11.6	10.4	7.2
4	3.5	6.6	8.5	10.0	11.2	12.1	12.7	13.0	12.6	9.9
3	2.3	4.8	6.8	8.5	10.1	11.6	13.0	14.2	15.0	13.8
2	1.2	3.1	4.8	6.6	8.5	10.5	12.7	15.1	17.8	19.9
1	0.4	1.3	2.4	3.8	5.5	7.7	10.6	14.6	20.6	33.2

Table 12-5 corresponds to a standardized regression coefficient $\beta = 0.56$. Example of use: Suppose two individuals have the same adult IQ but one is in the 9th decile in level of education ($x = 9$), while the other is in the 2nd decile ($x = 2$). Then the first individual is $15.0/4.8 = 3.12$ times as likely as the second to attain the 8th decile in economic success (column 9, row 8, divided by column 2, row 8).

Table 12-6

Differential probabilities of attaining economic success for individuals of equal early IQ but differing levels of social class background

Social class backgrounds by deciles

		x 10	9	8	7	6	5	4	3	2	1
	y 10	27.7	18.5	14.1	11.1	8.8	6.9	5.3	3.9	2.5	1.1
	9	18.2	15.8	13.8	12.1	10.5	9.0	7.6	6.1	4.5	2.4
	8	13.7	13.8	13.0	12.1	11.1	10.1	8.9	7.6	6.1	3.7
Economic success by deciles	7	10.7	12.0	12.1	11.8	11.3	10.7	9.9	8.9	7.5	5.0
	6	8.4	10.5	11.1	11.3	11.3	11.1	10.7	10.0	9.0	6.6
	5	6.6	9.0	10.0	10.7	11.1	11.3	11.3	11.1	10.5	8.4
	4	5.0	7.5	8.9	9.9	10.7	11.3	11.8	12.1	12.0	10.7
	3	3.7	6.1	7.6	8.9	10.1	11.1	12.1	13.0	13.8	13.7
	2	2.4	4.5	6.1	7.6	9.0	10.5	12.1	13.8	15.8	18.2
	1	1.1	2.5	3.9	5.3	6.9	8.8	11.1	14.1	18.5	27.7

Table 12-6 corresponds to a standardized regression coefficient β = 0.46. Example of use: Suppose two individuals have the same childhood IQ but one is in the 9th decile in social background while the other is in the 2nd decile. Then the first is 18.5/2.5 = 7.4 times as likely as the second to attain the top decile in economic success (column 9, row 10, divided by column 2, row 10).

differing levels of schooling have substantially different chances of economic success. Indeed the similarity of Tables 12-2 and 12-5 demonstrates the validity of our second proposition—that schooling affects chances of economic success predominantly by the noncognitive traits which it generates, or on the basis of which it selects individuals for higher education.[33]

The next step in our argument is to show that the relationship between social background and economic success operates almost entirely independently of individual difference in IQ. Whereas Table 12-3 exhibits the total effect of social class on an individual's economic success, Table 12-6 exhibits the same effect among individuals with the same childhood IQ. Clearly these tables are nearly identical. That is, even were all social class differences in IQ eliminated, a similar pattern of social class intergenerational immobility would result.[34] Our third proposition is thus supported: the intergenerational transmission of social and economic status operates primarily via noncognitive mechanisms, despite the fact that the school system rewards higher IQ—an attribute significantly associated with higher social class background.

The unimportance of the specifically genetic mechanism operating via IQ in the intergenerational reproduction of economic inequality is even more striking. Table 12-7 exhibits the degree of association between social class background and economic success that can be attributed to the genetic

Table 12-7

The genetic component of intergenerational status transmission, assuming the Jensen heritability coeffient, and assuming education operates via cognitive mechanisms alone.

Social class background by deciles

		x 10	9	8	7	6	5	4	3	2	1
	y 10	10.6	10.3	10.2	10.1	10.0	10.0	9.9	9.8	9.7	9.4
	9	10.4	10.2	10.1	10.1	10.0	10.0	9.9	9.9	9.8	9.6
	8	10.2	10.1	10.1	10.1	10.0	10.0	9.9	9.9	9.9	9.8
	7	10.1	10.1	10.1	10.0	10.0	10.0	10.0	9.9	9.9	9.9
	6	10.0	10.0	10.0	10.0	10.0	10.0	10.0	10.0	10.0	10.0
	5	10.0	10.0	10.0	10.0	10.0	10.0	10.0	10.0	10.0	10.0
	4	9.9	9.9	9.9	10.0	10.0	10.0	10.0	10.1	10.1	10.1
	3	9.8	9.9	9.9	9.9	10.0	10.0	10.1	10.1	10.1	10.2
	2	9.6	9.8	9.9	9.9	10.0	10.0	10.1	10.1	10.2	10.4
	1	9.4	9.7	9.8	9.9	10.0	10.0	10.1	10.2	10.3	10.6

(Left vertical axis label: Economic success by deciles)

Table 12-7 corresponds to 0.02 standard deviations difference in economic success per standard deviation difference in social class background, in a causal model assuming social class background affects early IQ only via genetic transmission, and assuming economic success is directly affected only by cognitive variables. Example of use: For an individual in the 95th percentile in social class background ($x = 9$), the probability of attaining between the 20th and 30th percentiles in economic success ($y = 3$), assuming only genetic and cognitive mechanisms, is 10.1 percent (the entry in column 9, row 8).

inheritance of IQ alone. This table assumes that all direct influences of socioeconomic background upon economic success have been eliminated, and that the noncognitive components of schooling's contribution to economic success are eliminated as well (the perfect meritocracy based on intellectual ability). On the other hand, it assumes Jensen's estimate for the degree of heritability of IQ. A glance at Table 12-7 shows that the resulting level of intergenerational inequality in this highly hypothetical example would be negligible.

The unimportance of IQ in explaining the relation between social class success, together with our previously derived observation that most of the association between IQ and economic success can be accounted for by the common association of these variables with education and social class, support our major assertion: IQ is not an important intrinsic criterion for economic success. Our data thus hardly lend credence to Duncan's assertion that "and meritnce . . . is not essentially different from that of achievement or status in the occupational sphere,"[35] nor to Jensen's belief in the "inevitable" association of status and intelligence, based on society's "rewarding talent and merit,"[36] nor to Herrnstein's dismal prognostication of a "virtually hereditary meritocracy" as the fruit of successful liberal reform in an advanced industrial society.[37]

IQ and the Legitimation of the Hierarchical Division of Labor

A Preview

We have disputed the view that IQ is an important causal antecedent of economic success. Yet IQ clearly plays an important role in the United States stratification system. In this section we shall argue that the set of beliefs surrounding IQ betrays its true function—that of legitimating the social institutions underpinning the stratification system itself.

Were the IQ ideology correct, understanding the ramifications of cognitive differences would require our focusing on the technical relations of production in an advanced technological economy. Its failure, however, bids us scrutinize a different aspect of production—its social relations. By the "social relations of production" we mean the system of rights and responsibilities, duties and rewards, that governs the interaction of all individuals involved in organized productive activity.[38] In the following section we shall argue that the social relations of production determine the major attributes of the US stratification system.[39] Here, however, we shall confine ourselves to the proposition that the IQ ideology is a major factor in legitimating these social relations in the consciousness of workers.

The Need for Legitimacy

If one takes for granted the basic economic organization of society, its members need only be equipped with adequate cognitive and operational skills to fulfill work requirements and provided with a reward structure motivating individuals to acquire and supply these skills. United States capitalism accomplishes the first of these requirements through family, school, and on-the-job training, and the second through a wage structure patterned after the job hierarchy.

But the social relations of production cannot be taken for granted. The bedrock of the capitalist economy is the legally sanctioned power of the directors of an enterprise to organize production, to determine the rules that regulate workers' productive activities, and to hire and fire accordingly, with only moderate restriction by workers' organizations and government regulations. But this power cannot be taken for granted, and can be exercised forcefully against violent opposition only sporadically. Violence alone, observe Lasswell and Kaplan, is inadequate as a stable basis for the possession and exercise of power, and they appropriately quote Rousseau:

"The strongest man is never strong enough to be always master, unless he transforms his power into right, and obedience into duty." Where the assent of the less favored cannot be secured by power alone, it must be part of a total process whereby the existing structure of work roles and their allocation among individuals is seen as ethically acceptable and even technically necessary.

The Thrust of Legitimation: IQ, Technocracy, and Meritocracy

We may isolate several related aspects of the social relations of production that are legitimated in part by the IQ ideology. To begin, there are the overall characteristics of work in advanced United States capitalism: bureaucratic organization, hierarchical lines of authority, job fragmentation, and unequal reward. It is highly essential that the individual accept, and indeed come to see as natural, these undemocratic and unequal aspects of the workaday world.

Moreover, the mode of allocating individuals to these various positions in United States capitalism is characterized by intense competition in the educational system followed by individual assessment and choice by employers. Here again the major problem is that this "allocation mechanism" must appear egalitarian in process and just in outcome, parallel to the formal principle of "equality of all before the law" in a democratic juridical system based on freedom of contract.

While these two areas refer to the legitimation of capitalism as a social system, they have their counterpart in the individual's personal life. Thus, just as individuals must come to accept the overall social relations of production, workers must respect the authority and competence of their own "superiors" to direct their activities, and justify their own authority (however extensive) over others. Similarly, just as the overall system of role allocation must be legitimated, so individuals must assent to the justness of their own personal position, and the mechanisms through which this position has been attained. That workers be resigned to their position in production is perhaps adequate; that they be reconciled is preferable.

The contribution of IQism to the legitimation of these social relations is based on a view of society that asserts the efficiency and technological necessity of modern industrial organization, and is buttressed by evidence of simi larity of production and work in such otherwise divergent social systems as the United States and the Soviet Union. In this view large-scale production is a requirement of advanced technology, and the hierarchical division of labor is the only effective means of coordinating the highly complex and interdependent parts of the large-scale productive system.

Not only is the notion that the hierarchical division of labor is "techni-cally necessary" (albeit politically totalitarian) strongly reinforced, but also the view that job allocation is just and egalitarian (albeit severely unequal) is ultimately justified as objective, efficient, and necessary. Moreover, the individual's reconciliation with his or her own position in the hierarchy of production appears all but complete: the legitimacy of the authority of superiors no less than that of the individual's own objective position flows not from social contrivance but from science and reason.

That this view does not strain the credulity of well-paid intellectuals is perhaps not surprising.[40] Nor would the technocratic/meritocratic perspective be of much use in legitimating the hierarchical division of labor were its adherents to be counted only among the university elite and the technical and professional experts. But such is not the case. Despite the extensive evidence that IQ is not an important determinant of individual occupational achievement, and despite the fact that few occupations place cognitive requirements on job entry, the crucial importance of IQ in personal success has captured the public mind. Numerous attitude surveys exhibit this fact. In a national sample of high school students, for example, "intelligence" ranks second only to "good health" in importance as a desirable personal attribute.[41] Similarly, a large majority chose "intelligence" along with "hard work" as the most important requirements of success in life. The public concern over the Coleman Report findings about scholastic achievement and the furor over the IQ debate are merely indications of the pervasiveness of the IQ ideology.

This popular acceptance, we shall argue, is due to the unique role of the educational system.

Education and Legitimation

To understand the widespread acceptance of the view that economic success is predicted on intellectual achievement we must look beyond the work place, for the IQ ideology does not conform to most workers' everyday experience on the job. Rather, the strength of this view derives in large measure from the interaction between schooling, cognitive achievement, and economic success. IQism legitimates the hierarchical division of labor not directly, but primarily through its relationship with the educational system.

The linking of intelligence to economic success indirectly via the educational system strengthens rather than weakens the legitimation process. First, the day-to-day contact of parents and children with the competitive, cognitively orientated school environment, with clear connections to the economy, buttresses in a very immediate and concrete way the technocratic perspective on economic organization, to a degree that a sporadic and impersonal testing process divorced from the school environment could not aspire. Second, by rendering the outcome (educational attainment) dependent not only on ability but also on motivation, drive to achieve, perseverance, and sacrifice, the status allocation mechanism acquires heightened legitimacy. Moreover, personal attributes are tested and developed over a long period of time, thus enhancing the apparent objectivity and achievement orientation of the stratification system. Third, by gradually "cooling out" individuals at different educational levels, the student's aspirations are relatively painlessly brought into line with his probable occupational status. By the time most students terminate schooling they have validated for themselves their inability or unwillingness to be a success at the next highest level. Through competition, success and defeat in the classroom, the individual is reconciled to his or her social position.[42]

The History of Legitimation: IQ, Education, and Eugenics

The relationship between schooling, IQ, and the stratification system is therefore by no means technologically determined within the framework of capitalist economic institutions. Nor did it arise accidentally. Rather, a growing body of historical research indicates that it grew out of a more or less conscious and coordinated attempt to generate a disciplined industrial labor force and to legitimate the rapid hierarchization of the division of labor around the turn of the century.[43]

This research strongly contests the dominant "liberal-technocratic" analysis of education. This "technocratic" view of schooling, economic success, and the requisites of job functioning supplies an elegant and logically coherent (if not empirically accurate) explanation of the historical rise of mass education in the process of industrial development. Because modern industry, irrespective of its political and institutional framework, consists in the application of increasingly complex and cognitively demanding operational technologies, these cognitive demands require an increasing level of cognitive competence on the part of the labor force as a whole. Thus the expansion of educational opportunity becomes a requisite of modern economic growth.[44] Formal education, by extending to the masses what had been throughout history the privilege of the few, opens the superior levels in the production hierarchy to all with the ability and willingness to attain such competencies. Hence the observed association between education and economic success reflects the achievement of a fundamentally egalitarian school system in promoting cognitive development.

Quite apart from the erroneous view that the determinants of job adequacy in modern industry are primarily cognitive, this interpretation of the rise of universal education in the United States finds little support in the historical record. Mass education made its beginning in cities and towns where the dominant industries required little skill—and far less cognitive ability—among the work force. The towns in which the skill-using industries were located were the followers, not the leaders, in the process of mid nineteenth-century educational reform and expansion.[45] Likewise in the late nineteenth-century rural West and South the expansion of schooling was associated not with the application of modern technology or mechanization to farming but with the extension of the wage labor system to agricultural employment.

Thus the growth of the modern educational system did not originate with the rising cognitive requirements of the economy. Rather, the birth and early development of universal education was sparked by the critical need of a burgeoning capitalist order for a stable work force and citizenry reconciled, if not inured, to the wage labor system. Order, docility, discipline, sobriety, and humility—attributes required by the new social relation of production—were admitted by all concerned as the social benefits of schooling.[46] The popular view of the economy as a technical system would await Frederick Taylor and his scientific management movement; the social Darwinist emphasis on intelligence appeared only in the "scientific genetics" of Benet and Terman. The integration of the IQ ideology into educational theory and practice had to await basic turn-of-the-century developments in the industrial order itself. The most important of these developments was the birth of the modern corporation, with its relentless pressure toward uniformity and objectivity in the staffing of ever more finely graded hierarchical positions. The rationalistic efficiency orientation of bureaucratic order was quickly taken over by a growing educational system.[47] Taylorism in the classroom meant competition, hierarchy, uniformity, and, above all, individual accountability by means of objective testing.

A second related source of educational change emanating from the economy was the changing nature of the work force. Work on the family farm or in the artisan shop continued to give way to employment in large-scale enterprises. And millions of immigrants swelled the ranks of the new working class. The un-American, undomesticated character of this transformed work force was quickly revealed in a new labor militancy (of which Sacco and Vanzetti are merely the shadow in folk history) and a skyrocketing public welfare burden.

The accommodation of the educational system to these new economic realities was by no means a placid process. Modern education was constructed on the rapidly disintegrating and chaotic foundations of the old common school. Geared to the small town, serving native American Protestant stock, and based on the proliferation of the one-room schoolhouse, the common school was scarcely up to supplying the exploding labor needs of the new corporate order. Dramatic was its failure to deal effectively with the seething urban agglomeration of European immigrants of rural and peasant origin.[48] As large numbers of working-class and particularly immigrant children began attending high schools, the older democratic ideology of the common school—that the same curriculum should be offered to all children—gave way to the "progressive" insistence that education should be tailored to the "needs of the child." In the interests of providing an education relevant to the later life of the students, vocational schools and tracks were developed for the children of working families. The academic curriculum was preserved for those who would later have the opportunity to make use of book learning either in college or in white-collar employment.

The frankness with which students were channeled into curriculum tracks on the basis of their race, ethnicity, or social class background raised serious doubts concerning the "openness" of the social class structure. The relation between social class and a child's chances of promotion or tracking assignments was disguised—though not mitigated much—by another "progressive" reform: "objective" educational testing. Particularly after World War I the increased use of intelligence and scholastic achievement testing offered an ostensibly unbiased means of measuring the product of schooling and stratifying students.[49] The complementary growth of the guidance counseling profession allowed much of the channeling to proceed from the students' own well-counseled choices, thus adding an apparent element of voluntarism to the system.

If the rhetoric of the educational response to the economic changes after the turn of the century was "progressive," much of its content and consciousness was supplied by the new science of "evolutionary genetics," in the form of the prestigious and influential eugenics movement.[50] Of course, as Karier notes, "the nativism, racism, elitism, and social class bias which were so much a part of the testing and eugenics movement in America were, in a broader sense, part of the *Zeitgeist* which was America." Yet its solid grounding in Mendel's Law, Darwin, and the sophisticated statistical methodologies of Pearson, Thurstone, and Thorndike lent it the air of scientific rigor previously accorded only to the Newtonian sciences.

The *leitmotiv* of the testing movement was the uniting constitutional character of human excellence, as rooted in genetic endowment. Moral character, intelligence, and social worth were inextricably connected and biologically rooted. In the words of the eminent psychologist Edward L. Thorndike, "to him that a superior intellect is given also on the average a superior character."[51] A glance at the new immigrant communities, the black rural ghettos, and the "breeding" of the upper classes could not but confirm this opinion in the popular mind. Statistical information came quickly from that architect of the still-popular Stanford-Binet intelligence test—Lewis M. Terman—who confirmed the association of IQ and occupational status. Study after study, moreover, exhibited the low intelligence of "wards of the state" and social deviants.

That a school system geared toward moral development and toward domesticating a labor force for the rising corporate order might readily embrace standardization and testing—to the benefit of the leaders as well as the led—goes without saying. Thus it is not surprising that, while the idealistic progressives worked in vain for a humanistic, more egalitarian education,[52] the bureaucratization and test orientation of the school system proceeded smoothly, well oiled by seed money from the Carnegie Corporation and other large private foundations, articulated by social scientists at prestigious schools of education[53] and readily implemented by business-controlled local school boards.[54]

The Reproduction of the Hierarchical Divisions of Labor

A Preview

Why is it that economically successful parents tend to have economically successful children? In this section we seek to explain how social class background interacts with schooling to influence an individual's chances of economic success and in so doing to reproduce a family's position in the hierarchical division of labor.

The argument may be briefly summarized at the outset. To get a job at any particular level in the hierarchy of production one has to meet two tests: first, one must be able and willing to do the work; and second, one must be of appropriate race, sex, age, education, and demeanor so that his or her assignment to the job will contribute to the sense that the social order of the firm is just. Thus criteria of worker adequacy reflect more than the employer's desire that workers be hardworking and capable. They reflect as well the need for acquiescence to the employer's monopolization of power. Thus the perpetuation and legitimation of the hierarchical division of labor within the enterprise is an important additional objective of employers in the selection and placement of workers. The smooth exercise of control from the top of the enterprise rests on the daily reconfirmation of the employee's sense of the just claim of his or her superiors, co-workers, and subordinates to their particular jobs.

The ability to operate well at a particular level in the hierarchy and the legitimate claim to one's place in the authority structure and to the rewards associated with it depend to a large extent on experiences in the home and at school. The enterprise is by no means a full-blown socialization agency capable of shaping worker consciousness and behavior to its needs; its control over recruitment and internal organization can but *reinforce* pattterns of consciousness developed in the larger society. That is, the particular structure of authority within the firm that will be seen as legitimate— whether based on distinctions of race, sex, educational credentials, age, manners of speech, or whatever—is an expression of broader social values and prejudices. And these too are both reflected in and dependent upon the structure of family life and schooling.

The Criteria of Hirability

We begin with an obvious point: in capitalist society the income and social position of the vast majority of individuals derive predominantly from the sale of their labor services to employers. An adequate explanation of the stratification process thus requires understanding (1) the criteria used by employers in hiring, tenure, promotion, and pay; (2) the processes whereby these criteria come to be seen as fair and legitimate; and (3) the process whereby individuals come to acquire those attributes relevant to employers' criteria.

The prime facie dimensions of job-relevant individual attributes are vast indeed. They include (at least) such features as ownership of physical implements (for example, the medieval knight owned his horse, armor and retinue), membership (for example, the feudal gild master), ascription (for example, sex, race, social class, age, taste, religion), and personal attributes (for example, skills, motivation, attitudes, personality, credentials). In capitalist society it is the last of these along with a few important ascriptive traits—sex, race, and age—that come to the fore. Indeed even the relationship between social class background and economic success operates in large measure through differences in personal characteristics associated with differential family status. Employers never ask about social background.[55]

Thus our inquiry into the stratification process must focus on the supply, demand, and production of those personal attributes and ascriptive traits that are relevant to getting ahead in the world of work. We may begin with the demand for personal attributes by employers. While employers may have certain restrictions in their hiring practices (child labor and antidiscrimination laws, union regulations, social pressures), by and large their sole objective in hiring is to insure the ability of individuals to perform adequately in the work role in question. The requirements of job adequacy in any job, of course, depend on the entire structure of work roles—that is, on the social relations of production within the enterprise.

Our analysis suggests five important sets of worker characteristics. First, we have noted the emphasis of the "technocratic perspective" on cognitive attributes—such as scholastic achievement—to which we may add concrete technical and operational skills (for example, knowing how to do typing, accounting, chemical engineering, or carpentry). Second, there are, parallel to cognitive attributes, a set of personality traits (such as motivation, perseverance, docility, dominance, flexibility, or tact) that enable the individual to operate effectively in a work role. Third, there are traits that we may call modes of self-presentation, such as manner of speech and dress, patterns of peer identification, and perceived "social distance" from individuals and groups of different social position. These traits do not necessarily contribute to the worker's execution of tasks, but may be valuable to employers in their effort to stabilize, validate, and legitimate the particular structure of work roles in the organization as a whole. Similar in function is our fourth set of traits: ascriptive characteristics such as race, sex, and age. Finally we may add to our list of attributes credentials, such as level and prestige of education, which like modes of self-presentation and the ascriptive traits, are a resource used by employers to add to the overall legitimacy of the organization.

The analytical problem, of course, is to determine the precise content of these five factors, and how each affects the stratification process. This problem is particularly difficult in that all five tend to occur together in a single individual. Thus an individual with more cognitive achievement and skills will also, on the average, be more capable personality-wise of operating on higher occupational levels, will speak, dress, and exhibit a pattern of loyalties befitting the corresponding social class, and will have proper credentials to boot (though she may be a woman!). But since there is still a great deal of variation among individuals in their relative possession of these various attributes, analysis is not impossible. Indeed a major statistically supported assertion of this essay is that cognitive attributes are not central to the determination of social stratification, and hence the association of cognitive level and access to higher level occupations must be largely a by-product of selection on the basis of others.

We believe that all four of the remaining types of personal attributes—personality traits relevant to the work task, modes of self-presentation, ascriptive traits, and credentials—are integral to the stratification process.

We do not yet understand precisely how these four noncognitive types of worker traits interact, or the extent to which each contributes to the stratification process. The strong association between education and economic success, plus the relative unimportance of cognitive achievement as a criterion of job placement, nevertheless convinces us of their overall decisive impact. We shall present evidence for the importance of each in turn, beginning with the job-relevant personality traits.

The personality traits required of "efficient" workers must correspond by and large to the requirements of harmonious integration into the bureaucratic order of the enterprise. This order exorder of the enterprise. This order exhibits four essential characteristics. First, the duties, responsibilities, and privileges of individuals are determined neither according to individual preference nor flexible cooperative decision by workers, but rather by a system of rules that precedes the individual's participation and sets limits on his or her actions. Second, the relations among individuals are characterized, according to the rules of the organization, by hierarchical authority and interdependence. An individual's actions are closely tied to the wills of his or her superiors, and the results of his or her actions have repercussions on large numbers of other workers. Third, while control from the top is manifested in rules, the principle of hierarchical authority implies that large numbers of workers have essential, though circumscribed, areas of decision and choice. Fourth, the formal nature of the organization and the fact that work roles are determined on the basis of profitability and compatibility, with control from the apex of the pyramidal organization, imply that workers cannot be adequately motivated by the intrinsic rewards of the work process.[56]

While these requirements hold for all workers, there are important qualitative differences among levels. These tend to follow directly from differences in the scope of independent decision making, which increases with hierarchical status. Thus the lowest level of worker must simply refrain from breaking rules. On the highest level it becomes crucial that the worker internalize the values of the organization, act out of personal initiative, and know when not to go by the book. In between, workers must be methodical, predictable, and persevering, and at a somewhat higher level must respond flexibly to their superiors, whose directives acquire a complexity transcending the relatively few rules that apply directly to their tasks. Thus we would expect the crucial determinants of job adequacy to pass from full-following to dependability-predictability to subordinateness to internalized values, all with an overlap of motivation according to external incentives and penalties (doubtless with penalties playing a larger role at the lower levels, and incentives at the higher).

Thus the doctor not only must cure but also must exude the aura of infallibility and dedication fitting for one whose critical acts intervene between life and death. Similarly, the supervisor not only must supervise but also must exhibit his inevitable distance from and superiority to his inferiors, and his ideal suitability for his position. Thus role fulfillment requires a dramatic "theatrical" performance—an impulse toward idealization of role—on a routinized and internalized basis. Goffman documents the importance of self-presentation in a vast array of social positions—those of doctors, nurses, waitresses, dentists, military personnel, mental patients, funeral directors, eighteenth-century noblemen, Indian castes, Chinese mandarins, junk peddlers, unionized workers, teachers, pharmacists, as well as in the relations between men and women and blacks and whites.[57]

The role of self-presentation in social stratification arises from a similar social treatment of "personal fronts." Social class differences in family and childhood socialization, as well as the informal organization of peer groups along social class lines,[58] are likely to develop career identities, symbols and ideologies, organization loyalties, and aspirations apposite to particular levels in the hierarchy of production.

We may now consider the importance of our last two sets of employability traits: ascriptive characteristics (race, age, sex) and acquired credentials (such as educational degrees or seniority). We have argued that the legitimation of the hierarchical division of labor, as well as the smooth day-to-day control over the work process, requires that the authority structure of the enterprise—with its corresponding structure of pay and privilege—respects the wider society's ascriptive and symbolic distinctions. In particular, socially acceptable relations of domination and subordination must be respected: white over black, male over female, old (but not aged) over young, and schooled over unschooled.

We make no claim that these social prejudices originated as a capitalist contrivance, although a strong case could probably be made that the form and strength of both sexism and racism here derive in large measure from the particular historical development of capitalist institutions in the United States and Europe.

The individual employer, acting singly, normally takes societal values and beliefs as data, and will violate them only where his long-term financial benefits are secure. The broader prejudices of society are thus used as a resource by bosses in their effort to control labor. In this way the pursuit of profits and security of class position reinforces the racist, sexist, and credentialist mentality. Thus black workers are paid less than whites with equivalent schooling and cognitive achievement[59] and similarly for women relative to men.[60] Likewise those with more schooling are given preference for supervisory jobs, in the absence of compelling evidence of the superior performance of those less educated.[61] Lastly pay and authority increase over most of a person's working life, out of all proportion to any conceivable on-the-job learning of increased skills.

How Worker Characteristics Are Acquired: The Correspondence Principles

Having surveyed the reasoning and evidence indicating the importance of our four sets of noncognitive worker traits—work-related personality characteristics, modes of self-presentation, ascriptive characteristics, and credentials—we turn now to our last question, how are these determinants of one's place in the stratification system acquired? The ascriptive traits are, of course, acquired at birth, or—in the case of age—inescapably as life progresses, so little need be said of them. The acquisition of credentials requires survival in the school system, and is an arduous, but not particularly complex, process. The way in which workers come to have a particular set of work-relevant personality characteristics or modes of self-presentation requires a more searching analysis.

We find the answer to this question in two correspondence principles, which may be stated succinctly as follows: the social relations of schooling and of family life correspond to the social relations of production.

We have suggested above that the social relations of schooling are structured similarly to the social relations of production in several essential respects.[62] The school is a bureaucratic order with hierarchical authority, rule orientation, stratification by "ability" (tracking) as well as by age (grades), role differentiation by sex (physical education, home economics, shop), and a system of external incentives (marks, promise of promotion, and threat of failure) much like pay and status in the sphere of work. Thus schools are likely to develop in students traits corresponding to those required on the job.

The differential socialization patterns in schools attended by students of different social classes, and even within the same school, do not arise by accident. Rather, they stem from the fact that the educational objectives and expectations of administrators, teachers, and parents, and the responsiveness of students to various patterns of teaching and control, differ for students of different social classes.[63] Further, class inequalities in school socialization patterns are reinforced by inequalities in financial resources. The paucity of financial support for the education of children from working-class families leaves more resources to be devoted to the children of those with commanding roles in the economy; it also forces upon the teachers and school administrators in the working-class schools a type of social relations that fairly closely mirrors that of the factory. Thus financial considerations in poorly supported working-class schools militate against small intimate classes, against a multiplicity of elective courses and specialized teachers (except disciplinary personnel), and preclude the amounts of free time for the teachers and free space required for a more open, flexible educational environment. The lack of financial support all but requires that students be treated as raw materials on a production line; it places a high premium on obedience and punctuality; there are few opportunities for independent, creative work or individualized attention by teachers. The well-financed schools attended by the children of the rich can offer much greater opportunities for the development of the capacity for sustained independent work and the other characteristics required for adequate job performance in the upper levels of the occupational hierarchy.

The Failure of Liberal Social Reform and the Future of the Stratification System

Social Reform in the 1960s: An Action Critique of Liberal Theory

In 1847 Karl Marx and Friedrich Engels wrote, "Wherever the bourgeoisie has risen to power, it has destroyed all feudal, patriarchal, and idyllic relationships . . . it has left no other bond betwixt man and man but crude self-interest and unfeeling cash payment."[64] Ironically the positive aspect of this historical pronouncement lies at the base of the liberal theory of stratification. Thus John Gardner, president of the Carnegie Corporation, later to become Secretary of the United States Department of Health, Education, and Welfare, could confidently state: "Most human societies have been

beautifully organized to keep good men down. . . . Birth determined occupation and status. . . . Such societies were doomed by the Industrial
Revolution."[65]

But by the early 1960s it was painfully evident that the heralded natural
trend toward equality had not fared well. Despite phenomenal economic
growth, a vast expansion (and equalization) of the educational system, and
the introduction of the "progressive" income tax, social security, and other
welfare state programs, inequality of income has remained essentially unchanged.[66] The introduction of taxes on inheritance has done little to alter
the distribution of wealth: the top one-half of one percent of wealth holders
hold about a quarter of all wealth; the top one percent hold about three-
quarters of all corporate stock.[67] Women's suffrage and a more liberal attitude toward "the woman's place" in the home and on the job did not prevent
a decline in the economic situation of women relative to men.[68] The attenua-
tion of racial prejudice—attested to in numerous recent surveys—and the
dramatic educational gains made by blacks have not resulted in occupational
or income gains for blacks relative to whites.[69] Finally the extension of public
elementary and secondary education and the growth of state-supported
higher education have not been accompanied by a reduction in the extent to
which one's family's social status determines one's own education opportunities.[70] Similarly, the correlation between the occupational status of individuals and their parents has not been reduced.[71]

Thus the decade of the 1960s was marked by the commitment to bring social policy to bear on the equalization of opportunity. In fulfilling this
commitment, liberal social policy has drawn on liberal social theory in three
essential respects. First, it has harbored an abiding optimism, flowing from
the theorists' separation of equality of opportunity and equality of outcome.
The hierarchical division of labor could be maintained while the atavistic
remains of bigotry and unequal social resources could be swept away via
additional legislation and more effective propaganda. Second, the technocratic orientation of liberal theory indicated that the crucial policy variables
were those related to differences in cognitive and psychomotor performance-
related skills—hence the emphasis on education and training. This, then,
provided the focus of the reforms of the 1960s. Third, the limits of social reform in this area, so the theory predicts, are dictated by genetic differences in
ability.

A less auspicious set of assumptions could scarcely have been chosen, for
the cognitive abilities central to the theory have turned out to be far less socially malleable than the liberals had hoped. By 1970 the hubris of the War
on Poverty, in the face of persistent failure, had vanished. In the area of educational policy, the "empirical finding" that differing levels of resources did
not significantly promote scholastic achievement[72] was quickly buttressed
by a host of dismal assessments of the performance of the major compensa-

tory educational programs—Title 1, Head Start, Follow Through, and others.[73]

These failures, of course, softened the liberal position for the inevitable conservative counterattack. This counterattack has been based on both pillars of the liberal theory of stratification: *willingness* and *ability* to perform in the impersonal industrial marketplace. The voguish "culture of poverty" school locates the blame for poverty in deeply rooted deficiencies of the poor themselves, limiting their willingness to perform.[74] Progressive social theory has been unable to defend itself against this thrust, as it lacks a firm understanding of the structural relations between the cultural subsystems in the work place in the larger society.[75] The assault of the "genetic school" discussed in this paper is based on the purported *inability* of the poor to perform. The proponents of liberal social policy cannot defend itself against the massive attack of the geneticists without reversing in midstream; for it had consistently posited "ability" and "performance" as the ideal criteria of employability and economic reward. This perspective has manifested itself particularly strongly in the more policy-related social science disciplines, especially in the economics and sociology of education. Thus the economic returns to schooling have been "corrected for ability" differences;[76] student quality has been measured by IQ, and school quality by contribution to cognitive achievement;[77] and cognitive indices have been taken as the basic output variables in educational production functions.[78] In the area of social policy the findings of the Coleman Report,[79] relying only on measures of cognitive achievement, were conceived, and are still consistently referred to, as basic to the solution to problems of poverty and inequality. Thus Moynihan and Mosteller, in the introduction to their massive reanalysis of the Coleman data, refer to the report as a "revolutionary document" whose growing achievement lies in its taking "educational output, not input alone . . . [as] the central issue."[80] Adding the critics of Jensen and Herrnstein to this list, we are faced with a degree of unanimity perhaps unparalleled in social science.

In earlier sections we argued that the liberal perspective on stratification is incorrect. Hence we are not surprised that social policy based on its premises has failed. Nor are we surprised at the success of the counterattack. The theoretical fallacy at the heart of liberal stratification theory, stated in policy-oriented terms, is the assertion that equality of opportunity is compatible with equality of outcomes. We have argued that neither "ability" nor "willingness" can be understood outside a total perspective in which social, racial, ethnic, and sexual differentiations and differential patterns of socialization interact with the hierarchical division of labor. Individuals, as well as their social subcultures, develop according to their relationship to the social division of labor. Our argument holds that the social relations of production are mirrored—via the correspondence principles—in the basic socialization agencies of family, community, and school. Thus inequality of opportunity is a by-product of the organization of production itself, and cannot be attached either to "dysfunctional" attributes of the underclasses or the self-interest, malfeasance, and unfeeling perversity of unprogressive social policy. In addition to performance-related individual capacities normally developed on a class basis, beneath the surface of rationality, meritocracy, and performance-oriented efficiency, the capitalist economic system operates on a subtle network of ascriptions and symbolic differentiations, quite as well articulated as the most complex caste system. Moreover, this "open caste system" is essential to the legitimation and operation of the hierarchical division of labor itself. Any particular element may be eliminated (such as racism), but new modes of status differentiation must arise to take its place. Such is the logic of our argument.

Contradictory Development and the Future of the Class Structure

Yet our analysis must be incomplete in one essential respect: it seems to propose that the system has little difficulty in fulfilling these preconditions for its own reproduction. Yet the political and social upheavals of the 1960s—including the black and women's movements, radical student revolts, rank-and-file unrest in the labor movement, the rise of the counterculture and a new mode of equality among youth—have ushered in growing consciousness directed against the stratification system, and even the hierarchical division of labor itself.[81] Clearly our analysis has been one-sided.

The problem? We have treated only the way in which the United States capitalist system reproduces itself, without dealing with the contradictions that inevitably arise out of the system's own successes—contradictions that lead to social dislocation and require structural change in the social relations of production for the further development of the social system.[82] The present seems to represent one of these crucial periods of contradiction.[83] We can do no more here than list some of these central contradictions.

First, the legitimacy of the capitalist system has been historically based in no small part on its ability to "deliver the goods." The ever-increasing mass of consumer goods and services seemed to promise constant improvement in levels of well-being for all. Yet the very success of the process has undermined the urgency of consumer wants; other needs—for community, for security, for a more integral and self-initiated work and social life—are coming to the fore. And these needs are unified by a common characteristic: they cannot be met simply by producing more consumer goods and services. On the contrary, the economic foundations of capital accumulation are set firmly in the destruction of the social basis for the satisfaction of these needs. Thus through "economic development" itself, needs are generated that the advanced capitalist system is not geared to satisfy.[84] Thus the legitimacy of the capitalist order must increasingly be handled by other social mechanisms, of which the meritocracy is a major element. It is not clear that the latter can bear this strain.

Second, the concentration of capital and the continuing separation of workers—white collar and professional as well as manual—from control over the production process has reduced the natural defenders of the capitalist order to a small minority.[85] Two hundred years ago over three-fourths of white families owned lands, tools, or other productive property; this fraction has fallen to about a third, and even among this group a tiny minority owns the lion's share of all productive property. Similarly, two hundred years ago almost all white male workers were their own boss. The demise of the family farm, the artisan shop, and the small store, and the rise of the modern corporation, has reduced the figure to less than 10 percent.[86] For most Americans the capitalist system has come to mean someone else's right to profits, someone else's right to work unbossed and in pursuit of one's own objectives. The decline of groups outside the wage labor system—farmer, artisan, entrepreneur, and independent professional—has eliminated a ballast of capitalist support, leaving the legitimation system alone to divide strata among the working class against one another.

Third, developments in technology and work reorganization have begun to undermine the main line of ideological defense of the capitalist system— namely the idea that the capitalist relations of production (private property and the hierarchical organization of work) are the most conducive to the rapid expansion of productivity.[87] Repeated experiments have shown that in those complex work tasks that increasingly dominate modern production, participatory control by workers is a more productive form of work organization.[88] The boredom and stultification of the production line and the steno pool, the shackled creativity of technical workers and teachers, the personal frustration of the bureaucratic office routine, increasingly lose their claim as the price of material comfort. The ensuing attacks on bureaucratic oppression go hand in hand with demystification of the meritocracy ideology as discussed in this paper. Support for capitalist institutions—once firmly rooted in their claim to superiority in meeting urgent consumption needs and squarely based on a broad mass of property-owning independent workers—is thus weakened by the process of capitalist development itself. At the same time powerful anticapitalist forces are brought into being. The accumulation of capital—the engine of growth under capitalism—has as its necessary companion the proletarianization of labor. The continuing integration of new groups into the worldwide wage labor system has not brought about the international working-class consciousness that many Marxists had predicted. But the process has introduced serious strains into the capitalist order. These may be summarized as a fourth and fifth set of contradictions.

Fourth, the international expansion of capital has fueled nationalist and anticapitalist movements in many of the poor countries. The strains associated with the worldwide integration of the capitalist system are manifested in the resistance of the people of Vietnam, in the rise of the Chilean left, in the socialist revolution in China and Cuba, and in political instability and guerrilla movements elsewhere in Asia, Africa, and Latin America. The United States role in opposition to wars of national liberation—particularly in Vietnam—has brought part of the struggle back home and exacerbated many of the domestic contradictions of advanced capitalism.[89]

Fifth, and cutting across all of the above, with the return to comparatively smooth capitalist development in the United States in the mid 1950s after the tumultuous decades of the 1930s and 1940s, the impact of far-reaching cumulative changes in the class structure is increasingly reflected in crises of public consciousness. The corporatization of agriculture and reduction of the farm population has particularly affected blacks, who are subjected to the painful process of forceful integration into the urban wage labor system. The resulting political instabilities are not unlike those following the vast wave of immigrants in the early decades of the century. Changes in the technology of household production and the vast increase in female labor in the service industries also portend a radically altered economic position of women. Finally, the large corporation and the state bureaucracies have replaced entrepreneurial, elite white-collar, and independent professional jobs as the locus of middle-class economic activity, and the effective proletarianization of white-collar labor marks the already advanced integration of these groups into the wage labor system.[90] In each case contradictions have arisen between the traditional consciousness of these groups and their new objective economic situations. This has provided much of the impetus for radical movements among blacks, women, students, and counterculture youth.

While searching for long-range structural accommodations to these contradictions, defenders of the capitalist order will probably be forced to place increasing reliance on the general legitimation mechanisms associated with the meritocratic-technocratic ideology. As a result it appears likely that the future will reveal increasing reliance on the "meritocratic" stratification mechanisms and the associated legitimating ideologies: IQism and educational credentialism. Efforts and resources will doubtless multiply toward the "full equalization of opportunity," but the results, if our arguments are correct, will be limited as long as the hierarchical division of labor perpetuates itself.

The credentialist and IQ ideology upon which the "meritocratic" legitimation mechanisms depend is thus already under attack. Blacks reject the racism implicit in much of the recent work on IQ; they are not mystified by the elaborate empirical substantiation of the geneticist position, nor by the assertions of meritocracy by functionalist sociologists. Their daily experience gives them insights that seem to have escaped many social scientists. Likewise women—indeed many poor people of both sexes—know that their exclusion from jobs is not based on any deficiency of educational credentials.

We have here attempted to speed up the process of demystification by showing that the purportedly "scientific" empirical basis of credentialism and IQism is false. In addition, we have attempted to facilitate linkages between these groups and workers' movements within the dominant white male labor force, by showing that the same mechanisms are used to divide strata against one another so as to maintain the inferior status of "minority" groups.

The assault on economic inequality and hierarchical control of work appears likely to intensify. Along with other social strains endemic to advanced capitalism, the growing tension between people's needs for self-realization in work and the needs of capitalists and managers for secure top-down control of economic activity opens up the possibility of powerful social movements dedicated to the elimination of the hierarchical division of labor. We hope our paper will contribute to this outcome.

Notes

1. The most explicit statement of the genetic interpretation of intergenerational immobility is R. Herrnstein, "I.Q.," *Atlantic Monthly* (September 1971): 43–64.

2. M. Katz in *The Irony of Early School Reform* (Cambridge: Harvard University Press, 1968), notes the historical tendency of genetic interpretation of social inequality to gain popularity following the failure of educational reform movements. On the rise of genetic interpretation of inequality towards the end of the Progressive Era, see C. J. Karier et al., "Testing for Order and Control in the Corporate Liberal State," *Educational Theory* 22: 2 (Spring 1972).

3. See L. Wirth, "Preface," in K. Mannheim, *Ideology and Utopia: An Introduction to the Sociology of Knowledge* (New York: Harcourt, Brace & World, 1936), pp. x–xxx.

4. A. R. Jensen, "How Much Can We Boost IQ and Scholastic Achievement?," *Harvard Educational Review*, reprint series no. 2 (1969): 126–34.

5. For example, H. J. Eysenck, *The I.Q. Argument* (New York: Library Press, 1971), and Herrnstein, "I.Q."

6. For a representative sampling of criticisms, see the issues of the *Harvard Educational Review* that followed the Jensen article.

7. Jensen, "How Much Can We Boost IQ?"; C. Bereiter, "The Future of Individual Differences," *Harvard Educational Review*, reprint series no. 2 (1969): 162–70; Herrnstein, "I.Q."; Eysenck, *I.Q. Argument*.

8. By IQ we mean—here and throughout this essay—those cognitive capacities that are measured on IQ tests. We have avoided the use of the word "intelligence" as in its common usage it ordinarily connotes a broader range of capacities.

9. A. R. Jensen, "Estimation of the Limits of Heritability of Traits by Comparison of Monozygotic and Dizygotic Twins," *Proceedings of the National Academy of Science* 58 (1967): 149–57.

10. Jensen, "How Much Can We Boost IQ"; C. Jencks et al., *Inequality: A Reas-*

sessment of the Effects of Family and Schooling in America (New York: Basic Books, 1972).

11. Eysenck, *I.Q. Argument*, p. 9.

12. J. S. Kagan, "Inadequate Evidence and Illogical Conclusions," *Harvard Educational Review*, reprint series no. 9 (1969): 126–34; J. M. Hunt, "Has Compensatory Education Failed? Has it Been Attempted?," *Harvard Educational Review*, reprint series no. 2 (1969): 130–52.

13. Does the fact that a large component of the differences in IQ among whites is genetic mean that a similar component of the differences in IQ between blacks and whites is determined by the former's inferior gene pool? Clearly not. First of all, the degree of heritability is an average, even among whites. For any two individuals, observed IQ differences may be due to any proportion of genes and environment—it is required only that they average properly over the entire population. For instance, all of the difference in IQ between identical twins is environmental, and presumably a great deal of the difference between adopted brothers is genetic. Similarly, we cannot say whether the average difference in IQ between Irish and Puerto Ricans is genetic or environmental. In the case of blacks, however, the genetic school's inference is even more tenuous. R. J. Light and P. V. Smith ("Social Allocation Models of Intelligence: A Methodological Inquiry," *Harvard Educational Review* 39: 3 [1969]) have shown that even accepting Jensen's estimates of the heritability of IQ the black-white IQ difference could easily be explained by the average environmental differences between the races. Recourse to further experimental investigations will not resolve this issue, for the "conceptual experiments" that would determine the genetic component of black-white differences cannot be performed. Could we take a pair of black identical twins and place them in random environments? Clearly not. Placing a black child in a white home in an overtly racist society will not provide the same "environment" as placing a white child in that house. Similarly, looking at difference in IQs of unrelated black and white children raised in the same home (whether black or white or mixed) will not tell us the extent of genetic differences, since such children cannot be treated equally, and environmental differences must continue to persist (of course, if in these cases, differences in IQ disappear, the environmentalist case would be supported; but if they do not, no inference can be made).

14. Most environmentalists do not dispute Jensen's assertion that existing large-scale compensatory programs have produced dismal results (see Jensen, "How Much Can We Boost IQ" and, for example, H. Averch et al., *How Effective Is Schooling? A Critical Review and Synthesis of Research Findings* [Santa Monica, Calif.: Rand Corporation, 1972]). But this does not bear on the genetic hypothesis. As Jensen himself notes, the degree of genetic transmission of any trait depends on the various alternative environments that individuals experience. Jensen's estimates of heritability test squarely on the existing array of educational processes and technologies. Any introduction of new social processes of mental development will change the average unstandardized level of IQ as well as its degree of heritability. For instance, the almost perfect heritability of height is well documented. Yet the average heights of Americans have risen dramatically over the years, due clearly to change in the overall environment. Similarly, whatever the heritability of IQ, the average unstandardized test scores rose 83 percent between 1917 and 1943 (see Jencks et al., *Inequality*.)

But compensatory programs are obviously an attempt to change the total array of environments open to children through "educational innovation." While existing large-scale programs appear to have failed to produce significant gains in scholastic achievement, many more innovative small-scale programs have succeeded. See Bereiter, "Future of Individual Differences"; C. E. Silberman, *Crisis in the Classroom* (New York: Random House, 1970); Averch, *How Effective Is Schooling?* Moreover, even accepting the genetic position should not hinder us from seeking new environmental innovation—indeed it should spur us to further creative activities in this direction. Thus the initial thrust of the genetic school can be at least partially repulsed; there is no reliable evidence either that long-term contact of blacks with existing white environments would not close the black-white IQ gap, or that innovative compensatory programs (that is, programs unlike existing white child-rearing or education environments) might not attenuate or eliminate IQ differences that are indeed genetic.

15. J. S. Coleman et al., *Equality of Educational Opportunity* (Washington, D.C.: U.S. Government Printing Office, 1966).

16. For example, E. Rows, *Social Control* (New York: Macmillan, 1924); L. M. Terman, "The Conservation of Talent," *School and Society* 19: 483(March 1924); J. Schumpeter, *Imperialism and Social Class* (New York: Kelley, 1951).

17. This is not meant to imply that all liberal social theorists hold the IQ ideology. D. McClelland, *The Achieving Society* (Princeton, N.J.: Van Nostrand, 1967), and O. Lewis, "The Culture of Poverty," *Scientific American* 215 (October 1966): 16–25, among others, explicitly reject IQ as an important determinant of social stratification.

18. Jensen, "Estimation of the Limits of Heritability," p. 19.

19. O. D. Duncan, "Properties and Characteristics of the Socioeconomic Index," in *Occupations and Social Status*, ed. A. J. Reisse (New York: Free Press, 1961), p. 142.

20. Jensen, "Estimation of the Limits of Heritability," p. 19.

21. Bereiter, "Future of Individual Differences," p. 166.

22. Herrnstein, "I.Q.," p. 51.

23. Jensen, "How Much Can We Boost IQ?," p. 75.

24. Herrnstein, "I.Q.," p. 63.

25. Ibid.

26. Ibid.

27. In Table 12-2, as throughout this paper, "adult IQ" is measured by scores on a form of the Armed Forces Qualification Test. This measure is strongly affected both by early IQ (in this paper measured by Stanford-Binet or its equivalent at age six to eight) and years of schooling, and hence can be considered a measure of adult cognitive achievement. Economic success is measured throughout as the average of an individual's income and the social prestige of his occupation as measured on the Duncan occupational status index, each scaled to have standard deviation equal to one. See Duncan, "Properties and Characteristics of the Socioeconomic Index." For a description of the independent behavior of income and status, see S. Bowles, "The Genetic Inheritance of IQ and the Intergenerational Reproduction of Economic Inequality," (Harvard Institute of Economic Research, 1972). We have chosen a weighted average for simplicity of exposition, and in recognition of their joint importance in a reasonable specification of economic success.

28. See P. Blau and O. D. Duncan, *The American Occupational Structure* (New

York: John Wiley, 1967); O. D. Duncan, D. L. Featherman, and B. Duncan, *Socioeconomic Background and Occupational Achievement: Extensions of a Basic Model*, Final Report Project No. 5-0074 (EO-191), Contract No. OE-5-85-072 (Washington, D.C.: U.S. Department of Health, Education and Welfare, Office of Education, Bureau of Research, 1968); S. Bowles, "Schooling and Inequality from Generation to Generation," *Journal of Political Economy* (May-June 1972); and Bowles, "The Genetic Inheritance of IQ," for a more complete description. Similar calculations for other age groups yield results consistent with our three main empirical propositions.

29. Jencks et al., *Inequality*: R. Hauser, K. G. Lutterman, and W. H. Sewell, "Socioeconomic Background and the Earnings of High School Graduates," Mimeographed (University of Wisconsin, August 1971); J. Conlisk, "A Bit of Evidence on the Income-Education-Ability Interaction," *Journal of Human Resources* 6 (Summer 1971): 358–62; Z. Griliches and W. M. Mason, "Education, Income and Ability," *Journal of Political Economy* 80: 3 (May-June 1972); O. D. Duncan and D. L. Featherman, "Psychological and Cultural Factors in the Process of Occupational Achievement," (Population Studies Center, University of Michigan, 1971).

A further word is in order on Tables 12-1 to 12-7. Most popular discussions of the relation of IQ and economic success (for example, Jensen, "How Much Can We Boost IQ?"; Herrnstein, "I.Q.").

30. Bowles, "The Genetic Inheritance of IQ."

31. In Table 12-3, as throughout this paper, socioeconomic background is measured as a weighted sum of parental income, father's occupational status, and father's income, where the weights are chosen so as to produce the maximum multiple correlation with economic success.

32. This is not to say that IQ is never an important criterion of success. We do not contend that extremely low or high IQs are irrelevant to economic failure or success. Nor do we deny that for some individuals or for some jobs, cognitive skills are economically important. Rather, we assert that for the vast majority of workers and jobs, selection, assessed job adequacy, and promotion are based on attributes other than IQ.

33. For a more extensive treatment of this point, using data from nine independent samples, see Gintis, "Education and the Characteristics of Worker Productivity."

34. For a more extensive demonstration of this proposition, see Bowles, "The Genetic Inheritance of IQ."

35. Duncan, "Properties and Characteristics of the Socioeconomic Index."

36. Jensen, "Estimation of the Limits of Heritability," p. 73.

37. Herrnstein, "I.Q.," p. 63.

38. For an explanation of the social relations of production, see A. Gorz, "Capitalist Relations of Production and the Socially Necessary Labour Force," in *All We Are Saying . . .* , ed. A. Lothstein (New York: Putnam, 1970), and H. Gintis, "Power and Alienation," in *Readings in Political Economy*, ed. J. Weaver (Boston: Allyn & Bacon, forthcoming).

39. See S. Bowles, "Unequal Education and the Reproduction of the Social Division of Labor," *Review of Radical Political Economy* 3 (Fall-Winter 1971), and "Contradictions in U.S. Higher Education," in *Readings in Political Economy*, ed. Weaver, for an explanation of the connection between the social relations of produc-

tion and the stratification system.

40. Jensen reports that a panel of "experts" determined that higher status jobs "require" higher IQ. See Jensen, "How Much Can We Boost IQ?"

41. O. G. Brim et al., *American Beliefs and Attitudes about Intelligence* (New York: Russell Sage Foundation, 1969).

42. See B. R. Clark, "The 'Cooling Out' Function in Higher Education," *American Journal of Sociology* 65: 6 (May 1960); P. Lauter and F. Howe, "The Schools are Rigged for Failure," *New York Review of Books* 20 (June, 1970).

43. For an extensive bibliography of this research, see H. Gintis, "Toward a Political Economy of Education: A Radical Critique of Ivan Illich's *Deschooling Society*," *Harvard Education Review* 42: 1 (February 1972); Bowles, "Unequal Education and the Reproduction of the Social Division of Labor"; C. Greer, *The Great School Legend* (New York: Basic Books, 1972).

44. See F. T. Carleton, *Economic Influences Upon Education Progress in the U.S., 1820–1850* (Madison: University of Wisconsin Press, 1908); T. W. Shultz, "Capital Formation by Education," *Journal of Political Economics* 68 (December 1960): 571-83. This ideology is discussed in its several variations in S. Bowles and H. Gintis, "The Ideology of Progressive School Reform," in *Work, Technology, and Education: Dissenting Essays in the Intellectual Foundations of Education*, ed. H. Rosemont and W. Feinberg (Urbana: University of Illinois Press, 1975), and Greer, *Great School Legend*.

45. See D. Bruck, "The Schools of Lowell" (Honors thesis, Harvard University, 1971). In his study of cotton mill workers in Lowell in the 1840s, H. Luft ("The Industrial Worker in Lowell," Mimeographed, Harvard University, 1972) revealed no relationship whatever between worker literacy and their physical productivity. Bowles's as yet unpublished study (jointly with Alexander Field) of nineteenth-century educational expansion in Massachusetts found that the leading towns were those with cotton industries and large concentrations of foreign-born workers.

46. Bowles, "Unequal Education and the Reproduction of the Social Division of Labor," develops this argument in more detail. This perspective on the use of education is supported by a growing number of historical studies. See Bruck, "The Schools of Lowell," and Katz, *Irony of Early School Reform*.

47. R. Callahan, *Education and the Cult of Efficiency* (Chicago: University of Chicago Press, 1962).

48. See M. Lazerson, *Origins of the Urban School* (Cambridge: Harvard University Press, 1971).

49. See Callahan, *Education and the Cult of Efficiency*; D. K. Cohen and M. Lazerson, "Education and the Corporate Order," *Socialist Revolution* (March 1972); and L. Cremin, *The Transformation of the School* (New York: Knopf, 1964).

50. For a short review of this movement and its relation to the development of the U.S. stratification system, see Karier et al., "Testing for Order and Control."

51. E. C. Thorndike, "Intelligence and Its Uses," *Harper's* 140 (January 1920).

52. Cremin, *Transformation of the School*.

53. Karier et al., "Testing for Order and Control."

54. G. S. Counts, "The Social Composition of Boards of Education," *Review and Elementary School Journal*, Supplementary Education Monographs no. 33 (1927); Callahan, *Education and the Cult of Efficiency*.

55. Warner et al., in their extensive empirical studies of stratification, place much emphasis on social class ascription. See W. Lloyd Warner et al., *Who Shall Be Educated?* (New York: Harper, 1944). Compare W. P. S. Lunt, *The Social Life of a Modern Community* (New Haven: Yale University Press, 1941). But this seems characteristic only of the "small-town" economic community, rapidly becoming past history.

56. See H. Gintis, "New Working Class and Revolutionary Youth," *Socialist Revolution* (May 1970).

57. See the work of Erving Goffman. Other studies may be cited. Gorz, "Capitalist Relations of Production," provides a cogent analysis of the self-presentation of technical workers. Offe's analysis (*Leistungsprinzip and Industrielle Arbeit*) includes evidence on the role of schools in codifying modes of self-presentation and promotability. Finally, Bensman and Rosenberg ("The Meaning of Work in Bureaucratic Society," in *Anxiety and Identity*, ed. M. Stein et al. [New York: Free Press, 1960]), analyze the importance of conscious manipulation of self-presentation among the upwardly mobile.

58. N. C. Alexander and E. Q. Campbell, "Peer Influences on Adolescent Educational Aspirations and Attainments," *American Sociological Review* 29 (August 1964): 568–75; R. P. Boyle, "On Neighborhood Context and College Plans," *American Sociological Review* 31 (October 1966): 706-07; E. Erickson, "A Study of the Normative Influence of Parents and Friends," in *Self-Concept of Ability and School Achievement*, ed. W. Brookover et al. (Cooperative Research Project 2381, Office of Research and Publications, Michigan State University, 1967), vol. 3; A. Haller and C. Butterworth, "Peer Influence on Levels of Occupational and Educational Aspiration," *Social Forces* 38 (May 1960): 285–95; W. H. Sewell and M. Armer, "Neighbourhood Context and College Plans," *American Sociological Review* 31 (April 1966): 159–68; A. Wilson, "Residential Segregation of Social Classes and Aspirations of High School Boys," *American Sociological Review* 24 (December 1959): 836–45.

59. See R. D. Weiss, "The Effect of Education on the Earnings of Blacks and Whites," *Review of Economics and Statistics* 52 (May 1970); P. Cutright, "Achievement, Military Service, and Earnings," Mimeographed (Harvard University, May 1969).

60. M. P. Goldberg, "The Economic Exploitation of Women," in *Problems in Political Economy*, ed. D. M. Gordon (Lexington, Mass.: D. C. Heath, 1971).

61. I. Berg, *Education and Jobs: The Great Train Robbery* (New York: Praeger, 1970).

62. For a more extended discussion, see Gintis, "Education and the Characteristics of Worker Productivity," and "Toward a Political Economy of Education"; S. Bowles, "Cuban Education and the Revolutionary Ideology," *Harvard Educational Review* 41 (November 1971).

63. That working-class parents seem to favor more authoritarian educational methods is perhaps a reflection of their own work experiences that have demonstrated that submission to authority is an essential ingredient in one's ability to get and hold a steady, well-paying job.

64. K. Marx and F. Engels, *Communist Manifesto* (New York: International Publishers, 1948).

65. J. W. Gardner, *Excellence* (New York: Harper, 1961).

66. G. Kolko, *Wealth and Power in America* (New York: Praeger, 1962); H. Miller, *Income Distribution in the United States*, 1960 Census mimeograph (Washington, D.C.: U.S. Government Printing Office, 1966).

67. R. Lampman, *The Share of Top Wealth Holders in the National Wealth* (Princeton, N.J.: Princeton University Press, 1962).

68. R. C. Edwards, M. Reich, and T. Weisskopf, *The Capitalist System* (Englewood Cliffs, N.J.: Prentice-Hall, 1972), p. 324.

69. M. Reich, "The Economics of Racism," in *Problems in Political Economy* (Lexington, Mass.: D. C. Heath, 1971).

70. W. G. Spady, "Educational Mobility and Access: Growth and Paradoxes," *American Journal of Sociology* (November 1967); Blau and Duncan, *American Occupational Structure*.

71. Blau and Duncan, *American Occupational Structure*.

72. Coleman et al., *Equality of Educational Opportunity*; F. Mosteller and D. P. Moynihan, *On Equality of Educational Opportunity* (New York: Random House, 1972). Whether additional school resources are in fact irrelevant to greater academic performance is still an unsettled question. See S. Bowles and H. Levin, "The Determinants of Scholastic Achievement: An Appraisal of Some Recent Evidence," *Journal of Human Resources* 3 (Winter 1968); J. Guthrie et al., *Schools and Inequality* (Cambridge, Mass.: MIT Press, 1971). Available studies shed no light whatsoever on the relation between school resources and performance outside the cognitive sphere.

73. H. Averch et al., *How Effective Is Schooling?*; D. Armor, "The Evidence on Busing," *The Public Interest* (Summer 1972); T. Ribich, *Poverty and Education* (Washington, D.C.: Brookings Institute, 1968).

74. E. Banfield, *The Unheavenly City* (Boston: Little, Brown, 1968); O. Lewis, "The Culture of Poverty," *Scientific American* (October 1966); D. P. Moynihan, *The Negro Family: The Case for National Action* (Cambridge, Mass.: MIT Press, 1967).

75. H. Gans, *The Urban Villagers* (New York: Macmillan, 1962); Greer, *Great School Legend*.

76. Z. Griliches, "Notes on the Role of Education in Production Functions and Growth Accounting," in *Education, Income and Human Capital, Studies in Income and Wealth*, vol. 35 (New York: National Bureau of Economic Research, 1970); Weiss, "Effect of Education."

77. For example, A. W. Astin, "Undergraduate Achievement and Institutional 'Excellence'," *Science* 161 (August 1963). For a survey, see Bowles, "Unequal Education and the Reproduction of the Social Division of Labor."

78. Thus Averch et al., in *How Effective Is Schooling?*, their Rand Corporation report to the President's Commission on School Finance, state: "[In our attempt] to assess the current state of knowledge regarding the determinants of educational effectiveness . . . [we find that] educational outcomes are almost exclusively measured by cognitive achievement," (p. ix).

79. Coleman et al., *Equality of Educational Opportunity*.

80. Mosteller and Moynihan, *On Equality of Educational Opportunity*, p. 27.

81. D. Gilbarg and D. Finkelhor, *Up against the American Myth* (New York: Holt, Rinehart & Winston, 1970); Edwards, Reich, and Weisskopf, *Capitalist System*; Gintis, "New Working Class and Revolutionary Youth"; Bowles, "Contradictions in U.S. Higher Education"; T. Roszak, *The Making of the Counter-Culture* (New York:

Doubleday, 1969).

82. On "reproduction" and "contradiction" in the analysis of the social system, see H. Gintis, "Counter-Culture and Political Activism," *Telos* (Summer 1972).

83. For a more extended treatment of the contradictions of advanced U.S. capitalism, see: Bowles, "Contradictions in U.S. Higher Education"; Gintis, "Counter-Culture and Political Activism."

84. For a more complete statement of their position see: Gintis, "Education and the Characteristics of Worker Productivity," *American Economic Review* (May 1971); Bowles, "Contradictions in U.S. Higher Education."

85. For a more elaborate statement of this problem see: Schumpeter, *Imperialism and Social Class*; Bowles, "Contradictions in U.S. Higher Education."

86. See J. T. Main, *The Social Structure of Revolutionary America* (Princeton, N.J.: Princeton University Press, 1965); Reich in Edwards, Reich, and Weisskopf, *Capitalist System*.

87. See Gorz, "Capitalist Relations of Production."

88. The evidence is summarized in Gintis, "Power and Alienation."

89. See Therborn, reprinted in Edwards, Reich, and Weisskopf, *Capitalist System*.

90. See Bowles, "Contradictions in U.S. Higher Education"; Gintis, "New Working Class and Revolutionary Youth"; Gintis, "Counter-Culture and Political Activism."

13

It Comes with the Territory:
The Inevitability of Moral Education in the Schools

David Purpel and Kevin Ryan

A major assumption of this book is that public schools are actively, continuously, and heavily involved in moral education. We will try in this chapter to support this assumption by specifying the various ways in which moral
concerns and viewpoints are expressed in the schools. The great bulk of these
moral education experiences and activities are very likely *not* considered to be
moral education by those involved. However, we are including in our concept
of moral education those events and activities that carry with them some explicit or implicit moral concern, position, or orientation. We are convinced
that on any given day anyone sensitive to moral issues will find a great deal
of moral education going on in any public school in the nation. There is in
effect really no point in debating whether there should be moral education in
the schools. What needs to be debated is what form this education should take
since we believe that moral education, in fact, "comes with the territory."

An important disclaimer needs to be made. To our knowledge there is not
very much in the way of systematic, precise data as to just how much and in
what ways moral issues are presented in the schools. We are basing this description on our own personal impressions, observations, and experiences
as well as those of others. The field very much needs much more precise and
detailed information on the moral life of schools, even though we are confident that our impressions have significant bases in reality.

Reprinted from *Moral Education . . . It Comes with the Territory*, ed. David
Purpel and Kevin Ryan. Copyright © 1976 by McCutchan Publishing Corporation.
All rights reserved.

In lieu of hard data, we invite our readers to join us in an imaginary visit to some imaginary schools. As we journey together, we feel confident that some of our observations will seem familiar and that some will not. We urge our readers to augment, correct, or revise our analyses. We are less concerned with convincing our readers that any particular practice does or does not have moral significance than with increasing general sensitivity and understanding of the moral implications of current school experiences.

We will begin our visit by examining and observing the most obvious and most accessible instances, namely those found in the formal curriculum and in the day-to-day instructional programs.

Moral Education in the Visible Curriculum

An increasing number of schools (no one really knows how many) are involved in curriculum programs that openly and directly deal with moral education. Our analysis, however, will *not* deal with formal programs in moral education but rather with morally laden curriculum that emerges from traditional school practices.

When one visits a school and concentrates on the program of study and the instructional content of classroom activities, he is very likely to encounter a great many instances of morally loaded content in virtually every aspect of the curriculum:

1. A debate on abortion in a biology class raises questions on the value and definition of life.
2. A discussion on the radical nature of the American Revolution in a history class deals with the question of when insurrection and disloyalty are justified.
3. A critical analysis of the values implicit in Huckleberry Finn's relationship to Jim, the runaway slave, in an English class raises questions of the conflict between law and human dignity.
4. A mock trial of Daniel Ellsberg in a civics class raises questions on the meaning of the First Amendment.
5. Any number of moral issues are embedded in discussions of any number of current events, such as Watergate, the My Lai massacre, the morality of terrorism.

These activities and others like them can be conducted with explicit and conscious attention to moral issues, but often the moral issues inevitably intrude even when not invited. Naturally, there is immense variation among teachers as to how these issues are handled, but one thing is evident—moral considerations are involved and moral messages are inevitably conveyed about them, deliberately or not.

What our visitors might note is that this kind of moral education goes on in most schools routinely and unchallenged, as accepted and legitimate elements of the formal curriculum.

As we walk through the school corridors we might come across some less traditional settings where moral issues arise easily and naturally. There are, for example, programs in career education and personal development which provide opportunities for students to directly and systematically reflect on their lives so as to help make more informed decisions. Stress is put on self-knowledge and realistic appraisal of self in relation to society, which inevitably involves a whole host of moral questions. For example, students are often asked to deal with such questions as:

1. Should one work for a career that pays well or one that pays not so well but involves considerable opportunities for public service?
2. Should one defer immediate concerns (for example, playing varsity football) for ones with longer range considerations (for example, studying for exams)?
3. Should one plan for a career that will increase the possibility of family alienation? For example, a student under pressure from home to work in the family hardware store contemplates a career in marine biology.

We might also chance to visit other discussion activities having such names as town meeting, class gathering, and show-and-tell that center on personal concerns. What these groups all have in common is an opportunity for students to express and examine personal concerns, many of which have significant moral implications. For example, a child's complaint of feeling friendless and rejected can lead to a discussion of the responsibilities of other class members to respond to the child's needs.

Or we might visit a class where an incident or event is being used as a learning situation, for example, a death in the school community, any number of school disciplinary actions, a field trip, petty thievery, or a plagiarism case.

Or we might see a number of other classroom events in which moral issues either intrude themselves or arise but are apparently not stressed. For example, many stories, myths, and folktales are told and retold in the schools and they inevitably reveal some moral emphasis or another:

1. George Washington and his fallen cherry tree are often used to extol the virtues of honesty and facing the music.
2. "Three Little Pigs" are often used to point up the value of careful planning and industry.
3. Bible readings (in some schools) are used to illuminate a variety of subjects including the divine bases of authority and goodness.
4. Cinderella is presumably rewarded for her patience, forbearance, modesty, and obedience—or is it because she's good looking?
5. "The Man Without a Country" finds that to reject one's nation is to invite despair and emptiness.
6. The little Dutch boy who saved his community from disaster by

plugging up a hole in the dike certainly demonstrates the importance of social responsibility and how every little thing helps.

An extended visit would probably give us an opportunity to hear (and see) a great number of exhortations, proverbs, mottos, homilies, and epigrams carrying with them some moral imperatives:

1. Waste not, want not.
2. Love thy neighbor.
3. You reap what you sow.
4. If at first you don't succeed, try, try again.
5. Patience is a virtue.
6. Think!
7. Make love not war.
8. To thine own self be true.
9. Have a nice day.
10. Busy hands are happy hands.
11. Fight for dear old P.S. 162.
12. Happiness is anyone or anything at all loved by you.

It's fun (and what's important, very easy) to make such lists. We urge our readers to make their own list of favorite and persistent memories of moral messages received in schools. Here's ours:

1. Patriotic songs like "God Bless America," "America the Beautiful," and "The Battle Hymn of the Republic" said something to us about God's special relationship with the U.S.A.
2. We still remember the Alamo, the Maine, and Pearl Harbor—lest foreign treachery and American bravery and steadfastness be forgotten.
3. King Arthur set on his round table for us a number of vivid instances of loyalty, persistence, dedication, and devotion to God, women, and a set of rules. (Usually *not* included, we found out later, were Arthur's marital difficulties.)
4. We were often reminded of the long-run advantages of the steady persistent pace of the turtle over the erratically brilliant lope of the easily distracted rabbit.
5. Robin Hood shot holes through the notion that stealing is categorically wrong.
6. Abraham Lincoln's childhood of poverty, honesty, and determination seemed to provide the necessary ingredients for a political career of emancipation, charity for all, and martyrdom.
7. The little engine that could proved that stubbornness and willfulness can overcome humility and modesty.
8. Squanto and his fellow Indians' assistance to the Pilgrims in 1620 became early models of: (a) giving technical assistance to underdeveloped nations, (b) assisting the culturally disadvantaged, and (c) Brotherhood Week.

Moral Education in the Hidden Curriculum

Our imaginary visit so far has been mostly limited to an examination of the formal curriculum and to classroom observations. We now need to widen our horizons and to examine those activities which have been labeled the "hidden curriculum." The hidden curriculum has been defined as what students learn that is not in the formal curriculum. It has to do with the relationships among students, teachers, administrators, and staff particularly as they relate to authority, rules, and the quality of interpersonal relations. We will use the term to include some aspects of school which are not really hidden, such as formal rules, as well as to designate the more subtle and informal activities. We shall divide this analysis into four parts: the classroom culture, other formal school activities, the student culture, and the school culture.

The Classroom Culture

In our visit we need to be mindful of how students, teachers, staff, and administrators relate to each other. Lots of very powerful things happen in classrooms that go beyond the formal course of study. Many verbal transactions inevitably involve moral issues. Students, like all institutional citizens, derive notions of fair play, justice, and morality from how they are treated by the institution, its representatives, and fellow constituents. Schools certainly do "teach" about authority, about justice, about what is right and wrong, and about priorities in the myriad of school policies and practices ranging from the trivial to the significant. Think of the moral implications of these school events:

1. An entire class of children is punished because one or a small group has misbehaved.
2. A teacher sets up groups of children to work collaboratively on projects.
3. A pregnant unmarried student is not allowed to attend school.
4. An applicant for the cheerleader squad is blackballed because of "poor citizenship."
5. A student is not allowed to make up an exam because he went on a family trip on the day of the exam.
6. A teacher apologized to a class for having insulted a student during an argument.
7. Some students with a history of trouble making are not allowed to go on a field trip.
8. Some students volunteer to tutor younger children with reading problems.
9. A teacher taunts a child for not being nearly as productive as another sibling.

10. A teacher allows a student fight to continue as a way of settling an issue "once and for all."
11. A civics class decides to work on Saturdays to clean up a local playground.

Further observation might reveal certain patterns that express certain moral views:

1. Teachers hugging, patting heads, and showing affection to kids who have been "good."
2. Students who "misbehave" are chastised, exiled, humiliated, and even beaten.
3. Students who achieve at a certain level are given special privileges like being eligible to participate in varsity sports, work on the school paper, or go on special trips.
4. Students who fight or cheat or argue are, by the same token, often deprived of certain privileges.
5. Students who get all their math problems right often get gold or blue stars on their papers.
6. Students who "try hard" are often singled out and recognized, a policy which often extends to passing any student who shows sufficient effort. In this value system, high achievement/low effort is not as appreciated as low achievement/high effort.

Other Formal School Activities

The school, obviously, formally provides opportunities for learning other than courses and subject matter. There are such functions as the counseling and guidance program, athletic programs, various extracurricular activities such as dramatics, band, or debating society. Any one of these programs provides opportunities for issues with strong moral overtones to be developed (for example, winning and losing in a program of competitive athletics; or deciding who gets the lead in the major school production, the talented but uncooperative or the modestly talented but even tempered). And just what would be an appropriate topic for the debating society: "Resolved, All Holidays Should Be Celebrated on Mondays" or "Resolved, Marijuana Sales Should Be Made Legal"?

We could very well see assemblies and pep rallies which attempt to involve students emotionally and experientially in issues with moral content. For example, the purpose of some Memorial Day exercises seems to be to involve participants in grieving for fallen warriors and for reaffirming the validity and majesty of giving one's life for one's country. Pep rallies are designed to generate the kind of enthusiasm, fervor, and identification that will produce deep and abiding support for athletic teams. If our visit were at Christmas time we might see a pageant in which students could be expected to experience piety, awe, and reverence.

Student Culture

The observant visitor will see how students themselves (unwittingly or not) become agents of moral education. Teachers very often cite certain youngsters as models to be emulated and admired for their character. (Within this category is the more specific and for some more vivid phenomenon of comparing a student with a sibling.) In addition, students by themselves and without prompting are affected and influenced by other students and are apt to derive notions of good behavior from those they admire. This is an area where subtle combinations of peer and teacher approval provide powerful reinforcements for modeling certain behaviors. Some examples are:

1. Kids beating up "tattletales."
2. Social cliques ostracizing individuals.
3. Kids taunting "show-offs" or "teacher's pets."
4. Kids developing and enforcing rules in playground games.
5. Kids threatening unruly peers lest all are punished.

The strength and power of the student culture is reflected in the increasing tendency of many teachers, particularly student and beginning teachers, to identify with their students. Many teachers find themselves torn between the traditions and forms of the school and the inclination to respond to students' needs and feelings. Students as a group do affect the quality of school life and their values, be they hedonistic or pietistic, represent another important strand in the moral fabric of the school.

Teachers and administrators often face the opposing values of the school as an institution and the needs of students, individually or collectively. The increasing stress on personal and civil rights has sharply strengthened sensitivity to student concerns and indeed has led to situations where students significantly share decision making responsibilities. This by itself represents a particular set of values, that is, the values of shared decision making and affording the individual an increased sense of self-worth.

School Culture

The individual school or school system as a whole conveys certain beliefs, attitudes, and tenets that represent moral positions. It is therefore important that we become aware of the operational principles of the school. We can do this by reading official publications like bulletins, codes, and regulations as well as becoming sensitive to the implicit mores of the school. Some examples:

1. Good "conduct" is as important as good achievement.
2. Punctuality and neatness are good.
3. Cheating is bad.

4. Regular attendance is good.
5. School loyalty is good.
6. Informing on misbehavior is good.
7. Respect for adults is good.
8. Overt aggression is bad.
9. Damaging books is bad.

Although there is no question that moral issues and responses are involved in these policies and practices, there is still considerable disagreement and confusion over whether a school ought to represent or stand for a particular moral orientation. It is one thing to say that moral issues are involved in what the schools do and another to maintain that schools ought to deliberately act as moral institutions, that is, to indicate their conception of moral behavior and to proceed accordingly. Should the school deliberately set up moral criteria and judge conduct by those criteria?

For example, one sometimes hears teachers and administrators characterize a particular class or subgroup as having unusual attributes. We have in mind such statements as, "this third grade is a particularly rambunctious group" or "this year's graduating class seems more interested in personal rather than school matters." Are such observations expressions of legitimate school concerns? Should the school intervene in such areas? For example, what should teachers do if a graduating class seems to be on the verge of not following the tradition of making a gift to the school?

Conclusion

We have tried in this chapter to accomplish two basic tasks: (1) to make a case for the extensive and pervasive ways in which moral education is willy-nilly going on in our public schools, and (2) to try to increase our sensitivities to moral concerns as expressed in school life. Our intention was not to take any particular position on the policies and practices used as examples but only to point up the inevitability of moral education in the schools. We are not criticizing the schools for being moral agents but rather are asking that they be more aware, systematic, and informed about their moral influence.

There is also the question of whether any intervention is appropriate, since the argument exists that intervention in the realm of values constitutes manipulation and control of a personal and profound nature. However, we have tried to demonstrate that moral education does in fact go on in schools, and that it inevitably goes on even when not desired or intended. It is our view that the professional must not look at the issue as "should we have moral education in the schools?" but rather "to what degree and in what dimensions and areas should we deal with moral education in the schools?" We need to become more aware of the implicit techniques and goals that are used, not so as to eliminate them but so as to provide us with a basis for making reasonable judgments no matter how complex and painful they may be.

The basic professional decisions, then, are in the realm of choosing an approach that approximates general school and community policy on moral education. Obviously, professionals need to participate in this policymaking since it is really not possible to separate goals from techniques. However, broad school policy on moral education should emerge from discussions with parents, students, and community representatives. We say this with full knowledge that it creates difficulties, controversies, and conflicts. Professionals, however, have a vital role to play in informing the public on the nature of the issues and the nature of the options.

The age, ability, and background of students affects the nature of the program, and many moral education programs stress verbal and intellectual abilities not found in younger children. Some programs require certain levels of emotional and personal maturity. Some goals of moral education can be reached through teaching specific skills, others may be more a matter of developmental growth and maturity. Some programs will require special understanding or training for teachers. A number of specific approaches have been developed with different theoretical frameworks utilizing combinations of techniques described above.* Any one of those approaches is a reasonable response to the requirement for a moral education program that is intellectually valid, pedagogically sound, and consistent with our democratic traditions.

---

*For a discussion of the more technical questions of approaches and programs, see David Purpel and Kevin Ryan, "Moral Education in the Classroom: Some Instructional Issues," in *Moral Education . . . It Comes with the Territory*, ed. id. (Berkeley, Calif.: McCutchan, 1976), pp. 35–67.

Section III

From the Hidden Curriculum to Moral Values in Pedagogy

The first two sections of this book have essentially dealt with the exposition of the concept *hidden curriculum* and how it has been applied in various settings and with different orientations. In this section, we respond to the question Jane Martin poses in her article: "What does one do when one finds the hidden curriculum?" It is our view that underneath all curriculum, explicit or implicit, lie basic moral beliefs. Indeed, a basic purpose of the first two parts of this book has been to demonstrate this point. It is also our conviction that these moral beliefs should *not* be hidden but rather uncovered and acknowledged as part of the process by which educators can openly choose, affirm, and celebrate a particular belief system.

We agree with Jane Martin's statement on the importance of consciousness raising as a way of responding to the hidden curriculum. It is the essence of the educative process to discover, to know, to be aware, and *not* to be deceived or deluded. Education could be described as a process through which the hidden, the implicit, the tacit, the elusive, and the unknown become vivid and known to us. However, it is not enough to know and understand—we must know with intention and purpose, and we must act with understanding and meaning. We must as educators give up the futile task of trying to be neutral and objective and instead take on the responsibility for directing our energies toward our ideals. It is time for educators to stop being coy and evasive about their moral postures toward the basic questions of dignity, freedom, justice, and equality. We have tried to show that school curriculum touches deeply on these issues *inevitably*.

The issue of conspiracy is in one sense irrelevant, the point being that the schools are in fact teaching and imparting important ideas on these basic questions however silent or inadvertent the process may be. It is imperative

277

that we be as keenly aware of the silent curriculum as of the explicit one, which then makes the development of the capacity to be aware a prime goal of our educational program. Moreover, as educators we must face up to our responsibilities not only to be aware but to make choices and to make them openly.

Many contemporary curriculum writers have used ideas from the German sociologist Jurgen Habermas as a framework for discussing various approaches to knowledge. Habermas has suggested three ways in which knowledge can be used to serve human interests—for control, understanding, and liberation. Knowledge can be used to help control our environment and provide ways of meeting our needs and wants. This kind of knowledge is basically technical, such as the knowledge that enables us to build machines and systems. Knowledge also helps us to understand our world and provides us with a body of common knowledge and beliefs that provide for continuity and community. Not only do we have knowledge of machines and systems, but we also have an understanding of how and why they work. Beyond that, knowledge can help us become liberated from understandings that unnecessarily restrict us and prevent us from exercising our own autonomy and selfhood. To be free from unnecessary controls and restrictive understandings is the purpose of liberating knowledge. Jane Martin's stress on consciousness raising in regards to the hidden curriculum would seem to reflect an emphasis on understanding and controlling those phenomena. We strongly agree with that position as far as it goes, but we do not think it goes far enough. We believe that we ought to use knowledge about the hidden curriculum to help in the process of human liberation as grounded in the values of personal dignity and social justice.

Several of the articles in this section deal specifically with what the meaning of education for human liberation is. However, it is useful to sketch in broad terms what we mean, particularly as it relates to the hidden curriculum in its moral dimensions. First, we mean liberated in the ideal-typical sense of being fully aware of both reality and possibility. There can be no covert hidden curriculum when people are liberated, for free people are informed and resistant to deception and delusion. There is always a tacit hidden curriculum because the truth is never fully or completely revealed; that is, there is *no end* to ideology. To be liberated means not only being savvy and aware but also being in touch with potential—not only sophisticated about what is going on but about what might go on. It is for these reasons that the development of a critical consciousness and the imagination are of crucial importance as will be shown in more detail in the articles in Section III. Critical consciousness allows us to have more awareness and understanding of the moral implications of the hidden curriculum, and imagination allows us to continually reconstruct a world in which there is a greater likelihood that personal dignity and social justice will flourish.

Second, human liberation requires being free from the social, economic, and cultural barriers to personal autonomy and meaning. What we have in mind here is interpersonal, political, and economic oppression in all of its forms—lack of love and understanding; lack of access to the decision-making process; and denial of individual worth.

Education must help to remove these unnecessary cultural, social, and political barriers to personal dignity by revealing the assumptions and biases that underlie any set of ideas, axioms, propositions, or beliefs. The hidden curriculum must be exposed so that it can no longer be used to oppress anyone. It is not that the hidden curriculum inevitably oppresses, but it is only by becoming aware of it that we can be sure that it does not. More positively, we need to explicitly and openly strive to help people become free, partly by helping develop strong intellectual and aesthetic capacities, partly by celebrating a commitment to personal dignity and social justice, and partly by trying to create a culture and society in which all this is possible. It is a vast chain—we need the commitment and moral energy that impels us to be vigilant and sensitive to misguided educational efforts; and we need the courage and endurance to keep working for the kind of society that itself is committed to personal dignity and social justice, which means an educational system that helps to instill such a commitment. We know schools have been shown to have limited impact on students, but we believe that most educators still have strong faith in the power of knowledge, understanding, and imagination to stir, inspire, and move to action. Certainly, the authors in this third section have that faith; but more than faith, they have powerful and compelling ideas on the relationship between education and human liberation that can help schools maximize their role in the quest for human liberation, however modest that role might be.

We have divided Section III into two parts—the first group of articles deals specifically with the meaning and validity of the notion of education for liberation. The second part includes articles that deal with the question of just what a curriculum for human liberation might look like. It is clear that an all-encompassing model for a curriculum of liberation has yet to be developed, but as these articles reveal, many of the key elements of such a model are emerging. We are optimistic that the ongoing resurgence of energy and commitment to liberation as the goal for education will continue and deepen, and eventually will produce a powerful and enduring model designed to make education a vital force in the development of a just and caring democratic community.

Part A
EDUCATION AS LIBERATION

14

The Banking Concept of Education

Paulo Freire

A careful analysis of the teacher-student relationship at any level, inside or outside the school, reveals its fundamentally *narrative* character. This relationship involves a narrating Subject (the teacher) and patient, listening objects (the students). The contents, whether values or empirical dimensions of reality, tend in the process of being narrated to become lifeless and petrified. Education is suffering from narration sickness.

The teacher talks about reality as if it were motionless, static, compartmentalized, and predictable. Or else he expounds on a topic completely alien to the existential experience of the students. His task is to "fill" the students with the contents of his narration—contents which are detached from reality, disconnected from the totality that engendered them and could give them significance. Words are emptied of their concreteness and become a hollow, alienated, and alienating verbosity.

The outstanding characteristic of this narrative education, then, is the sonority of words, not their transforming power. "Four times four is sixteen; the capital of Pará is Belém." The student records, memorizes, and repeats these phrases without perceiving what four times four really means, or realizing the true significance of "capital" in the affirmation "the capital of Pará is Belém," that is, what Belém means for Pará and what Pará means for Brazil.

Narration (with the teacher as narrator) leads the students to memorize mechanically the narrated content. Worse yet, it turns them into

Reprinted from *Pedagogy of the Oppressed*, by Paulo Freire (New York: Herder and Herder-Seabury Press, 1970), pp. 57–74. Reprinted by permission of The Continuum Publishing Company.

"containers," into "receptacles" to be "filled" by the teacher. The more completely he fills the receptacles, the better a teacher he is. The more meekly the receptacles permit themselves to be filled, the better students they are.

Education thus becomes an art of depositing, in which the students are the depositories and the teacher is the depositor. Instead of communicating, the teacher issues communiqués and makes deposits which the students patiently receive, memorize, and repeat. This is the "banking" concept of education, in which the scope of action allowed to the students extends only as far as receiving, filing, and storing the deposits. They do, it is true, have the opportunity to become collectors or catalogers of the things they store. But in the last analysis, it is men themselves who are filed away through the lack of creativity, transformation, and knowledge in this (at best) misguided system. For apart from inquiry, apart from the praxis, men cannot be truly human.[1] Knowledge emerges only through invention and reinvention, through the restless, impatient, continuing, hopeful inquiry men pursue in the world, with the world, and with each other.

In the banking concept of education, knowledge is a gift bestowed by those who consider themselves knowledgeable upon those whom they consider to know nothing. Projecting an absolute ignorance onto others, a characteristic of the ideology of oppression, negates education and knowledge as processes of inquiry. The teacher presents himself to his students as their necessary opposite; by considering their ignorance absolute, he justifies his own existence. The students, alienated like the slave in the Hegelian dialectic, accept their ignorance as justifying the teacher's existence—but, unlike the slave, they never discover that they educate the teacher.

The *raison d'être* of libertarian education, on the other hand, lies in its drive toward reconciliation. Education must begin with the solution of the teacher-student contradiction, by reconciling the poles of the contradiction so that both are simultaneously teachers *and* students.

This solution is not (nor can it be) found in the banking concept. On the contrary, banking education maintains and even stimulates the contradiction through the following attitudes and practices, which mirror oppressive society as a whole:
   a. The teacher teaches and the students are taught.
   b. The teacher knows everything and the students know nothing.
   c. The teacher thinks and the students are thought about.
   d. The teacher talks and the students listen—meekly.
   e. The teacher disciplines and the students are disciplined.
   f. The teacher chooses and enforces his choice, and the students comply.
   g. The teacher acts and the students have the illusion of acting through the action of the teacher.
   h. The teacher chooses the program content, and the students (who were not consulted) adapt to it.

    i. The teacher confuses the authority of knowledge with his own authority, which he sets in opposition to the freedom of the students.

    j. The [teacher] is the Subject of the learning process, while the pupils are mere objects.

It is not surprising that the banking concept of education regards men as adaptable, manageable beings. The more students work at storing the deposits entrusted to them, the less they develop the critical consciousness which would result from their intervention in the world as transformers of that world. The more completely they accept the passive role imposed on them, the more they tend simply to adapt to the world as it is and to the fragmented view of reality deposited in them.

The capability of banking education to minimize or annul the students' creative power and to stimulate their credulity serves the interests of the oppressors, who care neither to have the world revealed nor to see it transformed. The oppressors use their "humanitarianism" to preserve a profitable situation. Thus they react almost instinctively against any experiment in education which stimulates the critical faculties and is not content with a partial view of reality but always seeks out the ties which link one point to another and one problem to another.

Indeed, the interests of the oppressors lie in "changing the consciousness of the oppressed, not the situation which oppresses them";[2] for the more the oppressed can be led to adapt to that situation, the more easily they can be dominated. To achieve this end, the oppressors use the banking concept of education in conjunction with a paternalistic social action apparatus, within which the oppressed receive the euphemistic title of "welfare recipients." They are treated as individual cases, as marginal men who deviate from the general configuration of a "good, organized, and just" society. The oppressed are regarded as the pathology of the healthy society, which must therefore adjust these "incompetent and lazy" folk to its own patterns by changing their mentality. These marginals need to be "integrated," "incorporated" into the healthy society that they have "forsaken."

The truth is, however, that the oppressed are not "marginals," are not men living "outside" society. They have always been "inside"—inside the structure which made them "beings for others." The solution is not to "integrate" them into the structure of oppression, but to transform that structure so that they can become "beings for themselves." Such transformation, of course, would undermine the oppressors' purposes; hence their utilization of the banking concept of education to avoid the threat of student *conscientizacão*.[3]

The banking approach to adult education, for example, will never propose to students that they critically consider reality. It will deal instead with such vital questions as whether Roger gave green grass to the goat, and insist upon the importance of learning that, on the contrary, Roger gave green grass to the rabbit. The "humanism" of the banking approach masks the effort to turn men into automatons—the very negation of their ontological vocation to be more fully human.

Those who use the banking approach, knowingly or unknowingly (for there are innumerable well-intentioned bank-clerk teachers who do not realize that they are serving only to dehumanize), fail to perceive that the deposits themselves contain contradictions about reality. But, sooner or later, these contradictions may lead formerly passive students to turn against their domestication and the attempt to domesticate reality. They may discover through existential experience that their present way of life is irreconcilable with their vocation to become fully human. They may perceive through their relations with reality that reality is really a *process*, undergoing constant transformation. If men are searchers and their ontological vocation is humanization, sooner or later they may perceive the contradiction in which banking education seeks to maintain them, and then engage themselves in the struggle for their liberation.

But the humanist, revolutionary educator cannot wait for this possibility to materialize. From the outset, his efforts must coincide with those of the students to engage in critical thinking and the quest for mutual humanization. His efforts must be imbued with a profound trust in men and their creative power. To achieve this, he must be a partner of the students in his relations with them.

The banking concept does not admit to such partnership—and necessarily so. To resolve the teacher-student contradiction, to exchange the role of depositor, prescriber, domesticator, for the role of student among students would be to undermine the power of oppression and serve the cause of liberation. . . .

It follows logically from the banking notion of consciousness that the educator's role is to regulate the way the world "enters into" the students. His task is to organize a process which already occurs spontaneously, to "fill" the students by making deposits of information that he considers to constitute true knowledge.[4] And since men "receive" the world as passive entities, education should make them more passive still, and adapt them to the world. The educated man is the adapted man, because he is better "fit" for the world. Translated into practice, this concept is well suited to the purposes of the oppressors, whose tranquility rests on how well men fit the world the oppressors have created, and how little they question it.

The more completely the majority adapt to the purposes which the dominant minority prescribe for them (thereby depriving them of the right to their own purposes), the more easily the minority can continue to prescribe. The theory and practice of banking education serve this end quite efficiently. Verbalistic lessons, reading requirements,[5] the methods of evaluating "knowledge," the distance between the teacher and the taught, the criteria for promotion: everything in this ready-to-wear approach serves to obviate thinking.

The bank-clerk educator does not realize that there is no true security in his hypertrophied role, that one must seek to live *with* others in solidarity. One cannot impose oneself, nor even merely co-exist with one's students. Solidarity requires true communication, and the concept by which such an educator is guided fears and proscribes communication.

Yet only through communication can human life hold meaning. The teacher's thinking is authenticated only by the authenticity of the students' thinking. The teacher cannot think for his students, nor can he impose his thought on them. Authentic thinking, thinking that is concerned about *reality*, does not take place in ivory tower isolation, but only in communication. If it is true that thought has meaning only when generated by action upon the world, the subordination of students to teachers becomes impossible.

Because banking education begins with a false understanding of men as objects, it cannot promote the development of what Fromm calls "biophily," but instead produces its opposite: "necrophily."

While life is characterized by growth in a structured, functional manner, the necrophilous person loves all that does not grow, all that is mechanical. The necrophilous person is driven by the desire to transform the organic into the inorganic, to approach life mechanically, as if all living persons were things. . . . Memory, rather than experience; having, rather than being, is what counts. The necrophilous person can relate to an object—a flower or a person—only if he possesses it; hence a threat to his possession is a threat to himself; if he loses possession he loses contact with the world. . . . He loves control, and in the act of controlling he kills life."[6]

Oppression—overwhelming control—is necrophilic; it is nourished by love of death, not life. The banking concept of education, which serves the interests of oppression, is also necrophilic. Based on a mechanistic, static, naturalistic, spatialized view of consciousness, it transforms students into receiving objects. It attempts to control thinking and action, leads men to adjust to the world, and inhibits their creative power. . . .

Education as the exercise of domination stimulates the credulity of students, with the ideological intent (often not perceived by educators) of indoctrinating them to adapt to the world of oppression. This accusation is not made in the naive hope that the dominant elites will thereby simply abandon the practice. Its objective is to call the attention of true humanists to the fact that they cannot use banking educational methods in the pursuit of liberation, for they would only negate that very pursuit. Nor may a revolutionary society inherit these methods from an oppressor society. The revolutionary society which practices banking education is either misguided or mistrusting of men. In either event, it is threatened by the specter of reaction. . . .

Those truly committed to liberation must reject the banking concept in its entirety, adopting instead a concept of men as conscious beings, and consciousness as consciousness intent upon the world. They must abandon the educational goal of deposit making and replace it with the posing of the problems of men in their relations with the world. . . .

Through dialogue, the teacher-of-the-students and the students-of-the-teacher cease to exist and a new term emerges: teacher-student with students-teachers. The teacher is no longer merely the-one-who-teaches, but one who is himself taught in dialogue with the students, who in turn while being taught also teach. They become jointly responsible for a process in which all grow. In this process, arguments based on "authority" are no longer valid; in order to function, authority must be *on the side of* freedom, not *against* it. Here, no one teaches another, nor is anyone self-taught. Men teach each other, mediated by the world, by the cognizable objects which in banking education are "owned" by the teacher.

The banking concept (with its tendency to dichotomize everything) distinguishes two stages in the action of the educator. During the first, he cognizes a cognizable object while he prepares his lessons in his study or his laboratory; during the second, he expounds to his students about that object. The students are not called upon to know, but to memorize the contents narrated by the teacher. Nor do the students practice any act of cognition, since the object toward which that act should be directed is the property of the teacher rather than a medium evoking the critical reflection of both teacher and students. Hence in the name of the "preservation of culture and knowledge" we have a system which achieves neither true knowledge nor true culture.

The problem-posing method does not dichotomize the activity of the teacher-student: he is not "cognitive" at one point and "narrative" at another. He is always "cognitive," whether preparing a project or engaging in dialogue with the students. He does not regard cognizable objects as his private property, but as the object of reflection by himself and the students. In this way, the problem-posing educator constantly reforms his reflections in the reflection of the students. The students—no longer docile listeners—are now critical co-investigators in dialogue with the teacher. The teacher presents the material to the students for their consideration, and reconsiders his earlier considerations as the students express their own. The role of the problem-posing educator is to create, together with the students, the conditions under which knowledge at the level of the *doxa* is superseded by true knowledge at the level of the *logos*.

Whereas banking education anesthetizes and inhibits creative power, problem-posing education involves a constant unveiling of reality. The former attempts to maintain the *submersion* of consciousness; the latter strives for the *emergence* of consciousness and *critical intervention* in reality.

Students, as they are increasingly posed with problems relating to themselves in the world and with the world, will feel increasingly challenged and obliged to respond to that challenge. Because they apprehend the challenge as interrelated to other problems within a total context, not as [a] theoretical question, the resulting comprehension tends to be increasingly critical and thus constantly less alienated. Their response to the challenge evokes new challenges, followed by new understandings; and gradually the students come to regard themselves as committed.

Education as the practice of freedom—as opposed to education as the practice of domination—denies that man is abstract, isolated, dependent, and unattached to the world; it also denies that the world exists as a reality apart from men. Authentic reflection considers neither abstract man nor the world without men, but men in their relations with the world. In these relations consciousness and world are simultaneous; consciousness neither precedes the world nor follows it. . . .

In problem-posing education, men develop their power to perceive critically *the way they exist* in the world *with which* and *in which* they find themselves; they come to see the world not as a static reality, but as a reality in process, in transformation. Although the dialectical relations of men with the world exist independently of how these relations are perceived (or whether or not they are perceived at all), it is also true that the form of action men adopt is to a large extent a function of how they perceive themselves in the world. Hence, the teacher-student and the students-teachers reflect simultaneously on themselves and the world without dichotomizing this reflection from action, and thus establish an authentic form of thought and action.

Once again, the two educational concepts and practices under analysis come into conflict. Banking education (for obvious reasons) attempts, by mythicizing reality, to conceal certain facts which explain the way men exist in the world; problem-posing education sets itself the task of demythologizing. Banking education resists dialogue; problem-posing education regards dialogue as indispensable to the act of cognition, which unveils reality. Banking education treats students as objects of assistance; problem-posing education makes them critical thinkers. Banking education inhibits creativity and domesticates (although it cannot completely destroy) the *intentionality* of consciousness by isolating consciousness from the world, thereby denying men their ontological and historical vocation of becoming more fully human. Problem-posing education bases itself on creativity and stimulates true reflection and action upon reality, thereby responding to the vocation of men as beings who are authentic only when engaged in inquiry and creative transformation. In sum: banking theory and practice, as immobilizing and fixating forces, fail to acknowledge men as historical beings; problem-posing theory and practice take man's historicity as their starting point.

Problem-posing education affirms men as beings in the process of *becoming*—as unfinished, uncompleted beings in and with a likewise unfinished reality. Indeed, in contrast to other animals who are unfinished, but not historical, men know themselves to be unfinished; they are aware of their incompletion. In this incompletion and this awareness lie the very roots of education as an exclusively human manifestation. The unfinished character of men and the transformational character of reality necessitate that education be an ongoing activity.

Education is thus constantly remade in the praxis. In order to *be*, it must *become*. Its "duration" (in the Bergsonian meaning of the word) is found in the interplay of the opposites *permanence* and *change*. The banking method emphasizes permanence and becomes reactionary; problem-posing education—which accepts neither a "well-behaved" present nor a predetermined future—roots itself in the dynamic present and becomes revolutionary.

Problem-posing education is revolutionary futurity. Hence, it is prophetic (and, as such, hopeful). Hence, it corresponds to the historical nature of man. Hence, it affirms men as beings who transcend themselves, who move forward and look ahead, for whom immobility represents a fatal threat, for whom looking at the past must only be a means of understanding more clearly what and who they are so that they can more wisely build the future. Hence, it identifies with the movement which engages men as beings aware of their incompletion—an historical movement which has its point of departure, its Subjects and its objective.

The point of departure of the movement lies in men themselves. But since men do not exist apart from the world, apart from reality, the movement must begin with the men-world relationship. Accordingly, the point of departure must always be with men in the "here and now," which constitutes the situation within which they are submerged, from which they emerge, and in which they intervene. Only by starting from this situation—which determines their perception of it—can they begin to move. To do this authentically they must perceive their state not as fated and unalterable, but merely as limiting—and therefore challenging.

Whereas the banking method directly or indirectly reinforces men's fatalistic perception of their situation, the problem-posing method presents this very situation to them as a problem. As the situation becomes the object of their cognition, the naive or magical perception which produced their fatalism gives way to perception which is able to perceive itself even as it perceives reality, and can thus be critically objective about that reality.

A deepened consciousness of their situation leads men to apprehend that situation as an historical reality susceptible of transformation. Resignation gives way to the drive for transformation and inquiry, over which men feel themselves to be in control. If men, as historical beings necessarily engaged with other men in a movement of inquiry, did not control that movement, it would be (and is) a violation of men's humanity. Any situation in which some men prevent others from engaging in the process of inquiry is one of violence. The means used are not important; to alienate men from their own decision making is to change them into objects.

This movement of inquiry must be directed towards humanization—man's historical vocation. The pursuit of full humanity, however, cannot be carried out in isolation or individualism, but only in fellowship and solidarity; therefore it cannot unfold in the antagonistic relations between oppressors and oppressed. No one can be authentically human while he prevents others from being so. . . .

Problem-posing education, as a humanist and liberating praxis, posits as fundamental that men subjected to domination must fight for their emancipation. To that end, it enables teachers and students to become Subjects of the educational process by overcoming authoritarianism and an alienating intellectualism; it also enables men to overcome their false perception of reality. The world—no longer something to be described with deceptive words—becomes the object of that transforming action by men which results in their humanization.

Notes

1. *Praxis* means reflection and action upon the world in order to change it.

2. S. de Beauvoir, *La Pensée de Droite, Aujord'hui* (Paris); ST, *El Pensamiento politico de la Derecha* (Buenos Aires, 1963), p. 34.

3. The term *conscientizacão* refers to learning to perceive social, political, and economic contradictions and to take action against the oppressive elements of reality.

4. This concept corresponds to what Sartre calls the "digestive" or "nutritive" concept of education, in which knowledge is "fed" by the teacher to the students to "fill them out." See Jean-Paul Sartre, "Une idée fundamentale de la phenomenologie de Husserl: L'intentionalité," *Situations I* (Paris, 1947).

5. For example, some professors specify in their reading lists that a book should be read from pages 10 to 15—and do this to "help" their students!

6 F Fromm, *The Heart of Man* (New York: Harper & Row, 1966), p. 41.

15

Curriculum, Consciousness, and Social Change

James Macdonald

Three things cannot be retrieved—
The arrow once sped from the bow,
The word spoken in haste,
The missed opportunity.
—Islamic Proverb

It is becoming very fashionable to take a dim view of the field of curriculum and curriculum development. I suspect we are overly harsh on ourselves, perhaps because we have had high and unwarranted expectations of dramatic change. I believe we are, as the proverb suggests, missing opportunities to affect those aspects of the curriculum field that we are best able to influence.

It is important to note that although we in curriculum have always had our own special set of complexities and problems, we also share in a broader social and intellectual context, which is currently experiencing considerable disillusionment, anxiety, and confusion. Our alternatives seem fairly clear: we can give up the whole enterprise (negate it, if you wish) and simply live with whatever resolution occurs, or we can continue to try to provide better conceptualization and practice that can lead to the improvement of curriculum environments. I, personally, have not yet lost my passion for continuing the quest for improving curriculum.

Those of us who continue on this path confront a very difficult question: Is

Reprinted, by permission, from *Journal of Curriculum Theorizing* 3: 1 (Winter 1981): 143–53.

there anything we can do at the level of schooling that does not require prior or concomitant broad social change before meaningful improvements can occur? Or, stated in another way, perhaps we can modify George Count's "Dare the Schools Change the Social Order?" to "Can the Schools Change the Social Order?" If we decide we can make a difference, then we must justify the implicit "should" that rests in asking that question. Personally, I believe we both can and should attempt to change society.

So that I may focus on how I believe we can make a difference, I will not deal with the question of "should" at any length. Yet, I must at least say that although schooling is a major vehicle for socializing the young and for conserving and transmitting our culture, there is no reason why we ourselves must not act on the basis of the best values we are trying to communicate to the young.

I can see no reason to propose to the young that freeing the human spirit, mind, and body from arbitrary social and psychological constraints—that is, the liberation of human potential in a framework of democratic rights, responsibilities, and practices, which leads toward better realization of justice, equality, liberty, and fraternity—should not be reflected in our own work with schools. Thus, I think we should work toward change in the direction of human liberation.

Turning to the question of what we can do in curriculum and curriculum development in the schools, we must be clear about our expectations. In this article, I shall take an organic as opposed to a synthetic approach,* and I shall attempt to provide an analysis of the setting for the derivation of reasonable expectations; then I will suggest ways we might meet these expectations.

What Do We Expect?

In order to become involved in the work of curriculum for the sake of human liberation and social change rather than for shaping and controlling behavior or broadening our understanding of our problems, per se, as end points, we need to have our expectations (as distinguished from objectives) clearly in mind.

What we can expect to achieve is grounded in our conceptions of human nature and the nature of change in society and culture. I shall briefly explain, using the works of two rather disparate scholars, the position and thus the setting from which my expectations come.

---

*In doing so, I shall immediately be accused of liberal reformism rather than radical revolution. The weight isn't too heavy to carry, but I think there is a subtle difference between the position that will be developed here and traditional ideas of reform. In any case, what I propose seems to me the only sensible way to proceed.

The past 2,500 years of Western culture have witnessed a basic confrontation between various brands of idealism and realism. Pushed to their extremities, these positions may be called consciousness and materialism. At the extremes, the consciousness position may argue that reality rests in our consciousness and the material objects of the world are appearances. The extreme materialistic position would posit that reality is what it appears to be (what we sense) and mental phenomena are epiphenomena of our actions in the world. This is a continuing debate and the diversity in viewpoints on the problem are almost beyond cataloging.

I will use the work of Michael Polanyi[1] as a basis for illustrating the concept of human nature that I believe makes most sense in relation to the fundamental problem of consciousness and materialism, which for our purposes I have translated into the mind-body argument. Polanyi posits that all knowledge is personal knowledge. By this he does not mean that all knowledge is relative and idiosyncratic to individuals, but that all knowledge involves a person knowing (a knower). Further, knowing involves a focus for our coming to know and a tacit subsidiary ground or context is needed to form the elements of personal knowing. Polanyi combines a Gestalt psychology, perceptual understanding with an organismic biological orientation that posits a hierarchy of organization in organic systems whereby the higher-level systems are not the sum of their parts (though dependent on them) but provide an organizing function for lower levels. I shall not argue the case here, but I would like to present what Polanyi feels are the implications of his framework in terms of the mind-body problem or consciousness.

Polanyi states that the relation of mind to body has the same logical structure as that which exists in focal awareness and subsidiary awareness (that is, consciousness), since we all have those awarenesses. Polanyi concludes from his analysis that the mind or consciousness exists as a separate entity but is dependent on the body to which it serves as the higher principle in the organization of the organism's functions: "Though rooted in the body, the mind is, therefore, free in its actions from bodily determination— exactly as our common sense knows it to be free."

We may also look to the work of Antonio Gramsci for descriptions of the setting in which we project expectations. Gramsci was an Italian Marxist theoretician whose major work ranges from 1916 to 1937. His work has special relevance to my position here because it contributes, from a Marxist orientation on social and cultural change, the kind of perspective that helps us focus on resonable expectations for curriculum and curriculum development.

According to Carl Boggs,[2] Gramsci's major themes were:

1. To focus upon the active, political, and voluntarist side of a theory rather than fatalistically relying on the objective focus and scientific laws of capitalist development.

2. To focus less on historical analysis and empirical description and more on the issues of strategy and political methods necessary to destroy bourgeois society.

3. Revolution or change necessitates passionate emotional commitment, not just rational-cognitive activity, integrated through the concept of praxis.

4. Most important for our purposes here, Gramsci gave a high priority to the role of ideological struggle in the revolutionary process. He insisted that socialist revolution be conceived as an organic phenomenon, not as an event, and that transforming consciousness was an inseparable part of structural change (that is, economic and social conditions of work and production).

5. Thus, revolutionary change must embrace all aspects of society and culture, not simply the economic.

6. Further, he rejected the elitist and authoritarian tendencies in the community movement and strove to develop a "mass" party rooted in everyday social reality.

7. And, finally, he strove to build a theory that would be visibly relevant to the broad masses of people.

What is selectively critical for my purposes here is Gramsci's concept of ideological hegemony. Where many Marxists emphasized the dependence of politics, ideology, and culture on the economic substructure as a reflection of the material base, Gramsci clearly felt this was not broad enough to encompass the necessary analysis for change. By positing the idea of ideological hegemony, Gramsci meant to elucidate, as Boggs says:

. . . the permeation throughout civil society—including a whole range of structures and activities like trade unions, schools, the churches, and the family—of an entire system of values, attitudes, beliefs, morality, etc., that is in one way or another supportive of the established order and the class interests that dominate it. To the extent that this prevailing consciousness is internalized by the broad masses, it becomes part of "common sense" For hegemony to assert itself successfully in any society, therefore, it must operate in a dualistic manner: as a general conception of life for the masses, and as a scholastic program or set of principles which is advanced by a sector of the intellectuals.[3]

What Gramsci posits and develops through the context of his Marxist theory is the critical role of consciousness and the changes in values, attitudes, morality, and beliefs that are necessary for revolutionary change.

One additional point of Gramsci's theorizing should be noted for our purposes here—his conception of the role of intellectuals in the process of social change. Assuming that curriculum thinkers are intellectuals, his points may have relevance for us. Gramsci rejected the establishment of an elite group of theoreticians and proposed what he called an "organic intellectual," who would be immersed in the everyday activity of different groups of workers. Such a person would integrate new ideas into the fabric of the lifestyles, language, and traditions of workers in their work environments. As Idries Shah, the leader of the Sufis, says, "Please do not start to teach the blind until you have practiced living with closed eyes."

I will turn now to the problem of our own expectations for positive change in schools. The positions described by Polanyi and Gramsci, which originated from widely separate experiences and intentions, have provided a setting that is representative of many other scholars. The importance I wish to attach to these views may be summarized quickly. First, the existence of a separate entity called human consciousness is apparent. Second, change in human social consciousness is a necessary condition for later political change. And it is precisely in the realm of changing consciousness that I believe our expectations should reside.

Thus, in Jurgen Habermas's[4] terms, there are two moments in the dialectic—work and communication. If we utilize the concept of a dialectical relationship over longer periods of time between consciousness and structural change, it is at the "moment" of consciousness in this dialectic when we may expect to have any meaningful input in the change process. Our activities, efforts, and expectations should, in other words, be focused on the ideas, values, attitudes, and morality of persons in school in the context of their concrete, lived experiences, and our efforts should be directed toward changing consciousness in these settings to provide more liberating and fulfilling outcomes.

Furthermore, there is no one brand of liberation. There is no predictable, absolute outcome that we should expect from our efforts. On the contrary, a diversity and apparent inconsistency of comparative efforts can be expected. Any concrete or spontaneous concern on the part of educators for repressive or oppressive structures, practices, and ideas should also be treated as valid and as a point of entry for changing consciousness.

William Irwin Thompson[5] makes a similar point when he asks why our good intentions so often lead to evil outcomes. One answer to this, he feels, is simply that if the good is seen shining in the immediacy of the act itself, it should be adopted. All appeals to long-range goals, fixed outcomes, expediency, and efficiency are the foci that wreck our ideals. In terms of our activity then, the good of it for liberating human beings resides in the validity of the immediate activity in concrete contexts.

Our expectations then should be focused on the consciousness of educators. The educators should be stimulated through the analysis of existing conditions, by the introduction of new frameworks for looking at school life, and by providing leadership through which new experiences with these perspectives can be internalized in a wide variety of seemingly disparate activities. Let us examine some of these areas and activities.

Some of the Possibilities

The proposals and prescriptions I will present must obviously remain in the realm of possibilities. I believe we must be much more opportunistic, flexible, and adaptable to practical situations if we can hope to realize our expectations. To attempt to be definitive at this point would obviously be inconsistent with the view presented here. Nevertheless, I think there are some areas of activity and some potential alternatives within these areas that may be legitimately suggested.

The areas I see at this time as most relevant for changing consciousness toward a more liberating existence are: (1) ideas and perspectives, (2) personal growth, (3) substance or subject matter, (4) preference rules, and (5) constitutive rules. In addressing myself to these areas, I shall refer primarily to the roles of teachers and other workers in the curriculum field.

Perspectives

Perhaps the most important concern is our ideas and perspectives that influence our activity. Through my experience I have become convinced that a major prerequisite for liberating changes necessarily includes a rather dramatic altering of the consciousness of persons and a change in how they "see" the meaning of their participation in activities with students and colleagues. It is not enough to simply change the structures or to provide new techniques without acquiring new lenses of perception and conception.

What I propose is the attempt to shift the perspective of educators from the dominant quantitative achievement task-orientation toward nebulous future goals to a perspective that focuses directly on the quality of our everyday situations.

The quality of experience resides in the relationships in our lives. Thus, the way we relate to other people, the way we organize and administer power, the relationship of our work to our self-esteem, how we feel about what we are doing, and what meaning our lives have in concrete contexts are all ways of thinking about the quality of our experience.

After many frustrating years as a teacher at a university, I have realized that if one wishes to influence others' ideas and perspectives, one must literally embody those ideas and perspectives. By this I do not mean "teaching the way you recommend others teach." This old bromide is simplistic and futile. Our styles are our own, rooted in biography and personality. What we must reveal are our passions, our values, and our justifications. To focus only on our behavior is near to selling our souls to the devil at the price of our own vital energy.

What we must ask of ourselves then is to profess—to reveal and to justify from our own viewpoints what we believe and value. There need be no loss in setting forth others' views that differ from our own, but what we must risk is losing the posture of neutral scholarship suffused with the aridity of living an uncommitted life.

There are inherent dangers in this process. The temptation to slide from legitimating justification to propaganda and indoctrination is not always easy to resist, yet the very process of challenge and the creation of dissonance in the mind of the student, embodied in the living presence of another and infused in a living relationship, is often the source of the beginning of liberation. Most university teachers of my acquaintance would rather be neutral and offer readings with divergent views. I would reverse this posture if I hoped to guide students toward their own liberation and new liberating perspectives.

We are coming quite close at this point to the concept of transcendence. We are asking persons to transcend the limitations and restriction of their social conditioning and common sense and to venture beyond by seeing and choosing new possibilities. Thus, the human spirit becomes engaged in the direction of transcendent activity through the guidance of meaningful and valued goodness toward which these possibilities may lead.

Phillip Phenix[6] has spoken insightfully about curriculum transcendence. He posits that by our nature we are drawn toward transcending our present state via our consciousness of temporality. Thus, our impetus for choosing and becoming is not something that need be externally imposed; rather it is a process of helping others see possibilities and helping them to free themselves to go beyond their state of embedded existence.

Paulo Soleri[7] captures this eloquently in another context, which should be seen as an analogy for our purposes, when he says:

I do not bow to the death wish we exhibit cynically as a sign of existential responsibility, nor do I sympathize with the pietists sporting flowing robes, beards and sandals of the simple and the meek. I find the hard-headed technocrat utterly pulp-minded; and the politician too busy to know and be serious. I find him smothering the soul while flushing history into the past as if it were an undigestible but somehow homogeneable slut.

I see most of the equivocation, the inability to act, as the gap between the nuts and bolts fanatic and the spiritualist . . . the bridge between the matter and spirit is *matter becoming spirit*. This flow from the indefinite-infinite into the utterly subtle is the moving arch pouring physical matter into the godliness of conscious and metaphysical energy. This is the context, the place where we must begin anew.

If the reference point is spirit, then whenever spirit is not incremented, pollution is present in its most comprehensive form: Entropy. Entropy and pollution are one and the same.

What we ask of students is equally important. It should be clear by now that our goals, broadly conceived, should be to: (1) develop new liberating perspectives, (2) clarify values, (3) stimulate and develop educational thinking, and (4) communicate significant knowledge and ideas in the area we are dealing with. The statement of, or intent to achieve, highly specific goals in curriculum courses is neither necessary nor desirable, for this process is both fruitless and antithetical to freeing students to achieve our significant goals.

In the late 1920s, W. W. Charters, through analysis of the teaching role, produced approximately 1,000 teacher competencies. No one is quite sure what happened to those necessities of good teaching, but some say their ghosts have come back to haunt us today. At any rate, in my understanding about the phenomena of ghosts, they are more to be pitied than taken seriously and their only power resides in the fear they produce in the observer.

What is at stake here is close to the distinction Rene Spitz [8] makes between education and learning. He sees these processes as radically different, both structurally and developmentally. Spitz illustrates this from his work with infants and toilet training. In the 1930s the Children's Bureau recommended toilet training begin at two months of age. Babies actually learned when placed on the toilet to do their duty. By the end of the first year, the training broke down. At this time, says Spitz, training conflicted with the infant's developing personality and it proved exceedingly difficult to right the breakdown. Toilet training based on education calls for a later age, but it also requires an effective relationship that facilitates identification with a significant other's wishes and standards. Humanization can only occur via education, which comes through affect-charged relationships that help to develop self-governance, autonomy, and independence.

I shall share one general approach that I believe is a real possibility for achieving the broad liberating goals mentioned earlier. It is wholistic in that all the aforementioned goals are embedded in the same general approach. Students and school personnel in curriculum courses or in the field can be asked to develop and share their own creative models of educational contexts that are relevant to their own work. In the process they are asked to specify the basic intentions of the model, that is, control, understanding, or liberation. Value assumptions concerning the cosmos and human nature are also identified. The model itself, once constructed, must have boundaries, variables, and specify the relationships among the variables within the model. And, finally, each may be asked to state what new insights or what practical implications the model may have for them. These models are then shared and critiqued by a group of peers.

This form of curriculum activity engages the person not only in an exercise of thinking, but of revealing and clarifying values, searching for new perspectives, and engaging in moral, political, and aesthetic discourse; all of which are so needed in education, as Huebner[9] has pointed out.

Let us turn now to what might be loosely called the "content" of the liberating thrust.

There are at least four fundamental emphases that we must constantly attempt to recognize and analyze to encourage deeper understanding of their meaning at the levels of values, attitudes, morals, and ideological thought processes. These emphases are: (1) technological rationality, (2) bureaucracy, (3) human rights, and (4) economic substructures. All of these have meaning that should be focused on for improving the quality of experience in our lives.

Technological rationality refers to the dominant mind-set of our culture. It is in Marcuse's[10] terms a one-dimensional orientation toward tasks and problems characterized by a complete commitment to an instrumental thinking that separates means from ends. Thus, this empirical and socially behavioristic stance emphasizes the efficiency and effectiveness of measurable achievement and divorces human activity from the source of valued meanings or qualities. Thus, an irrational rationality predominates. In social terms this is both an ideological set and a political act of destroying the validity of possible change as concerns are narrowed to the efficiency of the domination of the status quo.

School personnel must be constantly alerted to this cultural mind-set. They must be helped to see where it enters our lives through such practices as behavioral objectives, behavioral modification, management by objectives, systems analyses, teacher competency approaches, accountability movements, and so forth. They must be constantly encouraged to shift from the "How?" to the "What?" and the "Why?"

In terms of bureaucracy we are witnessing a form of institutional organization that facilitates the rationalization and specialization necessary to carry technological rationality into social structures, work tasks, and communication networks. Thus, examination and analysis of the intentions and effects of bureaucratic practices are critical for developing liberating values and procedures.

There also exists in bureaucratic structures the phenomenon of displaced goals, which must be revealed and examined. Much of the policy and form of bureaucracy tends to become self-serving and related to the institution as a place of work, rather than to its professional goals or purposes. This too must be noted.

A third emphasis is a concern for human rights. If we are to affect the quality of our lives in schools, we must ask if the "Bill of Rights" should be parked at the door when we enter the school, as it tends to be in most other work situations. We have, I believe, relegated our concern for our rights as private citizens to our homes and to our participation in the political system. This is a critical aspect of domination, since the impact on our perceptions, attitudes, values, and morals in living in institutional work settings is a pervasive factor in our mind-set, or perspective. Thus, we must take every reasonable opportunity to raise the issue of human rights in the context of our conduct and the impact of that conduct on the quality of living in the environments we create.

The final major substantive emphasis concerns the economic system (and especially the substructure) of which we are a part. There can be little doubt that many of the policies, practices, and procedures we use in schools are built on a "factory" model or analogy. Further, the basic justification for schooling seems to be shifting more toward preparation for occupations. Also, there is the fact that education is a major "industry" itself, at least in the sense that the expenditure of monies is directly related to the private world of commerce through the purchase of books, materials, and so on.

The examination of the influence of these and other economic factors on our daily lives in schools is critical, and we should take every opportunity to examine and raise questions about our activity in relation to the economic forces in our society if we wish to acquire a clearer perspective on the potential for liberating experiences.

The four perspectives just mentioned are not only topics for study, but should be used as liberating lenses when we deal with the curricular substance of our courses and our work as curriculum persons.

Personal Growth

The second broad area of concern beyond building new perspectives is that of personal growth. Personal growth is not divorced from perspectives, of course, but I refer here primarily to the idea that there is little chance that persons will be concerned about liberating human potential in others unless they themselves are also involved in their own personal structures in a quest for liberation.

The work of Gramsci and many others clearly suggests that liberating social change necessarily involves breaking up conditioned and pre-set attitudes, values, and meanings attached to present social phenomena in a manner that allows people to sense the potential within themselves for change and growth, from powerlessness to power, and from alienation to relationship and commitment. I do not believe that there is any fundamental contradiction in the long run between those theorists who advocate a personal change position and those who advocate a social change orientation in terms of changing consciousness toward a liberating praxis. This assumes that the social approach does not involve a highly structured set of "new" meanings, nor does the personal growth approach involve restructuring to a highly individualistic orientation without meaning for communal living. Neither approach need be exaggerated to the point of excluding the other.

There is, thus, a need for us as curriculum teachers and workers to involve ourselves in the process of continuous liberating growth; and we should facilitate personal growth in those we work with through caring for them as people. We should also select working processes that enhance a person's self-esteem as well as select experiences that will facilitate developing an awareness of their potential for growth.

One relevant example comes from my year's experience as a member of the staff at the Curriculum Laboratory of Goldsmith College, University of London. Teachers and Heads, as teams from various schools, were brought on campus for twelve-week workshop sessions with one day a week back in their schools. They were attending in order to work on developing curricula for an innovative program loosely labeled "Interdisciplinary Inquiry."

I was immediately and forcefully struck, and puzzled, by the provision of about a third of the workshop time for the participants' engagement in various activities in the areas of arts and crafts. This came to be one of the most significant aspects of their "curriculum" work, for not only did they learn art and craft substance for building into interdisciplinary studies, but far more important, the activities provided a rich personal experience for exploring their own potentials and for seeing themselves as creative and growing persons.

Group sessions on the curriculum were organized to facilitate the kinds of issues, values, and decisions that were inherent in the task of curriculum development and design. The teams worked to develop their own plans in a full participatory manner in relation to their unique practical situations. In the broad context of attempting to innovate under the loose rubric of "interdisciplinary inquiry" toward a more liberating curriculum, the result was specific team plans that were widely varied.

The following year, I was asked to return to England to do a follow-up study of the approximately two hundred persons who had experienced the Goldsmith program. One technique used was an open-ended interview ranging over five years with a random selection of some forty participants. The most common response to their experience was its meaning to them personally, the impact upon the way they saw themselves as persons and professionals. Their judgments about the value of the actual curriculum plans produced and the subsequent implementation of these plans were much more varied.

A final note on personal growth refers to the use of such experiences as group therapy, encounter groups, and other similar activities. Frankly, I am not competent to fairly evaluate these possibilities. I should think, from what I know, that there exists a great potential for personal growth if these practices can be sensibly related to the tasks of curriculum teaching and working, but a caution, gleaned from the comments of Keen's remarks in Floyd Matson's "Behaviorism versus Humanism," is in order. He suggests that some varieties of the humanistic encounter group activities may be as dehumanizing as behavioristic techniques when they result in stripping all human dignity away from the person in the process.

Substance or Subject Matter

When we approach the task of providing liberating possibilities with the content of the curriculum, we must keep some fundamental epistemological assumptions clearly in mind. Among these epistemological assumptions are:

1. Knowledge is uncertain, not absolute.
2. Knowledge is personal.
3. Knowledge is for use, not simply storage.

And, perhaps of a slightly different order:

4. Knowledge of social arrangements is knowledge of human creations that reflect more than anything else historical accidents within the broad organizing trends of growing technology, sciences, industry, and religion.
5. Knowledge is not disparate or segmented in a broad human sense of lived meaning, but rather it is unitary. Only by specific highly rationalized human interests and tasks has it been segmented and highly disparate.

Given these epistemological assumptions (which I believe can be justified satisfactorily), we may look at the substance of the total curriculum plan or at any given aspect, area, or subject of it, while keeping in mind that the quality of lived experiences resides in relationships. In the case of curriculum, the relationships are basically: (1) persons to subject matter, (2) subject matter to subject matter, (3) society to subject matter, and (4) persons to society.

Kliebard,[11] at the Geneseo Conference, restates what he sees historically as the basic questions of curriculum: "What knowledge is of most worth?"; "How is this differentiated for learning?"; "How do we teach it?"; and "How is it integrated?" He says the central question is that of objectives.

I have little difficulty accepting the four questions as basic to curriculum, but I believe he is in error from a liberating point of view in the priority he attaches to the question of objectives. As a matter of fact, if one takes the questions in the order that Kliebard presents them, they can easily be transposed into the Tyler rationale, with the one notable exclusion being the evaluation question.

Care must be taken here to also note that these questions represent a "back to basics" in the curriculum field. It reflects a general trend to refocus the definition of curriculum back to the subject matter taught. One might suppose that this is related to the frustrations suffered over the past years in dealing with the complexities of experience and activity models of curriculum.

Accepting these four questions as central to curriculum for purposes here, I would posit that from a liberating value base the critical question must be the question of integration (or in terms used earlier—relationships). The questions of goals, procedures, and differentiation, it would seem to me, can be answered in the dynamics of relationships. It is this network of relationships that Maxine Greene[12] has spoken so eloquently about.

Given these comments we may turn to a possible set of suggested design guidelines that focus on the four relationships (that is, subject to subject, person to subject, society to subject, and person to society). These guidelines are not new. They would not only lead toward developing new consciousness for social change, but have also been known over the years to many persons as good, sound educational premises. What follows is an illustrative reminder.

1. Curriculum substance must be directly related to needs, interests, past experiences, and capabilities of persons.
2. Substance should be so organized as to allow for maximum possible variation between persons.
3. Substance should be organized so that it reveals to the greatest possible extent its instrumental and interpretive relevance to the social world.
4. Substance should be organized so that its meaning for the everyday living of the persons involved is apparent.
5. Substance should be organized so that the cognitive and affective relationships within and between usually disparate areas are apparent.
6. Substance should be organized so that all areas of the curriculum contribute directly to the creation of meaning structures that deal with the human condition.
7. And finally, substance should be organized so that the overall concern is the development of broad structures of meaning, human values, attitudes, and moral understandings.

This list by no means represents all of the possible guidelines. Designs that are consistent with these liberating guidelines go under such titles as: Core Curriculum, Interdisciplinary Inquiry, Open Education, Broad Fields, Emerging Needs, Affective Education, Problems of Living, and so on.

Essentially what is needed is a continued effort to help workers in curriculum see the meaning of these designs for freeing human potential and, thus, raising consciousness, but in a way that provides for creative development of their everyday lives in schools. We are, as I am sure many of us can testify, in desperate need of new and better design possibilities that will facilitate this movement.

Preference Rules and Constitutive Rules

The last two topics for discussion are the preference and constitutive rules, which I shall deal with together.

Michael Apple[13] has discussed the implication of these rules in relation to the hidden curriculum. Fundamentally, it amounts to recognition that there are rules that we may vary by preference, such as the rules for the use of toilet facilities, and rules that constitute basic boundaries that cannot be varied if the system or cultural mileu is to retain its integrity and function. One such constitutive rule in most settings is the rule against cheating.

I would posit that in the cause of liberation three things are necessary. First, that the distinction between these kinds of rules be brought into everyone's awareness; second, that constitutive rules be made cognitively accessible to all through analysis and discussion; and third, that to the degree possible, attempts be made to move constitutive rules into the realm of preference rules.

Apple's illustration of a chess game is useful here because, among other reasons, it is also used by Polanyi to establish the identity of consciousness. Chess is played with boundary conditions such as definition of the use of the spaces, the acceptable directions and procedures for moving different pieces on the board, and so on. On the other side, the strategy, sequence of moves, and the like are the preference of the players. In Polanyi's terms, one focuses consciously on the strategy (preference rules) from the subsidiary cues (ground rules). It would appear then that the boundaries or constitutive rules, once internalized, become a tacit dimension or, if you wish, a hidden curriculum.

The importance of the hidden curriculum in freeing human potential cannot be overestimated. It is at this juncture that many of the most pernicious practices and procedures reside. The "return to basics" referred to earlier is essentially a turning away from this critical aspect of schooling. It is probably a product or corollary of the general retrenchment of conservative stability that we are witnessing throughout our society.

Curriculum teachers and workers must continuously raise the reflective consciousness questions, "What are the constitutive and preference rules?," "Why do you have them?," and "What (if any) is their connection to the broader society and culture?" This can be done on an abstract level or through techniques such as observation, videotapes, self-descriptions of our own practices and procedures, and tapes and typed transcriptions of learning episodes.

One very good avenue for helping us to locate constitutive rules lies in our passions. It appears sensible to me that basic rules are those boundaries that are most apt to arouse our emotional judgments. Following the position espoused by Solomon, passions are not imposed upon us but are fundamental judgments, such as love, anger, anxiety, hate, envy, with which we have interpreted our situation and which provide a key through our reflection of our definition of the situation.

When we are pleased or disturbed by the actions of individuals or the way things are going, it would seem quite possible that we are touching basic boundaries or rules and making judgments in terms of those rules that reflect our perspectives, values, attitudes, and morals. Thus, schoolpeople can come to grips with identifying the constitutive rules in their activity via careful reflection on those very situations and actions that arouse our passions. This kind of reflective activity also has the merit of completing the human response to liberation by a momentary and sometimes tentative but real dissolution of the subject-object distinction so prevalent and humanly damaging in Western civilization.

There are two other critical areas that are of special importance. These concerns are the testing and the evaluation of plans and procedures, and the differentiation of hidden structures that are rationalized by goals and efficiency in procedure. The structures are hidden in the sense that their full intent in relation to what constitutes their existence is not revealed in their function. Thus, to many schoolpeople and students the structures seem "natural" rather than arbitrary value commitments.

One dimension of this problem is the clear realization that many of the grouping, labeling, and tracking procedures used in curriculum and instruction provide an unequal access to common knowledge. This has the effect of replicating the social structure in terms of a meritocracy and convincing the winners and the losers that they deserve the status they achieve. There exists a considerable lack of distributive justice in our schools or society—either materially or in terms of knowledge and consciousness.

In another sense, many of the constitutive rules, such as "work is more important than play," "the teacher is the final authority," "be on time," "don't skip school," and the like, are most probably functions of social conditioning for the work force, rather than necessary for stimulating and developing human creative potential or capabilities.

The evaluation dimension is at least as troublesome for persons concerned about human liberation, and perhaps it is the epitome of domination for all persons in schools. What it amounts to in practical terms is a system that can be characterized as a tyranny of knowledge and basic skills. It is interesting to note in passing that in the Business School at the University of North Carolina at Greensboro, the term "evaluation" is defined as control, perhaps a more honest approach than we take.

I am reasonably sure that technical rationales and the use of behavioristic approaches are dominant in curriculum because they are logically, though not necessarily empirically, the most advantageous approaches to control. Further, the concerns for specifying and managing by objectives are not essentially related to the questions of "What knowledge is of most worth" or "What relationships enhance the quality of living," but these concerns become important only in the control nexus of evaluation. Though evaluation is often made to seem a necessary adjunct to reaching goals, I am afraid that statements of objectives are much more apt to be necessary adjuncts to the system of evaluative control.

There is really no point in detailing the problems with accountability, behavioral objectives, behavioral modification, management by objectives, systems analysis, teacher competencies, and other control and evaluation-oriented procedures. Let it just be said that they are the tools of domination for the tyranny of cognitive knowledge and skills in our schools.

Neither shall I, at this point, suggest strategies or procedures for changing evaluation procedures, for I am not sure that positive alternatives within the control orientation are even possible. What I shall say is that if evaluation were truly an adjunct to the goals of human liberation, its value would reside in the provision of data from the consequences of our actions, which could serve as a basis in our consciousness for further reflection and praxis.

Conclusion

In closing, I would like to reiterate the major points I have presented. I believe that things are not hopeless and curriculum thinking is not moribund. Improving curriculum environments is essentially a matter of our expectations, and our expectations should be focused on the development of cultural consciousness. Further, I assume that the major meaning of education relates to the liberation of human potential and not to the control of human behavior, which to me is training.

Consciousness is an essential entity of human beings, though existent in a material base. Any quest for liberating persons from arbitrary domination by others calls for a basic change in attitudes, values, morals, and perspectives, as well as for change in social and economic structures. We in our roles as curriculum teachers and workers can only expect to have influence in the realm of consciousness, but this influence is both a necessary and significant contribution.

Changing consciousness toward liberating activity can be effected by focusing upon school persons' ideas and perspectives, personal growth, subject matter, and upon the preference and constitutive rules, with the intent of using our analysis to improve the quality of the relationships in our school lives.

The avenues and aspects will be manifold, but essentially any change in consciousness or practice that moves one step closer to freeing ourselves from arbitrary domination by social structure or other persons may be counted as a legitimate step toward liberation. What we must do, if we are concerned about these matters, is to become somewhat more humble, but continue to work for what we believe is right. We must, as Erich Fromm[14] says, keep up our hope, which he defines as the willingness to keep working for what we believe in with the full realization that we may never see it come to fruition in our lifetime.

Notes

1. M. Polanyi, *Personal Knowledge* (Chicago: University of Chicago Press, 1958); id., *The Tacit Dimension* (Garden City, N.Y.: Doubleday Anchor Books, 1967).

2. C. Boggs, *Gramsci's Marxism* (London: Pluto Press, 1976).

3. Ibid., p. 39.

4. J. Habermas, *Knowledge and Human Interest* (Boston: Beacon Press, 1971).

5. W. I. Thompson, *Evil and World Order* (New York: Harper & Row, 1976).

6. P. Phenix, "Transcendence and the Curriculum," *Teachers College Record* 73: 2 (December 1971): 271–82.

7. P. Soleri, *Matter Becoming Spirit* (Garden City, N.Y.: Doubleday Anchor Books, 1973), pp. 2, 4.

8. R. Spitz, *Fundamental Education Play and Development,* ed. M. Piers (New York: W. W. Norton, 1977).

9. D. Huebner, "Curricular Language and Classroom Meanings," *Languages and Meaning,* ed. J. Macdonald (Washington, D.C.: The Association for Supervision and Curriculum Development, 1966), pp. 8–26.

10. H. Marcuse, *One Dimensional Man* (Boston, Mass.: Beacon Press, 1964).

11. H. Kliebard, "Curriculum Theory: Give Me a 'For Instance'," *Curriculum Inquiry* 6: 4 (1977): 257–68.

12. M. Greene, "Curriculum and Consciousness," *Teachers College Record* 73: 2 (December 1971): 253–69.

13. M. Apple, "The Hidden Curriculum and the Nature of Conflict," *Interchange* 2: 4 (1971): 27–40.

14. E. Fromm, *The Revolution of Hope* (New York: Harper & Row, 1968).

16

The Moral Content of American Public Education

Israel Scheffler

The title of this essay is to be taken not as a declaration but as a question: What should be the purpose and content of our educational system insofar as it relates to moral concerns? This is a very large question, with many and diverse ramifications. Only its broadest aspects can here be treated, but a broad treatment, though it must ignore detail, may still be useful in orienting our thought and highlighting fundamental distinctions and priorities.

Education in a Democracy

The title refers to education as American. But the latter designation is simply geographical; it provides little in the way of distinguishing criteria relevant to our problem. What is more pertinent is the commitment to the ideal of democracy as an organizing principle of society. This commitment has radical and far-reaching consequences, not only for basic political and legal institutions, but also for the educational conceptions that guide the development of our children. All institutions, indeed, operate through the instrumentality of persons; social arrangements are "mechanisms" only in a misleading metamorphical sense. Insofar as education is considered broadly, as embracing all those processes through which a society's persons are developed, it is thus of fundamental import for all the institutions of society, without exception. A society committed to the democratic ideal is one that

Reprinted from *Educational Research: Prospects and Priorities* (Washington, D.C.: U.S. Government Printing Office, 1972).

makes peculiarly difficult and challenging demands of its members; it accordingly also makes stringent demands of those processes through which its members are educated.

What is the democratic ideal, then, as a principle of social organization? It aims so to structure the arrangements of society as to test them ultimately upon the freely given consent of its members. Such an aim requires the institutionalization of reasoned procedures for the critical and public review of policy; it demands that judgments of policy be viewed not as the fixed privilege of any class or elite but as the common task of all, and it requires the supplanting of arbitrary and violent alteration of policy with institutionally channeled change ordered by reasoned persuasion and informed consent.

The democratic ideal is that of an open and dynamic society: open, in that there is no antecedent social blueprint which is itself to be taken as a dogma immune to critical evaluation in the public forum; dynamic, in that its fundamental institutions are not designed to arrest change but to order and channel it by exposing it to public scrutiny and resting it ultimately upon the choices of its members. The democratic ideal is antithetical to the notion of a fixed class of rulers, with privileges resting upon social myths which it is forbidden to question. It envisions rather a society which sustains itself not by the indoctrination of myth, but by the reasoned choices of its citizens, who continue to favor it in the light of a critical scrutiny both of it and its alternatives. Choice of the democratic ideal rests upon the hope that this ideal will be sustained and strengthened by critics and responsible inquiry into the truth about social matters. The democratic faith consists not in a dogma, but in a reasonable trust that unfettered inquiry and free choice will themselves be chosen, and chosen again, by free and informed men.

The demands made upon education in accord with the democratic ideal are stringent indeed; yet these demands are not ancillary but essential to it. As Ralph Barton Perry has said,

Education is not merely a boon conferred by democracy, but a condition of its survival and of its becoming that which it undertakes to be. Democracy is that form of social organization which most depends on personal character and moral autonomy. The members of a democratic society cannot be the wards of their betters; for there is no class of betters. . . . Democracy demands of every man what in other forms of social organization is demanded only of a segment of society. . . . Democratic education is therefore a peculiarly ambitious education. It does not educate men for prescribed places in life, shaping them to fit the requirements of a preexisting and rigid division of labor. Its idea is that the social system itself, which determines what places there are to fill, shall be created by the men who fill them. It is true that in order to live and to live effectively men must be adapted to their social environment, but only in order that they may in the long run adapt that environment to themselves. Men are not building materials to be fitted to a preestablished order, but are themselves the architects of order. They are not forced into Procrustean beds, but themselves design the beds in which they lie. Such figures of speech symbolize the underlying moral goal of democracy as a society in which the social whole justifies itself to its personal members.[1]

To see how radical such a vision is in human history, we have only to reflect how differently education has been conceived. In traditional authoritarian societies education has typically been thought to be a process of perpetuating the received lore, considered to embody the central doctrines upon which human arrangements were based. These doctrines were to be inculcated through education; they were not to be questioned. Since, however, a division between the rules and the ruled was fundamental in such societies, the education of governing elites was sharply differentiated from the training and opinion-formation reserved for the masses. Plato's *Republic,* the chief work of educational philosophy in our ancient literature, outlines an education for the rulers in a hierarchical utopia in which the rest of the members are to be deliberately nourished on myths. And an authoritative contemporary Soviet textbook on *Pedagogy* declares that "Education in the USSR is a weapon for strengthening the Soviet state and the building of a classless society. . . . the work of the school is carried on by specially trained people who are guided by the state."[2] The school was indeed defined by the party program of March 1919 as "an instrument of the class struggle. It was not only to teach the general principles of communism but 'to transmit the spiritual, organizational, and educative influence of the proletariat to the half- and nonproletarian strata of the working masses'."[3] In nondemocratic societies, education is two faced: it is a weapon or an instrument for shaping the minds of the ruled in accord with the favored and dogmatic myth of the rulers; it is, however, for the latter, an induction into the prerogatives and arts of rule, including the arts of manipulating the opinions of the masses.

To choose the democratic ideal for society is wholly to reject the conception of education as an *instrument* of rule; it is to surrender the idea of shaping or molding the mind of the pupil. The function of education in a democracy is rather to liberate the mind, strengthen its critical powers, inform it with knowledge and the capacity for independent inquiry, engage its human sympathies, and illuminate its moral and practical choices. This function is, further, not to be limited to any given subclass of members, but to be extended, insofar as possible, to all citizens, since all are called upon to take part in processes of debate, criticism, choice, and cooperative effort upon which the common social structure depends. "A democracy which educates for democracy is bound to regard all of its members as heirs who must so far as possible be qualified to enter into their birthright."[4]

Implications for Schooling

Education, in its broad sense, is more comprehensive than schooling, since it encompasses all those processes through which a society's members are developed. Indeed, all institutions influence the development of persons working within, or affected by, them. Institutions are complex structures of actions and expectations, and to live within their scope is to order one's own actions and expectations in a manner that is modified, directly or subtly, by that fact. Democratic institutions, in particular, requiring as they do the engagement and active concern of all citizens, constitute profoundly educative resources. It is important to note this fact in connection with our theme, for it suggests that formal agencies of schooling do not, and cannot, carry the whole burden of education in a democratic society, in particular moral and character education. All institutions have an educational side, no matter what their primary functions may be. The question of moral education in a democracy must accordingly be raised not only within the scope of the classroom but also within the several realms of institutional conduct. Are political policies and arrangements genuinely open to rational scrutiny and public control? Do the courts and agencies of government operate fairly? What standards of service and integrity are prevalent in public offices? Does the level of political debate meet appropriate requirements of candor and logical argument? Do journalism and the mass media expose facts and alternatives, or appeal to fads and emotionalism? These and many other allied questions pertain to the status of moral education within a democratic society. To take them seriously is to recognize that moral education presents a challenge not only to the schools but also to every other institution of society.

Yet the issue must certainly be raised specifically in connection with schools and schooling. What is the province of morality in the school, particularly the democratic school? Can morality conceivably be construed as a *subject*, consisting in a set of maxims of conduct, or an account of current mores, or a list of rules derived from some authoritative source? Is the function of moral education rather to ensure conformity to a certain code of behavior regulating the school? Is it, perhaps, to involve pupils in the activities of student organizations or in discussion of "the problems of democracy"? Or, since morality pertains to the whole of what transpires in school, is the very notion of specific moral schooling altogether misguided?

These questions are very difficult, not only as matters of implementation, but also in theory. For it can hardly be said that there is firm agreement among moralists and educators as to the content and scope of morality. Yet the tradition of moral philosophy reveals a sense of morality as a comprehensive institution over and beyond particular moral codes, which seems to me especially consonant with the democratic ideal, and can, at least in outline, be profitably explored in the context of schooling. What is this sense?

It may perhaps be initially perceived by attention to the language of moral judgment. To say that an action is "right," or that some course "ought" to be followed, is not simply to express one's taste or preference; it is also to make a claim. It is to convey that the judgment is backed by reasons, and it is further to invite discussions of such reasons. It is, finally, to suggest that these reasons will be found compelling when looked at impartially and objectively, that is to say, taking all relevant facts and interests into account and judging the matter as fairly as possible. To make a moral claim is, typically, to rule out the simple expression of feelings, the mere giving of commands, or the mere citation of authorities. It is to commit oneself, at least in principle, to the "moral point of view," that is, to the claim that one's recommended course has a point which can be clearly seen if one takes the trouble to survey the situation comprehensively, with impartial and sympathetic consideration of the interests at stake, and with respect for the persons involved in the issue. The details vary in different philosophical accounts, but the broad outlines are generally acknowledged by contemporary moral theorists.[5]

If morality can be thus described, as an institution, then it is clear that we err if we confuse our allegiance to any particular code with our commitment to this institution; we err in mistaking our prevalent code for the *moral point of view* itself. Of course, we typically hold our code to be justifiable from the moral point of view. However, if we are truly committed to the latter, we must allow the possibility that further consideration or new information or emergent human conditions may require revision in our code. The situation is perfectly analogous to the case of science education; we err if we confuse our allegiance to the current corpus of scientific doctrines with our commitment to scientific method. Of course we hold our current science to be justifiable by scientific method, but that very method itself commits us to holding contemporary doctrines fallible and revisable in the light of new arguments or new evidence that the future may bring to light. For scientific doctrines are not held simply as a matter of arbitrary preference; they are held for reasons. To affirm them is to invite all who are competent to survey these reasons and to judge the issues comprehensively and fairly on their merits.

Neither in the case of morality nor in that of science is it possible to convey the underlying *point of view* in the abstract. It would make no sense to say "Since our presently held science is likely to be revised for cause in the future, let us just teach scientific method and give up the teaching of content." The content is important in and of itself, and as a basis for further development in the future. Moreover, one who knows nothing about specific materials of science in the concrete could have no conception of the import of an abstract and second-order scientific method. Nevertheless, it certainly does not follow that the method is of no consequence. On the contrary, to teach current science without any sense of the reasons that underlie it, and of the logical criteria by which it may itself be altered in the future, is to prevent its further intelligent development. Analogously, it makes no sense to say that we ought to teach the moral point of view in the abstract since our given practices are likely to call for change in the future. Given practices are indispensable, not only in organizing present energies, but in making future refinements and revisions possible. Moreover, one who had no concrete awareness of a given tradition of practice, who had no conception of what rule-governed conduct was, could hardly be expected to comprehend what the moral point of view might be, as a second-order vantage point on practice. Nevertheless, it does not follow that the latter vantage point is insignificant. Indeed, it is fundamental insofar as we hold our given practices to be reasonable, that is, justifiable in principle upon fair and comprehensive survey of the facts and interests involved.

There is, then, a strong analogy between the moral and the scientific points of view, and it is no accident that we speak of reasons in both cases. We can be reasonable in matters of practice as well as in matters of theory. We can make a fair assessment of the evidence bearing on a hypothesis of fact, as we can make a fair disposition of interests in conflict. In either case, we are called upon to overcome our initial tendencies to self-assertiveness and partiality by a more fundamental allegiance to standards of reasonable judgment comprehensible to all who are competent to investigate the issues. In forming such an allegiance, we commit ourselves to the theoretical possibility that we may need to revise our current beliefs and practices as a consequence of "listening to reason." We reject arbitrariness in principle, and accept the responsibility of critical justification of our current doctrines and rules of conduct.

It is evident, moreover, that there is a close connection between the general concept of *reasonableness* underlying the moral and the scientific points of view, and the democratic ideal. For the latter demands the institutionalization of "appeals to reason" in the sphere of social conduct. In requiring that social policy be subject to open and public review, and institutionally revisable in the light of such review, the democratic ideal rejects the rule of dogma and of arbitrary authority as the ultimate arbiter of social conduct. In fundamental allegiance to channels of open debate, public review, rational persuasion, and orderly change, a democratic society in effect holds its own current practices open to revision in the future. For it considers these practices to be not self-evident, or guaranteed by some fixed and higher authority, or decidable exclusively by some privileged elite, but subject to rational criticism, that is, purporting to sustain themselves in the process of free exchange of reasons in an attempt to reach a fair and comprehensive judgment.

Here, it seems to me, is the central connection between moral, scientific, and democratic education, and it is this central connection that provides, in my opinion, the basic clue for school practice. For what it suggests is that the ' fundamental trait to be encouraged is that of reasonableness. To cultivate this trait is to liberate the mind from dogmatic adherence to prevalent ideological fashions, as well as from the dictates of authority. For the rational mind is encouraged to go behind such fashions and dictates and to ask for their justifications, whether the issue be factual or practical. In training our students to reason we train them to be critical. We encourage them to ask questions, to look for evidence, to seek and scrutinize alternatives, to be critical of their own ideas as well as those of others. This educational course precludes taking schooling as an instrument for shaping their minds to a preconceived idea. For if they seek reasons, it is their evaluation of such reasons that will determine what ideas they eventually accept.

Such a direction in schooling is fraught with risk, for it means entrusting our current conceptions to the judgment of our pupils. In exposing these conceptions to their rational evaluation we are inviting them to see for themselves whether our conceptions are adequate, proper, fair. Such a risk is central to scientific education, where we deliberately subject our current theories to the test of continuous evaluation by future generations of our student-scientists. It is central also to our moral code, *insofar as* we ourselves take the moral point of view toward this code. And, finally, it is central to the democratic commitment which holds social policies to be continually open to free and public review. In sum, rationality liberates, but there is no liberty without risk.

Let no one, however, suppose that the liberating of minds is equivalent to freeing them from discipline. Laissez-faire is not the opposite of dogma. To be reasonable is a difficult achievement. The habit of reasonableness is not an airy abstract entity that can be skimmed off the concrete body of thought and practice. Consider again the case of science: scientific method can be learned only in and through its corpus of current materials. Reasonableness in science is an aspect or dimension of scientific tradition, and the body of the tradition is indispensable as a base for grasping this dimension. Science needs to be taught in such a way as to bring out this dimension as a consequence, but the consequence cannot be taken neat. Analogously for the art of moral choice: The moral point of view is attained, if at all, by acquiring a tradition of practice, embodied in rules and habits of conduct. Without a preliminary immersion in such a tradition, an appreciation of the import of its rules, obligations, rights, and demands, the concept of choice of actions and rules for oneself can hardly be achieved. Yet the prevalent tradition of practice can itself be taught in such a way as to encourage the ultimate attainment of a superordinate and comprehensive moral point of view.

The challenge of moral education is the challenge to develop critical thought in the sphere of practice and it is continuous with the challenge to develop critical thought in all aspects and phases of schooling. Moral schooling is not, therefore, a thing apart, something to be embodied in a list of maxims, something to be reckoned as simply another subject, or another activity, curricular or extracurricular. It does, indeed, have to pervade the *whole* of the school experience.

Nor is it thereby implied that moral education ought to concern itself solely with the general structure of this experience, or with the effectiveness of the total "learning environment" in forming the child's habits. The critical questions concern the *quality* of the environment: What is the *nature* of the particular school experience, comprising content as well as structure? Does it liberate the child in comprising content as well as structure? Does it liberate the child in the long run, as he grows to adulthood? Does it encourage respect for persons, and for the arguments and reasons offered in personal exchanges? Does it open itself to questioning and discussion? Does it provide the child with fundamental schooling in the traditions of reason, and the arts that are embodied therein? Does it, for example, encourage the development of linguistic and mathematical abilities, the capacity to read a page and follow an argument? Does it provide an exposure to the range of historical experience and the realms of personal and social life embodied in literature, the law, and the social sciences? Does it also provide an exposure to particular domains of scientific work in which the canons of logical reasoning and evidential deliberation may begin to be appreciated? Does it afford opportunity for individual initiative in reflective inquiry and practical projects? Does it provide a stable personal milieu in which the dignity of others and the variation of opinion may be appreciated, but in which a common and overriding love for truth and fairness may begin to be seen as binding oneself and one's fellows in a universal human community?

If the answer is negative, it matters not how effective the environment is in shaping concrete results in conduct. For the point of moral education in a democracy is antithetical to mere shaping. It is rather to liberate.

Notes

1. R. Barton Perry, *Realms of Value* (Cambridge: Harvard University Press, 1957), p. 425.

2. B. P. Yesipov and N. K. Goncharov, *Pedagogy*, 3rd ed., 1946. Quoted in G. S. Counts and N. P. Lodge, *I Want To Be Like Stalin* (New York: John Day, 1947).

3. F. Lilge, "Lenin and the Politics of Education," *Slavic Review* XXVII: 2 (June 1968): 255.

4. Perry, *Realms of Value*.

5. See, for example, K. Baier, *The Moral Point of View* (Ithaca: Cornell University Press, 1958); W. K. Frankena, *Ethics* (Englewood Cliffs, N.J.: Prentice-Hall, 1963); R. S. Peters, *Ethics and Education* (Glenview, Ill.: Scott, Foresman & Co., 1967); I. Scheffler, ed., *Philosophy and Education*, 2d ed. (Boston: Allyn & Bacon, 1966).

Part B
CURRICULUM AND LIBERATION

17

Critical Theory and Rationality in Citizenship Education

Henry Giroux

In the classical Greek definition of citizenship education, a model of rationality can be recognized that is explicitly political, normative, and visionary. Within this model, education was seen as intrinsically political, designed to educate the citizen for intelligent and active participation in the civic community. Moreover, intelligence was viewed as an extension of ethics, a manifestation and demonstration of the doctrine of the good and just life. Thus, in this perspective, education was not meant to train. Its purpose was to cultivate the formation of virtuous character in the ongoing quest for freedom. Therefore, freedom was always something to be created, and the dynamic that informed the relationship between the individual and the society was based on a continuing struggle for a more just and decent political community.[1]

If we were to use citizenship education in the Greek sense against which to judge the quality and meaning of civic education in this country, a strong case could be made that, for the most part, it has been a failure.[2] This is not meant to suggest that liberal democratic theory has not supported noble ideals for its citizens, for it has. It is simply to assert that such ideals have not

Prepared for a Symposium on Citizenship and Education in Modern Society. Mershon Center, Ohio State University, April 1980.

Reprinted from *Curriculum Inquiry* 10: 4 (Winter 1980): 329–66. Copyright © 1980 by The Ontario Institute for Studies in Education. Reprinted by permission of John Wiley & Sons, Inc.

found their way, in general, into the day-to-day practices of schools, either historically or in more recent times.

The role that schools have played historically in reproducing the rationality of social control and class dominance has been developed extensively and need not be repeated here.[3] But there is one interesting note worth mentioning. Prior to the advent of the twentieth century and the rise of the scientific management movement that swept the curriculum field, there was no pretense on the part of educational leaders as to the purpose and function of public schooling. Schools, with few exceptions, were training grounds for character development and economic and social control.[4] Unlike the notion of social control later articulated by Dewey in which schools provide noncoercive forms of persuasion in order to develop intellectual growth consistent with psychological development in students,[5] the educators of the early republic equated social control with obedience and conformity. Edward Ross captured the nature of this sentiment when he referred "to education as an inexpensive form of police."[6] Moreover, the language of justification in nineteenth-century public school rationales made the intent and purpose of schooling quite clear. In other words the "hidden curriculum" during this part of the history of American education was at least "partially" revealed in public school rationales.

. . . for much that is today called a hidden function of the schools was previously held to be among the prime benefits of schooling. . . . A society newly in conflict over its own identity could respond to such an appeal. Education continued to be justified more as a means of social control than as an instrument of individual betterment. The quest for the one best system precluded any acknowledgment of local differences and aspired instead to a uniformity of experience. In 1891 the Commissioner of Education, William Torrey Harris, frankly admitted that a major purpose of schools was to teach respect for authority and that forming the "habits of punctuality, silence, and industry" was more important than understanding reasons for good behavior.[7]

The comparison between the Greek and early American notions of citizenship reveals telling differences in political ideals. At the same time, the interaction among schooling, politics, and citizenship is quite clear. The visibility of this interaction was lost, however, when educational theory and practice in the twentieth century shifted the philosophical basis of schooling from the political to the technical. Schooling was no longer justified in terms of political values and concerns; the theoretical pillars upon which a new rationale was constructed were efficiency and control. With the age of scientific management came the celebration of a new rationality and the removal of "the political" from the terrain of schooling. William Lowe Boyd in his study of curriculum policymaking captures the essence of this stance with this observation:

. . . since, the reformers believed that there was "no Republican or Democratic way to pave a street, only a right way," the business of running a city or a school system was viewed as just that, a business matter and not something appropriate for politics. The prompt, business-like dispatch of the decision-making tasks facing school boards . . . was facilitated by their view that a wide range of educational questions were essentially technical matters beyond the capacity of the laity to decide.[8]

This philosophical shift in the purpose and function of schooling not only abstracted schools from the context of the wider society, it also ushered in a mode of rationality that relegated the political nature of schooling to the anteroom of educational theory and practice. Citizenship education became entwined in a "culture of positivism," one that displayed little interest in the ways in which schools acted as agents of social and cultural reproduction in a society marked by significant inequities in wealth, power, and privilege.[9]

This article argues that if citizenship education is going to revitalize itself in the interest of creating a more noble and just society, it will have to free itself from the burden of its own intellectual and ideological history. In doing so it will have to develop a new rationality and problematic for examining the relationship between schools and the wider society. Questions of technique, objectivity, and control will have to give way to a rationality based on the principles of understanding and critique; likewise, within this rationality a more critical problematic will have to be developed, one that generates new categories and raises questions that could not be raised within the old rationality.

At the core of this new rationality should be a serious attempt to reformulate citizenship education by situating it within an analysis that explores the often-overlooked complex relations among knowledge, power, ideology, class, and economics.[10] Such an appraisal would have to use and demonstrate the importance of social and political theory for its analysis of schooling and citizenship education.

In approaching this task, I will examine the following aspects of rationality in the order listed: that which can be termed the "American ideology"; the political nature of different types of rationality; and the ways in which these particular forms of rationality roughly characterize a number of existing traditions in citizenship education. Then I will outline the foundation of a more radical rationality, one that attempts to unravel the relationship among the educational system, the economic system, and the class structure. Finally, I will explore how these rationalities might be integrated into a set of radical educational practices that might be used as a foundation for developing a more viable theory of citizenship education.

Theoretical Foundations in Educational Theory and Practice

Any notion of rationality has to be defined not only in regard to the truth claims commanded by its major assumptions and ensuing practices, but also by its relationship to what might be called the dominant rationality of a given society at a particular moment in history. This methodological approach is crucial because it illuminates the interconnections that exist between a dominant rationality and the institutions that function in a given society to reproduce it.[11] Such interconnections politicize the notion of rationality by questioning how its ideology supports, mediates, or opposes the configuration of existing sociopolitical forces that use the dominant rationality to legitimize and sustain their existence.

Rationality

By rationality, I mean a specific set of assumptions and social practices that mediate how an individual or group relates to the wider society. Underlying any one mode of rationality is a set of interests that define and qualify how one reflects on the world. This is an important epistemological point. The knowledge, beliefs, expectations, and biases that define a given rationality both condition and are conditioned by the experiences into which we enter. Of crucial importance is the notion that such experiences only become meaningful within a mode of rationality that confers intelligibility on them. Modes of rationality "bind" in a nonmechanistic way. As Althusser points out, "it is not the material reflected on that characterizes and qualifies a reflection . . . but the modality of that reflection, the actual relation the reflection has with its objects.[12] The importance of the notion of rationality becomes clear when its definition is extended to include the concept of the "problematic."[13]

Problematic

All modes of rationality contain a problematic, which is a conceptual structure that can be identified both by the questions that it raises and the questions that it is incapable of raising. The concept of the problematic suggests that any mode of rationality can be viewed as a theoretical framework, the meaning of which can be understood by analyzing both the system of questions that command the answers given as well as the absence of those questions that exist beyond the possibility of such a framework. Boyne captures the importance of this dialectical concept with this comment:

A word or concept cannot be considered in isolation; it only exists in the theoretical or ideological framework in which it's used; its problematic . . . is centered on the absence of problems and concepts within the problematic as much as their presence. . . . The notion of absence indicates that what the problematic excludes is as important as what it includes. The problematic defines the field of the visible within which errors, oversights, and individual blindness are possible, and can be corrected. At the same time it defines the boundary of the invisible, the correlate of the visible, the realm of the necessarily absent. This invisibility relates crucially to the production of problems; within any problematic there are problems which cannot be posed.[14]

A mode of rationality and its given problematic represent a response not simply to the problematic's internal logic, but also to the objective struggles, tensions, and issues posed by the historical times in which the problematic operates. The limits of a mode of rationality, particularly one that poses as being universal, become evident when we realize that the intelligibility of its claims cannot "speak" to the issues or questions that threaten to undermine its basic assumptions. This often happens when what had been given as a solution is now posed as a problem. For instance, this happened when it became clear to Lavoisier that Priestly's new gas was not "dephlogisticated" air but oxygen, or more recently, when the new sociology of education rejected the notion of "objective" curriculum knowledge and argued for a curriculum theory based on a recognition of the social construction of knowledge and the negotiation of classroom meaning.[15]

The American Ideology

Before analyzing the different modes of rationality that dominate citizenship education, I want to provide a brief description of the rationality that appears to dominate American social science,[16] the curriculum field and the social studies field in particular.[17] By focusing on the dominant rationality in American society, it is possible to get a better understanding of the nature of schooling as a societal process. This approach is not meant to deny the invaluable contributions of numerous traditional studies of schools as socialization agents; it is simply a matter of acknowledging that these studies have generally failed to lay bare the complex relationships between ideology and power in the dominant society and the related, though far from mechanistic, use of knowledge and power at the level of school organization and classroom practice.

Social and Cultural Reproduction in Schools

The recognition that schools are agencies of socialization is an assumption shared by all proponents of citizenship education, but this assumption is incomplete in itself as an analytical tool for unraveling the societal functions of schooling. A more analytical approach, studied in much of the socialization literature, analyzes the socialization process as a vehicle of economic and cultural reproduction; that is, as a process that mediates the social practices and cultural beliefs necessary to maintain the dominance of certain groups and power structures.[18] A more recent reconceptualization of the socialization process embedded in schools is echoed in Jean Anyon's comment that "what is important about school socialization is what school practices and assumptions it entails, and conversely, what those school assumptions and practices reveal about the society in which the schools are embedded."[19]

If the perspective advocated by Anyon and others strips schools of their innocence, the more traditional studies on socialization enshrine such innocence in a position that suffers from what Nietzsche once termed "the dogma of the immaculate perception." In the latter views, school knowledge is either treated unproblematically or the focus is limited to how different forms of knowledge, usually what is narrowly termed *moral knowledge*, is acquired in school settings. Talcott Parsons and Robert Dreeben stand out as examples of this tradition.[20]

A more fundamentally political and critical approach to school socialization would begin with the premise that one of the critical elements in the power of a dominant class resides in its ability to impose, though not mechanistically, its own set of meanings and social practices through the selection, organization, and distribution of school knowledge and classroom social relationships. The conceptual basis for investigating such an issue requires a more precise definition than educators generally have of how power functions in distinct and interrelated ways in schools and the wider social order. One promising focus of investigation has been articulated by Michael F. D. Young in his argument that there is a "dialectical relationship between access to power and the opportunity to legitimize certain dominant categories, and the processes by which the availability of such categories to some groups enables them to assert power and control over others."[21]

The importance of the above perspective, largely articulated in radical critiques of schooling, is that it not only situates the relationship between schools and other social institutions in a basically political framework, but it also makes problematic the very nature of citizenship itself. It provides the basis for analyzing how a given conception of what it means to be a citizen is conveyed through the dominant rationality in a given social order. Thus, it calls into question not simply what the school claims it does, but what in fact schools may unintentionally do as institutions that exist in a particular relationship with the state. The nature of their relationship, of course, is contained in one of the fundamental questions at the heart of any notion of citizenship education. Kant has said it as well as anyone with his proclaimed principle that students "ought to be educated not for the present but for a future condition of the human race, that is for the idea of humanity."[22]

Dominant Rationality

The dominant rationality that presently permeates American society appears to be incompatible with Kant's suggestion. The democratic labels and slogans that are echoed so cheerily at sports events and in early morning school pledges belie the reality that hides behind them. Furthermore, one finds in the practices of systems management, inquiry learning, back to basics, and other curriculum approaches a different set of messages that appear to dissolve the human subject and the promise of critical thinking and action into what Sartre once referred to as the "bath of sulphuric acid."

H. T. Wilson has referred to the dominant rationality as "the American Ideology":

The American ideology is composed of the following elements: 1) an anti-reflexive and anti-theoretical bias already noted which in more "liberal" times extended to virtually *all* intellectual activity; combined, paradoxically, with 2) a more recent concern for accumulating "knowledge," understood as exploitable observations (or observations in principle) having immediate application and "relevance"; undergirded jointly by 3) a false commitment to "objectivity" in the absence of the object being aspired to, derived from scientific rationalism with its unreflexive notion of neutrality, scepticism, and freedom from values and interests; and by 4) a vision of social and political processes as the product of a "piecemeal," trial and error approach concerned with procedural legitimacy for its own sake and prone to value a reformist posture toward social change understood as a set of activities played out within the rules of a game which sociological and political knowledge (and knowing) *must* emulate and thereby legitimize; 5) a derived contemporary view of this "open" society as eminently exportable, a negation of this very openness which justifies itself by invoking economics, sociology, and politics as disciplines which demonstrate a coming convergence of world societies and cultures and the supremacy and longevity (not to mention permanence) of the American-type Western society.[23]

The central issue is not how this rationality permeates and functions in American society; the literature on this issue is abundant. Rather, the issue is how this type of rationality is embedded in the rationalities that characterize major traditions of citizenship education and how the problematics raised by these rationalities are incomplete. I will examine this issue and focus on a newly emerging rationality that holds more promise for building a theory of citizenship education. Before articulating the meaning of these rationalities a few points must be clarified.

Though the models of citizenship education discussed below represent ideal types that are described in distinct terms, this should not suggest the absence of variation and subtle differences among teachers and other educational workers who might combine any one of a number of them. Nor should it suggest an inclusive coverage of all the diverse citizenship programs and models which were developed in the 1960s. Such a coverage would be impossible within the confines of this article. Moreover, simply because I have asserted that the essence of any approach to citizenship education can, in part, be unraveled by examining its relationship to the dominant societal rationality that is not meant to imply that *any* rationality simply mirrors the imperatives of a dominant ideology; instead it suggests a *particular* relationship to the latter. Finally, it is important to note that the relationships and distinctions among the forms of rationality to be outlined below should not imply that any one of them should be universalized to the exclusion of the others. The important task is to identify what is progressive in each of them and to develop a higher level of synthesis where the limitations and possibilities of each become clear.

Three Modes of Rationality

Most models of citizenship education can be categorized under what can be termed three modes of rationality: the technical, the hermeneutic, and the emancipatory.[24] Each of these rationalities represents different processes of social inquiry and is determined by specific knowledge interests. They will be explained briefly, along with the models of citizenship education that correspond to each of them.

Technical Rationality

Technical rationality is linked to principles of control and certainty. Its knowledge constitutive interest lies in "controlling the objectified environmental world."[25] Technical rationality uses the natural sciences as its model of theoretical development, and rests on a number of interrelated assumptions which, when translated into educational theory and practice, take the following form.

First, educational theory should operate in the interests of lawlike propositions which are empirically testable. A major assumption here is that theory should contribute to the mastery and control of the environment through a set of deductively derived operations aimed at discovering the regularities that exist among isolated variables under study. In this case, theory becomes enshrined in the logic of the formula, and observation and technique become starting points for theoretical practice.[26] This is an important point because the mediating link between theory and practice not only appears primarily as a technical one, that is, mastery, but the foundation for such an approach also points to an epistomology in which "knowledge starts from the concrete and is raised to general propositions through a process of abstraction/generalization."[27] Marcuse captures the essence of this assumption in his claim "as a result of this twofold process, reality is now idealized into a 'mathematical manifold': everything which is mathematically demonstrated with the evidence of universal validity as a pure form (reine Gestalt) now belongs to the true reality of nature."[28]

Second, knowledge, like scientific inquiry, is regarded as value-free. Thus knowledge should be objective and described in neutral fashion. The assumption here is that knowledge can be reduced to those concepts and "facts" that exist a priori and then can be translated to operational definitions and precise meanings. Thus, the hallmarks of knowledge and theoretical inquiry become steeped in a notion of objectivity, one that measures [the] strength of its meaning against the degree to which it is objectively testable. "Hard" data becomes the focus of explanation and discovery, while other forms of knowledge such as those that cannot be universalized intersubjectively are banished to the realm of mere "speculative" wisdom. The application of this assumption to educational theory is well stated by Suppes when he argues that educators "do not need wisdom and broad understanding of the issues that confront us. What we need are deeply structured theories of education that drastically reduce, if not eliminate the need for wisdom."[29]

Third, causation in this approach is linked to a notion of prediction that makes the process a linear one. That is, since knowledge of the social world is objective and consists of isolated and distinctly separable parts that interact according to lawlike regularities, which simply have to be discovered, then the relationship among these variables is an empirical one that can be reduced to predictable outcomes.

Finally, there is the belief that educators themselves can operate in a value-free manner by separating statements of values from the "facts" and "modes of inquiry" which must be objective.

Technical Rationality and Citizenship Education

Two traditions in citizenship education that are strongly wedded to the basic assumptions of technocratic rationality include the citizenship transmission model and the citizenship as social science model.[30] While it is indisputable that there are basic differences in orientations between these two models, there appears to be a nucleus of ideas that link both to the principle of technocratic rationality.

Citizenship Transmission. The citizenship transmission model represents the oldest and still most powerful tradition in citizenship education. Historically it can be seen in the writings of Mann and many of the early proponents of the curriculum field in general.[31] It appears to have reached its heyday in the hysteria of the McCarthy period, and with the demise of the innovative curriculum and social studies movements of the sixties, it once again is gaining expression in the current back-to-basics movement.

The essence of this model is captured in the concept of transmission. Knowledge, in this view, is situated above and beyond the social realities and relationships of the people who produce and define it. It is fixed and unchanging in the sense that its form, structure, and underlying normative assumptions appear to be universalized beyond the realm of historical contingency or critical analysis. Appearing in the guise of objectivity and neutrality, it is rooted in the precious adulation of the fact or facts, which simply have to be gathered, organized, transmitted, and evaluated. We get a better sense of the implications of this model for citizenship education if it is viewed not simply as a pedagogical veil for incompetent teaching or teacher "mindlessness," but as a "historically specific social reality expressing particular production relations among men."[32] That is, if we view how this model defines notions of power and meaning as expressed in its treatment of knowledge, human beings, values, and society, we get a more accurate idea of what its political and pedagogical commitments might be.

Knowledge in this perspective resides in a notion of objectivity and detachment that renders questions concerning the production and legitimation of its form and content irrelevant.[33] Consequently, it supports a notion of knowing that ignores that facts have to be mediated, that they are never accessible in their immediacy. The question of who legitimizes "the facts" of a given social order, in this case, is removed from the context of classroom pedagogy and discussion. This is an important point because such a posture violates one of the basic preconditions of all freedom of thought: the necessity for the mental space and reflection one needs to see "beyond" the arbitrary constructs of a society in order to understand the source and genesis of their historical development and the interests they support. The importance of this issue for a more radical notion of citizenship education is captured by Herbert Marcuse in his claim that "if 'education' is to be more than simply training for the status quo it means not only enabling man to know and understand the facts which make up reality but also to know and understand the factors that establish the facts so that he can change their inhuman reality."[34]

Not only is knowledge objectified in this rationality, but it is usually reduced to the mastery of technical decisions for ends already decided. Ends are affirmed rather than explained as a social reality. In the name of transmitting cherished beliefs and values, this model of citizenship education ends up supporting, through its methodologies and content, behavior that is adaptive and conditioned, rather than active and critical.

The reification of knowledge and the flawed epistemology that characterize this approach find their practical counterpart in the passive model of human behavior they support in classroom social relationships. A pedagogical model built on the transmission of a given body of information, values, and beliefs does not ask whether the latter are warranted, it asks under what conditions they can be maintained. Teachers and students within this context are expected to be either passive consumers or transmitters of knowledge, rather than negotiators of the world in which they work and act. Built into these pedagogical relationships are a series of messages and norms that constitute a hidden curriculum, one that in its unexamined body of knowledge and social relationships concretizes and legitimizes human powerlessness. Some critics have argued that the real significance of this approach has more to do with what it omits than what it includes, and they point out that what it really teaches is a form of unrealistic civic education.[35]

The citizenship transmission model expresses the core of its ideology and relationship to the dominant rationality in its view of change and stability in the wider society. Wedded to a Parsonian notion of faunctionalism, this model supports a notion of consensus and role socialization that downplays both the notion of social conflict and the underlying contradictions that characterize the existing society.[36] The roles and relationships that are worthy of attention, in this view, are those that are functional for the present social order. As one functionalist puts it: "functionalism . . . seeks to do no more than assay the place of a particular element of culture or societal institution in relation to other elements. The question may then be posed as to whether an institution leads to or assists int he perpetuation of the social entity in which it appears."[37]

The functionalist dimension in the citizenship transmission model not only closes its "eyes" to the falsehoods perpetuated in many social studies textbooks—falsehoods that present students with a view of society that is as saccharine as it is ideological—it also supports a model of role socialization which, in fact, is a "refinement of role conformity."[38] The existential reality of teachers, students, and others in the world of schooling and the social forces that both constrain and shape that reality are lost in this model.[39] In its place stands the compromised language of "integration" and harmony.

Beneath the "Olympian" harmony of the citizenship transmission model stands a perception of teachers' and students' roles as relatively fixed and permanent. This becomes particularly evident in much of the research in the educational field. That is, the economic, social, and political forces that bear on pedagogical theory and practice disappear in this research, which focuses almost exclusively on the individual and the study of cognitive processes framed within the narrow boundaries of educational psychology.[40]

Finally, an important failing in this citizenship education model is that it neither recognizes nor responds to social and structural dysfunctions; instead, social and institutional failings are translated into personal ones. This is manifest in those educational research studies that conjure up categories that arbitrarily absorb structural failings under a pseudoscientific litany of semiotic mystifications. As Jean Anyon says: "This concept of individual culpability . . . is embedded in educational evaluation and psychological findings that attribute to 'lack of student interest,' low 'ability,' 'different or deficient family language or culture,' or to 'teacher indifference,' what may in fact be economically compatible failure to provide all groups or social classes successful pedagogy and/or 'complete personal development.'"[41]

Social Science Model. What is paradoxical about the citizenship education as social science model is that on one level it attempts to rescue students as active and critical thinkers; but on a more significant level it falls prey to certain presumptions about knowledge and meaning that results in its merely recycling, albeit in a more sophisticated package, the very assumptions it tries to redress.

Emerging in the United States in the 1960s, the social science model[42] was heavily influenced by Jerome Bruner's structuralist notion that the essence of learning lies in understanding the basic principles governing the structure of specific academic disciplines.[43] Learning in this approach is based on students mastering the basic ideas and body of knowledge that represent the "deep" structure of a particular discipline. Though initially designed for science curricula, Bruner's structuralism readily found its way into the social science field. In part, by attempting to situate social studies curricula in the "rigorous" foundation of the social science disciplines, the "new" social studies provided a more sophisticated epistemological framework than the rather "crude" rationale provided by the transmission model of citizenship education.

Attempting to free social studies knowledge from the theoretical strait-jacket of the "transmission" thesis, advocates of the new social studies put forth a number of assumptions that supported their claims to an improved approach to citizenship education. These include (1) a claim to high status knowledge and equality with other academic disciplines based upon a firm commitment in the social sciences; (2) a claim to the "truth" based upon a view of social science knowledge as "correct" in a relatively unproblematic way; (3) support for an epistemology based on a reflectionalist notion of learning in which the mastery of specific social science knowledge and skills would offset the half-truths and mystifications inherent in "common sense" knowledge; (4) support for a hierarchical view of knowledge and a concomitant view of social relationships. Experts provided the knowledge, and teachers and curriculum developers "helped" students to "discover" the answers to predesigned curricula and the problems they posed.[44]

While this approach to learning was a significant improvement over the transmission model in that it attempted a more rigorous definition of social science knowledge, it failed in a number of ways to live up to its claim as a pedagogy for improved citizenship education. Since this position has been extensively criticized elsewhere, my criticisms will be limited to some of the more relevant points.[45]

What counts as valued knowledge in this perspective is grounded in a notion of objectivity that results in a pedagogy that celebrates inquiry, concept discovery, and various other forms of inductive thinking. While this may appear at first to make this model of citizenship education incompatible with the tenets of technocratic rationality, such is not the case. Celebrating not the production of meaning but the consumption of "objective" meanings sanctified by experts, inquiry and skill-oriented pedagogy belies its own intentions. What appears to be discovery learning ends up as a series of pedagogical methods in which knowledge is depoliticized and objectively "fixed." Having limited possibilities to question the conditions under which knowledge is socially constructed, the social science model of citizenship education ignores both the social constraints that distort knowledge and the connection between knowledge and social control. Cleo Cherryholmes raises this issue in his critique of one inquiry model.

. . . as interesting as it is in many ways, [it] does not illuminate the issues involved in citizenship education for the simple reason that the wrong question was asked. The appropriate question is, what knowledge and skills do students need in order to make predictions that will increase their individual and social effectiveness in a democratic society?[46]

It is by studying the contradictions of daily life that the mediations between individuals and their society take on meaning and set the stage for political action. The first step in developing a pedagogy that makes this possible involves forms of analysis that seek knowledge and social reality as a human product. Both the transmission model and the social science model of citizenship education are trapped in a problematic that separates facts from values and by doing so canonizes the very knowledge it should be questioning. To view knowledge as the priestly domain of warrior scholars is to forfeit the possibility of questioning the normative and political nature of the knowledge and social interests they legitimize. What we often find in these approaches is a gross insensitivity to the experiences and "history" that students bring with them to the classroom. As a result, this model of citizenship education often ends up substituting general concepts for social concepts and then "hawks" the importance of "analytical" skills as the answer to critical thinking. What usually results is a process whereby the judgments made by authors who use these methods are not questioned. Instead, concepts are used along with "inquiry skills" that eventually elicit confirmation from students on problems governed by answers that can barely be challenged. Tom Popkewitz in analyzing Edwin Fenton's *Comparative Political Systems: An Inquiry Approach* found the following:

The instructional approach uses concepts of leadership, ideology, and decision making to compare different political systems. However, investigation of the text reveals that judgments are already made by the authors. The purpose of children's "analytical" work is simply to make the teacher's answers plausible. . . . For example, a dichotomy is established between the leaders of the Soviet Union and the United States. The personal characteristics of the U.S. political leaders are characterized as energy, tact, ability to tend to many things at once, ability to operate effectively under tension and so on. On the other hand, a Soviet leader is described as one "not given to resistance, who is a little above average in energy and intelligence and below average in imagination." Under the guise of "social theory," a dichotomy is established which seems to prevent critical scrutiny rather than nurture it.[47]

Critical thinking not only "slips away" in this approach, so does the concept of social conflict. This model of citizenship education easily fits Adorno's critique that "social concepts are taken 'as such' and then classified according to general concepts. In the process, social antagonists invariably tend to be glossed over."[48]

Lost in these two citizenship education models are the normative, political, and historical landscapes that give them meaning. In spite of all the clatter about the importance of student choice making in these models, the latter are reduced to a faint echo that does little to illuminate how dominant values work through and are mediàted by teachers, students, and curriculum materials. Lacking any vestige of critical theory, these approaches to citizenship education fail to break through their own false objectivism to examine critically the assumptions that wed them to the precepts of technocratic rationality and the "American ideology."

Hermeneutic Rationality

Paraphrasing Alvin Gouldner,[49] I think it is accurate to argue that every rationality has within it another problematic struggling to get out. The "caged" problematic that represents the Achilles' heel of technocratic rationality is the very notion of meaning itself, for it is in the struggle to unshackle the concepts of "meaning" and experience from the "fossilized" notion of objectivity that hermeneutic rationality is grounded.

Hermeneutic rationality does not take as its starting point the production of monological knowledge; instead, it has a deep-seated interest in understanding the communicative and symbolic patterns of interaction[50] that shape individual and intersubjective meaning. Rather than focusing on or taking for granted the a priori forms of knowledge, its constitutive interest lies in understanding how the forms, categories, and assumptions beneath the texture of everyday life contribute to our understanding of each other and the world around us.

Meaning in this mode of rationality is not removed from the worlds of the social actors who constitute, shape, and live within its definitions. Instead, it is seen in its most crucial form as something which is constantly negotiated and renegotiated by human beings as they mutually produce and define the constitutive rules that shape their interactions. Central to this form of rationality are the concepts of appropriation, intentionality, and intersubjectivity.

Human beings are never seen as passive recipients of information. Hermeneutic rationality is sensitive to the notion that through the use of language and thought human beings constantly produce meanings as well as interpret the world in which they find themselves. Therefore, if we are to understand their actions, we have to link their behavior to the intentions that provide the interpretative screen they use to negotiate with the world. Thus, as Geoff Whitty has argued, this form of rationality rejects the wider culture of positivism and is based on an epistemology in which

truth and objectivity are seen as nothing but human products, and man rather than nature is seen as the ultimate author of "knowledge" and "reality." Any attempt to appeal to an external reality in order to support claims for the inferiority of one way of seeing over another is dismissed as ideological. Knowledge is inexplicably linked to methods of coming to know and any supposed dichotomy between them is therefore false.[51]

Hermeneutic rationality has generated a number of important concerns for educational theory and practice. First, it has challenged many of the commonsense assumptions that teachers, students, and other educational workers use to guide, structure, and evaluate their day-to-day pedagogical experiences. Second, it has refocused attention on the normative and political dimensions of teacher-student classroom relationships. Third, it has established a relationship between epistemology and intentionality, on the one hand, and learning and classroom social relationships on the other. In other words, knowledge is treated as a specific social act with its underlying social relationships. Finally, hermeneutic rationality has played a significant role in helping educators unravel the latent and manifest dimensions of classroom knowledge and classroom relations.[52]

Reflective Inquiry Approach. The tradition in citizenship education in the United States that has been influenced by this type of rationality falls under the general label of the "reflective inquiry approach."[53] This approach relies heavily upon what has generally been called decision making in a sociopolitical context. The importance of the stress on decision making is further defined by pointing to the unique burdens imposed by this process in a "democracy." "The assumption is that democracy imposes a unique burden; we cannot escape the requirement of making decisions. Sometimes decisions relate to the making of legislation or the selecting of legislators; that is, of course, an inherent part of our government—what it means to live in a self-governing, democratic society."[54]

In contrast to the positivist assumptions inherent in the transmission and social science models previously mentioned, the traditions that fall roughly under a hermeneutic rationality stress negotiation, participation, and the importance of values in citizenship education. For instance, various supporters of this position invoke the general trinity of knowledge, participation in decision making, and values/attitudes as the basis for citizenship education. The pedagogical approaches following from these assumptions have recently been outlined in detail by a number of theorists and need only brief mention here.[55]

In this rationality, there is a strong emphasis on the social construction rather than the imposed nature of classroom knowledge. As such, students are encouraged to explore their own values and either to define problems within the context of their experiences or to relate social problems to the day-to-day texture of their lives.[56] On the other hand, the concrete vehicle for expressing the latter emphasis rests on its support and use of the problem-solving process as the principal pedagogical tool. In fact, the only absolute value in this pedagogical approach appears to lie in the decision-making process itself,[57] best summed up by the notion that "the orientation of the social scientist is that of research."[58]

Reflective inquiry suggests a number of useful and constructive insights, and makes important contributions to an analysis of the meaning and purpose of citizenship education. But in the end, it is trapped in a problematic that is defined less by what it advocates than by what it ignores. As a theory that attempts to situate the meaning of schooling in a wider context, it appears as a well-intentioned, but, in the final analysis, naive and incomplete mode of rationality.

On one level some of its weaknesses can be traced to the nature of its epistemology. In celebrating the notions of intentionality in the exploration of human behavior, it has failed to move beyond a relativistic notion of knowledge. That is, although this position sees through the arbitrary division between objective and subjective forms of knowing posited by technocratic rationality, it does not analyze the history of this division or develop a form of critique that is capable of revealing the ideology embedded in it. As Cherryholmes has pointed out, in this view there is "no clearly identifiable position regarding knowledge claims."[59]

By focusing on the subjective intentions of the individual while simultaneously encouraging the importance of the social construction of knowledge, this position fails to understand how such meanings are maintained or how they might distort rather than comprehend reality. Moreover, such a posture tends to overlook how ideological and structural constraints in the larger society are reproduced in schools so as to mediate against the possibility of critical thinking and constructive dialogue. Thus, by reducing power and democratic action to the level of an epistemology that supports a form of subjective idealism, the reflective inquiry approach emerges as a one-sided theory of citizenship education which has "miraculously" abstracted its social epistemology from such troublesome concepts as ideology, power, struggle, and oppression. As a result, the basic nature of existing social arrangements in the wider society go unquestioned or are questioned in relatively narrow terms. The limits of this position are partially identified in Elizabeth Cagen's remark:

While liberal reformers tend to use education to promote equality, community, and humanistic social interaction, they do not confront those aspects of the schools which pull in the opposite direction. Their blindness to these contradictions may stem from their class position: as middle-class reformers they are unwilling to advocate the kind of egalitarianism which is necessary for a true human community.[60]

I am not so sure that middle-class reformers act as intentionally as Cagen suggests they do; it is more likely that they are caught within a rationality that "blinds" them to the nature of their own ideology. This can be partly demonstrated by looking at how the reflective inquiry approach deals with a theory of the state and the concept of pluralism.

Harold Berlak has pointed out that few educators have come to terms with the notion that schooling in America takes place in one of the most powerful industrial capitalist states in the world, one that is characterized by an enormous concentration of political and economic power.[61] In spite of this, the relationship between the state and public schools is often articulated in simplistic and one-dimensional terms. While it is stressed repeatedly in the rationales of reflective inquiry advocates that schools can and must educate students to participate in the shaping and running of the state, they say practically nothing about how the state affects and reproduces the ideology of dominant social and economic interests in the schools. A number of social theorists have raised questions about the particular relationship between schools and the wider society that puts in high relief the complex relations that exist between schools and the state.

Nicos Poulantzas has argued that schools are part of an ideological state apparatus that both reproduces and mediates the social divisions of labor and the dominant ideology which supports it.[62] Schools by the very nature of their position in a class-based society are politically and structurally bound to a relationship with the state and its ruling interests. This relationship must be understood if we are to be clear about what schools actually do in this society. The broader nature of this relationship has been explored by Althusser, who claims that schools produce the modes of consciousness, know-how, and ideological dispositions necessary to function in a capitalist economy.[63] On the other hand, Bowles and Gintis stress the importance of specific structural features of schools—the classroom social relationships—in reproducing the social relations of production.[64] Bernstein and Apple have argued that the principles involved in both the structure and content of curriculum, pedagogy, and evaluation constitute specific message systems that are ultimately dependent on the allocation of power and resources of a dominant class.[65]

Bourdieu and Passeron take one dimension of this analysis a bit further by arguing that schools institutionalize, through the rules and meanings that constitute the day-to-day working of classroom experience, the dominant cultural capital.[66] Cultural capital, in this sense, refers to those systems of meanings, linguistic and social competencies, and elements of style, manner, taste, and disposition that are permeated throughout society by the dominant class as being the most legitimate.[67] In this analysis, schools play a crucial role in reproducing the unequal distribution of cultural capital.[68] Instead of providing compensatory education to the students with different cultural capital, the school, while appearing neutral, asks them to think and perform in a way that is quite alien to their own background. If Bourdieu is right, and there is a significant amount of evidence suggesting that he is, classroom knowledge has little to do with the negotiated outcomes and critical thinking skills that the reflective inquiry rationality sees as the essence of schooling; instead, its essence lies in the imposition of meanings and specific modes of behavior by the school. Of course, there are modes of resistance and contradictions in the schools. There are also ideologies that are ethnic, gender, and community specific that mediate and alter the dominant ideology.[69] But what results in the absence of political action are piecemeal and minor victories, which leave the constitutive rules of the dominant ideology unchallenged.

This mode of citizenship education is wedded to a one-sided notion of determination. It argues that schools can educate students to exert political influence on the state, but it ignores how the state places constraints of a *specific* political, ideological, and structural nature on the schools. This becomes most evident in the support for pluralism found among advocates of this group. Arguments of this sort reveal their own ideology by denying the very conditions that make the struggle for pluralism imperative. Pluralism as a philosophy of equality and justice is a noble political ideal. But when the ideal is not measured against a society that rests on fundamental inequalities in wealth, power, and participation, it tilts over into ideology or empty formalism, one "that presupposes that society is without those antagonisms that are of its essence."[70] This concept fits badly into a view of citizenship education that is based on democratic principles of justice and political participation. Pluralism ignores the tension between political democracy and economic inequality. That is, it fails to acknowledge that equality of opportunity and the importance of human reflectiveness may be impeded by particularistic private interests in the economic sphere that use the state to impose severe constraints on certain segments of the population.[71] The limited pedagogical insistence on decision-making skills that emerge from this position are inherited from a priori assumptions about the existence of a pluralistic society. What is missed is the way the "invisible" hand of dominant political and economic interests affect the nature of what is to be decided. Peak and Zeigler in their critique of "unrealistic civic education" illuminate this issue with this argument:

Pluralists have taken a hard-headed approach in insisting that the only legitimate datum is the decision. . . . By focusing entirely upon the process whereby highly contested decisions are reached, pluralists ignore . . . the more mysterious "nondecisions" . . . which are of more importance upon the overall political style of a community than the more spectacular and tangible decisions.[72]

What this suggests is that there is a "hidden curriculum" which functions to favor the reproduction of the dominant society by establishing the boundaries within which conflict can take place and questions can be raised. Of course, the emphasis on critical thought in the work of the moral development advocates under the reflective inquiry approach points to the hidden curriculum as something to be overcome in order to promote critical thinking. But by defining critical thinking as a psychological characteristic reduced to matters of cognitive developmental psychology, we are left with a perspective that lacks the benefit of critical sociology or political theory.[73] How the nature and structure of social relationships in the wider society are revealed in the political structure of classroom life and schools are missing from this perspective.

The problematic that characterizes the reflective inquiry approach fails to examine the nature of its own ideology, and in doing so it has not been able to raise fundamental questions about the nature of the relationship between the state and schooling, the mechanisms of ideological and structural domination in schools, or how the relationship among class, culture, and ideology in schools serves to reproduce the institutional arrangements of the status quo.

The dialectical relationship that interconnects the dynamics of the state, economics, and ideology with the concept of citizenship education demands a theoretical framework grounded in a rationality that truly challenges the existing American ideology. The foundation for such a rationality can be found in what may be called emancipatory rationality.

Emancipatory Rationality

Though hermeneutic rationality has disposed of the illusion of objectivism, it has failed to develop an analysis that unravels how the relationship among power, norms, and meaning function within a specific sociohistorical context to promote forms of self-misunderstanding as well as to support and sustain modes of structural domination. The hermeneutic mode of rationality does not ask the central question: How is it that a social system steeped in domination can legitimize itself through a set of meanings and practice that prevent the development of an open, self-critical community of inquiring citizens?

The issue here is that emancipatory rationality does not renounce the primacy of intentionality and meaning central to hermeneutic interests; instead it attempts to locate such meaning and action in a societal context in order to explore how the latter might place specific limitations and constraints upon human thought and action. Sharp and Green illuminate the problematic at the heart of emancipatory rationality:

The correct perspective should enable one to ask the question "Under what historical conditions can men break through the structure of determination?" Such a perspective retains the model of man as active, with intentionality, while socially locating him within a context which may resist, block or distort his projects. To realize his values as an acting subject who seeks to control his situation, he forces the constraining effect of others in this situation, the institutionalized consequences of his and others' actions, the sanctions that can be used against him, and the conditions of his non-social environment.[74]

Emancipatory rationality, in this context, is based upon the principle of critique and action. It is aimed at criticizing that which is restrictive and oppressive while at the same time supporting action in the service of individual freedom and well-being. This mode of rationality is construed as the capacity of critical thought to reflect on and reconstruct its own historical genesis, that is, to think about the process of thinking itself. More specifically, the capacity to think about thinking points to a mode of reasoning aimed at breaking through the "frozen" ideology that prevents a critique of the life and world on which rationalizations of the dominant society are based. Similarly, emancipatory rationality augments its interest in self-reflection with social action designed to create the ideological and material conditions in which nonalienating and nonexploitative relationships exist. This suggests a view of citizenship education based on a different view of sociability and social relations than those that presently exist.

Sociability will have to be rescued from the limited notion of closeness it presently occupies. In other words, sociability currently defined solely in terms of family images and relationships, against which it is difficult to conceive of strangers as social, will have to be viewed as a position at odds with a democratic notion of citizenship.[75] In addition, citizenship education based on an emancipatory form of rationality will have to reproduce and stress the importance of social relationships in which men and women are treated as ends and not means. Both positions represent ethical principles linked to the development of radical needs and the ideological and material conditions needed to support them.[76]

Emancipatory Rationality and Citizenship Education

A number of radical educational theories have developed under this mode of rationality that either directly or indirectly address questions relevant to citizenship education. All these theories share a critical stance toward the existing social order and support, though in different ways, what may be called theories of reproduction and transformation. Madeleine MacDonald captures the focus of these theories with this comment:

The assumption underlying most of the "reproduction" theories is that education plays a mediating role between the individual's consciousness and society at large. These theorists maintain that the rules which govern social behavior, attitudes, morals, and beliefs are filtered down from the macro level of economic and political structures to the individual via work experience, educational processes, and family socialization. The individual acquires a particular awareness and perception of the society in which he lives. And it is this understanding and attitude towards the social order which constitute his consciousness. The concept has therefore taken on particular significance within the context of theories of social and cultural reproduction. . . . By acquiring an awareness both of the nature of social conditioning and the potential for acting upon it, the individual or groups of individuals in a social class, it is argued, can learn not only to formulate alternatives but also to bring about change. The different emphases placed . . . on social order or social change, on macro levels or micro processes, on structural or interactional features derive from a variety of conceptions of the ability or inability of individuals and social classes to act in and upon the social world. In the context of educational strategies for change, these theories have different implications, for in each a particular relationship between schooling and society is postulated.[77]

Two broad traditions can be abstracted from this radical mode of pedagogy, of which neither one by itself is adequate to lay the theoretical foundation for a form of citizenship education based upon an emancipatory rationality. But by combining elements of the two traditions, the possibilities for such a project exist. Since it is impossible here to outline in full the basic components of both traditions,[78] each will be described briefly, and then a more detailed outline of the theoretical guidelines for an emancipatory mode of citizenship education will be given. The first tradition will arbitrarily be called the political economy position, and the second will be labeled the culturalist position.

Political Economy Position. The political economy tradition focuses its attention upon macrostructural relationships and how they interconnect and mediate to reproduce the class relations in a given society. In this analysis, modes of social and cultural reproduction are traced back to the political-economic structural configurations that govern them. Studies of this sort tend to concern themselves with the organizational features of institutions and how they function to produce certain roles, affect social mobility, and structure social stratification. In many of these studies, specifically those of a functionalist or structuralist nature, the object gains primacy over the subject, and structures tend to be given a more fundamental role in shaping human behavior than social processes explained through the intentions and consciousnesses of human actors. The structural analyses that emerges from these studies do us a theoretical service by focusing on forces that affect human behavior but cannot be traced by referring solely to the immediate context or consciousness of the human subject. While this position helps to throw into high relief the "deep" structures that influence and "bind" human action it sometimes treats the day-to-day workings of institutions such as schools as if they were "black boxes" and does little to illuminate how people negotiate and define their daily activities.

Culturalist Position. Culturalists, on the other hand, focus their attention on the experiences of subjects and how notions of consciousness, ideology, and power enter into the way human beings constitute their day-to-day realities. Culturalists have done a great deal to rescue human behavior from the tendency of radical functionalist accounts that would reduce consciousness to a mere reflex of the mode of production. Culturalists have attempted, in part, to explain how human actions within the grip of structures such as schools escape, resist, and transform the effects of the latter.

Summary. In simplistic terms, both positions if dialectically related provide the possibility for understanding how schools function as institutions roughly determined by the structural requirements of the imperatives of a capitalist state. On the other hand, schools can be studied as cultural realms that exist within a particular, nonmechanistic relationship with the wider society. This means focusing on the complex way in which schools mediate on a daily basis the ideological and material forces that are produced directly from within the contexts and sites in which they exist. The implications this has for developing a theory of citizenship education can now be explored.

Notes Toward a Theory of Citizenship Education

First, it is important to point out that what is put forth in this section does not represent a final program. The focus is on larger comprehensive issues that provide the foundation for establishing a theory of citizenship education that is more adequate than those that presently occupy the field.

The major struggle to develop and implement such a theory rests, in fact, with overcoming the rather dreadful legacy that has shaped it over the last century. Notions about citizenship education are complex and rather unwieldy. Citizenship education cuts across disciplines and is rooted in a myriad of political and normative issues. Unfortunately, it has been largely influenced, as I have mentioned previously, by the culture of positivism, with its underlying technocratic rationality. Hence, educators have generally retreated from engaging its most complex issues and have reduced theorizing about this issue mainly to questions of technique, organization, and administration.

Changing Society

A theory of citizenship education will have to redefine the nature of educational theorizing as it presently exists. In its place, it will have to construct a view of theory that integrates the artificial constructs that separate the academic disciplines. It will have to draw upon a more dialectical structure of knowledge in order to establish a theoretical center of gravity that provides a comprehensive analysis of what the nature and conduct of education is all about. Hence, as I have indicated previously, such a theory will be political and social. This becomes clear if we engage citizenship education at what has to be the starting point for any further theoretical development. That is, citizenship education's own problematic must begin with the question of whether or not this society should be changed in a particular way or be left the way it is. In fundamental concrete terms, it raises important questions that each individual must confront. Questions range from issues concerning how free one is in a given society to those that inquire as to what kind of understanding is necessary regarding the political basis, nature, and consequences of one's actions. Regardless of the answer, the core of the issue is fundamentally political and normative; it speaks to the need to confront assumptions concerning the aims of education—assumptions regarding who is going to be educated, and assumptions about what kinds of knowledge, values, and social relationships are going to be deemed legitimate as educational concerns.

These questions are not meant to be simply abstractions; their significance is linked to both the history and the existing social-political conjuncture that gives them context and meaning. Educational theorists and, more precisely, a theory of citizenship education will have to combine historical critique, critical reflection, and social action. This theory will have to recover the political determinants of what citizenship education has become and then decide what it does not want to be in order to emerge as a more viable mode of theorizing. In part, I have traced its history, and indicated what it has become. If it is going to provide both vision and hope for the citizens of this country, it will have to be redefined so that it can work in the interest of changing this society. In other words, it will have to measure the promise against the reality and then demonstrate the viability of such a struggle. This may not be an easy task, but it is certainly a necessary one.

Teacher Consciousness

In addition to being committed to building a better society, the next step in developing a notion of citizenship education that focuses on schools will have to address concerns about expanding the theoretical perceptions of teachers and other educational workers. That is, teachers rather than students should represent a starting point for any theory of citizenship education. Most students exercise very little power over defining the education experiences in which they find themselves. It is more appropriate to begin with those educators who both mediate and define the educational process. This is not meant to deny that students represent an important concern in both the development and effects of such a theory; in fact, it is precisely this concern that demands that we construe a theoretical framework giving teachers and others involved in the educational process the possibility to think critically about the nature of their beliefs and how these beliefs both influence and offset the day-to-day experiences they have with students. Similarly, it is important that teachers situate their own beliefs, values, and practices within a wider context so that their latent meanings can be better understood. This dialectical situating, so to speak, will help illuminate the social and political nature of the structural and ideological constraints that teachers face daily. What is needed then is a more comprehensive theory of totality; it is to this that I will now turn.

Theory of Totality. A theory of totality would avoid the pitfall of treating schools as if they existed in a political and social vacuum. Instead, schools would be analyzed, both historically and sociologically, in regard to their interconnections with other economic and political institutions. In concrete pedagogical terms, this means that educators need to situate the school, curriculum, pedagogy, and the role of the teacher within a societal context that reveals both their historical development and the nature of their existing relationship with the dominant rationality. Central to this analysis is that teachers view the evolution of schools and school practices as part of a historical dynamic, one in which different forms of knowledge, social structures, and belief systems are seen as concrete expressions of class-specific interests. Of course, this is not meant to reduce schooling to a reflex of the imperatives of certain powerful groups. Such a characterization ignores the active nature of resistance in human beings and often flattens out the complex relationship between schools and the dominant society. What is at stake here is the need to provide a theoretical focus for developing more critical categories that can be used to understand the linkages between how a society is controlled and organized and the principles that structure school experience. Inherent in this approach is the notion that schools act as agents of social and cultural reproduction. But if the concepts of reproduction and the notion of totality are to move beyond a "radical" functionalist account, it will be necessary to develop a more comprehensive analysis of the interconnections between culture, power, and transformation.

On one level this means that if the notion of totality is to be defined as more than a science of interconnections, it has to illuminate how the ideological and structural dimensions of existing school practices can be traced to their social, political, and economic determinants in the wider society. This approach not only helps us to see educational practices as historical and social products, it also raises questions as to how these determinants reveal themselves in the commonsense perceptions of teachers, in the social relations of the classroom, and in the form and content of curriculum materials. In a society marked by the pervasive presence of social class and inequality, the relevance of such questions to a notion of citizenship education concerned with economic and social justice is no small matter. Sharp and Green cite the importance of developing a notion of totality specifically related to the concept of transformation:

[We] want to stress that a humanist concern for the child necessitates a greater awareness of the limits within which teacher autonomy can operate and to pose the questions: "What interests do schools serve, those of the parents and children, or those of the teachers and headmaster?" and "What wide interests are served by the school?" and, possibly more importantly, "How do we conceptualize interests in social reality?" Therefore instead of seeing the classroom as a social system and as such insulated from wider structural process, we suggest that the teacher who has developed an understanding of his (or her) location in the wider process may well be in a better position to understand where and how it is possible to alter that situation. The educator who is of necessity a moralist must preoccupy himself with the social and (economic) preconditions for the achievement of his ideals.[79]

Hence, schools can be seen as part of the universe of wider cultural meanings and practices. This perception becomes a powerful heuristic and political tool for a theory of citizenship education only if we rescue the concept of culture from the depoliticized status that it now occupies in mainstream social science theory.

Politics of Culture. In short, a reform of citizenship education involves a reform of educators as well; this is a political task whose purpose is to make educators better informed citizens and more effective agents for transforming the wider society. It also points to and increases the possibility for helping students develop a greater social awareness as well as a concern for social action. An important step in realizing both tasks is to politicize the notion of culture. This is a critical imperative for a theory of citizenship education. When culture is stripped of its political innocence and seen as *one form* of political domination, the opportunity exists for educators not only to understand the normative dimensions of their own classroom experience, but also to trace such normative underpinnings back to structural determinants and values in the wider sociopolitical sphere. Moreover, the politicization of culture provides teachers with the opportunity to develop a pedagogy that is sensitive to the dynamics of the hidden curriculum and the biographies of their students.

Traditionally, mainstream social theorists have defined culture simply as a people's total way of life, that is, the entirety of those goods, services, and labor produced by human beings. Such a definition not only lacks any general validity, it also tilts over into a blank check that endorses the status quo when it is reduced to this level of explanation. In the latter case, not only does culture become a concept that is less than critical, but it serves to reflect reality rather than comprehend it. Divorced from notions of class, power, and conflict, it ends up as an empty social science category that hides more than it reveals.

A less mystifying approach to this issue would acknowledge that the distinction between power and culture is a false one that needs to be abolished. A critical analysis would demonstrate how social power can manifest itself in schools as "class cultural control."[80] But the beginning of such an analysis demands a redefinition of the relationship between society and culture. In this case, culture would be subsumed within the category of society itself. Rather than viewing culture as the general expression of the entire society, culture would be defined in terms of its functional relationship to the dominant social formations and power relations in a given society. Hence, in a class-specific society the *dominant* culture becomes an expression of the dominant interests and is revealed as a legitimating, motivational structure. In this case, secondary cultures have to be defined in their particular relationship to the dominant culture. Culture as a political phenomenon then refers to the power of a specific class to impose and distribute throughout society specific meanings, message systems, and social practices in order to "lay the psychological and moral foundations for the economic and political system they control."[81] Within the dominant culture, meaning is universalized and the historically contingent nature of social reality appears as self-evident and fixed. Of course, there are conflicts within the dominant cultural capital just as there is resistance from classes who stand in opposition to the dominant view of the world; but this should not be interpreted in ways to either relativize the different forms of culture capital or to underestimate the significance of the dominant culture as a moment "in the process of social domination and capital accumulation."[82]

As a heuristic tool for an emancipatory form of citizenship education, the politicization of culture provides the opportunity for teachers to reformulate the concept of power in terms of both its meaning and its use as a vehicle of domination or praxis. Power as a form of cultural domination has been captured in Gramsci's concept of ideological hegemony, a concept that helps to reassert the centrality of the interconnection among politics, culture, and pedagogy.[83] Carl Boggs explains Gramsci's notion of ideological hegemony as:

. . . the permeation throughout civil society—including a whole range of structures and activities like trade unions, schools, the churches, and the family—of an entire system of values, attitudes, beliefs, morality, etc., that is in one way or another supportive of the established order and the class interests that dominate it to the extent that this prevailing consciousness is internalized in any society, therefore, it must operate in a dualistic manner: as a general conception of life for the masses, and as a scholastic program or set of principles which is advanced by a sector of intellectuals.[84]

The implications this concept has for teachers become clear if the notion of culture as ideological hegemony is qualified. Hegemony does not simply refer to the content found, for instance, in the formal curriculum of schools.

It is that and much more; it also refers to the way such knowledge is structured. In addition, it refers to the routines and practices embedded in different social relationships; finally, it points to the notion of social structures as natural configurations which both embody and sustain forms of ideological hegemony. If we translate this insight into specific forms of pedagogy for citizenship education, the following theoretical practices for educators could be developed.

School Knowledge and Citizenship Education. Teachers would have to analyze school knowledge as part of a wider universe of knowledge and try to determine to what degree it reflects class interests. For instance, Anyon's work points to "a whole range of curriculum selections (which) favor the interest of the wealthy and powerful."[85] Next, school knowledge must be analyzed to determine to what degree its form and content represent the unequal presentation of the cultural capital of minorities of class and color: that is, how does classroom knowledge embody modes of language, systems of meaning, and cultural experiences so as to invalidate directly or indirectly other forms of cultural capital. This suggests that educators who assign a false equivalency to "all cultures" may be falling into the trap of cultural pluralism. That is, they depoliticize the notion of culture by abstracting the concept from the societal formations that give it meaning. The real issue to be raised focuses less on the equivalency of all cultures than on the question of how the dominant culture, as a form of power and control, mediates between itself and other secondary cultures. This kind of inquiry focuses on questions aimed at understanding what kind of reproductive functions exist between the dominant culture and the culture institutionalized by the schools. Questions that emerge from this type of analysis may take the following form: Whose culture gets distributed at schools? How is it legitimated? How is it distributed? How do its meanings relate to assumptions in the wider social parameter? What are its social, economic, and historical origins? In what way does this culture distort or reflect the realities of other cultures?

Teachers must also attempt to unravel the ideological principles embedded in the structure of classroom knowledge. As a social construction, curriculum materials consist of specific form and content. The internal organizing devices that go into their assemblage must be uncovered to lay bare the ideology they embody. Wexler argues that teachers must learn to identify the structuring concepts that lurk silently within a text, film, or any other form of curriculum material.[86] These materials must be decoded not only in terms of their content but in terms of their form and composition as well. Basil Bernstein, for example, points to the way curriculum knowledge is classified and insulated.[87] He argues that the rigid boundaries between categories of knowledge and different forms of knowledge carry messages of social control by reducing ways of knowing to static and seemingly unrelated representations of reality.[88]

Hidden Curriculum and Citizenship Education. The dominant culture is not simply embedded in the form and content of knowledge. It is also reproduced through what is called the hidden curriculum. The hidden curriculum in schools refers to those underlying norms, values, and attitudes that are often transmitted tacitly through the social relations of the school and classroom. Bowles and Gintis and others have pointed to the hidden curriculum, particularly its stress on rule conformity, passivity, and obedience, as one of the major socialization forces used to produce personality types willing to accept social relationships characteristic of the governance structures of the work place.[89]

It must be emphasized that the hidden curriculum is not removed from the Gramscian notion of ideological hegemony; it simply represents another dimension of it. Sharp and Green illuminate this point in their claim that cultural domination

. . . is produced not simply through ideas but in the everyday practices in which people are involved. . . . an approach to . . . curriculum which does not give equal emphasis to the forms and social practices involved in the transmission of knowledge has failed to develop the heuristic potential of the Gramscian concept of hegemony.[90]

If teachers are going to implement a more comprehensive notion of citizenship education they will have to understand not only the linkages that exist between the hidden and formal curricula, but also the complex connections that exist between both curricula and the principles that structure similar modes of knowledge and social relationships in the larger society. We can illuminate the nature of these complex linkages through an ethnographic portrayal of citizenship education in a kindergarten class analyzed by Ray Rist.[91]

Mrs. Caplow, the teacher, as part of her unit on citizenship has appointed a student to be the "sheriff" for a trip her kindergarten class is to take. (Caplow told Rist that the point of the lesson was to teach the children "respect for the law.") Frank willingly accepts this role and literally pushes, shoves, and yells at other students who step out of line. Frank, in this case, happens to be a middle-class student, while the other students are from the "lower class."

Rist interprets this in the following way. "When the rhetoric of 'learning respect for the law' is stripped away, it is obvious that middle-class children were learning how to shuffle in the face of superior power."[92] The ideology underlying this notion of citizenship education should be clear. But the interrelationship between the classroom social relationships that Mrs. Caplow established and the message she wanted to reinforce come into sharper focus in this exchange among Mrs. Caplow, another student, and Frank:

"David, can you tell Mr. Rist why you are wearing the star?" David responds, "Cause I the sheriff." Mrs. Caplow continues, "Can you tell him how you got to be the sheriff?" "By being a good citizen." "David, what do good citizens do?" "They check up on others." Mrs. Caplow: "Well that is not all they do . . ." Caplow repeats the question for Frank. Frank stands up and says, "Good citizens obey the rules." Mrs. Caplow responds, "Yes, that is right, Frank. Good citizens obey the rules, no matter what they are."[93]

This suggests that if teachers are going to be able to analyze the nature and degree of distributive injustice in schools, they will have to pay close attention to those basic, tacit, constitutive rules that establish the more obvious factors that structure classroom choices. It is the constitutive rules that silently structure and make impervious the conditional nature of the grouping, tracking, and labeling that goes on in schools. The nature of these rules must be analyzed in light of the political choices they reflect. For this type of analysis to emerge, teachers will have to pay close attention to the type of rationality that shapes their own assumptions and how it mediates between the "rules" of the dominant culture and the classroom experiences provided for students.

Power and Transformation. Finally, an analysis of power and transformation must be made an integral part of a theory of citizenship education. Teachers must attempt to understand the meaning of the contradictions, dysfunctions, and tensions that exist in both schools and the larger social order; moreover, they must focus on the underlying conflicts in both schools and society and investigate how these can contribute to a more radical theory of citizenship education. Too often, radical theorists have portrayed the use of power in schools in strictly negative and one-dimensional terms.[94] This easily slips into an Orwellian nightmare in which students submit readily and passively to the imperatives of the dominant culture. This not only distorts the reality of schools; it ends up being a more "radical" version of management ideology which sees human beings as infinitely malleable. Power in the service of domination is *never* as total as this image suggests. Richard Johnson writes insightfully about the dialectical nature of domination and resistance in schools:

. . . typically, under capitalism, schools seem to reproduce instead of the perfect worker in complete ideological subjection, much more the worker as bearer of the characteristic antagonisms of the social formation as a whole. Schools, in other words, reproduce forms of resistance too, however limited or "corporate" or unselfconscious they may be.[95]

Neither students nor teachers resemble the "social puppet" image that emerges in the writings of the reproduction theorists. Both teachers and students demonstrate forms of resistance in the context of cultural hegemony. Willis and others have provided research on how the informal culture, for instance, of working-class students rejects consistently the sum of the messages and values embedded in the formal and hidden curricula.[96] Likewise, there is a great deal of evidence pointing to the wide scope and degree of worker resistance that takes place at the site of production itself.[97] The similarities in the different modes of resistance should be studied both historically and sociologically to see how they have been diffused in the past and how their radical potential can be developed for the future. The crucial question is how do these contradictions offer the possibility for raising the consciousness of both teachers and students? In other words, how can they be used to reveal the workings of power and domination in the school culture? Madeleine MacDonald puts the question another way when she argues that educators must develop an

. . . understanding of how stability occurs despite conflict, how order is maintained over and above the face of change. Any system of reproduction insofar as it operates within a cultural hegemony must be struggled for, won and maintained in the context of opposition. The nature of the victory is uncertain unless we can define the source and the force of the opposition.[98]

It is clear that much of the opposition in both schools and the work place represents forms of symbolic resistance, that is, the struggle is thereby limited to the world of cultural symbols of dress, taste, language, and the like. In order for such opposition to move to a more effective level of action, it will have to be extended into a form of resistance linked to political action and control. That is, citizenship education will have to help students become aware of the political roots of their opposition, they will have to learn to identify the political nature of the contradictions that demanded rebellion in the first place. This is not simply a call for classroom consciousness raising. Subjective intentions alone pose little threat to the concrete and objective structures of domination that underlie the existing sociopolitical order. Social action is needed, but it must be preceded by those subjective preconditions that make the need for such action intelligible. Thus, social awareness represents the first step in getting students to act as '"engaged" citizens willing to question and confront the structural basis and nature of the larger social order. It is also an important step in teaching students about the complex nature of power itself. Power in this case is extended far beyond the subjective confines of thought itself. As Foucault says, "The problem is not one of changing people's 'consciousness' or what's in their heads; but the political, economic, institutional regime of the production of 'truth'."[99]

Hence, conflicts and contradictions must be studied and analyzed by teachers as issues to be problematized and used as points for classroom discussion and vehicles for connecting classroom practices to larger political issues. As mentioned, these contradictions exist not only in the competing forms of cultural capital unevenly distributed in schools, but also in the daily practices and life experiences of different classes outside the schools. These contradictions must be linked and used as an integral dimension of citizenship education. Such an approach would take more seriously the ways by which students and teachers define their experiences within specific class-room settings. It would be more sensitive to the nature of their discourses, their *own* views of school activities, their modes of resistance, and the way in which they serve to reproduce and sustain the dominant ideology. Within this theoretical framework, citizenship education would be better able to highlight how specific institutional practices both restrict and offer possibilities for citizenship growth and action.

In conclusion, citizenship education must be grounded in a reformulation of the role that teachers are to play in schools. As suggested, a new theoretical model that includes a theory of totality, a redefinition of culture and power, and a more insightful understanding of the contradictions and mediations that lie beneath the surface of educational theory and practice must be developed. Needless to say, these theoretical elements only become meaningful if they are wedded to a firm commitment to the development of economic and political justice in both schools and the wider social order. I now want to turn briefly to some classroom practices that follow from the above theoretical assumptions.

Classroom Pedagogy and Citizenship Education

If citizenship education is to be emancipatory, it must begin with the assumption that its major aim is not "to fit" students into the existing society; instead, its primary purpose must be to stimulate their passions, imaginations, and intellects so that they will be moved to challenge the social, political, and economic forces that weigh so heavily upon their lives. In other words, students should be educated to display civic courage, that is, the willingness to act *as if* they were living in a democratic society. At its core, this form of education is political, and its goal is a genuine democratic society, one that is responsive to the needs of all and not just of a privileged few. Agnes Heller illuminates the meaning of civic courage in the following comment:

. . . one should think and act as if one were in a real democracy. The fundamental bravery of this way of life is not military heroism but civic courage. Whoever says no to the dominant prejudices and to the oppressing power, and when necessary (and it is often necessary) to public opinion, and practices this throughout his life and in his life-conduct has the virtue of civic courage.[100]

In more concrete terms, students should learn not only how to weigh the existing society against *its own* claims, they should also be taught to think and act in ways that speak to different societal possibilities and ways of living. But if the development of civic courage is the bedrock of an emancipatory mode of citizenship education, it will have to rest on a number of pedagogical assumptions and practices that need to be somewhat clarified.

First, the active nature of students' participation in the learning process must be stressed. This means that transmission modes of pedagogy must be replaced by classroom social relationships in which students are able to challenge, engage, and question the form and substance of the learning process. Hence, classroom relations must be structured so as to give students the opportunity to both produce as well as criticize classroom meanings. Under such conditions, knowing must be seen as more than a matter of learning a given body of knowledge; it must be seen as a critical engagement designed to distinguish between essence and appearance, truth and falsity. Knowledge must not only be made problematic, stripped of its objective pretensions, it must also be defined through the social mediations and roles that provide the context for its meaning and distribution. Knowledge in this sense becomes the mediator of communication and dialogue among learners.

Second, students must be taught to think critically. They must learn how to move beyond literal interpretations and fragmented modes of reasoning. Not only must they learn to understand their own frame of reference; in addition, they must learn how the latter has both developed and how it provides a "map" for organizing the world. Depending of course upon grade levels, students can learn to juxtapose different world views against the truth claims that each of them makes. In an age when thought is being reduced to its technical dimensions, that is, the operatives of technocratic rationality, it is crucial that students are taught to think dialectically. That is, rather than being enslaved to the concrete, to the fact, they must learn to move beyond viewing issues in isolation. Facts, concepts, issues, and ideas must be seen within the network of connections that give them meaning. Students must learn to look at the world holistically in order to understand the interconnections of the parts to each other. As Maxine Greene says, students must learn an epistemology that allows them to draw from different subject areas and to "engage in new kinds of questioning and problem posing appropriate to an overly dominated human world."[101]

Third, the development of a critical mode of reasoning must be used so as to enable students to appropriate their own histories, that is, to delve into their own biographies and systems of meaning. This means that a critical pedagogy must draw upon the cultural capital that students bring to the classroom. The possibility to act and think must begin by acknowledging the politics of the concrete. That is, a critical pedagogy must provide the conditions that give students the opportunity to speak with their own voices, to authenticate their own experiences.[102] The will to act precedes the need to act. When the will is deadened, questions about critical thinking become empty chatter. Once students become aware of the dignity of their own perceptions and histories, they can make a leap to the theoretical and begin to examine the truth value of their meanings and perceptions, particularly as they relate to the dominant rationality.

Fourth, students must learn not only how to clarify values, they must also learn why certain values are indispensable to the reproduction of human life. Moreover, they must comprehend the source of their own beliefs and action. They must also learn how values are embedded in the very texture of human life, how they are transmitted, and what interests they support regarding the quality of human existence.

Fifth, students must learn about the structural and ideological forces that influence and restrict their lives. Denis Gleeson and Geoff Whitty speak to this issue when analyzing the role social studies can play in addressing it:

A radical conception of social studies starts with the recognition that social processes, both within school and outside it, influence and restrict the life chances of many students. What social studies can do is to help them become more aware of their assumptions and more politically articulate in the expression of what it is they want out of life. This can direct them towards an active exploration of why the social world resists and frustrates their wishes and how social action may focus upon such constraints.[103]

Inherent in Whitty's suggestion are a number of valuable insights that can be used here. Students must be taught how to act collectively to build political structures that can challenge the status quo. Fred Newmann has both actively pursued this line [of] reasoning and rightly criticized other educators for ignoring it.[104] Moreover, this kind of pedagogy must be infused by a passion and optimism that speak to possibilities. Too much of the literature in the citizenship education field borders on despair; not only does it lack any vision, but it seems "frozen" by its own inability to dream, imagine, or think about a better world. The endless studies on the sad state of citizenship education and the existing political consciousness of students are paraded before us as if there was nothing that could be done. These should be treated as starting points and not as terminal commentaries on the state of the nation's health.

The vitality of any field is measured, in part, by the intensity of the debate that it wages about its most basic assumptions and goals. Citizenship education is in dire need of such a debate. The price to be gained goes far beyond the merits of intellectual dialogue and insight. What appears to be at stake at the present moment in history is the ability of future generations of Americans to think and act in ways that speak to age-old precepts of freedom and democracy. The task of developing a mode of citizenship education that speaks to this challenge appears awesome. But when one looks at the consequences of not meeting this challenge, there appears the possibility of a barbarism so dreadful that we can do nothing less than act as quickly and thoughtfully as possible. It is in the spirit of what is just, necessary, and possible that we will have to move forward to meet this challenge.

Notes

1. For an excellent discussion of the classical doctrine of politics, see S. S. Wolin, *Politics and Vision* (Boston: Little, Brown, 1960); J. Habermas, *Theory and Practice* (Boston: Beacon Press, 1973); L. B. Iglitzin, "Political Education and Sexual Liberation," *Politics and Society* (Winter 1972): 241–54.

2. The literature on this issue is much too extensive to cite thoroughly. Informative summaries of these findings can be found in B. M. Franklin, "The Curriculum Field and the Problem of Social Control, 1919–1938: A Study in Critical Theory" (Ph.D. dissertation, University of Wisconsin-Madison, 1974); D. B. Tyack, *The One Best System* (Cambridge: Harvard University Press, 1974); J. Spring, *The Sorting Machine: National Educational Policy Since 1945* (New York: David McKay, 1976); J. V. Torney, A. N. Oppenheim, and R. F. Farmen, *Civic Education in Ten Countries* (New York: John Wiley, 1975); F. B. Brown, *Education for Responsible Citizenship: The Report of the National Task Force on Citizenship Education* (New York: McGraw-Hill, 1977); National Assessment of Educational Progress, *Changes in Political Knowledge and Attitudes, 1969–1976* (Denver, Colo.: National Assessment of Educational Progress, 1978); D. J. Metzger and R. D. Barr, "The Impact of School Political Systems on Student Political Attitudes," *Theory and Research in Social Education* 6:1 (June 1978): 48-79; J. P. Shaver, O. L. Davis, and S. W. Helburn, "The Status of Social Studies Education: Impressions from Three National Science Foundation Studies," *Social Education* 43 (February 1979): 150–53; L. H. Ehrman, "Implications for Teaching Citizenship," *Social Education* 43 (November–December 1979): 594–96.

3. Studies that exemplify the revisionist historians' view include M. Katz, *The Irony of Early School Reform* (Boston: Beacon Press, 1968); C. Greer, *The Great School Legend* (New York: Basic Books, 1972); J. Spring, *Education and the Rise of the Corporate State* (Boston: Beacon Press, 1972); S. Bowles and H. Gintis, *Schooling in Capitalist America* (New York: Basic Books, 1976). A recent critique of the revisionist position can be found in D. Ravitch, *The Revisionists Revised: A Critique of the Radical Attack on Schools* (New York: Basic Books, 1978). Some of the more recent works that use the revisionist perspective to examine classroom practices include M. Apple, *Ideology and Curriculum* (Boston and London: Routledge & Kegan Paul, 1979); H. A. Giroux and A. N. Penna, "Social Education in the Classroom: The Dynamics of the Hidden Curriculum," *Theory and Research in Social Education* 7 (Spring 1979): 21-42; J. Benet and A. Kaplan Daniels, ed., *Education: Straitjacket or Opportunity* (New Brunswick, N.J.: Transaction Books, 1980); J. Anyon, "Social Class and the Hidden Curriculum of Work," *Journal of Education* 162: 1 (Winter 1980): 67–92.

4. The notion of social control is an ambiguous term and its usage needs to be qualified. Social control is not always a negative phenomenon, particularly when it is seen as an inherent part of any social system. A more precise definition of the term would focus on whether it was used to maximize democratic and economic rights in a country or to further the privileges, power, and wealth of one social group at the expense of other groups. It is in the latter sense that the term is being used in this essay. For an elaboration of this issue, see W. Feinberg, *Reason and Rhetoric: The Intellectual Foundations of Twentieth Century Liberal Reform* (New York: John

Wiley, 1975); Franklin, "The Curriculum Field and the Problem of Social Control"; H. M. Kliebard, "The Drive for Curriculum Change in the United States, 1890–1958: The Ideological Roots of Curriculum as a Field of Specialization," *Journal of Curriculum Studies* 2: 3 (1979): 191–202; H. A. Giroux, "Teacher Education and the Ideology of Social Control," *Journal of Education* 162: 1 (Winter 1980): 5–27.

5. This theme is particularly developed in chapters 4 and 5 of J. Dewey's *Experience and Education* (New York: Collier Books, 1971).

6. J. Spring, *American Education* (New York: Longman, Inc., 1978), p. 11.

7. E. Vallance, "Hiding the Hidden Curriculum: An Interpretation of the Language of Justification in Nineteenth-Century Educational Reform," *Curriculum Theory Network* 4: 1 (1973–1974): 5, 12, 13.

8. W. L. Boyd, "The Changing Politics of Curriculum Policy Making for American Schools," *Review of Educational Research* 48: 4 (Fall 1978): 580, 581.

9. The term *positivism* has gone through so many changes since it was first used by Saint-Simon and Comte that it is virtually impossible to narrow its meaning to a specific school of thought or a well-defined perspective. Thus, any discussion of positivism will be broad and devoid of clearcut boundaries. However, we can speak of the "culture of positivism" as the legacy of positivistic thought, a legacy which includes those convictions, attitudes, techniques, and concepts that still exercise a powerful and pervasive influence on modern thought. In the sense that the term is used here, it appropriates the different dimensions of positivism that are both historical and epistemologically specific. That is, it refers to a legacy of thought that looks at the commonalities that join epistemological, sociological, economic, and political dimensions of positivism. Epistemologically, we can see positivism emerge from the writings of Comte to the Vienna School to the present-day writings of "reflectionist" theorists. In schools, we see the residue of this type of positivism in curricula which objectify knowledge, support a transmission form of pedagogy, and separate conception from execution. Sociologically, we see the legacy of positivism in social relationships that were first systematically structured under the notion of the scientific management movement of the 1920s. In schools, we see the legacy of this movement in those types of social encounters in which roles are hierarchically arranged in rigid fashion and where the emphasis is on individual performance rather than collective interaction. Economically, the changing nature of positivism has moved from a science of management control in which workers performed isolated tasks on machines to forms of atomized behavior which program machines designed to regulate other mechanized aspects of the labor process. Politically, the legacy of positivism carries with it changing social relationships and social formations based on a separation of power and a division of labor rooted in class-specific interests. See H. A. Giroux, "Schooling and the Culture of Positivism: Notes on the Death of History," *Educational Theory* 29: 4 (Fall 1979): 263–84.

10. C. Cherryholmes, "Social Knowledge and Citizenship Education: Two Views of Truth and Criticism," *Curriculum Inquiry* 10: 2 (Summer 1980): 115–41.

11. M. F. D. Young and G. Whitty, eds., *Society, State, and Schooling* (Sussex, United Kingdom: Falmer Press, 1977); R. Williams, *Marxism and Literature* (London: Oxford University Press, 1977); C. Mouffe, ed., *Gramsci and Marxist Theory* (London and Boston: Routledge & Kegan Paul, 1979).

12. L. Althusser, *For Marx* (London: Penguin Press, 1969), p. 68.

13. This concept has received its most extensive treatment in G. Bachelard, *The Philosophy of No* (New York: Orion Press, 1968); Althusser, *For Marx*; E. Laclau, *Politics and Ideology in Marxist Theory* (London: New Left Books, 1977); M. Castells and E. De Ipalo, "Epistemological Practice and the Social Sciences," in *Critical Sociology*, ed. J. W. Freiberg (London: Halsted Press, 1979).

14. R. D. Boyne, "Breaks and Problematics," *Philosophy and Social Criticism* 6: 2 (Summer 1979): 206.

15. M. F. D. Young, ed., *Knowledge and Control* (London: Macmillan, 1971).

16. H. Marcuse, *One Dimensional Man* (Boston: Beacon Press, 1964); J. Habermas, *Toward a Rational Society* (Boston: Beacon Press,1964); J. Habermas, *Toward a Rational Society* (Boston: Beacon Press, 1971); R. J. Bernstein, *The Restructuring of Social and Political Thought* (Philadelphia: University of Pennsylvania Press, 1976); H. T. Wilson, *The American Ideology* (London and Boston: Routledge & Kegan Paul, 1977).

17. W. F. Pinar, "Notes on the Curriculum Field, 1978," *Educational Researcher* 7 (September 1978): 5-12; T. S. Popkewitz, "Paradigms in Educational Science: Different Meanings and Purpose in Theory," *Journal of Education* 162: 1 (Winter 1980): 28-46.

18. P. Bourdieu and J. Passeron, *Reproduction in Education, Society, and Culture* (London: Sage Publications, 1977); B. Bernstein, *Class, Codes and Control, Vol. 3: Towards a Theory of Educational Transmissions*, 2d ed. (Boston and London: Routledge & Kegan Paul, 1977); M. MacDonald, *The Curriculum and Cultural Reproduction* (Milton Keynes, United Kingdom: Open University Press, 1977).

19. J. Anyon, "Structure and the Power of Individuals," *Theory and Research in Social Education* 7: 1 (Spring 1979): 49.

20. T. Parsons, "The School as a Social System: Some of Its Functions in American Society," *Harvard Educational Review* 29: 4 (Fall 1959): 297–318; R. Dreeben, *On What Is Learned in Schools* (Reading, Mass.: Addison-Wesley, 1968).

21. Young, *Knowledge and Control*, p. 8.

22. H. Marcuse, *Counter-Revolution and Revolt* (Boston: Beacon Press, 1972), p. 27.

23. Wilson, *The American Ideology*, p. 15.

24. J. Habermas, *Knowledge and Human Interest* (Boston: Beacon Press, 1971); id., *Communication and the Evolution of Society*, trans. T. McCarthy (Boston: Beacon Press, 1979); K. Apel, *Towards a Transformation Philosophy* (Boston and London: Routledge & Kegan Paul, 1980); S. C. Brown, ed., *Philosophical Disputes in the Social Sciences* (Sussex, United Kingdom: Harvester Press, 1979).

25. K. Apel, "Types of Social Science in the Light of Human Cognitive Interests," in *Philosophical Disputes in the Social Sciences*, ed. Brown, p.6.

26. Habermas, *Theory and Practice*.

27. Laclau, *Politics and Ideology in Marxist Theory*, p. 66.

28. H. Marcuse, "On Science and Phenomenology," in *The Essential Frankfurt School Reader*, ed. A. Arato and E. Gebhardt (New York: Urizen Books, 1978), p. 471.

29. P. Suppes, "The Place of Theory in Educational Research," *Educational Researcher* 8 (June 1974): 8.

30. R. D. Barr, J. L. Barth, and S. S. Shermis, *Defining the Social Studies* (Washington, D.C.: National Council for the Social Studies, 1977).

31. See Apple, *Ideology and Curriculum*; and B. M. Franklin, "Education for Social Control," *History of Education Quarterly* 14 (Spring 1974): 131–36. An exceptional critique of the "new technology" movement in recent curriculum writings can be found in B. Andrews and D. Hakken, "Educational Technology: A Theoretical Discussion," *College English* 39 (September 1977): 68–109.

32. M. F. D. Young, "Curriculum Change: Limits and Possibilities," *Educational Studies* 1: 2 (June 1975): 129.

33. J. Friedman, "The Epistemology of Social Practice: A Critique of Objective Knowledge," *Theory and Society* 6: 1 (July 1978): 75–90.

34. H. Marcuse, "Repressive Tolerance," in *A Critique of Pure Tolerance*, ed. R. Paul Wolff, B. Moor, Jr., and H. Marcuse (Boston: Beacon Press, 1969), pp. 122–23.

35. W. Peak and H. Zeigler, "The Political Functions of the Educational System," *Sociology of Education* 43: 2 (Spring 1970): 115–42.

36. J. Anyon, "Ideology and U.S. History Textbooks," *Harvard Educational Review* 49: 3 (August 1979): 361–86.

37. R. Spencer, "Nature and Value of Functionalism," in *Functionalism in the Social Sciences*, ed. D. Martendale (Philadelphia: American Academy of Political and Social Sciences, 1965), p. 1.

38. R. H. Turner, "Role Taking: Process vs. Conformity," in *Human Behavior and Social Process*, ed. A. Rose (London and Boston: Routledge & Kegan Paul, 1962), p. 37.

39. G. Grace, *Teachers, Ideology, and Control: A Study in Urban Education* (Boston and London: Routledge & Kegan Paul, 1978).

40. U. Lundgren, "Background: The Conceptual Framework," in *Codes, Context, and Curriculum Processes*, ed. id. and Stan Peterson (Stockholm: Liber, 1979).

41. Anyon, "Ideology and U.S. History Textbooks," p. 52.

42. Representative examples of the work under analysis here include E. Fenton, "A Structure of History," in *Concepts and Structure in the New Social Science Curriculum*, ed. I. Morrisett (New York: Holt, Rinehart & Winston, 1966); P. Hanna and John Lee, "Generalizations from the Social Sciences," in *Structure in the Social Studies* (Washington, D.C.: National Council for the Social Studies, 1968); R. Price, W. Hickman, and G. Smith, *Major Concepts for the Social Studies* (Syracuse, N.Y.: Social Studies Curriculum Center, 1965).

43. J. Bruner, *The Process of Education* (Cambridge: Harvard University Press, 1960).

44. D. Gleeson and G. Whitty, *Developments in Social Studies Teaching* (London: Open Books, 1976).

45. Ibid.; J. Anyon, "Ideology and U.S. History Textbooks"; id., "School Curriculum: Political and Economic Structure, and Social Change," *Social Practice* (Spring 1980): 96–108.

46. Cherryholmes, "Social Knowledge and Citizenship Education," p. 120.

47. T. S. Popkewitz, "The Latent Values of the Discipline-Centered Curriculum," *Theory and Research in Social Education* 5: 1 (April 1977): 48.

48. T. W. Adorno, *Prisms* (London: Spearman, 1967), p. 38.

49. A. Gouldner, *Two Marxisms: Contradictions and Anomalies in the Development of Theory* (New York: Seabury Press, 1980).

50. The Hermeneutic tradition finds its strongest philosophical expression in H. Gadamer, *Philosophical Hermeneutics,* trans. D. E. Linge (Berkeley: University of California Press, 1977); A. Schutz, *The Phenomenology of the Social World* (Evanston, Ill.: Northwestern University Press, 1967); P. Winch, *The Idea of a Social Science and Its Relation to Philosophy* (London: Routledge & Kegan Paul, 1972). A good collection of writings can be found in M. Douglas, ed., *Rules and Meaning* (London: Penguin Books, 1973).

51. G. Whitty, "Sociology and the Problem of Radical Educational Change," in *Educability, Schools, and Ideology,* ed. M. Flude and J. Ahier (London: Croom Helm, 1974), p. 120.

52. In the United States this type of work is probably best represented by a number of traditions ranging from the free-school movement of the early 1960s, the open-school movement, various offshoots that support a Freire-like approach to education, and various branches of humanistic pedagogy. An analysis of these traditions can be found in H. A. Giroux, "Beyond the Limits of Radical Educational Reform: Toward a Critical Theory of Education," *Journal of Curriculum Theorizing* 2: 1 (Winter 1980): 20–46.

53. Barr, Barth, and Shermis, *Defining the Social Studies,* p. 64.

54. Ibid.

55. See R. C. Remy and M. J. Turner, "Basic Citizenship Competencies: Guidelines for Educators, Policymakers, and Citizens," *Mershon Center Quarterly Report* 5 (Autumn 1979): 1–8. A critical overview of these positions can be found in F. M. Newmann, "Political Participation: An Analytical Review and Proposal," in *Political Education in Flux,* ed. J. Gillespie and D. Heater (London: Sage Publications, 1980).

56. J. L. Barth and S. S. Shermis, "Defining Social Problems," *Theory and Research in Social Education* 7: 1 (Spring 1979): 1–19.

57. The enthusiasm for this approach sometimes appears to reach dizzying heights. For example, Metzger and Barr seem to believe that the essence of citizenship education lies in a combination of positive political attitudes in students and the support the latter receive in open school environments which encourage decision making and participation. The concept of false consciousness and the notion that student participation may take place within narrowly defined parameters of power appear to disappear in these studies. See Metzger and Barr, "Impact of School Political Systems."

58. See S. Engle, "Decision Making: The Heart of Social Studies Instruction," *Social Education* 24 (November 1960): 301–04, 306. The positivist nature of this assumption, that radical decision making should assume higher priority in the social studies than Verstehen and social reconstructionism, compromises much of the hermeneutic rationality underlying this mode of citizenship education.

59. C. Cherryholmes, "Citizenship Education as Critical Decision Making" (Paper presented at the annual meeting of the American Educational Research Association, San Francisco, April 1979).

60. E. Cagen, "Individualism, Collectivism, and Radical Educational Reform," *Harvard Educational Review* 48: 2 (May 1978): 227–66.

61. H. Berlak, "Human Consciousness, Social Criticism, and Civic Education,"

in *Rationales for Citizenship Education*, ed. J. P. Shaver (Arlington, Va.: National Council for the Social Studies, 1977).

62. N. Poulantzas, *Classes in Contemporary Society* (London: Verso, 1978).

63. L. Althusser, "Ideology and State Apparatus," in *Lenin and Philosophy and Other Essays*, trans. B. Brewster (New York: Monthly Review Press, 1971.)

64. Bowles and Gintis, *Schooling in Capitalist America*.

65. Bernstein, *Class, Codes and Control*; M. Apple, "Curricular Form and the Logic of Technical Control: Building the Possessive Form and the Logic of Technical Control: Building the Posessive Individual" (Unpublished paper, University of Wisconsin, Madison, 1980).

66. Bourdieu and Passeron, *Reproduction in Education, Society and Culture*.

67. An interesting discussion of Bourdieu's notion of cultural capital and schooling can be found in M. MacDonald, "Cultural Reproduction: The Pedagogy of Sexuality," *Screen Education* 32 (Autumn/Winter 1979–1980): 141–53.

68. Anyon, "School Curriculum."

69. H. A. Giroux, "Beyond the Correspondence Theory: Notes on the Dynamics of Educational Transformation and Reproduction," *Curriculum Inquiry* 10: 3 (Fall 1980): 225–47.

70. R. Jacoby, *Social Amnesia* (Boston: Beacon Press, 1975), p. 73.

71. Two excellent critiques of the notion of pluralism can be found in R. P. Wolff, "Beyond Tolerance," in *A Critique of Pure Tolerance*, ed. id., B. Moore, Jr., and H. Marcuse (Boston: Beacon Press, 1969); B. Clark and Herbert Gintis, "Rawlsian Justice and Economic Systems," *Philosophy and Public Affairs* 7: 4 (Summer 1978): 302–325.

72. Peak and Zeigler, "Political Functions of the Educational System," p. 122.

73. This is particularly true of the work of Kohlberg and his associates. See L. Kohlberg and R. Mayer, "Development as the Aim of Education," *Harvard Educational Review* 42: 4 (November 1972): 449–96; R. Mosher, "A Democratic High School: Damn It, Your Feet Are Always in the Water," in *Value Development . . . as the Aim of Education*, ed. N. Sprinthall (New York: Character Research Press, 1978).

74. R. Sharp and A. Green, *Education and Social Control* (Boston and London: Routledge & Kegan Paul, 1975), p. 28.

75. J. Donzelot, *The Policing of Families*, trans. R. Hurley (New York: Pantheon, 1980).

76. A. Heller, *Theory of Need of Marx* (London: Allison & Busby, 1974).

77. MacDonald, *Curriculum and Cultural Reproduction*, p. 60.

78. Overviews of these positions can be found in ibid.; R. Johnson, "Histories of Culture/Theories of Ideology: Notes on an Impasse," in *Ideology and Cultural Production*, ed. M. Barrett et al. (New York: St. Martin's Press, 1979); G. Whitty and M. Young, *Society, State and Schooling* (Sussex, United Kingdom: Falmer Press, 1977).

79. Sharp and Green, *Education and Social Control*, p. x.

80. R. Johnson, "Notes on the Schooling of the English Working Class 1780–1850," in *Schooling and Capitalism: A Sociological Reader*, ed. R. Dale, G. Esland, and M. MacDonald (Boston and London: Routledge & Kegan Paul, 1976).

81. H.P. Dreitzel, "On the Meaning of Political Culture," in *Beyond the Crisis*,

ed. N. Birnbaum (New York: Oxford University Press, 1977), p. 88.

82. P. Wexler, "Structure, Text, and Subject: A Sociology of School Knowledge" (Unpublished paper, n.d.), p. 6.

83. A. Gramsci, *Selections From the Prison Notebooks*, ed. and trans. Q. Hoare and G. Smith (New York: International Publishers, 1971).

84. C. Boggs, *Gramsci's Marxism* (London: Pluto Press, 1976), p. 39.

85. Anyon, "Ideology and U.S. History Textbooks," p. 379.

86. Wexler, "Structure, Text, and Subject."

87. Bernstein, *Class, Codes and Control.*

88. See H.A. Giroux, ed., "Education, Ideology, and the Hidden Curriculum," *Journal of Education* 162: 1 (Winter 1980).

89. Bowles and Gintis, *Schooling in Capitalist America*; Bernstein, *Class, Codes and Control*; Giroux, "Education, Ideology, and the Hidden Curriculum."

90. Sharp and Green, *Education and Social Control*, pp. 41–42.

91. R. Rist, *The Urban School: A Factory for Failure* (Cambridge, Mass.: MIT Press, 1977).

92. Ibid., pp. 145, 146.

93. Ibid., pp. 146, 150.

94. I have analyzed the work of a number of these theorists in Giroux, "Beyond the Correspondence Theory." See also E. Bredo and W. Feinberg, "Meaning, Power and Pedagogy," *Journal of Curriculum Studies* 11: 4 (1974): 315–32.

95. Johnson, "Histories of Culture," p. 52.

96. P. Willis, *Learning to Labour: How Working Class Kids Get Working Class Jobs* (England: Saxon House, Teakfield, 1977).

97. S. Aronowitz, *False Promises* (New York: McGraw-Hill, 1973); R. Edwards, *Contested Terrain* (New York: Basic Books, 1979).

98. MacDonald, *Curriculum and Cultural Reproduction*, p. 104.

99. M. Foucault, *Power, Truth, and Strategy* (Sydney, Australia: Federal Publications, 1979), p. 17.

100. A. Heller, "Marx's Theory of Revolution and the Revolution in Everyday Life," in *The Humanization of Socialism: Writings of the Budapest School*, ed. id. et al. (London: Allison & Busby, 1967).

101. M. Greene, *Landscapes of Learning* (New York: Teachers College Press, 1978), p. 59.

102. W. F. Pinar, "The Abstract and the Concrete in Curriculum Theorizing," in *Curriculum and Instruction: Alternatives in Education*, ed. H. A. Giroux, A. N. Penna, and W. F. Pinar (Berkeley: McCutchan, 1981).

103. Gleeson and Whitty, *Developments in Social Studies Teaching*, p. 102.

104. Newmann, "Political Participation."

18

Conflict and Liberation: Personal Aspects of the Mathematics Experience

Marshall Gordon

Any situation in which some men prevent others from engaging in the process of inquiry is one of violence. The means used are not important; to alienate men from their own decision-making is to change them into objects.
—*Paulo Freire*

When we view the formal presentation of mathematics, whether in a textbook or classroom, typically we find clear demonstrations, logical relationships, and solutions that are errorless, if not elegant. The experience is offered as objective, lucid, and unequivocal. What is recognized and established by appropriate action is that "mastery of truths has to do with getting the appropriate beliefs; acquisition of methods and operations involves getting the right skills. For each subject there are characteristic and peculiar truths as well as distinctive and appropriate skills. To find these and to state them is to produce a curriculum."[1]

I would like to express my appreciation to Joyce Haroutunian-Gordon, David E. Purpel, James B. Macdonald, and Richard Mullaney for their valuable comments, and to Graham Orpwood and Joel Weiss for their fine editorial assistance.

Reprinted from *Curriculum Inquiry* 8: 3 (1978): 251–71. Copyright © by the Ontario Institute for Studies in Education. Reprinted by permission of John Wiley & Sons, Inc.

We are asking as Scheffler has, "What could be more familiar—or more misguided?"[2] At the same time, we find books such as *Mathematics Without Tears* and *The I Hate Mathematics Book* that are written for students who "never understood mathematics" and who have "mathophobia"—a fear of a discipline unique to mathematics.

How is one to make sense of both of these perceptions? To what extent does this antinomy have validity? In response to this apparent contradiction, I suggest that we view the mathematics experience from both an epistemological and an axiological context. I am particularly concerned that we do not separate knowing from valuing inasmuch as I believe that one does not "follow truth wherever it may lead," rather truth follows from personal intention. While this view of knowledge is most closely associated with what Lamm refers to as the "radical approach to knowledge in education,"[3] in contrast to the views of knowledge as having practical use or intrinsic value, the pragmatic or essentialist views of knowledge—it does not exclude the latter. Moreover, the notion of radical is intended in the sense of going back to the roots, the subjective roots of the mathematics experience. As Lamm notes, "creativity as a mode of life, subjectivity as a test of the validity of knowledge, and self-awareness as its goal are the dimensions of knowledge in the radical conception of education."[4] Specifically, the view developed in this article argues that mathematics and all knowledge have both intrinsic and practical value to the person in the experience of creating that knowledge in that the experience becomes part of the person, enriches the person's lived experience, and relocates the person's effort in and toward the world.

Toward Locating the Conflict

It is my contention that although mathematics is viewed and presented as a deductively determined body of knowledge, it is nevertheless fundamentally a personal experience; the "terror and triumph" of constructing mathematical knowledge clearly signal its subjective dimension. In my estimation, this confict—both personal and epistemological—derives from a failure to acknowledge the personal acts of choosing and valuing in our finely polished, impersonal mathematics curriculum—acts which are paramount in providing personal, adequate evidence for knowing, not only evidence for substantiation but, more importantly, evidence that clarifies personal (as versus a weak or surface) understanding and tests the taken-for-granted reality.

The human acts of teaching and learning are shared acts of presenting and accepting oneself and others in coming to a particular way of knowing. As acts of control, they make us submerge our awareness of our existence. As acts of and toward understanding, they make us acutely aware of our human capacity and need for meaning and explanation of our experience. As liberating acts, they require honesty and, as honest acts, they require sensitivity to and recognition of subjectivity. To view the mathematics experience in both "repair and transcendence"[5] is to understand that liberation requires the creation of personal meaning which, subsidiarily, tests the taken for granted. I examine this conflict emphasizing the personal aspects of constructing mathematical meaning. I hope to suggest some ways in which the mathematics experience may be offered as a liberating experience, both in itself and in its connection to the world we inhabit and create.

Dimensions of the Mathematics Experience

Belief

What is the relationship between belief and mathematical knowledge? Consistent with a twentieth-century view held by many research mathematicians, Israel Scheffler describes what he believes is the essence of propositional knowledge. He chooses the following, by now well known, conditions of knowledge:[6]

1. (person) X believes (proposition) P
2. P is true
3. X has adequate evidence for P

What it means then, according to Scheffler and most practicing mathematicians and mathematics educators, is that for X to have a "strong" sense (knowledge) of P (it would be "weak" if condition 3 was not met), X has to have justified the belief of P. So, for example, we say that X knows that $2 + 2 = 4$ but not that $2 + 1 = 4$ because in the latter case the truth condition is not met. Similarly, we say that X only has a weak sense if it is accepted that $2 + 2 = 4$ without having any adequate evidence for knowing that $2 + 2 = 4$. Notice that it is implied that *belief* or *value* are taken on by the person from the proposition itself. The proposition exists and one is then said to know if the belief has been justified. It is within belief where we find if one is open to accepting the logical argument—and as such has a more profound role to play in coming to what we know than argued by Scheffler. I am saying that if X does not believe it is worth knowing P, then X will not reason (to P); and, if X believes in P, X will seek to find reasons to claim P. As Whitehead observed: "Our reasoning grasps at straws for premises and floats on gossamers for deduction." And, why "grasp" and "float" if not for beliefs?

Side Path 1. To gain a strong sense of what is to be developed here, consider the following elementary problem from plane geometry: If the circumference of the earth is approximately 25,000 miles, how much distance would there be between the surface of the earth and a concentric circle (having the same center as the earth and assuming the earth is circular) whose circumference is 25,000 miles + 30 feet? We wish to determine x from Figure 18-1. Would you guess that $x =$ one inch, less, much less—how much? Guess whatever you *believe* might be the case. (The circles are drawn so that the distance x can be discerned and should not be taken as a scale drawing.) As we want to determine the difference between the lengths of the radii ($r_2 - r_1 = x$), we have to find r_1 and r_2. Recall (ah, sweet memory) that the circumference of a circle $= 2 \pi r$. As 25,000 miles = 132,000,000 ft.,

$$132,000,000 = 2 \pi r_1;$$
$$66,000,000 = \pi r_1,$$

and

$$r_1 \approx 21,008,470 \text{ ft.}$$

Now $r_2 = r_1 + x$, is determined by solving for r_2 where

$$132,000,000 + 30 = 2 \pi r_2;$$

or

$$132,000,030 = 2 \pi r_2.$$

Then

$$66,000,015 = \pi r_2,$$

or

$$r_2 = 21,008,475 \text{ ft.}$$

We find $r_2 - r_1 = 5$. That is, one who is 5 feet tall could walk on the surface of the planet and one's head would just touch the outer circumference created by adding only 30 feet to the total—an increase which is seemingly infinitesimal: 30 feet added to 132 million feet. Well, you have the adequate evidence for P; the arithmetic confirms that P is true, do you believe it? What type of knowing do you have? Weak? Strong? Something else?

   The basic problem is this: a formal attitude prevails in the presentation of mathematics today in North America—with its emphasis on a logical, rigorous model and a disavowal of the essential role of belief and value in constructing mathematical knowledge. I argue that failure to recognize commitment and belief in constructing knowledge results in failure to recognize that they are essential conditions for knowing and that to exclude them from the mathematics experience is misguided at best. The following instance aids us in locating the epistemological and personal conflict.

   Side Path 2. Most if not all of us saw in our study of geometry that the sum of the measures of the angles of a triangle is 180° (see Figure 18-2). As it is a short proof, it is presented here in a form consistent with modern presentation:

1. Draw a line through A parallel to segment BC (through a point not on a line there is one and only one line that can be drawn parallel to that line).
2. Angle 1 has the same measure as angle ABC, and angle 2 as angle ACB (if lines are parallel, the alternate interior angles formed by those parallel lines are of the same measure).
3. Angle 3 has the same measure as angle BAC (reflexive property of equality).
4. Since the sum of the measures of angles 1, 2, and 3 equal 180° (sum of the measures of a straight angle), then the sum of angles B, C, and BAC also must equal 180° (substitution of equal quantities for equal quantities).
5. Therefore, the sum of the angles of a triangle is 180°.

Figure 21-1
Side Path 1

It is clear and direct; its logic demands its acceptance. However, it is the clarity and directness which hides the difficulty of coming to know the proof. Einstein, at the age of eleven, read this proof and remarked later that he realized that "something deep and profound is hidden here." Notice that the first step of the proof is not the conclusion of a logical inference, nor is it a definition or statement of a prior theorem; rather, it is an insight found through intuition, grounded in a belief that this knowledge was worth pursuing and creating. Without this insight, the direct logical implications found in the rest of the proof would never come to be. Without acknowledging this insight, the direct logical implications do not warrant our belief. Without this emphasis, there is no reason to believe that anyone has learned anything from this proof about constructing mathematics. Both the presentation and acceptance of this proof in only its logical context engender an empty epistemological experience and a diminishing personal experience. Epistemologically it is empty for we cannot know what we do not believe. Personally it is diminishing for we are forced to accept what we do not understand.

The conditions of knowledge alluded to earlier can lead one (and often do in mathematics) to thinking that knowing and inquiring are constituted by the same acts. In this confusion the condition of belief comes after the fact; I would suggest it comes both before and after and that adequate evidence is, at bottom, a personal choice often grounded in aesthetics, personal experience, and, ultimately, belief—the "hard facts" are always theory laden.[7] The significance of the inquiry, presented as knowledge in this example, can be seen in the denial of a number of vital contexts: one is the energy, the personal commitment to give part of one's life to this pursuit; another is that in this particular proof lies the determinant of Euclidean geometry—it is the assumption presented as the reason for the acceptability of the first step which determined the path of the entire body of knowledge known as Euclidean geometry; and, for the particular student, there is little, if any, possibility that the experience, as it is, provided any personal meaning.

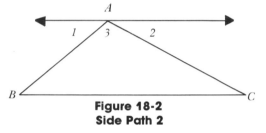

Figure 18-2
Side Path 2

To particularize these significant aspects of inquiry and to exemplify the integral relationship of believing, valuing, and knowing, we will take a closer look at the rich past of the first assumption. Saccheri, a Jesuit priest and amateur mathematician, was a devout believer in Euclidean geometry, as both historical and personal evidence had demonstrated the accuracy with which Euclidean geometry explained physical space. However, during those two thousand years, mathematicians were not convinced that Euclid's fifth postulate (the reason given for the first step in the proof) was self-evident— the essential characteristic of postulates.[8] Thus, during those years many tried to show that this postulate was in fact a theorem; that is, it could be deduced from the earlier postulates and the rules of logic. This belief was strengthened by the knowledge that the converse of this postulate was demonstrable. Saccheri, who strongly believed that the postulate was true (for he believed that Euclidean geometry was the geometry to explain the world of phenomena), chose to pursue proving it by using a *reductio ad absurdum* proof; that is, he would assume it was not true in the hope that this assumption would lead to a logical contradiction. He died believing he had constructed such a proof, and the year of his death, 1733, his work entitled, "Euclid Cleared of Every Flaw," was published. However, he hadn't succeeded in doing what he had thought. The proof was not logically complete.

The development of his proof led him to certain conclusions which, although not logically contradictory, were so foreign to an understanding of physical reality that he concluded that some findings were "repugnant to the nature of a straight line." What in fact Saccheri had found were theorems of a non-Euclidean geometry; that is, the choice he made in attacking the problem led him to generate true statements within another geometry rather than a contradiction as he had thought and believed. On the one hand, it is true that Saccheri's preconceptions and beliefs overrode his reason and led him to see what he believed; on the other hand, with history and reality clearly on his side, the logical argument he constructed seemed in belief to lead to such absurdities as to question the foundations of reality and logic. His logical error comes from thinking and believing that the logic constructed by the human mind and a geometry constructed by the reality it perceives could not be at odds. Is this simply a logical error? Or is it a manifestation of the strength of belief irrevocably embedded in the acts of coming to know? Belief, I am suggesting, is an essential and inextricable part of the fabric we call logic. The human need for continuity, consistency, and completeness is greater than logic, for the need creates the logic. This case shows how deeply felt beliefs can lead one to reject the dictates of logic, for belief precedes and transcends logic. The following will emphasize how belief, not rigor, can lead to the creation of new mathematics.

The Greeks, and especially the followers of Pythagoras, believed that numbers and their relationships ruled and explained the universe. However, a discovery of irrational numbers—numbers which cannot be located exactly on a number line—was such an anathema to the Greeks that they designated these incommensurate numbers as *unutterable*; it is written that those who mentioned these unutterables were drowned. Their belief led them to reject irrational numbers as numbers and to translate them into lengths. "In fact they converted all of algebra into geometry in order to work with lengths, areas, and volumes that might otherwise have to be represented numerically by irrationals, and they even solved quadratic equations geometrically."[9] This graphically demonstrates the deep roots at which mathematical formulations can operate. Numbers were not in this nature formal, objective tools but aspects of spiritual truths and human aspirations. The cosmic relationship of numbers to human spirit continues today with hypernumbers as the focus.[10]

Side Path 3. To present and view mathematics in only a logical framework is to deny personal conviction and commitment. We find this denial in many, if not most, mathematics textbooks. For example, we find irrational numbers developed, rationally and logically, in the following two ways: either one is led to solve equations of the type $x^2 - 2 = 0$ (which leads to finding $\sqrt{2}$), or irrational numbers are constructed as those numbers which can be represented as nonrepeating infinite decimals (versus rational numbers, which can be represented as either finite decimals—$\frac{1}{4} = 0.25$, or as infinite but repeating decimals—$\frac{1}{3} = 0.\overline{33} \cdots$). These logical explanations are constructed after the fact and provide no historical or personal reality of the profound effect such discoveries created. Interestingly, some texts do include the story of drowning those who dared to mention these unutterables.[11] That in one paragraph irrational numbers are developed so reasonably, and in a footnote one is told what was done to those who spoke of them, must leave the student or reader wondering what is really going on. To create a number is to open a crack in the objective egg—and those who have given their energies and commitment, and possibly created their meaning of the universe in conjunction with a particular number system, can obviously be devastated when a new paradigm is forced upon them. One does not know initially, in the tentative, troubling stages of inquiry, if in fact the future will unfold in such a way as to negate the past and one's efforts, values, and beliefs along with it.

Intuition

Poincaré raises and responds to an important question: "Can one ever understand a theory if one builds it up right from the start in the definitive form that rigorous logic imposes, without some indications of the attempts which led to it? No; one does not really understand it; one cannot even retain it or one retains it only by learning it by heart."[12] My concern is not only with whether the individual understands the mathematics but, just as important, with the psychological effects on a person who comes to that experience with a desire to know and a sense of self, how this affects the way a person will go, about seeking to know, and the society he or she will seek to create. The continual commitment and attitude of the formal approach, which does not admit our subjectivity, most assuredly minimizes the opportunity for providing the individual with experiences which are valuable in developing personal knowledge. And the emphasis on formal operational thought only submerges the creative inquiry spirit in all of us.

To know that one wants to commit oneself to know is the first and essential act in coming to know. But the formal perspective and the personal perspective call for divergent considerations. To begin with the logical demonstration, which is the conclusion of the inquiry, cannot make personal sense; it is a clever approach allowing for verification only to those who know, and inauthentic and dishonest to those who do not. The problem that is solved is not the problem the student wants solved. The student wants to know "is this (the formal description) the way I should or must start?" and "why isn't what I think considered?" This inner disturbance should take precedence for, if unanswered, it will leave the person confused about mathematics and one's own awareness and ability to make personal as well as mathematical meaning.

The commitment to the logical or technical exposition, without response to the inherent role of intuition in determining knowledge, may in part be due to the fact that intuition is not readily accessible as a product of experience and hence not offered within the rational presentation of mathematical knowledge. But to fail to recognize the value of intuition in constructing knowledge is also to fail to recognize that "rigor will not refine an intuition which has not been allowed to function freely."[13]

The following situation emphasizes the duality which exists between the knowledge as presented and the possible experience involved. This duality is caused by acknowledging an ideal of the formal presentation of essential knowledge; to redirect it is to acknowledge the dignity of the human being. It is to share the experience as being human.[14] If we are to reveal personal intention or thought and not just impersonal reason or proof, it is necessary, as the mathematician J. L. Synge states, to take away the "austere and unrevealing mask." For "behind that mask there are quick jumps of intuition and much mental stumbling and confusion."[15]

Side Path 4. The formal perspective presents addition of fractions with the following:

$$a/b + c/d = (ad + bc)/db$$

The child is presented with this information in elementary, junior, and senior high school. But when one asks many adults "how much is $2/3 + 5/7$?," there is usually silence coupled with an embarrassed look. What is most disturbing is not that they do not know how to add fractions given the constant exposure but that they blame themselves for forgetting the rule.

The system that presented the mathematics without considering the person's experience and belief system in developing meaning is at fault. Consider the following situation: David won 2 out of 3 games on Monday and 5 out of 7 games on Tuesday. Is it possible that this sort of experience would suggest that $2/3 + 5/7 = (2 + 5)/(3 + 7)$; that is, David won 7 out of the 10 games played? While a child may know this on a preconscious level and may ask why can't one add numerators and denominators [that is, $a/b + c/d = (a + c)/(b + d)$], many teachers, without personal understanding and unabetted by the formal curriculum, respond, "you can't add apples and oranges." As one graduate student explained, "I learned you can't add apples and oranges but when I was in junior high school (and learned that $a/b \times c/d = ac/bd$), I learned that you can multiply them!" The meaning made here is the result of an insensitive, nonintuitive presentation; moreover, it is destructive. While the person cared about keeping score and tallying the game scores, there was no thought given to learning this algorithm of formal arithmetic. The person was told what to believe; that is, that this belief was important to hold, but devoid of any value orientation other than institutional reward or punishment.

While I have unsuccessfully tried to follow Goedel's (1931) proof,[16] the import of the theorem, as I understand it, is worth our consideration here. Goedel demonstrated that a logically rigid system, such as the one devised by Russell and Whitehead for arithmetic,[17] must necessarily contain propositions that are undecidable or undemonstrable within the system. Thus, we cannot determine whether the axioms will not lead to contradictions some time in the future. In essence, what is involved to prove a system S not contradictory from within the system requires that we know that S is not contradictory; for if it were, then anything could be proved including the non-contradictory nature of S. This is impossible to prove within the system. Let us entertain some implications from this exciting insight.

It appears that there is little reason to believe humans could construct a machine which would provide a substitute for living intelligence.[18] The implications of this view perhaps provide a valuable perspective in the argument for whether our brains work serially or in parallel. Inasmuch as computers are constructed with serial arrangements which contain logical connectives for decision making and proof making, Goedel's proof suggests that the machine could not draw certain logical inferences. Then the argument for thinking in parallel, which includes thinking intuitively, appears to gain added support. The connection seems to me to be thus: we construct logical mechanisms, such as the computer using serial organization, because serial organization is logically available to our understanding. We cannot construct a computer which operates in a parallel mode because we do not understand the logical constructions and perhaps, more importantly, it would be contradictory to think otherwise. If we could construct a logic in response to parallel thought, such as intuition, we would necessarily have to conclude that intuition is logical. The intuitive process in itself transcends our logic and language and thus must be explained, if at all, from an aesthetic consciousness and conduct that is grounded in personal belief. Hence, the presentation of only a formal perspective has its limits, as does language (which we have long agreed). Thus to act in good faith requires providing environments where neither logic nor proof is the ultimate judge or exclusive goal. As the mathematician Lebesgue has said, "logic makes us reject certain arguments but it cannot make us believe any argument." The incompleteness theorem of Goedel moreover suggests that if one acts only on the basis of logic, so that emotion, belief, and commitment are neutered, one's actions and thoughts must be necessarily incomplete; the logic of logic is and can be always negated by the logic of choice.

Subjectivity

In one sense, the abstract metaphysical quality of mathematics provides an objective distance from reality. At this distance, mathematics is under no obligation to reality; it is free to create relationships, needing to satisfy only its own requirements where the choices are grounded in subjectivity. In another sense, the visions that are seen while soaring at this height inevitably turn out to be valuable for science and technology (which may be seen as a metaphor for our experience). What seems necessary then is to allow subjectivity to become part of accepted experience and be presented as part of the mathematics experience. The following considerations will emphasize that what we can know through experience and intuition we may not be able to know through logic and that personal meaning does not lie in a system but in our reflections about the system.

Side Path 5. Russell and Whitehead,[19] in three volumes, attempted to develop arithmetic from a particular set of axioms with their ultimate goal being to prove that all of mathematics can be generated from a small number of logical principles (Goedel's work not having been done at this time). In the first volume, they define number in the following way: "The number belonging to a class C is the class of all the classes in a one-to-one correspondence with C."[20] However, the notion of one-to-one correspondence is, as I see it, dependent upon the concept of number.[21] Is it possible that Russell and Whitehead's commitment to logical exposition narrowed their understanding? Although this query can remain only a conjecture,[22] the point I wish to make is that total commitment to an explicit logic or a language has serious limitations. As Polanyi notes, "we can know more than we can tell,"[23] and this is evident when, without definition but through intuition and personal experience, there is a deep rather than surface understanding.

The fact that there are still intuitionists and formalists, as neither group is able to dispel the beliefs of the other, exemplifies the subjectivity that is at the foundation of mathematics. What one group may accept as a proof or an axiom the other may not. This dichotomy should not be taken lightly. It is powerful enough to cause humans to destroy each other. For example, the formalist findings of Cantor were so abhorrent to the intuitionist Kronecker that he used his considerable influence to deprive Cantor of publication and a deserved position—treatment which ultimately contributed to Cantor's mental breakdown. Sometimes belief makes us reject certain logical arguments. The antinomies of present-day mathematics will be resolved by mathematical logicians, indeed by their creativity, but moreover by their belief that what they do is worth doing; their belief will lead to another axiom or another system which will explain and possibly eliminate the problems of the former system. Nevertheless, the activity of doing mathematics will continue, grounded in subjectivity.

Another context for subjectivity can be found in examining the parallel relationships between mathematical postulates and personal beliefs. Here we find that beliefs lead to personal statements and actions, as postulates to mathematical theorems. Disagreement between people, as between mathematical systems, is profound when the differences are grounded in beliefs or postulates, and logic is not powerful enough to resolve the schisms; only understanding grounded in belief can appreciate the disparity. Our earlier discussion of Saccheri is a case in point. Euclidean geometry and the non-Euclidean, created but emotionally unaccepted by Saccheri, came into existence with the choice of the parallel postulate. From that point on, the geometries differ in their development and perspective. Newton worked within the confines of Euclidean space believing, as did Kant, that one could explain physical space in this perspective. Einstein developed a richer perspective within a non-Euclidean space, and there is no reason to believe that the search has ended, or that it ever will. It would take more than logic for Newton to understand Einstein; it takes a subjective acceptance of another perspective, a richer perspective that is only available if one is personally open and accepting. The question then is to what extent can a prepackaged rigorous curriculum allow for a reality which is open and accepting?

The Person and the Formal Mathematics Experience

I have indicated that presenting mathematics formally, with little or no consideration given to intuition, belief, and subjectivity, is dishonest with respect to the ways in which mathematics is created. It is my belief that Davis's indictment of the traditional ninth-grade algebra course may be extended to the major portion of the student's formal mathematics experience, if we extend our view of tricks to include epistemological, logical, and operational tricks: "it is based on a sequence of tricks to get children to write down on paper what appear to be correct answers, although the student more often than not does not know what it all means, if anything."[24] An example of how this may come about and is perpetuated is the following: Imagine teachers having a "weak sense" of belief in, or knowledge of, what to present, due to their own experience as students with a formal curriculum; and, not being able to reconcile this personal knowledge, present what is in the textbook in the belief that they are not personally responsible for these tricks. In essence, the teacher becomes a thing—"neither consenting or resisting."[25] For the student the situation is much the same. The student is aware of being there but, for the most part, does not understand the purpose behind the acts being performed; at the same time the student is aware of playing at being a student, which does not require understanding, for memory will suffice; of accepting a state of being in which the choices are true to the role of the student but not true to the self. Thus one tries to escape the situation, the feelings, and the knowledge that one does not know.

These beliefs lead to fear—the fear is not of mathematics *qua* mathematics, as I understand it; rather, this self-destructive condition derives from the fear of not knowing believing that one should know, and from the fear of being discovered, of not being able to defend oneself. These students and teachers bear the burden built on the contradictions one finds when one is involved in coming to know mathematics in contrast to the usual logical demonstration which has little, if anything, in common with experience. However, it has become common practice to dismiss the personal experience and accept the authoritative presentation. Herein lies the root of "mathophobia": trying to believe what one does not believe, that mathematics is as it is presented. If this were not the case, why can't even good students "give examples, construct counter-examples, and solve special problems" although they can "spout correct statements of theorems, and remember correct proofs"?[26] Spouting and memorizing are the products of misleading experiences, while constructing, posing, and solving are acts of deep understanding. And acts of deep understanding require that the "presentation of mathematics should be . . . free . . . from forbidding dogmatism which refuses to disclose motive or goal and which is an unfair obstacle to honest effort."[27]

The operational difficulty is clear: when the formal model of argument does not allow for false starts, dead ends, and confusion, it is ineffective, especially when the student loses the accepted path. Teachers who are torn between being responsible to the student or to the formal curriculum (they are mutually exclusive), and choose the latter, necessarily teach so that "the classroom performance . . . makes everything look, at once, too easy and too hard."[28] The personal difficulty is also clear: these acts force the self to a denigrating position. The operational and personal problems are the result of acting dishonestly in the misguided belief that one's social survival will be safeguarded. Presenting and accepting mathematics in an attitude and a model, which is what it is not, are acts of bad faith which can only lessen who we are and might become. Our obligation is to make the educational experience a liberating one, and this requires that we acknowledge meaning as transcending language, logic, and experience. Making meaning is the activity of an emerging consciousness.

Toward a Liberating Mathematics Experience

I begin by contrasting and comparing the relationship between ways of teaching mathematics and their implications for students with respect to a particular mathematical situation. That is, we first consider possible presentations or experiences of considering dividing a fraction by a fraction from the contexts of teaching for control, understanding, and liberation.[29]

In teaching where control is the emphasis, that is, where the student is dependent upon the teacher to create meaning, knowledge is usually presented in a fragmented nature. That is, knowledge presented one day may or may not be related to knowledge presented the next. The student has no sense of integration, no understanding of the intrinsic value of the knowledge nor how the knowledge is applicable or was created. In the particular situation we are considering, the student would come to know that when one has to divide a fraction by another fraction one "inverts and multiplies." That is, there is an operational procedure to follow which can be mastered, but the student lacks any mathematical comprehension. In a personal sense the student has been wired to perform as a machine: present a particular problem in a form which is identical to what was memorized and get a particular response provided that the pattern has been reinforced. At this stage of knowledge the student is incapable of separating belief from knowledge and knowledge from belief, for what has been emphasized is that the knowedge which is presented is to be believed and beliefs presented are to be held as true—thus, it is *all* questionable.

When we consider a second level—teaching for understanding—the emphasis is on relational knowledge in the sense that the student comes to see why "things are the way they are." Whereas in the control stage subjectivity is muted by training, in the understanding stage it is muted by valuing objectivity. The instrument, mathematics, becomes the mediating influence between the situation and the person and explains how things are. Thus the emphasis is upon adjustment so that one can and would function objectively (within the normal paradigm of the status quo),[30] that is as everyone else, given the same mathematical situation. While in the control stage one fills in blanks, in the understanding stage one solves problems. For example, when presented with the problem of simplifying a fraction divided by another fraction the student comes to understand why one "inverts and multiplies." The student comes to know that the object is to create a denominator with a value of one; thus, one inverts the denominator fraction and must multiply both numerator and denominator in order to keep constant the same fraction value. In this way the student comes to understand why one solves the particular type of problem the way one does. If students have really understood this process, then they can operationalize it in contexts requiring a ratio simplification. Here they have come to see that belief is requisite for knowing and that one holds only beliefs which can be shown to be true. And this is what the "modern" mathematics approach seeks to offer.

At a third level, however, in teaching for liberation it is necessary to establish that the particular mathematics is interesting and important for the student. In this situation the concern is for the personal construction of knowledge. Here, rather than being a problem solver, one is a problem poser/chooser. One appreciates that belief is instrumental in determining what and how one comes to know. Given that the student wants to consider the problem of simplifying a ratio with a fraction in both the numerator and the denominator, it is the student who pursues the possibility of creating meaning. The emphasis here is that there is not a prepackaged approach to the problem solution. One need not come to understand that the "object is to get a value of one in the denominator." Nor would the prescription be that one must multiply by the reciprocal of the denominator to obtain the value of one—for example, one could attempt to add, subtract, or do a number of operational procedures in order to begin to come to know how to simplify the expression. Here concepts of justice and equality can be seen in the contexts of symmetry and equivalence. For example, those readers of a mathematical bent could consider adding a fractional value to the denominator to gain a sum of one and then, having a sense of equality and symmetry, add the same value to the numerator. We could then ask, in what sense is mathematical equivalence met? Does the addition of equal quantities to the numerator and denominator do justice to the complex fraction? (That is, what is justice here?) Suppose, in our musing and daydreaming, one decides to invert the numerator and multiply by the denominator. Instead of being told immediately that this is not "the way," one could ask under what conditions would the product be equal to the quotient; that is, when would, if ever,

$$\frac{b}{a} \bigg/ \frac{c}{d} = \frac{b}{a} \times \frac{c}{d}.$$

The pervasive concern is to provide students with an opportunity to locate themselves in the process of inquiry, to re-create and re-view from many perspectives, to gain a fuller sense of the particular experience and moment in which they as individual human beings seek to have a personally meaningful experience. As the process of exploration continues students are aware of their choosing, of the personal commitment to locate meaning. The teacher could be involved in exploring with the students how they have come to choose one approach as opposed to another—intuition being appreciated— or/how the particular experience relates both personally and epistemologically to similar experiences they may have had or may presently have. If, for example, students decide not to continue the pursuit, then it might be valuable to explore with them how they deal with other situations which they find difficult—for instance, have they found it valuable to leave a problem alone and return to it another time, as many mathematicians do, or are they rejecting the experience because they have come to view themselves as a person who cannot do this problem, or any other perspective that the experience of the teacher and the personal insights of the students might offer as a means by which the students come to know more about themselves and the rich nature of inquiry (for example, do they care about pursuing the inquiry?).

In general, the mathematics curriculum, in concerned response to those involved in coming to know, should be constructed so as to encourage students to become aware of the ways in which people "find out how challenges are recognized and how questions are asked"[31] and, moreover, how they come to be recognized. For the mathematics experience to be seen and felt as liberating, the curriculum must share how and why mathematical knowledge is developed, with special emphasis on its grounding in belief, intuition, and subjectivity, and facilitate our understanding of the world in which we live and create and of the beliefs we act upon.

The first perspective of the knowledge lens requires that the mathematics curriculum be sensitive to the acts of choosing and valuing and emphasize the value of personal attempts and rationales for constructing knowledge. To sanction and encourage the personal aspects of the mathematics experience requires emphasizing what I call catalytic knowledge within the development of accepted knowledge. This knowledge includes aspects of our experience in constructing accepted knowledge: the approaches that didn't work, the approaches we thought worked but didn't, the inquiries we raised and pursued, the emotions and reflections we experienced in the process of coming to know. Brown aptly contrasts standard and nonstandard knowledge.[32] However, I am using the terms catalytic and accepted knowledge to emphasize the interactive, generative, tenuous, personal qualities of the inquiry or knowledge process. *It is this knowledge which explains how we have come to acquire that which we do know about ourselves and our experience.* In this way personal history or biography becomes, as it should, part of one's present.[33] Catalytic knowledge represents concretely the role of belief and the commitment to know that precedes and transcends accepted objective knowledge, the latter being a small part of what we know. It is integral to having personal adequate evidence for knowing. For it is not so much the reasons of an argument that persuade us but rather the process and discussion (with the self and others) and aesthetic perspective which provide us with the personal knowledge for this acceptance.

This perspective provides us with a way to reexamine and redefine the form of the mathematical model of inquiry as it now exists. At present, it follows the function of generating accepted knowledge. That is, the hypothetico-deductive model of inquiry explains how one logically progresses to demonstrate that some hypothesis is in fact that case. However, it would appear that if its function were to be one of also sharing catalytic knowledge, then the form would necessarily have to change. It would have to share the person in the presentation. To include catalytic knowledge, and thus to personalize the model of proof, would begin to liberate both student and teacher for deep understanding. It is essential, as I see it, for mathematics to be seen as liberating, that it be presented in terms of the contexts and processes that produced it and gave it meaning (and each of these from a personal, aesthetic, historical, and epistemological focus).

We are always in transition from coming to know and going to know. Part of our catalytic knowledge consists of ways in which we respond to complexity; if we are to become more capable and comfortable in coping with complexity, then our reflections on the ways we respond, and our reflections on our reflections, require our concerned attention. The mathematics experience needs to be viewed as a dual-dialectical process[34] in which ideas, beliefs, and accepted and catalytic knowledge are blended into new ways of understanding ourselves and phenomena, to generate new inquiries which will enrich our personal history and knowledge. As E. C. Moore said, "education must shift its attention from things and minds, to the relation between the experiencing subject and the experienced object."

The second perspective involves the interrelationships of mathematics and the sciences—physical and social—with regard to the ways humans construct explanations and relations of phenomena (including ideas), their grounding in belief, and the tenuousness of these constructions. This requires consideration of the rationales and decisions of inquiring minds in the process of developing knowledge, rather than as products of inquiry. For example, in comparing numeration systems, it is not enough to contrast calculations; it is also necessary to reflect upon the choice of symbols and how that choice reflects a society, a past, a way of making meaning. Imagine the world that would be open to our understanding if the numeration system could not have had arithmetic as we understand it today; furthermore, it would take more than logic for us to understand their knowledge and beliefs—required is an aesthetic concern to gain a strong sense. And it is this aesthetic concern which determines how numbers are used today.

This perspective suggests that we are free at any time to create and change postulates, just as with beliefs, if we are willing to pursue the personal and formal implications. This is not to imply that the parallelism between beliefs and postulates, and their capacity to generate knowledge, is complete. It is not; we think and respond within a richer and subtler logic than that accepted in mathematical logic today. Whereas beliefs are weighted according to the strengths of our convictions, mathematical logic responds to a bivalent system of acceptance or rejection which denies, by the absence of acknowledgment, our catalytic knowledge.[35] Nevertheless, mathematics, as any other way of making sense, deserves our attention both as a body of knowledge and as a process where we are made aware and appreciative of choosing and valuing. But, it is a presumption to say that students in mathematics should "learn how to guess"—this view presumes that the problems already exist and have already been accepted as problems. But we must first ascertain whether or not our students believe that the problem is worth considering. If not, they should pose/choose the problems and become the creators of the situation, if we truly believe that one must have freedom to be responsible and to challenge the taken-for-granted logic.[36]

In the educational experience, we need to come to a better understanding and appreciation of our (collective) past actions and decisions, how they affect our present, and what they suggest for our future. If we think of mathematical operations as actions, then we can ask, "Why would one do that?" If we think of mathematics or scientific relationships as ways of making meaning, we can ask, "Why would anyone want to know that?" If we think of ourselves as we live the mathematics experience, and I think we must, then we should ask, "What does this experience mean to me?" The pursuit of these inquiries is meaningful when and if students are willing to commit themselves to the inquiry. At bottom they call on the individual to pose questions and possible ways of pursuit to make the experience part of one's personal history. To conclude the experience with only a logical description is to diminish the experience and the person. On some level we can know a body of mathematical knowledge, but for it to have personal meaning, we must know it in terms of how we came to that pursuit, what the experience meant to us and to our understanding of that pursuit, and what it suggests both about ourselves and human beings. For to create knowledge is to know more about ourselves.

In this regard consider, briefly, the role that language plays and could play in being an integral part of the liberative mathematics experience. The liberating nature of mathematics is located, in part, in the volitional context of its language. Consider that all mathematics begin with expressions such as "what if?," "suppose," "let"—suggestive of the way in which mathematics provides for its own liberation, creation, and aesthetic excitement.

Unfortunately, the mathematics experience offered in the formal setting vulgarizes both, replacing them with an almost arbitrary control and tension. Most often the classroom mathematics effort is expressed as a collection of facts, techniques, and procedural relationships which reflect the diminution of personal effort toward chosen sustained inquiry. There one accumulates disjoint fragments, hardly gaining a sense of how the parts fit into a whole, why anyone might bother with some of the parts, and how one is to apprehend this experience as being educational. Thus the expression of freedom potentially contained in its language is submerged, while priority is given to "practice problems," "covering the curriculum" (as if it would ever be finally covered), and emphasizing formal operational thought to the exclusion of personal exploration and the initiative and concomitant emotion and reflection.

Toward suggesting that each person is an agent of life, schooling, and society, I suggest reconnecting the person as the initiator of the journey. For example, toward relocating the personal and collective effort we could replace these expressions as follows: "what if" with "what if I," "let" with "if I let" or "if we let." It is we who create the world, school, and mathematics. But the person is never alluded to in mathematics textbooks, except for those famous individuals whose efforts have been singular. What can we say then? Is it that only certain efforts are to be appreciated? If so, it behooves the author(s) to express why this is the case, and if not, why not. Rather than just present versions of mathematics, I would suggest that certain ideational features of the mathematical physiognomy be offered from an aesthetic, heightened consciousness; for example, "This theorem is really important, interesting, and aesthetic to me for the way in which it extends X, connects back to Y, and includes a suggestion toward Z." That is, the dynamic nature of mathematics must be given space. It is not an arbitrary collection of techniques, or a rational or logical collection of facts and methods created linearly. The dynamic liberative nature can be expressed and appreciated, provided one is given the opportunity to connect personally to the mathematics experience. We hardly, if ever, gain a sense of the person(s) who wrote the textbook—for example, in terms of this person coming to decide upon a particular arrangement for presentation that others considered but rejected, or in the attending rationales for the choices of what material to include; and with regard to those aspects which excited and intrigued the person, and so on. Most often the language of the mathematics textbook reflects the behaviorist expression: seemingly noncommittal, objective, but direction giving. We often find mathematics which has an elegance, excitement, and integrity re-presented in institutional packets as a service no one asked for, a gift no one wants, and an offering no one can refuse. However, as Komisar notes,[37] this perspective permeates the entire educational experience and the connection of content to context deserves our continued attention.

We have read and heard of how mathematics is often presented as if it were magic—providing no source for the rabbit that comes out of the hat.[38] I would ask also about the hat—where did it come from? That is, in addition to seeking to understand how the mathematical argument was constructed, we need to ask about what is given. While the "given" format is most reminiscent of our geometry experience, it extends to all areas of mathematics and our reality. The language here denies a crucial dimension—that of the intention which came to create a beginning. For what is a beginning if not a response to that which has past? What I am suggesting here is that in this exploration one gains a sense that the "givenness" is an expression of choice and, as such, should be open to communication and possible reconceptualization. Students may well gain a deeper sense of the nature and structure of mathematics and society if they are given the opportunity to examine the roots of what is labeled "given." In this way they may come to see that some "given" is not as powerful or just or aesthetic as some other "given"; that it is often difficult to separate fact from belief; and perhaps to ask in whose interest was the "given" created and for what purpose. Here we can begin to explore the concept of "the given" not only within its mathematical context but against the backdrop of school and society as well.

The universal nature of mathematics often submerges the personal initiative of the experience. This difficulty is compounded in schools which seek to transmit certain information from one source to another, without taking a close look at the negative energy which often accompanies the transmission attempt. For example, consider the student who doesn't "get it." The committed teacher will try to help the student. Before long, this help results in the loss of time and ground and the message conveyed is that learning mathematics involves, at bottom, a race. That is, too often the course is seen as a racecourse or survival course—and especially an obstacle course—all of which demean the individual and the possibility for communication and understanding. The nature of the course as the taken-for-granted reality provides a context within which oppressive and denigrating action subvert even the best of intentions. The language of mathematics, especially that which serves to initiate the inquiry, is thick with suggestions as to the real nature of the mathematics experience but is often muted by the language of institutional or formal efficiency.

What is "given" as an expression of objectivity is concomitantly an expression of the status quo. In challenging the status quo of the taken-for-granted reality, one necessarily risks one's sanity. This is true in mathematics as anywhere else. The construction of Lobachevskian geometry, which Lobachevski called "imaginary geometry," was indeed such an expression. The great mathematician Gauss would only praise Lobachevski in private correspondence but not in public for fear of personal embarrassment.[39] To express the development of mathematics as the calculus of formal thought is to make what is not reality the reality. The revolution created in mathematics out of a personal revelation grounded in belief and commitment transcends the logic and order of the time; it is above formal operational thought. Here, one necessarily challenges one's sanity by testing what is given. But what is "given" is an expression of our "what if" and "suppose." Thus the language which constitutes mathematical reality no more keeps us confined to what is there than does the language of our social reality. That school and society could be so constituted as to be alive with considerations which can be seen and felt as intriguing, beautiful, exciting, interesting, and important are denied by the language of institutional thought. The emphasis on formal operational thought keeps each of us from testing the truth of the given—once one practices the prevailing logic and makes this the goal, one has lost sight of the genesis and meaning of the enterprise itself.

Mathematics, both in its particular and collective expression, is a pristine manifestation that knowledge is value laden, that we do not have to settle for what is not in our best interest, that consciousness and reality are of each other, and that we determine how the parts fit into the whole we want. Goedel's effort can be taken to offer a profound insight—that logic without passion and commitment is necessarily incomplete. I think we can find this corroborated in the work of Leibniz. Leibniz demonstrated that given any finite sequence there exists an infinite number of possibilities for the next term in the sequence. This to me suggests our freedom as the creators of meaning, who need not accept the given framework or situation nor provide the determined response. The creation and study of mathematics—an expression of a personal aesthetic endeavor—is blurred by the institutional given. It should not be uncritically accepted—one has this choice in mathematics as in life. If we continue to spend our effort away from rather than toward locating the integrity and meaning that each of us seeks in the mathematics classroom, as well as in society and the world, we will continue to attempt to resolve conflict only with what works—threat, and when that fails, destruction—the language of oppressed people everywhere.

Notes

1. I. Scheffler, "Basic Mathematical Skills: Some Philosophical and Practical Remarks," *Teachers College Record* 78: 2 (December 1976): 205.

2. Ibid.

3. Z. Lamm, "The Status of Knowledge in the Radical Conception of Education," in *Curriculum and the Cultural Revolution*, ed. D. Purpel and M. Belanger (Berkeley: McCutchan, 1974), p. 128.

4. Ibid., p. 136.

5. From personal communication with Maxine Greene.

6. See Scheffler, *Conditions of Knowledge: An Introduction to Epistemology and Education* (Chicago: Scott, Foresman & Co., 1965), for a discussion of the relationship between belief and knowing. However, I will argue shortly that belief is not only a condition for knowing but a determinant of what and how one will know.

7. See Gordon and Mullaney, "On Scientific Eggs and Cracks Therein" (Paper presented at the curriculum conference, "The Disciplines and Freeing Human Potential," University of North Carolina at Greensboro, 1978).

8. The quality of being self-evident is derived from personal intention and not logical necessity.

9. M. Kline, "Logic versus Pedagogy," *American Mathematical Monthly* 77: 3 (March 1970): 267.

10. C. Musés, "Working with the Hypernumber Idea," in *Consciousness and Reality*, ed. C. Musés and A.M. Young (New York: Discus Books, 1974), chapter 26.

11. For further discussion of the historical background of mathematics, see W. M. Setek, Jr., *Algebra: A Fundamental Approach* (Philadelphia: W.B. Saunders, 1977).

12. H. Poincaré, *Science and Method* (New York: Dover, 1952), p. 121.

13. M. Kline, "Mathematics and Axiomatics," in *Role of Axiomatics and Problem Solving in Mathematics*, ed. Conference Board of the Mathematical Sciences (Boston: Ginn, 1966), p. 58.

14. Compare M. Gordon, "Toward Providing an Honest, Personal Mathematics Experience," in *Reflections on the Mathematics Experience*, ed. id. (Unpublished manuscript, n.d.).

15. Musés, "Working with the Hypernumber Idea," p. 459.

16. See E. Nagel and J. R. Newman, "Goedel's Proof," in *The World of Mathematics* vol. 3, ed. Newman (New York: Simon & Schuster, 1966), pp. 1, 695.

17. B. Russell and A. N. Whitehead, *Principia Mathematica* (Cambridge, England: Cambridge University Press, 1903).

18. Nagel and Newman, "Goedel's Proof."

19. Russell and Whitehead, *Principia Mathematica*.

20. Ibid., p. 114.

21. Musés relates: "Through time man learned number. Hence the first number man factually learned was the number '2' since tallying is pairing, and the simplest possible tally involves two things: the object and the mark referring to it." In Musés, "Working with the Hypernumber Idea," p. 108.

22. For example, see J. S. Hadamard, *An Essay on the Psychology of Invention in the Mathematical Field* (New York: Dover, 1945), for a discussion of mathematics created "from attention too narrowly directed," (p. 50).

23. M. Polanyi, *The Tacit Dimension* (Garden City, N.Y.: Doubleday Anchor Books, 1966), p. 4.

24. R. B. Davis, "Mathematics Teaching—With Special Reference to Epistemological Problems," *Journal of Research and Development in Education*, monograph (Athens, Ga.: University of Georgia, 1967), p. 16.

25. J. Sartre, *Being and Nothingness: An Essay on Phenomenological Ontology*, trans. and intro. H. E. Barnes (New York: Philosophical Library, 1956).

26. P. R. Halmos, "The Problem of Learning to Teach," *American Mathematical Monthly* 82: 5 (May 1975): 467.

27. R. Courant and H. Robbins, *What Is Mathematics?: An Elementary Approach to Ideas and Methods* (London: Oxford University Press, 1941), p. v.

28. N. Noddings, "Cognitive Premises and Curriculum Construction," (Paper presented at the annual meeting of the American Educational Research Association, San Francisco, 1976), p. 46.

29. For an examination of these contexts in the social setting, see J. Habermas, *Knowledge and Human Interests* (Boston: Beacon Press, 1971).

30. R. Poole, *Toward Deep Subjectivity* (New York: Harper & Row, 1974).

31. K. F. Riegel, "The Dialectics of Human Development," *American Psychologist* 31: 9 (September 1976): 696.

32. S. I. Brown, "Discovery and Teaching a Body of Knowledge," *Curriculum Theory Network* 5: 3 (1976): 191–218.

33. For development of a process in which personal biography becomes part of the educational experience, see W. Pinar, "Search for a Method," in *Curriculum Theorizing*, ed. id. (Berkeley: McCutchan, 1975).

34. For further development of the dual-dialectical process, see J. B. Macdonald, "A Transcendental Development Ideology of Education," in *Heightened Consciousness, Cultural Revolution, and Curriculum Theory*, ed. W. Pinar (Berkeley: McCutchan, 1974).

35. This perspective of logic is being extended by the development of modal logic, created by C. I. Lewis and enhanced by the exciting work of Saul Kripke.

36. For consideration of problem posing in mathematics, see S. I. Brown and M. Walter, "What If Not?" *Mathematics Teaching* 46 (Spring 1969): 38–45. On problem posing in general and the applications for human beings, see P. Freire, *Pedagogy of the Oppressed* (New York: Herder & Herder, 1970), pp. 70–71. Freire writes, "In problem-posing education, men develop their power to perceive critically *the way they exist* in the world *with which* and *in which* they find themselves; they come to see the world not as a static reality, but as a reality in process, in transformation."

37. B. Paul Komisar, "Is Teaching Phoney?" *Teachers College Record* 70: 5 (February 1969): 407–11.

38. Compare G. Polya, *How to Solve It* (Garden City, N.Y.: Doubleday Anchor Books, 1957).

39. C. B. Boyer, *A History of Mathematics* (New York: John Wiley, 1968), p. 589.

19

The Humanities and Emancipatory Possibility

Maxine Greene

The land shifts. What we believed to be a "consensus" on human rights has shown itself to be ephemeral. A certain mean-spiritedness is finding expression in the public space, as compassion diminishes and "humanism" becomes a suspect term. Not only are food stamps cut and jobs for the young eliminated; support for the arts and humanities is eroded. Self-interest and self-concern triumph over social consciousness. Like Nathaniel Hawthorne's Ethan Brand, we are losing our hold "of the magnetic chain of humanity." We are no longer brother-persons or sister-persons, "opening the chambers or the dungeons of our common nature by the key of holy sympathy."[1]

Where do we turn in this time of technicism and brutal laissez-faire? How can we who are committed to educating countervail against the lack of care? How can we provide people with what are sometimes thought of as ethical shields? How can we make "goodness happen" among them, as it happened during the Nazi occupation in the village of Le Chambon?[2] It is natural to turn toward literature and the humanities as an antidote to positivism and technical domination. Yet, if we do so, we have to pay heed to such voices as George Steiner's, warning us that the literary imagination does not automatically resist barbarism:

The simple yet appalling fact is that we have very little solid evidence that literary studies do very much to enrich or stabilize moral perception, that they *humanize*. We have little proof that a tradition of literary studies in fact makes a man more humane.[3]

Reprinted, by permission, from *Journal of Education* 163: 4 (Fall 1981): 287–305.

We have to attend to scholars like Albert William Levi, writing of the classical scholars who killed Cicero, the humanists responsible for the death of Thomas More, for the St. Bartholomew massacre, and other atrocities. Levi, too, has written that "acquaintance with the humane tradition is no guarantee of moral wisdom and human decency."[4]

There are survivors who speak to us, witnesses like Herman Melville's Ishmael, who have "escaped to tell. . . ."[5] Terrence des Pres, among others, tells us of witnesses whose testimony is intended to enter public consciousness, "therefore modifying the moral order to which it appeals. . . ."[6] He was talking about concentration camp survivors; and, since the holocaust, there have been others, too many others; survivors of the Gulag; Jacobo Timerman of Argentina; Chileans, Salvadoreans, South Africans, Filipinos, with stories—unendurable stories—to tell. But all the stories, all the testimony, even if they have entered into the public consciousness, have not altered the "moral order" to any significant degree. There still exists the indifference to human suffering that makes holocausts and torture chambers possible. There are, increasingly, systems judged by the efficacy of their controls and the promise of their markets. Feelings of powerlessness, desperation, and anomie are probably more widespread than they were a decade ago. Somehow or other, the "plague" has to be confronted once again, and whatever the "plague" now signifies. (Tarrou, in Albert Camus's *The Plague,* says that "each of us has the plague within him; no one, no one on earth is free from it. And I know, too, that we must keep endless watch on ourselves lest in a careless moment we breathe in somebody's face and fasten the infection on him. What's natural is the microbe. All the rest—health, integrity, purity (if you like)—is a product of the human will, of a vigilance that must never falter.")[7] Yes: indifference, statistical thinking, manipulations. Not only do educators have to ponder, as never before, the "study of what is most human";[8] we have to consider what is demanded of us by the creation of new teaching situations, the kind that might release persons to pursue "a fuller humanity."[9]

A decade ago, radical educators were railing against the humanist's claim to disinterestedness, against the "enclave" he or she inhabited,[10] about the isolation of intellectuals. There were proposals (then thought reasonable) for participation in transforming action in society and in educational institutions. Today, the signs of disinterestedness multiply, even where the so-called humanists protest the decline of support. There are numerous intimations of a return to formalism where literary studies are concerned.[11] The social sciences are being insistently mathematicized as computerization and "artificial intelligence" are put to use. There is the persistent depersonalization of analytic philosophy; there are the objectifications of behaviorism; there are the "norms" of efficiency and quality control.

All of this cannot but intensify the defensiveness of humanities scholars, especially those struggling to hold on to their "enclaves." The great art historian, E. H. Gombrich, for example, has warned the humanities against emulating the sciences, talked of "the range of texts and monuments" that still concern the humanist, and called the young to the "true religion of scholarship."[12] Many humanities people, nonetheless, find themselves arguing for the "utility" of what they do, if they are not trying to justify the claim that their research and teaching hold "intrinsic" worth. Meanwhile, their doctoral candidates are forced to look to corporations for employment. Vocationalization goes on apace; and the students in humanities courses tend increasingly to be those who are practically oriented and lacking skills in general literacy. For many scholars, the new constituencies in their classrooms represent the enemy. They are forcing the proponents of the "true religion" out of their enclaves, out of their ivory towers; and those who were once elite see the specter of proletarianization hovering overhead, demanding that they create themselves anew (or go into retirement much too soon).

In the high school classrooms there are similar tensions being experienced: tensions between allegiance to what has been thought of as the "humanist ideal" and the obligation to teach a diverse group of media-reared, skeptical young people driven by desires to "play it safe" and "play it cool." My interest is in the teaching of humanities in situations like this, with both high schools and colleges in mind. My interest is in the role of the humanities in relation to the ideological mystifications and the "lying in politics"[13] marking our time. To speak about that role is also to confront the institutional pressures afflicting teachers and students, the effects of intensified "channeling,"[14] the impacts of the prevailing management ethos and whatever constitutes "market demand." Richard Shaull wrote, some years ago, with respect to such concerns:

There is no such thing as a *neutral* educational process. Education either functions as an instrument which is used to facilitate the integration of the younger generation into the logic of the present system and bring about conformity to it, or it becomes "the practice of freedom," the means by which men and women deal critically and creatively with reality and discover how to participate in the transformation of their world.[15]

How are we to conceive the humanities, if we are committed to "the practice of freedom"? Surely it is not enough to talk of the study of "texts and monuments" (fundamental though this may be), even in the "mixed communities of scholars" Gombrich would like to see.[16] Nor will it do to derive a definition from the concept of *humanitas*. Those who speak of *humanitas* assume that there exists some fundamental characteristic, some distinctive essence that sets human beings apart from animals (and from immortal beings). Drawing from the classical tradition, they often choose to conceive of that essence in the light of Man's fullest actualization, what they would call his perfection. Since that perfection was traditionally understood to involve an abandonment of practical and material concerns, the closer a man came to a condition of pure contemplation, to total rationality, the more actualized he was considered to be. *Humanitas,* in the Renaissance framework, was frequently used to describe that rare achievement; and the so-called liberal arts, with their emphasis on languages, literatures, and logic, were intended to liberate a talented few to know the True and the Good and the Beautiful through the exercise of reason. But what of the others? What of those lower down on the "great chain of being" or in the hierarchies of the state? It seems evident to me that an assumption of a human essence—and a linking of that essence to an arbitrary notion of perfection—subsumes all human beings under an abstraction. Moreover, it fixes and freezes the ends of human life. I prefer to acknowledge that human nature cannot be defined. It is protean and cannot be captured by any category. Conceiving human beings as always in pursuit of themselves, always futuring, always struggling to create themselves in the changing situations of their diverse lives, I want to define the humanities in the light of human incompleteness, human possibility.

I am aware that all definitions and all classifications are in some sense arbitrary; but I nevertheless would include among the humanities only those works concerned, as Merleau-Ponty put it, "with giving voice to the experience of the world. . . ."[17] This means, for me, those works that are articulations of some human consciousness thrusting into the world, aware of a contact with things that precedes all thinking *about* things. This contact with things, of course, refers to perceived reality, the primordial "landscape" underlying what is conceptually grasped and understood.[18] It is the contact we associate with "lived reality"[19] or with what Dewey spoke of as the "qualitative."[20] To remain in touch with it is to be present to oneself; it is to be grounded in the world.

Imaginative writers, painters, composers, sculptors, choreographers, even some film-makers are paradigmatic where "giving voice" and where "landscape" are concerned, and their works lie at the core of what I choose to call the humanities. But I would include certain types of literary and aesthetic criticism as well, as I would incorporate certain modes of doing history and sociology and philosophy. And indeed there are a number of scientists and mathematicians whose formulations stem as much from their being in the world as from their use of standard protocols and techniques; and I would include them as well. Excluded would be any writer or maker or thinker devoid of perspective on his or her grounding in experience. Saying that, I have in mind all those who are affected by the positivist tendency to separate the knower from the known, to lay their primary stress on what is finished, objective, purportedly *given.* I have in mind those who overlook or deny the fact that descriptions and explanations, no matter how highly schematized, arise out of and refer back to some human experience, that all knowledge is interpretive, perspectival, and in some way incomplete. This is not in any sense to underestimate the power of explanation, prediction, and rational controls. It is only to suggest that that power would in no way be diminished if, for all the "neutrality" and necessary "objectivity" of the scientist, there were some acknowledgment that such power can only be exercised by *situated* beings. Although I surely would not demand that all natural and social scientists give evidence of being grounded (as J. Bronowski has done, Lewis Thomas, Michael Polanyi, Werner Heisenberg, and a number of others), and although I would not be likely to include all those I considered to be nonpositivistic under the rubric of the humanities, I believe that the very existence (and dominance) of the positivist mode must affect a contemporary effort at definition or any effort to map the several fields.

Before going on to matters of teaching and learning, I wish to suggest some names of critics, philosophers, historians, and sociologists, simply to indicate how wide the range can be. The list must be taken as suggestive and provisional. Those who teach in the humanities must themselves create their own sources and origins, even as they identify (and perhaps incarnate) their own particular texts. Among literary critics, I would include those like Virginia Woolf and Henry James, who evaluated visibly against their own consciousness of being writers and alive; contemporary writers like Geoffrey Hartman, who talks openly of his own struggles to "see," Harold Bloom, who formulates his own ambivalences and "anxiety" even as he sheds light. I would add sections of Lionel Trilling's work, Leo Marx's, F. A. O. Matthiessen's, Ann Douglas's, George Steiner's—the writings of all of those who do not separate themselves as subjects from the created forms they are trying to unveil. Where philosophers are concerned, I would view (at least among the moderns) William James, George Moore, John Dewey, Ludwig Wittgenstein (in certain guises), Stuart Hampshire, Iris Murdoch, Jean-Paul Sartre, Maurice Merleau-Ponty, Marjorie Grene, Paul Ricoeur, Stanley Cavell, as thinkers among the large group that ought to be included in the humanities because their voices are somehow audible, and because they at times communicate a sense of their lived worlds. As for historians, I would consider those like E. H. Carr, who perceive the doing of history as a dialogue; certain liberal historians like Richard Hofstadter and Charles and Mary Beard; Oscar Handlin, Marc Bloch, Herbert Muller, John Herman Randall, Peter Gay. The lists may be endless. The crucial test has to do with articulated consciousness, a visible and embodied sense of being in the world. Wayne C. Booth says, probably correctly, that "every discovery or invention in any field, considered as a human achievement, becomes 'a humanity'." And then:

Whenever anyone does something that other people can't do, or can't do easily—

whether making better mousetraps, better juggling acts, better constitutions, better ideas, or better poems—and whenever other people talk about it with a sense that the *quality* of the making or doing matters—there you have the humanities.[21]

But what sorts of teaching situations might free persons for awareness of human possibility, for authentic talk about what they choose as "quality," for widening perspectives, for moving beyond? How do we launch diverse individuals on their own searches for meanings? In Walker Percy's *The Moviegoer*, there is one kind of suggestion:

What is the nature of the search, you ask? Really, it is very simple, at least for a fellow like me; so simple it is easily overlooked. The search is what anyone would undertake if he were not sunk in the everydayness of his own life. This morning, for example, I felt as if I had come to myself on a strange island. And what does such a castaway do? Why he pokes around the neighborhood and he doesn't miss a trick.[22]

Clearly, this narrator is talking about a search for meaning in the recognition that whatever means are conceivable are those human beings consciously pursue, those they create through shared undertakings and the work they do in the world. He is also saying that too many live submerged in everydayness, in the taken-for-granted. They accede to the world as it is given to them, labelled and marked off by others, objectively and unchangeably *there*. What is needed is a shift of vantage point, a move (for a while at least) to a "strange island." The narrator here feels as if he has come to himself (and that is important) when he looks afresh at what has seemed unquestionable. He sees his world, not in its taken-for-grantedness, but differently; and this is what moves him to poke around (to inquiry, to exploration) and never miss a trick.

There is a metaphor here for the type of experience that might be associated with the humanities, if they are thought of as occasions for emancipation. Many students, due in part to the manner of their early socialization, in part to the mystifications that have affected them, are indeed sunk in everydayness. Great numbers of them (like masses of their adult compatriots) are capable of only passive attention. They are therefore either unwilling to pose or are incapable of posing questions that reach beyond the self-evident. Acceding to the arrangements they see around them, accepting them indifferently or cynically or hopelessly, such persons are unlikely to reflect upon their own life situations in a mood of curiosity or critique. They may have been told, say, about inflation and about the "cuts" and the unemployment necessary to control what is presumably wrong. The anchormen have told them; the official voices have reiterated it, sometimes in a kind of "doublespeak," sometimes as if sermonizing on a mount. What is transmitted through it all is a message about the "nature of things." The official explanations take on the status of natural laws: the relation between cuts in social expenditures and economic upturn, like the necessity for an expanded "defense" budget, seems to be as unalterable and fixed as the law of gravity. And this is just one example of the perceived *givenness* of the public world, a *givenness* that tends to be "naturally" ascribed to everyday reality or the common sense world.[23]

Enmeshed in their everydayness, individuals have no way of realizing that the extremes of wealth and poverty that seem so "natural," the school bureaucracies, the work patterns, the rush hours, the movie lines all constitute a *constructed* social reality. Everything that makes up daily life, in fact, is part of an intersubjective world "experienced and interpreted by Others, our predecessors, as an organized world," as Alfred Schutz has put it. Then he went on: "Now it is given to our experience and interpretation. All interpretation of this world is based upon a stock of previous experiences of it, our own experiences and those handed down to us by our parents and teachers, which in the form of 'knowledge at hand' functions as a scheme of reference."[24] It is an organized world, a totality because those who inhabit it have learned how to attend it in a similar fashion, to select out certain aspects of what surrounds them and suppress others, to place some things in the foreground and keep others in the background. Perhaps oddly, most people posit a "normal" world, the same for everyone, as if their biographical backgrounds made no difference—or their location in society, or the work they happen to do. This is largely because the training and the schooling they have experienced have deflected their attention from their personal histories and the perspectives to which they may have given rise. Just as young children are compelled to adapt their rhythms and activities to clock time, to abandon the sense of their own inner time, so are older students taught to *accommodate to* what is called "objective," to an often standardized version of "reality."

Now it is clear enough that we inhabit an object world. Things, artifacts, phenomena of all sorts surround us and condition us, offering resistances we try to overcome through the efforts we exert in our lives. I want to emphasize the fact, however, that what we conceive to be real is *interpreted* experience; we can be sure of nothing beyond the grasp of human consciousness, beyond what some human consciousness intends. Too many disciplinary specialists and teachers, like the media and government agencies, obscure (either through neglect or by design) the contingency of what is thought to be real. Minimal attention is paid to the significance of standpoint and perspective, to the influence (say) of class membership on perspective, or to the effect of work or project on what is seen. (It should be clear, for instance, that the bricklayer sees the construction job differently from the foreman, that the superintendent of schools sees the classroom differently from the members of the third grade, that Chicanos in Los Angeles view Beverly Hills real estate differently from movie stars. Yet, almost without exception, the person with more power, more access to the public space, is thought to have the *true* perspective. Like the calculative thinkers of our time, or the systems analysts, those who are dominant at any given moment tend to do the naming of the world.) The consequence of all this for the ordinary person, be he or she child or adult, is an apprehension of the real as predefined, in some strange way opaque. Accepting it as unalterable, as part of his or her condition, the individual may simply stop paying heed. At that point he or she becomes (like Percy's narrator) "sunk in the everydayness" of his or her own life.

I think we have to assume that many of our students are in precisely that position. They may be motivated to train for future jobs; they may be in quest of status or material success; they may simply want to get along, to survive. Very few, however, enter classes in the humanities with any inclination to problematize, to question what is taken for granted in the surrounding culture, or even to wonder when they feel bored or diminished or shamed. The society most of them inhabit seems to me to be a kind of flatland, like Hans Castorp's Hamburg in Thomas Mann's *The Magic Mountain*. Mann wrote with respect to Hans Castorp:

A man lives not only his personal life, as an individual, but also, consciously or unconsciously, the life of his epoch and his contemporaries. He may regard the general, impersonal foundations of his existence as definitely settled and taken for granted, and be as far from assuming a critical attitude toward them as our good Hans Castorp really was; yet it is quite conceivable that he may none the less be vaguely conscious of the deficiencies of his epoch and find them prejudicial to his own moral well-being. . . . Now, if the life about him, if his own time seem, however outwardly stimulating, to be at bottom empty of such food for his aspirations; if he privately recognizes it to be hopeless, viewless, helpless, opposing only a hollow silence to all the questions man puts, consciously or unconsciously, yet somehow puts, as to the final, absolute, and abstract meaning in all his efforts and activities; then, in such a case, a certain laming of the personality is bound to occur. . . .[25]

Hans Castorp, you will recall, became vaguely ill and underwent a hermetic transformation in a mountain sanitarium, at a distance from the flatland and the everyday world. Not only was he provided opportunities for looking through new, often contesting perspectives at his own lived life, he reached heights and depths of experience he had never suspected before; he learned what it meant to be with others, to dream, to lose himself in music, to come awake. And, when he descended from the mountain to become a member once again, he was no longer a "delicate child of life"; he had transcended; he was transformed.

I am not eager for our students to get sick (although I do distrust those like the manager in Joseph Conrad's *Heart of Darkness*, people who proudly say they "never get sick"[26]). But I am eager for them to know what it is to move to a mountain or a "strange island," to experience the productive alienation brought about by engagement with the humanities and the several arts. Herbert Marcuse has written about the ways in which art forms (especially authentic modern art forms) may enlarge alienation and harden the incompatibility of such works with "the given reality." That is how they fulfill, he said,

the cognitive function of Art (which is its inherent radical "political" function), that is, to name the unnameable, to confront man with the dreams he betrays and the crimes he forgets. The greater the terrible conflict between that which is and that which can be, the more will the work of art be estranged from the immediacy of real life, thought, and behavior—even political thought and behavior. . . .[27]

He was referring to the standpoints that may be created by engagement with works of art (and, I would add, certain works in the humanities), standpoints that make it possible to see the gap between what is and what might be. Sartre meant very much the same thing when he talked about the ways in which works of literature address themselves to the "freedom" (and often the indignation) of their readers. This is defined as the "aesthetic imperative," Sartre wrote. A work of literature may be seen "as an imaginary presentation of the world insofar as it demands human freedom."[28] To make such a demand is to require of human beings that they transcend what appears to determine and define and limit them. It is to require them to refuse indifference, to act to close the gaps that exist, to pursue justice, to repair the insufficiencies in their lived worlds.

Now it seems clear enough that this cannot happen if the humanities are presented as "texts and monuments" to be reverently examined and disclosed. Nor will it happen if students are treated as barbarians or suppliants, waiting humbly outside the "house of intellect," hoping to be admitted by the guardians of the treasure within. In my view, attention must be directed to the students' own life situations, to what (preferably) is lived in common, if a work is to make any significant demand. Lukacs has made the related point that the aesthetic process always has a "social substratum" (mystified, he said, by "the subjective idealism of the bourgeois epoch"). Because human personality and human situations are social in character, the content and activity of any work are "the experience of the individual in the manifold riches of life in society and—mediated by the essentially new features of clearly defined human relations—his existence as a part and a moment of man's development, as a concise abbreviation of it."[29] This in no sense diminishes the importance of the individual perceiver's biography or perspective. It simply points to the crucial fact that any work—be it *The Iliad* or Toni Morrison's *Song of Solomon*, Beowulf or John Cheever's *Falconer*, Rousseau's *Confessions* or Hannah Arendt's *The Human Condition*—refers to a human reality that is social, always fundamentally historical. An individual can only enter into the created world that is a novel, poem, or personal essay in the light of his or her own temporality, by means of his or her own intentionality. Lending the characters in the work (or the speaker of the work) his or her own life, feeling his or her experiences broaden and deepen as this slowly takes place, the individual reader or beholder gains the opportunity to ground his or her own *social* identity.

When I think of today's young people in colleges, community colleges, or in high schools, I think of persons who are being "channeled," as Marcus Raskin puts it. He has described the school on all levels as a training instrument for the existing political, social, and economic order; and he has pointed out that the substance of what is learned "is less indelible . . . than other lessons which are taught and internalized."

In school, students are readied for adult life through the synthetic process of tension with themselves about whom they are supposed to be in the pyramid. They are in dialectic with their records and profiles, which they come to believe are the definition of who they are.[30]

According to this view, the records and profiles are intended to serve the needs of "the authority system"; and students are urged "to fulfill an achievement profile of themselves" mainly derived from the requirements of the "system." I believe this is largely the case, although I do not believe many students are fully conscious of it. They are, of course, vaguely aware that school records do not describe their subjective feelings or what they may think of as their "private selves"; and these they express in pursuits of heightened sensations (going to horror movies, watching scenes of violence, experimenting with drugs), erotic experiences, amplified rock music (communal, and their very own). Like many people in our culture, old as well as young, they are often drawn to privatist, even narcissistic enjoyments, now that the days of hope and protest are past. I am somehow reminded of John Dewey writing about what he called a "social pathology" linked to mystification, a pathology, he said, that "works powerfully against effective inquiry into social institutions and conditions." He went on:

It manifests itself in a thousand ways; in querulousness, in impotent drifting, in uneasy snatching at distractions, in idealization of the long established, in a facile optimism assumed as a cloak, in riotous glorification of things "as they are" . . . ways which depress and dissipate thought all the more effectually because they operate with subtle and unconscious pervasiveness.[31]

There are alternative ways of describing the flatland, alternative ways of describing the submergence with which I am concerned. It seems to me that too many young persons accept their "everydayness" indifferently, even fatalistically. But they talk cynically at the same time; they frequently seem as disillusioned as the very old. Some of them remind me of what Graham Greene described as "a burnt-out case."[32] Others remind me of Ernest Hemingway heroes, who tried desperately "not to think about it" and sought solace in all-night cafés, bullfights, going hunting in the woods. And still others resemble that other Hemingway character, the narrator in "A Clean, Well-Lighted Place," who says: "What did he fear? It was not fear or dread. It was a nothing that he knew too well. It was all a nothing and a man was nothing too. . . . Hail nothing full of nothing, nothing is with thee. . . ."[33] And still others are simply bored.

What kinds of situations can be created to move such people to the alienation Marcuse had in mind? How can the bored, the privatist, the disenchanted be engaged with the humanities in a way that might liberate—and move them to critique? I believe that the first step should involve an adaptation of Paulo Freire's dialogical method—a method intended, not only to move persons to reflection, but to engage them "in developing the pedagogy of their liberation."[34] Now I am not for one moment suggesting that American students suffer the debilitating oppression to which the Brazilian peasant seems to have been born. Nor am I suggesting that they have internalized the same diminished images of themselves. According to Raskin, students tend to accept the intrusion of "measurements" of themselves; and they become "slaves to the hierarchic other which becomes part of themselves."[35] Whether this is precisely so or not, it does seem clear that young people rarely question the classification system, the institutional structures, the very existence of hierarchy, the preoccupation with "winning" and success. I believe that attention must be drawn to these phenomena, and that it can only properly be drawn if students' subjectivities (now reserved for "free time" in the outside world) are involved in the critical reflection the objective world requires. That is partly why I believe the dialogical method to be so crucially important when we are preparing the ground for encounters with the humanities.

Like Freire, I believe that the educator's efforts "must coincide with those of the students to engage in critical thinking and the quest for mutual humanization."[36] If he or she is interested in enabling students to unveil the reality they have assumed to be "given" and to understand the role of interpretive acts, the teacher must have more trust in those who are present as learners than teachers normally have. He or she must, as Freire has said, become a partner with the students in a shared effort to unveil their lived worlds. That means, as I see it, that the teacher ought to play his or her own self-reflective part in clarifying what it means to submit to an authority structure, what it signifies to want to rise in a meritocracy whose governing ethos is scarcely understood. Efforts should be made to do on-site research, where possible, at nearby institutions: clinics in large public hospitals; welfare agencies; food-stamp offices; institutes like the Rand Institute or similar centers; military installations; the offices of the Board of Education. Not only should the human reality of such places (the submissive, weary people waiting in line; the cries of children; the clink of bottles and the rattle of typewriters and the clang of file cabinet drawers) become part of the perceptual reality of those who attend. Questions should be invented—personal questions, incisive questions, embarrassing questions—to elicit from clerks and managers and clients clues as to how they constitute their shared realities.

This, as I see it, might prepare the ground for the kind of distancing and the kind of incarnations we associate with the humanities. I want to make clear that, interested though I think we must be in disclosures of living actualities, there is no necessity to select out from the humanities according to a criterion of simple relevance. There is no need, for instance, to seek out the few novels that deal explicitly with the welfare system, unless those novels are seen as complex works of art. There is no need to turn, simply, to a film like *Hospital* or even to Frederic Wiseman's documentary on the hospital, in order to launch people into the productive alienation I have in mind. There may be a place for the explicitly relevant; there may be a role for relatively thin-textured, topical works when the ground is being prepared. But I believe that trust in ourselves—and trust in our students—ought to enable us to confront all kinds of young persons with intricate, multi-dimensional structures—complicated, many-windowed worlds. I should like to suggest a few, only to communicate some notion of what might be done in the treatment of the humanities as emancipatory.

Because I have systems in mind, and because I am particularly eager to find ways of breaking with the everyday and the mundane, I wish to start, as an example, with Tom Stoppard's play, *Rosencrantz and Guildenstern Are Dead*. In this play, the "system" is represented by Shakespeare's *Hamlet*, itself an imaginary structure, here ascribed a kind of solid, almost objective reality. Rosencrantz and Guildenstern tell how they were awakened by a messenger one morning with an urgent "royal summons" they did not understand. They meet the Players, find themselves at the castle, watch an undone Hamlet chase a troubled Ophelia, receive strange instructions from King Claudius, lose their sense of direction, keep cherishing "the irrational belief that somebody interesting will come on in a minute. . . ."[37] They do not know what the game is, what the rules are. They meet Hamlet, do not understand him, try to figure out what he said to them about Denmark and ambition and a hawk and a handsaw. "Half of what he said meant something else," Rosencrantz remarks, "and the other half didn't mean anything at all."[38] Finally, at the end, after hopeless watching, trying to make sense of a closed system that makes no sense at all to them, they (*because* they are Rosencrantz and Guildenstern, characters in *Hamlet*) are required to die. The last word is Guildenstern's: "Our names shouted in a certain dawn. . . .

a message . . . a summons. . . . There must have been a moment, at the beginning, when we could have said—no. But somehow we missed it. (He
looks around and sees he is alone)."[39]

Among the many things to attend to in this play, there is the suggestion
of multiple—and questionable—realities. It is not difficult at first to take for
granted the preexistent ordering of things, until the significance of the first
scene sinks in: Rosencrantz and Guildenstern are tossing coins, and the coins
always come up "heads." The loser is thunderstruck and afraid; the winner
is relatively unperturbed—because he can at least "count on self-interest as a
predictable factor." Guildenstern says that "the scientific approach to the
examination of phenomena is a defence against the pure emotion of fear";[40]
and he speculates that they are being controlled by "un-, sub- or supernatural
factors." He talks about the confidence instilled by knowledge of the law of
probability and the way in which it "related the fortuitous and the ordained
into a reassuring union we recognized as nature."[41] If the beholder or the
reader permits himself or herself to realize it, he or she is already confronting
scientific fictions, human modes of ordering, all the problematic barriers
against fear. Then there is the strange inexorability of the dramatic fiction
named *Hamlet,* whose reality is a function of changing interpretations over
the centuries. For all the changes, however, the incidental roles played by
Rosencrantz and Guildenstern (like their interchangeability) are among the
givens. They enter Elsinore from "outside"; they are manipulated into the
conspiracy; they are destroyed. Could they, could anyone have conceivably
said no? What did they somehow miss: what moment, what beginning?

As another example of a work that might enable readers to pose questions
relevant to their own situations, there is Paul Nizan's novel, *Antoine Bloyé.*
It is Nizan's effort to bring to life his own dead father, a French railroad
worker, the son of Breton peasants. Silent, unaware, he has been schooled to
rise in the hierarchy of the railway company; and he moves up into middle
management as the years of his life pass by "in the most insidious peace of
all," the peace of good conscience and false duty. Tied to his parents and
their conservative tradition, conditioned by the demands and commands of
the company, he keeps hoping something will happen; but he never chooses;
he never acts on possibility. Moreover, he is the kind of person who never allows himself the leisure to ask what he is doing on the earth, what he is good
for, where he is heading. He reads nothing but technical manuals; his very
language is full of engineers' turns of speech. "Like many men," Nizan
writes, "he was impelled by demands, ideas, and decisions connected with
his job. . . ."

There was no time to think about himself, to meditate, to know himself and know
the world. He did no reading, he did not keep himself *au courant.* . . . He glanced at
the newspapers casually. The events they told of belonged to another planet and did
not concern him. . . . He was alive, no doubt. Who is not alive? To go through the

motions of life, all you need is a well-fed body. He, Antoine, moved and acted, but the springs of his life, and the drive of his actions were not within himself."[42]

Although he has a job, always a fairly good job, Antoine has found no life work; or he has, perhaps, abandoned it. He does not, as the author keeps suggesting, use his own capacities. He is moved about by the railroad company, confined by a respectable, habit-constricted marriage. He lives "within . . . fortifications reared around . . . the good husband, around the good worker. . . . He has been a party to the conspiracy in favor of . . . that life that was not life."[43] He is presented as a deserter, a kind of traitor to his class, to himself, and also as someone mutilated, alienated. He is a human being, an ordinary man, who—for most of his life—never questions, who perceives the "fortifications" as insuperable.

He has not defined a purpose for himself; he has not, he will not in the future. He has always believed that "something will happen"; but he has never acted to transform his life situation. This is largely because he has scarcely reflected upon it; he has had neither the concepts nor the words. It is only at the end of his life, when he has been summarily dismissed from the railroad, that he puts his old certainties to doubt, spurns the "protecting hedges," realizes the emptiness and the waste. "All lives," says Nizan, "that do not attain fullness are relegated to the shadows of attempts that have failed."[44] Few readers can read that, can feel the underlying rage throughout the book, without asking themselves (if not the ghost of prematurely dead Paul Nizan) sometimes furious questions. Antoine does have choices in certain of the situations of his life: he could have stayed with the vital, life-affirming Marcelle in Paris in-stead of marrying the depot-master's daughter, bourgeois little Anne; he could have taken a job in Cardiff near the sea; he could even have gone to China at one point; he could have refused to side with the company during a railroad strike. . . . But he was constrained, made helpless by his felt obli-gations to his parents, by convention, by the huge overwhelming "system" (exemplified by the railroad tracks crossing and crisscrossing the open fields), by his busyness, his wordlessness, his fatigue. And in some dread way he was mystified, from the moment he receives a prize on graduating from the Arts and Trades School as a boy. The prize is a book, which he opens at random:

"Man is free" he reads, "he is ever aware of his power not to do what he does do and to do what he does not do."
Antoine reflects on these words and on some others besides. He ill understands them. Is his father free not to be poor, not to work nights, not to go where he does go? Is his mother free not to have her back ache from work, not to be tired out and old before her time? He himself—in what way is he free? To be free means simply not to be poor, and not always ordered about. The rich enjoy a form of freedom. People with an income. . . . He shuts M. Jules Simon's gilt-edged book, never to open it again."[45]

There is no answer; there is never an answer spelled out in a work of literature. I would insist, however, that persons who have been moved to attend to their own predicaments may be able to respond at a distance to a kindred predicament symbolized and set in aesthetic space. Much depends, again, upon how it is offered. Much depends upon the willingness of the teacher to take risks as he or she maintains a dialogue. There is always a risk when a teacher posits the freedom and the potential indignation of his or her students; there is always some tension as he or she attempts to make the work available, understandable, even while respecting students' perspectives—and encouraging each one to constitute his or her own imaginary world.

I want to take one more example, still another novel, and go on briefly to suggest how other modes of discourse can be used as well. The novel is George Konrad's *The Case Worker,* having to do with a social worker in charge of young children at a Hungarian state welfare organization. He is trapped in bureaucratic structures, dominated by files and forms and rulebooks; and yet he yearns, sometimes desperately, to identify with the individuals for whom he presumably works:

I question, explain, prove, disprove, comfort, threaten, grant, deny, demand, approve, legalize, rescind. In the name of legal principles and provisions I defend law and order for the want of anything better to do. . . . I repudiate the high priests of individual salvation and the sob sisters of altruism, who exchange commonplace partial responsibility for the aesthetic transports of cosmohistorical guilt or the gratuitous slogans of universal love. . . . My highest aspiration is that a medium-rank, utterly insignificant civil servant should, as far as possible, live with his eyes open.[46]

Again, there is no answer; but there is the possibility of transcendence, at least the transcendence of wide-awakeness, of being able to see. And to live with "eyes open" is something other than living submerged. It may be that engagement with literary texts can open eyes and counter "aesthetic transports"; and those with open eyes may at least be in a position to transform— or begin to transform—their lived worlds.

The question arises, then, of what is actually to be understood in such a text. Paul Ricoeur,[47] who is concerned about the matter of "distance" from such a work as Konrad's or Nizan's (or any one that is encountered as a work of art), talks about the ways in which such reading experiences can affect the way we know:

Not the intention of the author, which is supposed to be hidden behind the text; not the historical situation common to the author and his original readers; not the expectations . . . of these readers; not even their understanding of themselves as historical and cultural phenomena. What has to be appropriated is the meaning of the text itself, conceived in a dynamic way as the direction of thought opened up by the text. In other words, what has to be appropriated is nothing other than the power of disclosing a world that constitutes the reference of the text. In this way we are as far as possible from the Romanticist ideal of coinciding with a foreign psyche. If we may be said to coincide with anything, it is not the inner life of another ego, but the disclosure of a possible way of looking at things, which is the genuine referential power of the text.[48]

"A possible way of looking at things. . . .": it is this that gives the humanities their power to challenge the taken-for-granted, to move those who attend beyond their limiting horizons. Sartre has made the point that it is only when human beings become aware of what might be, of what is possible, that they become capable of conceiving "failures and lacks." He wrote: "It is on the day that we can conceive of a different state of affairs that a new light falls on our troubles and our suffering and that we *decide* that these are unbearable."[49] In another sense, we decide to act upon our freedom, to move beyond, to transform our lives.

If we can make this awareness of possibility live for our students, there will be reason enough for them to pose questions requiring exploration in several domains, in other "provinces of meaning" beyond the one identified with the arts. Suppose, again, the fundamental concern has to do with the order of things, the authoritarian structures, the "system," however conceived. Hannah Arendt's description of the "rule by Nobody" that characterizes bureaucracy[50] may help to illuminate what has been opaque; so might Jacques Ellul's work on technique, or R. D. Laing's, or Robert Heilbroner's, or Trent Schroyer's, or Jurgen Habermas's, or Karl Marx's. The sources are almost limitless; but they will be of significance only if they are used in response to deeply felt questions, if they are read against the background of lived lives.

The themes are endless; the sources are as multiple as the traditions at hand. I have been concerned with finding ways of arousing students from submergence, awakening them to critical consciousness and to the possibility of praxis in a world they share. There can be no guarantees that the humanities will "improve" those who engage with them; nor can there be guarantees that wide-awakeness will increase. But there is an obligation, I think, on the part of all who educate to address themselves, as great artists do, to the freedom of their students, to make demands on them to form the pedagogy of their own liberation—and to do so rigorously, passionately, and in good faith. Merleau-Ponty poses more hard questions: "Shall I make this promise? Shall I risk my life for so little? Shall I give up my liberty in order to save liberty?" And then he says:

There is no theoretical reply to these questions. But there are these *things* which stand, irrefutable, there is before you this person whom you love, there are these men whose existence around you is that of slaves, and *your* freedom cannot be willed without leaving behind its singular relevance, and without willing freedom *for all*. Whether it is a question of things or of historical situations, philosophy has no function other than to teach us once more to see them clearly. . . . But what is required here is silence, for only the hero lives out his relation to men and the world. . . . Your abode is your act itself. Your act is you . . . It is your duty, your hatred, your love, your steadfastness, your ingenuity. . . . Man is but a network of relationships, and these alone matter to him.[51]

There is only the hope of freedom and action. There is, as Merleau-Ponty says, "no theoretical reply." But the humanities offer themselves as possibility. They call to men and women in the way Rilke said poetry spoke to them; the call says, "You must change your life."

Notes

1. N. Hawthorne, "Ethan Brand," in *Hawthorne Short Stories*, ed. N. Arvin (New York: Vintage Books, 1946), p. 326.

2. P. P. Hallie, *Lest Innocent Blood Be Shed: The Story of the Village of Le Chambon and How Goodness Happened There* (New York: Harper & Row, 1979).

3. G. Steiner, *Language and Silence* (New York: Atheneum, 1967), p. 61.

4. A. William Levi, "The Uses of the Humanities in Personal Life," *The Journal of Aesthetic Education* 10: 1 (Jan. 1976): 6.

5. H. Melville, *Moby Dick* (New York: Random House, 1930), p. 823.

6. T. des Pres, *The Survivor* (New York: Oxford University Press, 1976), p. 47.

7. See A. Camus, *The Plague* (New York: Alfred A. Knopf, 1948), p. 229.

8. "Report of the Commission on the Humanities (1964)," quoted in M. A. Topf, The NEH and the Crisis in the Humanities," *College English* 37: 3 (November 1975): 231.

9. P. Freire, *Pedagogy of the Oppressed* (New York: Herder & Herder, 1970), p. 32.

10. L. Kampf, "It's Alright, Ma (I'm Only Bleeding): Literature and Language in the Academy," *PMLA* (Spring 1972): 377–83.

11. See, for example, G. Graff, "Fear and Trembling at Yale," *The American Scholar* (Fall 1977): 467–78; id., *Literature against Itself: Literary Ideas in Modern Society* (Chicago: University of Chicago Press, 1979); F. Lentricchia, *After the New Criticism* (Chicago: University of Chicago Press, 1980).

12. E. H. Gombrich, "Research in the Humanities: Ideals and Idols," *Daedalus (The Search for Knowledge)*, (Spring 1973): 1–10.

13. H. Arendt, "Lying in Politics," in *Crises of the Republic* (New York: Harcourt Brace Jovanovich, 1972).

14. M. G. Raskin, *Being and Doing* (New York: Random House, 1971), pp. 342–77.

15. R. Shaull, "Foreword," in Freire, *Pedagogy of the Oppressed*, p. 15.

16. Gombrich, "Research in the Humanities," p. 9.

17. M. Merleau-Ponty, "Metaphysics and the Novel," in *Sense and Non-Sense* (Evanston, Ill.: Northwestern University Press, 1964), p. 28.

18. Id., "The Primacy of Perception," in *The Primacy of Perception* (Evanston, Ill.: Northwestern University Press, 1964), p. 25.

19. See W. James, "Percept and Concept—The Importance of Concepts," in *Some Problems of Philosophy* (New York: Longmans, Green, 1947), pp. 47–74; id., "The Perception of Reality," in *The Principles of Psychology*, Vol. II (New York: Dover, 1950), pp. 283–324.

20. See J. Dewey, "Qualitative Thought," in *Philosophy and Civilization* (New York: Minton, Balch & Co., 1931), pp. 93–116.

21. W. C. Booth, "An Arrogant Proposal: A New Use for the Dyshumanities," in *Profession 77* (New York: Modern Language Association of America, 1977).

22. W. Percy, *The Moviegoer* (New York: Noonday Press, 1977), p. 13.

23. A. Schutz, "Common-Sense and Scientific Interpretation of Human Action," in *Collected Papers I, The Problem of Social Reality* (The Hague: Martinus Nijhoff, 1967), pp. 3–47.

24. Schutz, "On Multiple Realities," in *The Problem of Social Reality*, p. 208.

25. T. Mann, *The Magic Mountain* (New York: Alfred A. Knopf, 1955), p. 32.

26. J. Conrad, "Heart of Darkness," in *Three Great Tales* (New York: Modern Library Paperbacks, n.d.), p. 253.

27. H. Marcuse, "Art as a Form of Reality," in *On the Future of Art* (New York: S. R. Guggenheim Museum, 1970), pp. 132–33.

28. J. Sartre, *Literature and Existentialism* (New York: Citadel Press, 1965), p. 63.

29. G. Lukacs, "Art as Self-Consciousness in Man's Development," in *Marxism and Art,* ed. Berel Lang and Forrest Williams (New York: David McKay, 1972).

30. M. Raskin, *Being and Doing*, p. 112.

31. J. Dewey, *The Public and Its Problems* (Chicago: Swallow Press, 1954), p. 170.

32. G. Greene, *A Burnt-Out Case* (Harmondsworth, Eng.: Penguin Books, 1963).

33. E. Hemingway, "A Clean, Well-Lighted Place," in *The Short Stories of Ernest Hemingway* (New York: Charles Scribner's Sons, 1954), p. 383.

34. Freire, *Pedagogy of the Oppressed*, p. 333.

35. Raskin, *Being and Doing*, p. 114.

36. Freire, *Pedagogy of the Oppressed*, p. 62.

37. T. Stoppard, *Rosencrantz and Guildenstern Are Dead* (New York: Grove Press, 1967), p. 41.

38. Ibid., p. 57.

39. Ibid., p. 125.

40. Ibid., p. 17.

41. Ibid., p. 18.

42. P. Nizan, *Antoine Bloyé* (New York: Monthly Review Press, 1973), p. 113.

43. Ibid., p. 224.

44. Ibid., p. 208.

45. Ibid., p. 54.

46. G. Konrad, *The Case Worker* (New York: Harcourt Brace Jovanovich, 1974), p. 169.

47. P. Ricoeur, *Interpretation Theory: Discourse and the Surplus of Meaning* (Fort Worth: Texas Christian Press, 1976), p. 71.

48. Ibid., p. 92.

49. J. Sartre, *Being and Nothingness* (New York: Philosophical Library, 1956), pp. 434–35.

50. H. Arendt, "On Violence," in *Crises of the Republic* (New York: Harvest Books, 1972), p. 137.

51. M. Merleau-Ponty, *Phenomenology of Perception* (New York: Humanities Press, 1967), p. 456.

20

Teacher Education and
the Ideology of Social Control

Henry Giroux

Introduction

Teacher-education programs are caught in a deceptive paradox. Charged
with the public responsibility of educating teachers who will enable future
generations learn the knowledge and skills necessary for building a principled and democratic society, they represent a significant agency for the
reproduction and legitimation of a society characterized by a high degree of
social and economic inequality.[1] Unfortunately, the source of this paradox
remains an enigma to most educators. In part, the "hidden" meaning of the
paradox can be explained by the ambiguous position that teacher-education
programs occupy in this country. On the one hand they, along with the entire educational system, speak to a very real need on the part of all socioeconomic classes to learn about and to transform the nature of their existence.
On the other hand, schools and their various programs exist within a con-
stellation of economic, social, and political institutions that make them a
fundamental part of the power structure.[2]

This essay is dedicated to John DeBiase (d. 1973) and Armand Giroux (d. 1978),
each of whom knew something about the "dark" side of culture and ideology. It
is also lovingly dedicated to Jeanne Brady whose very existence makes me believe
in the future.

Reprinted, by permission, from *Journal of Education* 162: 1 (Winter 1980).

As public and private institutions, teacher-education programs and their respective schools of education provide the appearance of being neutral,[3] yet they operate within a social structure that disproportionately serves specific ruling interests.[4] Thus, teacher-education programs embody structural and ideological contradictions that are related to a larger social order caught in a conflict between the imperatives of its social welfare responsibilities and its functional allegiance to the conditions of capitalism. Such a posture testifies not only to the political nature of these programs, it also points to the necessity to unravel the multifaceted ways in which they both serve and contradict the latent as opposed to the overt functions of the existing society.

It is within this political and economic framework that I want to examine the relationship between teacher education and the ideology of social control. I believe that the nature, function, and the possibility for reforming such programs can only be grasped through an analysis of the ways in which power, ideology, biography, and history mediate between schools and the social and economic determinants of the dominant social order. Through such an analysis, I want to begin to lay the theoretical groundwork for a theory of ideological and material constraints. At the core of this theoretical scheme is an acknowledgment of the importance of the dialectical interplay between human consciousness and objective reality. There is also a further concern with institutional structures as representations of social relationships that are both shaped by and in turn shape human actions.

Social and Cultural Reproduction

The starting point for understanding this perspective rests with the assumption that the principles governing the organization of social practices, knowledge, and normative criteria in teacher-education programs represent a selection from corresponding principles in the wider society. Within this context teacher-education programs, like the universities and colleges of which they are a part, embody collective traditions and social practices that are linked to notions of meaning and control that can be traced in both historical and contemporary terms to specific economic and social interests. If questions of meaning can be associated with notions of authority and control, the issue can be raised as to whose sets of meaning stalk behind and legitimate the organization and structure of teacher-education programs. In more specific terms, how are these meanings sustained? How are they modified and altered? What are the value assumptions that lie hidden beneath the form and content of such programs? And, finally, what material and ideological forces obscure the latent functions of these programs?

This should not suggest that such programs simply mirror and reproduce the beliefs, values, and social practices of larger socioeconomic interests; nor should it suggest that teachers and students are merely "social puppets" in the machinery of domination.[5] Both positions are vulgar and mechanistic.

Moreover, they ignore the multiplicity of social and personal forces that both influence and are influenced by human actions. But it is important to stress that while there are a number of contradictions between teacher-education programs and the wider society, these contradictions only point to the "relative autonomy" of such programs and fail, in the final analysis, to posit a convincing case for examining them as "free-floating," existing outside of the imperatives of class and power in which they are embedded.

More recently a number of educational theorists have attempted to analyze education and history within a political and ideological context that functions in the interest of social and economic reproduction. In essence they have attempted to discover how institutions that serve as agencies of socialization function to help reproduce the division of labor that permeates existing social and institutional arrangements. Representing one mode of analysis, political economists such as Bowles and Gintis have analyzed and demonstrated how the varied ideological and economic outcomes of schools reproduce social and economic inequality.[6] Rejecting the consensus view of functionalist sociology, neo-Marxists have interpreted educational change as the outcome of class conflict and struggle. Moreover, they have explored how schools utilize certain selective principles such as testing, IQ scores, and tracking in order to discriminate against minorities of class and color. In this view, the educational system through its differential distribution of knowledge and nonacademic skills, awarded along class, racial, and sexual lines, functions to legitimate rather than ameliorate the injustices of the larger society. Representing a similar concern, but using a different mode of analysis, a number of social theorists, influenced by the new sociology of education in England, have examined the political function of schools through an analysis of how social reality is constructed and negotiated at the day-to-day level of the classroom encounter.[7] Both positions provide important conceptual insights and new critical categories for examining teacher education and the function of schooling. Yet neither position is without its respective flaws, flaws that must be overcome in order for educators to develop a more comprehensive framework for the study of educational theory and practice.

The economistic view, it has been rightly argued, often presents an overdetermined model of correspondence between schooling and the economic structures of society.[8] Moreover, in this view men and women appear to be eliminated as active, interpretive agents, and the institutions under analysis appear to be abstracted from the specifically conditioned social relationships they represent. Consequently, what we sometimes get from this perspective is a kind of melodrama in which a unified and "wicked" ruling class imposes its will on the complacent masses. Thus, while it is to the credit of economistic theorists that they have politicized the notion of schooling while similarly providing a theory of *class* reproduction, their analysis fails in the end because concrete individuals and social groups have a way of disappearing and schools end up being treated like "black boxes."[9]

Using a different approach, the new sociology of education theorists have illuminated the concrete ways in which teachers, students, and educational researchers both produce and work through socially constructed definitions of curriculum, pedagogy, and evaluation.[10] But this perspective also has serious shortcomings. In effect the new sociologists have failed to ground their view of domination in an adequate theory of class and social reproduction.[11] Similarly, the new sociology, in many cases, seems so intent in concentrating on how students and teachers construct and negotiate meanings in daily classroom encounters that both groups appear to "get lost" in the myriad of everyday classroom life. Consequently, we are often left with the notion that liberation can simply be willed into being, that is, objective structural and ideological forces that limit one's choices and actions become merely paper barricades to be blown away with a little gust of intentionality. In summary, both views posit an unwarranted division between the subject and the object, and in so doing eliminate the subject from reality.[12]

Beyond Methodology Madness

It is essential to understand that questions about meaning and purpose in teacher-education programs are political in nature. Such questions provide teacher educators and their students with value-laden "paradigms" that establish the foundation for addressing everyday school practices. In the most general sense, teacher-education systems represent socializing agencies that embody rules and patterns for constructing and legitimizing categories regarding competence, achievement, and success. Moreover, they serve to define specific roles (teacher, student, principal) through the language they use and the assumptions and research they consider essential to the teaching profession. Unfortunately, the basic premises and rules that underlie such programs are usually viewed as commonsense perceptions; they go unquestioned and often result in many problems in the teaching arena to be defined as basically technical ones.[13] Popkewitz captures both the spirit and consequence of this when he writes:

The technical definitions to educational problems and the procedural responses to reform in teacher education are legitimated by much of the research in the field. Most research tends to view teaching as a problem of human engineering and teacher education as the most efficient way to provide new recruits with the specific behaviors and attitudes of the people who practice teaching . . . the conduct of schooling, the system of status and privilege of the occupation, and the social and political implications of institutional arrangements are obscured through a process of reification. Teaching and teacher education are treated administratively. . . . What is ignored are the ways in which teacher education imposes work styles and patterns of communication which guide individuals as to how they are to reason and to act in their relationships in the setting of schooling. The language, material organization, and social interactions of teacher education establish principles of authority, power, and rationality for guiding occupational conduct. These patterns of thought and work are not neutral and cannot be taken for granted.[14]

The overall effect on teacher education of the social engineering approach has been considerable and is far removed from the vision of John Dewey, George Counts, and other progressive educators who stressed the ethical, experiential, and emancipatory dimensions of such programs. A number of educators such as Stanley Aronowitz have recently decried the rampant "methodology madness" that appears to dominate the field of teacher education.[15] Overly anxious about presenting students with "seven" approaches to empirical research, "six" dimensions of curriculum, and endless approaches to constructing behavioral objectives, too many courses in these programs are silent about the assumptions embedded in these varied approaches, not to mention the interests they serve or the ethical consequences of their use. The results suggest not a more comprehensive level of thought, but the debasement of thinking itself. As Aronowitz points out:

The stress on critical thinking . . . offering the student a chance to construct his own reality, has been debased by the emphasis on "methods" rather than content in the preparation of teachers by teachers colleges. This approach to the curriculum has contributed to the training of several generations of elementary and secondary school teachers whose main skill has become maintaining control over the class rather than understanding the cognitive and effective process of learning. Moreover, thousands of young teachers suffer from intellectual ignorance; they bring few resources to their work and often fall back on police-like behavior toward students to compensate for their inability to teach.[16]

While there are numerous exceptions to Aronowitz's charge, the question of whether teacher-education programs are based on valuative and cognitive principles that undermine critical thought and take for granted that which its task is to explain is no small matter. If educators have been blind to the role and function of teacher education, it is in part due to the study by mainstream educators of such programs under microsocial categories that ignore the historical and political context in which they exist. Thus, we are treated to studies that suggest that the quality of teacher-education programs can improve only if they select students with higher SAT test scores.[17] In the same vein, it has been suggested that we can improve teacher education if a process of psychological screening for entrants is built into the admission policies of such programs.[18] Such responses are characteristic of the rationality that dominates educational theory and practice. Divorced from the language of power, history, and critical sociology these positions appear deaf to the assumptions that generate the questions they formulate, not to mention the answers they provide. The basic, constitutive nature of these programs seems to disappear in studies of this sort. The basic assumptions that give meaning and legitimacy to teacher education are relegated to the realm of common sense.

A more worthwhile approach to examining teacher education will have to begin by utilizing macrosocial categories that reveal how the underlying economic and political structures of the larger society influence the "here and now" ideology and culture that are part of the tissue of everyday life in these programs.

New Critical Categories for
Examining Teacher Education

The form and content of teacher education are inextricably linked to notions of power, culture, ideology, and hegemony. An investigation of these concepts provides the basis for examining not only how such programs function as agencies of economic and cultural reproduction, but also how the contradictions and tensions in these programs point to possible reforms and modifications.

It has been pointed out that mainline curriculum theorists rarely understand what the linkages are between curriculum theory and cultural reproduction,[19] and that this leads to some puzzlement on their part as to why the notion of culture should be bracketed in the first place. Part of the problem lies with the depoliticized notion of culture that permeates mainstream social science. In this view culture is defined as simply a people's total way of life, the entirety of those goods, services, and labor produced by human beings. Adorno sums up this definition well when he writes, "Culture is viewed as the manifestation of pure humanity without regard for its functional relationship to society."[20] Divorced from notions of class, power, and ideology, such a definition becomes an empty social science category that relegates "culture" "to the atmosphere of a presumably harmonious Olympus."[21] A less mystifying approach would subsume "culture" within the category of society so as to reveal its functions as a legitimating, motivational structure that provides members of the dominant society with symbolic message systems and institutions to "lay the psychological and moral foundations for the economic and political system they control."[22] Culture as used here suggests not the existence of one "whole social process" happily produced by all members of society, but different layers of meanings and practices mediated by the inequitable distribution of wealth and power. Thus, one cannot speak of one culture or of a multiplicity of cultures; it is more accurate to speak of a dominant culture (with its own contradictions, of course), and of the existence of minority cultures, all mediated by considerations of power and control.[23]

The concept of dominant culture takes on a particular clarity in the writings of Korsch and Gramsci.[24] In their view, the state wields its power through a combination of force and *consent*. In this context the notion of cultural reproduction becomes more clearly linked to the state's political and economic functions. That is, state power relies less upon the use of physical repression than it does upon the use of belief and value systems to organize public consent for its policies and practices. Gramsci called this form of control hegemony. Hegemony is an ideology that defines the limits of discourse in a society by positing specific ideas and social relationships as natural, permanent, rational, and universal. Ideology as hegemony is in part a form of false consciousness because it represents "the repression of society in the formation of concepts . . . an academic confinement of experience, a restriction of meaning."[25] Hegemony, then, is an ideology that has been institutionalized by the state.[26] But it must be stressed that hegemony refers to more than dominant belief and value systems, it also refers to those routines and practices that saturate people's daily experiences. Raymond Williams captures the latter point when he writes:

Hegemony is then not only the articulate upper level of "ideology" nor are its forms of control only those ordinarily seen in "manipulation" or "indoctrination." It is a whole body of practices and expectations, over the whole of living: our senses and assignments of energy, our shaping perceptions of ourselves and our world. It is a lived system of meanings and values—constitutive and constituting—which as they are experienced as practices appear as reciprocally confirming. . . . It is, that is to say, in the strongest sense a "culture," but a culture which has also to be seen as the lived dominance and subordination of particular classes.[27]

The concept of hegemony and its implications for studying the ideology of social control in teacher education would be incomplete without a definition and analysis of ideology. First, I want to reject outright the orthodox Marxist notion of ideology as a set of illusions or lies. The concept recaptures its critical spirit if it is viewed as a form of social reconstruction. This means that ideology is a set of beliefs, values, and social practices that contain oppositional assumptions about varying elements of social reality, that is, society, economics, authority, human nature, politics, and so on.[28] Moreover, ideology is now seen as a critical view of the world that is value-laden, a view which points to the contradictions and tensions in a society from the perspectives of its own world view: that is, liberalism, communism, socialism, anarchism, and others.[29] Ideologies become hegemonic when they are institutionalized by the dominant society.[30] At this point, they are stripped of their oppositional power and serve to legitimize existing institutional arrangements and social practices. "Hegemonic ideologies smooth over the rough edges of reality and provide an idealized view . . . Hegemonic ideology presents private interests as public goods."[31] Through its structured silence about what ought to be, hegemonic ideology elevates "common sense" to a universal truth.

The concept of hegemonic ideology strips teacher-education programs of their purported innocence. This becomes clear if we raise questions about how hegemonic ideologies are created and distributed in a society. Social theorists such as Gramsci and Althusser have attempted to answer such questions by pointing to the "ideological state apparatus" as the primary reproducer of hegemonic ideology.[32]

Agencies considered part of the ideological state apparatus act as vehicles of socialization, either directly or indirectly, and while trading in ideas and values, they function to mediate between the summits of power and everyday life. The ideological state apparatus includes churches, schools, trade unions, media, work places, and the family. At the core of this perspective is the insight that advanced industrial countries such as the United States inequitably distribute not only economic goods and services but certain forms of cultural capital as well, that is, "that system of meanings, abilities, language forms, and tastes that are directly and indirectly defined by dominant groups as socially legitimate."[33] If we view the distribution of knowledge and social practices as a form of capital linked (though not mechanistically) to the concept of hegemony, I think we can get a clearer understanding of the role that schools play in this society. Bernstein and others have argued that schools are the primary agents of ideological control.[34] This raises specific questions about teacher-education programs since they "train" those intellectuals who play a pervasive and direct part in socializing students into the dominant society. The implications of the view would certainly dispel the perspective voiced by educators such as Tyler and R. S. Peters that schools simply "transmit" culture.[35] The term "transmit" hides the reality that lies behind the notion of "reproduction." As was mentioned earlier, schools do not transmit culture, instead they play a fundamental role in reproducing the dominant culture.[36] This has led a number of critics to raise substantive questions about schools and their relationship to the dominant culture.[37] These inquiries focus on questions such as: Whose culture gets distributed in the schools? Who benefits from such culture? What are the historical, social, and economic roots of this culture? How is this culture distributed? How is it sustained in the curriculum?

In short, teachers at all levels of schooling are part of an ideological region that has enormous importance in legitimizing the categories and social practices of the dominant society. Hence, the fundamental question now becomes, "How does the dominant ideology manifest itself in teacher-education programs?" I believe we can answer that question by first pointing to the rationality that dominates such programs; secondly, we can examine how this rationality ties these programs to wider societal interests. Through such an analysis, the theoretical framework will be developed for examining how this type of rationality can be countered in order to restructure teacher education as it presently exists.

The Dominant Rationality in Teacher Education

Any attempt at defining the dominant rationality underlying teacher education has to begin with an essential qualification. The rationality described below is portrayed in ideal-essence terms. In the extended political and cultural sense, it represents a form of dominance, but it is not all-engulfing, total, or exclusive. There are many contradictions and permeations that merge with the dominant rationality and give it a different "face" or "texture." Various forms of systems-management pedagogy or knowledge-based curriculum approaches are but two examples of so-called innovative approaches to classroom instruction that at heart are simply recycled and repackaged forms of the existing rationality that has dominated schools and teacher-education programs since their inception. Similarly, different contexts produce varied responses to such a rationality. For instance, rural and small teachers colleges may embrace such a rationality with a different degree of intentionality than schools of education that are part of metropolitan university systems. Moreover, this rationality as a form of hegemonic ideology does not represent a set of categories or "rules"—it is much more than that. At its core it represents the ideological expression of real social relationships and human encounters. As such, it is not static but constantly changing and modifying itself in the face of changing sociohistorical conditions.

The strength and pervasiveness of the rationality that presently dominates educational theory and practice can be grasped in the increasing national support of competency-based systems of instruction, behavioristic models of pedagogy, and the various versions of systems-theory models in curriculum development and evaluation. At first glance, this mode of rationality, hereafter referred to as technocratic rationality, appears to be a post-sputnik trend. A closer examination reveals that such is not the case. Technocratic rationality has a long history in curriculum theory and practice, and was initiated by many of the curriculum field's early founders, Franklin Bobbitt, W. W. Charters, Edward L. Thorndike, Charles Peters, and others. What is significant about the history of this form of rationality is that it reveals its roots in models of industrial psychology and control patterned after the scientific management movement of the 1920s.[38] Not only does the language of this mode of rationality conceptualize the nature and function of schooling in industrial terms (that is, schools are seen as factories, students as raw material), it also supports modes of behavior and goals premised on the need for a form of social control dedicated to social homogeneity and group conformity. The historical record shows that the demands of industrialization for cheap and docile labor provided the school with the "ideal" task of instilling "the immigrants with specific values and standards of behavior."[39] While the interests behind the historical development of technocratic rationality are rather clear, it appears that the historical roots of its more contemporary versions have been forgotten by many teacher educators. This form of "social amnesia" not only characterizes technocratic rationality, it also shapes the conditions under which it sustains itself. The consequences for teacher education are no small matter.

The importance of what passes as a legitimating rationality in teacher education cannot be overstated. Any form of rationality suggests specific limits and boundaries on the areas one sees fit for investigation, the questions one deems important for study, and the modes of investigation to be used. All forms of rationality, in one sense, provide *both* the definition and legitimation for the categories and assumptions that give expression and create opportunities for investigating the world. As Popkewitz points out, "What passes as reason and rationality in teacher-education has important implications to the meaning held in larger society."[40] This becomes evident when the basic assumptions that characterize technocratic rationality are made clear.

Assumptions Behind Technocratic Rationality

In broad general terms, a number of assumptions characterize technocratic rationality: (1) Educational theory should operate in the interests of lawlike propositions which are empirically testable. A major assumption here is that empirical-analytic research can identify lawlike regularities in the social world "which can be identified and manipulated as with objects in the physical world."[41] (2) The natural sciences provide the "proper" model of explanation of the concepts and techniques of educational theory, design, and evaluation. This becomes clear in the work of Suppes, Popham, and other major educational researchers in the field who decry methods of investigation not based upon the technical principles or interests of prediction, control, and certainty.[42] Variables that cannot be formally expressed in quantitative terms, such as philosophical analyses, historical inquiry, mystery, awe, forms of transcendence, are seen as "soft" data, not fit for serious inquiry. Eliot Eisner brings this point out in claiming that "the belief that educational research is a form of inquiry whose conclusions can be couched only in numbers is so pervasive that, of the 47 articles published in the *American Educational Research Journal* during 1974–1975, only one was non-statistical."[43] The failure to appreciate that there are fundamental interests in teacher education other than those of explanation, prediction, and technical control is what ties most educators to this rationality that shapes their view of pedagogy and teacher education. (3) Knowledge should be objective and capable of being described in neutral fashion. Knowledge in this form of rationality is reduced to those concepts and "facts" that can be operationally defined, that is, they have precise meanings and definitions. This has led to a celebration of techniques whose aim is to identify the different subsets of knowledge and put them together in order to produce knowledge about the whole. Knowledge defined this way sets the stage for separating the knowing subject from the known object. One consequence of this is that it becomes difficult to conceptualize how the subject and object are mutually influenced and transformed in the "act of knowing." On the other hand, the notion of value-free knowledge speaks to knowledge that has to be discovered and transmitted. There is a certain dogmatism here reinforced by the assumption that knowledge is the exclusive province of those who know; human consciousness and activity appear to surrender themselves to the guardians of the "truth." (4) Finally, educators can and must separate statements of value from the "facts" and "modes of inquiry," which ought to be objective.

These assumptions represent the driving force of a form of rationality that views itself as scientific, objective, and functional to the demands of teacher-education programs. Of course, the notion of functional becomes meaningful only when measured next to how this perspective views the larger relationship between teacher education and wider institutional arrangements. This view has been expressed quite well by Talcott Parsons who saw such programs as fitting the existing needs of the present society;[44] thus the relationship was a functional one. Inherent in this form of rationality is a definition of society that stresses consensus, equilibrium, and order. Consequently, the value of teacher-education programs is measured in terms "of their contributions to basic system requirements."[45] Lost from this type of analysis is the language of power and control. For example, society may be held together less by shared values than by ideological and material restraints. To ignore the latter is to accept as a given the basic norms and assumptions that shape existing socioeconomic institutions. Moreover, this perspective sees the socialization of prospective teachers as primarily a technical one, that is, "to transform the human raw material of society into good working members."[46]

Absent from such a view is any attempt to question the nature and quality of the society that teacher-education programs so cheerfully support. Similarly, the underlying emphasis on consensus and control in these programs generates models of socialization and role performance that downplay notions of social conflict and competing socioeconomic interests. In addition, by failing to make problematic the basic beliefs, values, and structural socioeconomic arrangements characteristic of American society, technocratic models of socialization and role performance depoliticize the nature of the teaching experience as well as the relationship between teacher education, schooling, and wider societal interests. Anyon illuminates the nature of the problem when she writes:

[Theories] . . . of school socialization that do not make problematic relationships between the reproduction of an unequal socio-economic order, practical and symbolic ideologies in school, and the construction of personal opportunity and identity, not only circumvent analysis of education and U.S. society, but trivialize our notions of childhood socialization.[47]

Within the theoretical boundaries of technocratic rationality the concept of socialization supports a passive view of students and an overly integrated perception of society.[48] The role of the teacher is often seen as one that can be universally defined in measurable terms and generally applied to any class or school, notwithstanding different levels of schooling. Roles for the prospective teacher are often viewed as "fixed" and objectively given. In this case, teacher roles are treated like "things," and the socialization process simply provides students with the skills and requirements to carry out these predefined roles efficiently.[49] The hidden curriculum here is that role theory becomes "a refinement of conformity theory";[50] characteristically, the teacher is not viewed as a creator of values but simply as the receiver and transmitter of "institutional" norms.[51] Consequently, the teacher's own existential reality becomes lost amidst a form of socialization and role theory that is blind to its own ideology. This position fails to acknowledge that there are no universally acceptable "roles" and "methodologies" that can be placed in gridlike fashion on any context. Gerhard Arfwedson points to the reason for the latter in his statement:

The contextual setting of teacher situations varies in so many different dimensions and directions that what is a "good" personality, role or method in one situation may be almost the "worst" in another situation. . . . These active contextual factors, which define the limits and possibilities that characterize the teacher's working situation, are found not only within the school as a place of work or within the educational system. The actual local society, too, as well as society in a broader sense (i.e., the state and the country) have to be taken into account when a survey of determining factors in teachers' work is to be made.[52]

Theory and Teacher Education

Unfortunately, the nature and role of theory in many teacher-education programs provide little or no explanatory power for students to reflect critically on how pedagogy is informed by theory or on how specific ideological and material conditions inside and outside of the schools play a determining part in shaping as well as constraining different pedagogies. The contours of the technocratic notion of theory are too one-dimensional. What is missing is a theory in which the relational structure of teacher and context, school and society, can be explained in terms of the possibilities and limitations that exist in correspondence and tension with each other. The contours of such a theory have been explained by Ulf Lundgren:

What we have is the contours of a theory in which the development of an educational system and of a curriculum can be explained in relation to processes for cultural reproduction, the need for qualification, the development of educational systems as a part of the state apparatus, and the demands on education for differentiation of labour.[53]

Steeped in the language and assumptions of the strict sciences, most teacher-education programs operate within parameters in which "problems that do not lend themselves to measurement or to scientific solution (are) considered intellectually ill-conceived."[54] This message is not only verified in the research models that dominate the education field but also in the curriculum models that dominate teacher education and public school pedagogy.[55]

The political and ethical function of theory is subsumed in this perspective amidst a trivializing concern with methodology and models. Supported by claims of objectivity and impartial scientific research, students in teacher education find themselves operating out of predefined categories and styles of thought that make curriculum appear to have a life of its own. Instead of being seen for what it is, a specific social reality expressing a distinct set of social relations and assumptions about the world, curriculum appears as something which exists in a suprahistorical vacuum.[56] The claims to objectivity and science that support this view are both false and mystifying. They are false because any notion about curriculum and pedagogy is value-laden and historically grounded, and unavoidably so. They are mystifying because by claiming to be objective such assertions falsify the meaning of "science" in order to be silent about the underlying politics and interests in which they are grounded.[57] By not making its basic assumptions problematic, technocratic rationality places itself beyond the realm of criticism and debate. Thus its posture has little to do with objectivity and a great deal to do with "objectivism," which as Gouldner describes it, is "communication that conceals the presence of the speaker, . . . thinking that ignores the language or theory about which thought is taking place."[58]

While it is impossible to fully detail how technocratic rationality promotes conformity and social control in teacher education, it is important to attempt to illuminate in concrete terms the effect it has had on the way teacher-education programs view knowledge and classroom pedagogy.

Knowledge and Classroom Pedagogy

A major criticism of both teacher education and public schooling has focused on how specific forms of knowledge and meanings are selected and distributed in their respective settings. These criticisms are not meant to imply that discussions about the selection, form, and content of knowledge go unexamined. Such is not the case. It is the criteria used in such programs that warrant criticism. For instance, Harris claims that teacher educators give high priority to variables involved in trying to answer the question "What knowledge is of most worth?"[59] The problem lies with the restricted assumptions and criteria used in formulating and answering such a question. The assumptions that shape the criteria and ensuing questions support the notion that knowledge is objective, "out there" to be learned and mastered. As Popkewitz points out, "These discussions are often related to questions about the structure of knowledge,"[60] or to the technical organization of content. The language used in this case represents the language of internal criticism, it is confined to solving the "puzzles" within its own symbolic space, and as such cannot step outside of the assumptions that legitimate it. Put another way, it is not a dialectical language, one that can choose among competing paradigms and disciplines in order to think about the subject or processes in use.[61]

It has been argued that such a static view of knowledge and students is both elitist and conservative. This view fails to provide a theoretic stance for analyzing the way teacher-education knowledge is selected, organized, distributed, and evaluated.[62] Instead of perceiving knowledge as a study in ideology, linked to socially constructed human interests, technocratic rationality ignores the relationship between power and school knowledge and often ends up celebrating, in both the overt and hidden curricula, knowledge that supports existing institutional arrangements. Popkewitz, Anyon, Apple,[63] and others have done extensive studies illuminating the biases and ideologically laden categories and assumptions that permeate textbooks and classroom practices. The responsibility for the latter cannot be placed on teachers' shoulders exclusively. In many respects teacher-education programs have simply not given teachers the conceptual tools they need in order to view knowledge as problematic, as a historically conditioned, socially constructed phenomenon. Similarly, the objectification of knowledge is usually accompanied by the objectification of the classroom social encounter. Knowledge is not just content; its use also suggests specific kinds of classroom social relationships. When knowledge is seen as objective and "out there," it is usually accompanied by top-to-bottom forms of pedagogy in which there is little dialogue or interaction.[64] But the way pupils construct meaning, the importance of subjectivity, and the value of knowledge outside of the "rationality" of strict science are important dimensions of the process of curriculum and instruction. These modes of knowing represent important pedagogical principles that future educators need to understand in order to be able to shape their *own* lives in a self-determining manner.

This leads to one final criticism. Knowledge in the technocratic rationality view is defined and used so as to be separated from the lived histories and biographies not only of teachers but of students.[65] Thus knowledge is used not only to mask the role that it plays in shaping how people view themselves and others, it also serves to ignore how important the relationship is among knowledge, context, and learning. For instance, knowledge that goes unexamined does more than hide the social interests it supports; it also militates against the use of social relationships that generate meanings from the perceptions and voices of different cultural actors involved in the "learning" process. This means that teachers are neither trained to recognize nor to use the cultural capital of others as a central category for dialogue and personal affirmation in their teaching. The result is a form of pedagogical violence that prevents teachers from establishing conditions which allow students to speak with an authentic voice.[66] Similarly, the notion of "objective" knowledge not only fails to reveal how knowledge is culturally bound, it also serves to buttress normative and intellectual support in teacher-education programs for the ethos of "professionalism."[67] The latter refers to the cult of "experts" and "professionals" who became avatars trained to guard as well as "transmit" the sacred knowledge and language to prospective educators, who in turn make *their* expertise available to members of the public. If the metaphor seems overdrawn, it is only because there is a real necessity to break down the pompous and dangerous ideology of professionalism that is so ingrained in teacher education. As Lasch, Bledstein, and Edelman have pointed out, the growth of professionalism in education has done little to benefit the public and a great deal to serve the narrow interests of educators themselves.[68] The latter interests include: increased hierarchical differentiation in the teaching profession, a growing standardization of school practices, and an increasing call for the legitimation of the value of "certified" knowledge. In general, the growth of the ideology of professionalism has only been matched in the field of education by the tendency of its members "to work toward inertia."[69]

Implications for Teacher-Education Programs

Teacher-education programs, it has been argued in this essay, function as agencies of social control. They do the latter to the degree that they directly or indirectly "educate" future generations of teachers to accept uncritically those skills, attitudes, and dispositional qualities that support the dominant social order. Of course, this is not meant to suggest that such programs mechanistically and awesomely reproduce the social and cultural imperatives of the state. Nor does this position suggest that students are so malleable and powerless that they willingly submit to their own victimization. Teacher-education programs operate within parameters that are severely constraining, but they also contain options for creating new possibilities and social realities. In other words, the seeds exist within teacher education for developing "critical intellectuals" who can begin the task of generating a more radical and visionary consciousness among their fellow workers, friends, and students. It is crucial to recognize that teacher-education programs not only exist in dialectical tension with the rest of society; they also mediate tensions and contradictions specific to their own interests and concerns. Teacher-education programs, then, both embody and demonstrate contradictions and correspondences with wider societal interests.[70] It is the tensions and contradictions in these programs that testify to their relative autonomy, and it is within the context of this relative autonomy that "radical" teachers can find the political space to develop innovative courses and alternative modes of pedagogy. It is an opportunity that should not be ignored.

Prospective reform in teacher education must begin by giving students the theoretical and conceptual tools to combat all forms of mystification and alienation. In both structural and intellectual ways, students should be able to penetrate beneath the commonsense, surface realities that, in part, shape their day-to-day experiences. Similarly, students should be given the opportunity to generate their own meanings, speak with their own voices, and come to understand "that there is always more to see and hear and feel, that the quality of our enjoyment is to some degree a function of what we know."[71] Students in teacher education must learn that knowledge is a socially constructed phenomenon and that methodological inquiry is never value-free. Moreover, they must be given the opportunity to learn how specific classroom social relationships not only are value-laden, but, in part, represent material-ideological configurations characteristic of the work place and other agencies of socialization and social control. But these heuristic devices are incomplete unless they are coupled with an affirmation of the importance of social justice and social action. With the latter in mind, a deepening attitude of self-awareness and justice must link the biographical with the social, the private with the sense of community. Maxine Greene perceptively captures the importance of such a dialectic when she writes:

There must be a perception of the ways in which persons locate themselves in the world in the light of their own particular biographical situations, the experiences they have built up over time. Every individual interprets the realities he or she confronts through perspectives made up of particular ranges of interests, occupations, commitments, and desires. Each one belongs to a number of social groups and plays a variety of social roles. His or her involvements—the work he or she has done, the schools he or she has attended, his or her race and class membership—affect the way "the stock of knowledge at hand" is used. Particular persons make use of it to order, to interpret from particular vantage points; as they do so, a common meaning structure is built up among them; they share a common world. . . . Whatever efforts can be made to enable teachers-to-be to speak for themselves and confront the concreteness of their lives ought to play into the critique that challenges mystification. And in time, this might be carried into the classrooms of the schools or wherever such problems finally work.[72]

If teacher educators and their students are encouraged to think about the self-formative processes that underlie their own thinking, this may also help them to reflect critically on the constraints that limit the possibilities they are attempting to develop and implement. It is a theory of ideological and material constraints that requires the need for the heuristic to be complemented by the political.[73] Furthermore, empirical investigations in education can only be useful when they are subordinated to the heuristic and political questions that determine their meaning and function. Adorno clearly expressed this point when he wrote: "But one must not confer autonomy upon them or regard them (empirical investigations) as a universal key. Above all, they must themselves terminate in theoretical knowledge."[74] The existence of material and ideological constraints should not be viewed as a limit situation, but as a starting point from which teacher educators can assess and act on those beliefs and structural forces that both legitimate and reproduce the worst dimensions of technocratic rationality. In more specific terms I will point to some broad suggestions that teacher educators might want to consider.

Teacher educators and their students must learn to think dialectically.[75] This means that they must develop a satisfactory theory of totality. Schools must be seen as part of a wider societal process. But to posit the importance of interconnections is merely a valuable methodological precept. More important,

to ask for a theory of totality is to ask how a society reproduces itelf, how it perpetuates its conditions of existence through its reproduction of class relationships and its propagation of ideologies which sanction the status quo.[76]

The dialectic involved here is a crucial one. The interplay of power, norms, and values will have to be connected with a more relational view of academic knowledge. The artificial constructs that characterize the ordering and boundaries of subject matter must give way to more fluid interconnections. But this must be preceded by an understanding that *both* knowledge and people are "processed" in schools, and if such an understanding is to become a viable starting point for a critical sociology of education, then the central task of teacher education will be "to relate those principles of selection and organization that underlie curricula to their institutional and interactional setting in schools and classrooms to the wider social structure."[77] The latter task demands that teacher educators reconstruct more critical categories for educational theory and practice. For instance, categories such as social class, ideology, false consciousness, and hegemony must be linked to others such as oppression, emancipation, freedom, and indoctrination.[78]

Similarly, teacher educators and their students must draw as much as possible from other disciplines in order to examine social reality. As Greene writes: "They must be enabled to look through the perspectives opened by history, sociology, anthropology, economics and philosophy; they must learn how consciously to order the materials of their experience with the aid of such perspectives."[79]

It is also crucial that students in these programs learn to use in their work theoretical models not based exclusively on the interests of prediction and control. Needed are theoretical models that flush out the political and ethical questions that implicitly or explicitly provide the foundation for educational theory, development, and evaluation. One approach would be to provide students with theoretical models that support interests such as human understanding, contextual inquiry, aesthetic literacy, and social reconstructionism. Such models can be drawn from fields such as hermeneutics, symbolic interactionism, phenomenology, semiotics, and neo-Marxism. Classroom and curricula activities that allow students to examine issues from a variety of perspectives, and to test the truth claims of these perspectives, at least provide the climate for dialogue and critique, and the latter are important pedagogical principles.

Another crucial point centers around providing students with heuristic devices based on different languages and different modes of rationality. It is imperative that future teachers be able to understand the "full range and varieties of rationality of which humans are capable, that are not limited to one set of assumptions about how we come to know."[80] For instance, Huebner suggests five modes of rationality that should play an integral role in both understanding and shaping educational theory and practice—technical, political, scientific, aesthetic, and ethical.[81] Each not only has its own language, but calls for a different and complex mode of interpretation. Pioneering examples of the attempt to link educational theory with modes of rationality in the arts and in critical psychology can be found in the work of Grumet and Pinar.[82] The more students in teacher-education programs learn to understand both the distinctiveness as well as the interconnections among these modes of rationality, the greater will be their range of heuristic and political abilities.

In addition, I think it is imperative that teacher educators and their students develop pedagogical approaches that enable them to understand the value and experience that each brings to the classroom experience. Teaching must be viewed, in part, as an intensely personal affair.[83] This suggests that prospective teachers be given the concepts and methods to delve into their own biographies, to look at the sedimented history they carry around, and to learn how one's own cultural capital represents a dialectical interplay between private experience and history. Methods of curriculum design, implementation, and evaluation must be seen as a construction in values and ideology. This approach provides the foundation for future teachers to analyze how their own values mediate the classroom structures and student experiences they work with.

Finally, teacher-education programs must stress as well as demonstrate the importance of historical sensibility as a tool for critical thinking. The value of making educational theory and practice problematic represents one important step towards demystifying the ideology of technocratic rationality, but it is not enough. If the "death trap" of pedagogical relativism is to be avoided, educators must turn to history to trace how school knowledge, modes of school organization, modes of evaluation, and classroom social relationships have developed out of specific social assumptions and political interests. Teachers, students, even the forms and shapes of schools themselves, carry the weight of history. And it is this "weight" that breaks into the moment as an objective and universal consideration. If teacher education is to move in the direction of a critical science, it will have to trace the interests and historical roots of the fields that it supports. Every field, whether it be curriculum, social education, or reading and language, is steeped in dominant paradigms that can only be understood and analyzed if their respective social and political assumptions and orientations are placed in a historical context. By doing so, it becomes relatively clear that the study of "the field" quickly becomes the study of the historical development of specific social relationships operating at particular conjunctures during specific sociohistorical periods. The historical sensibility represents an attempt to trace the self-formative genesis of any field. Thus it is at once historical and critical. Such a sensibility raises new questions and provides new possibilities. Raising questions such as How did systems management get into the curriculum field? What are the historical roots of the existing testing paradigm? Whose interests does the testing paradigm serve? How does technocratic rationality work in the interest of the state? What were the conditions under which it changed its form and content? What is the history of educational psychology in the curriculum field? What were the social theories and beliefs of the founders of the curriculum movement? will help students to unravel the multiple socioeconomic and ideological connections that mediate between schools and the wider social structure. Moreover, they point to the possibility of both critique and transformation.

These suggestions are meant to be no more than tentative guidelines that can be used to illuminate the limits of teacher education as well as establish the conditions for a dialogue over possible reforms. They argue strongly for recognizing the political nature of teacher education and the schools of which they are a part. Moreover, these suggestions represent a call to both students and teachers in such programs to redefine their roles and to work toward making teacher education, in the Kantian spirit, a "battleground" where future generations of teachers can be educated to "fight" for the building of a better and more just society for everyone.

Notes

1. S. Bowles and H. Gintis, *Schooling in Capitalist America: Educational Reform and Contradictions of Economic Life* (New York: Basic Books, 1976).

2. L. Althusser, "Ideology and Ideological State Apparatuses," in *Lenin and Philosophy and other Essays*, ed. id., trans. Ben Brewster (New York: Monthly Review Press, 1971); P. Bourdieu and J. Passeron, *Reproduction in Education, Society, and Culture* (Beverly Hills, Calif.: Sage, 1977).

3. For instance, this idea can be found in the work of educators such as Arthur Jensen and Charles Silberman. Jensen believes that problems with schooling can be traced to the intellectual capacities of the students. In A. R. Jensen, *Educability and Group Differences* (New York: Harper & Row, 1973). Silberman traces the source of school problems to the mindlessness of teachers. C. Silberman, *Crisis in the Classroom: The Remaking of American Education* (New York: Random House, 1970). Both views treat schools in a decontextualized fashion; such perceptions are ahistorical, as well as apolitical and end up abstracting schools from the society in which they exist.

4. C. Jencks, *Who Gets Ahead* (New York: Basic Books, 1979).

5. D. Gleeson, "Curriculum Development and Social Change: Towards a Reappraisal of Teacher Action," in *Teacher Decision-Making in the Classroom*, ed. John Eggleston (London: Routledge & Kegan Paul, 1979); H. A. Giroux, "Beyond the Limits of Radical Educational Reform: Toward a Critical Theory of Education," *Journal of Curriculum Theorizing* 2: 1 (1979).

6. Bowles and Gintis, *Schooling in Capitalist America*.

7. B. Bernstein, *Class, Codes, and Control, Vol. 3. Towards a Theory of Educational Transmission*, 2d ed. (London: Routledge & Kegan Paul, 1977); M. F. D. Young, ed., *Knowledge and Control* (London: Collier-Macmillan, 1971); M. MacDonald, *The Curriculum and Cultural Reproduction* (Milton Keynes, England: Open University Press, 1977).

8. C. Loparte, "Approaches to Schools: The Perfect Fit," *Liberation* (September/October 1974): 26–32; S. Gorelick, "Schooling Problems in Capitalist America," *Monthly Review* 29 (1977): 20-36; Giroux, "Limits of Radical Education Reform."

9. H. Mehan, *Learning Lessons: Social Organization in the Classroom* (Cambridge: Harvard University Press, 1979).

10. Young, *Knowledge and Control*; N. Keddie, "Classroom Knowledge," in *Knowledge and Control*, ed. Young.

11. R. Sharp and A. Green, *Education and Social Control* (London: Routledge & Kegan Paul, 1975).

12. J. Israel, *The Language of Dialectics and the Dialectics of Language* (London: Harvester Press, 1979).

13. G. Grace, *Teachers, Ideology and Control: A Study in Urban Education* (London: Routledge & Kegan Paul, 1978); M. W. Apple, *Ideology and Curriculum* (Boston: Routledge & Kegan Paul, 1979).

14. T. Popkewitz, "Teacher Education as Socialization: Ideology or Social Mission" (Paper presented at the American Education Research Association annual meeting in San Francisco, April 1979), pp. 1-3.

15. S. Aronowitz, *False Promises* (New York: McGraw-Hill, 1973).

16. Ibid., p. 314.

17. W. T. Weaver, "In Search of Quality: The Need for Talent in Teaching," *Phi Delta Kappan* (September 1979): 29–32, 46.

18. D. C. Lortie, *Schoolteacher* (Chicago: University of Chicago Press, 1975).

19. Apple, *Ideology and Curriculum*.

20. T. W. Adorno, "Culture and Administration," *Telos* 37 (1978): 93.

21. F. Ferrarotti, "The Struggle Against Total Bureaucratization," *Telos* 27 (1976): 159.

22. H. P. Dreitzel, "On the Political Meaning of Culture," in *Beyond the Crisis,* ed. Norman Birnbaum (New York: Oxford University Press, 1977), p. 88.

23. C. Sinba, "Class, Language, and Education," *Ideology and Consciousness,* no. 1 (May 1977): 77–92.

24. K. Korsch, *Marxism and Philosophy* (New York: Monthly Review Press, 1970); A. Gramsci, *Selections from Prison Notebooks,* ed. and trans. Q. Hoare and G. Smith (New York: International Publishers, 1972).

25. H. Marcuse, *One Dimensional Man* (Boston: Beacon Press, 1966), p. 208.

26. J. W. Freiberg, "Critical Social Theory in American Conjuncture," in *Critical Sociology,* ed. id. (New York: Irvington Press, 1979).

27. R. Williams, *Marxism and Literature* (New York: Oxford University Press, 1977), p. 110.

28. B. Kaufman, "Piaget, Marx, and the Political Ideology of Schooling," *Journal of Curriculum Studies* 10 (1978): 19–44.

29. A. Gouldner, *The Dialectic of Ideology and Technology* (New York: Seabury Press, 1976).

30. D. Kellner, "Ideology, Marxism, and Advanced Capitalism," *Socialist Review* 8 (1978): 36–65.

31. Ibid., p. 54.

32. Gramsci, *Selections from Prison Notebooks;* Althusser, "Ideological State Apparatuses."

33. Apple, *Ideology and Curriculum,* p. 496.

34. Bernstein, *Class, Codes, and Control.*

35. R. Tyler, *Basic Principles of Curriculum and Instruction* (Chicago: University of Chicago Press, 1949); R. S. Peters, *Ethics and Education* (London: Allen & Unwin, 1966).

36. J. Anyon, "Ideology and United States History Textbooks," *Harvard Educational Review* 49 (1979): 361–86; H. A. Giroux, "Dialectics and the Development of Curriculum Theory," in *Ideology, Culture, and the Process of Schooling* (Philadelphia: Temple University Press, 1981); Bourdieu and Passeron, *Reproduction in Education, Society, and Culture.*

37. MacDonald, *Curriculum and Cultural Reproduction;* Apple, *Ideology and Curriculum.*

38. E. Vallance, "Hiding the Hidden Curriculum," *Curriculum Theory Network* 4 (1973/74): 5–21; B. Franklin, "Technological Models and Curriculum Field," *The Educational Forum* (March 1976): 303–12.

39. Apple, *Ideology and Curriculum*, p. 73; Michael B. Katz, *The Irony of Early School Reform* (Boston: Beacon Press, 1968).

40. Popkewitz, "Teacher Education as Socialization."

41. T. Popkewitz, "Paradigms in Educational Science: Different Meanings of Social Theory and Implications" (Speech prepared for the American Educational Research Association annual meeting in San Francisco, April 1979), p. 9.

42. P. Suppes, "The Place of Theory in Educational Research," *Educational Researcher* 3 (1974): 3–10; J. W. Popham, "Objectives-Based Management Strategies for Large Educational Systems," in *Perspectives on Management Systems*, ed. Albert Yee (Englewood Cliffs, N.J.: Educational Technology Publications, 1973).

43. E. Eisner, *The Educational Imagination* (New York: Macmillan, 1979), pp. 10–11.

44. T. Parsons, "The School as a Social System: Some of Its Functions in American Society," *Harvard Educational Review* 29 (1959): 297–318.

45. Sharp and Green, *Education and Social Control*, p. 2.

46. Popkewitz, "Teacher Education as Socialization," p. 6.

47. Anyon, "Ideology and United States History Textbooks," p. 39.

48. C. A. Bowers, "Curriculum and Our Technocracy Culture: The Problem of Reform," *Teachers College Record* 78 (1977): 53–67.

49. Popkewitz, "Teacher Education as Socialization."

50. R. H. Turner, "Role Taking: Process vs. Conformity," in *Human Behavior and Social Processes*, ed. A. Rose (London: Routledge & Kegan Paul, 1962), p. 37.

51. Grace, *Teachers, Ideology and Control*.

52. G. Arfwedson, "Teachers Work," in *Codes, Context, and Curriculum Processes*, ed. U. P. Lundgren and S. Petterson (Stockholm: Liber, 1979), pp. 88–89.

53. U. Lundgren, "Background: The Conceptual Framework," in *Codes, Context and Curriculum Processes*, ed. id. and Petterson, p. 33.

54. Eisner, *Educational Imagination*, p. 15.

55. W. F. Pinar, "*Currere:* Toward a Reconceptualization," in *Curriculum Theorizing: The Reconceptualists* (Berkeley: McCutchan, 1975).

56. M. F. D. Young, "Curriculum Change: Limits and Possibilities," *Educational Studies* 1 (1975): 129–38.

57. Apple, *Ideology and Curriculum*; Gouldner, *Dialectic of Ideology and Technology*.

58. Gouldner, *Dialectic of Ideology and Technology*, p. 49–50.

59. K. Harris, *Classroom Knowledge* (London: Routledge & Kegan Paul, 1979).

60. Popkewitz, "Teacher Education as Socialization," p. 20.

61. F. M. Connelly and D. Roberts, "What Curriculum for Graduate Instruction in Curriculum?" *Curriculum Theory Network* 5 (1976): 173–89; Israel, *Language of Dialectics*.

62. H. A. Giroux, "Schooling and the Culture of Positivism: Notes on the 'Death' of History," in *Ideology, Culture, and the Process of Schooling* (Philadelphia: Temple University Press, 1981).

63. T. Popkewitz, "The Latent Values of the Discipline-Centered Curriculum in Social Education," *Theory and Research in Social Education* 5 (1978): 41–60; Anyon, "Ideology and United States History Textbooks"; Apple, *Ideology and Curriculum*.

64. P. Freire, *Pedagogy of the Oppressed* (New York: Seabury, 1973).

65. M. Greene, *Landscapes of Learning* (New York: Teachers College Press, 1978).

66. C. Brown, *Literacy in 30 Hours: Paulo Freire's Process in Northeast Brazil* (Chicago: Alternative Schools Network, 1978).

67. M. Edelman, *Political Language: Words that Succeed and Policies that Fail* (New York: Academic Press, 1977).

68. C. Lasch, *Haven in a Heartless World* (New York: Basic Books, 1977); B. J. Bledstein, *The Culture of Professionalism* (New York: W. W. Norton & Co., 1976); Edelman, *Political Language.*

69. Popkewitz, "Paradigms in Educational Science."

70. P. Willis, *Learning to Labour: How Working Class Kids Get Working Class Jobs* (England: Saxon House, Teakfield Ltd., 1977).

71. M. Greene, "From the Lincoln Center Institute: A Summary of Talks," A series of speeches presented at the Lincoln Center Institute, July 1979.

72. Greene, *Landscapes of Learning,* p. 70.

73. P. Ricoeur, *Political and Social Essays* (Athens: Ohio University Press, 1974).

74. T. W. Adorno, "Scientific Experiences of a European in America," in *The Intellectual Migration: Europe and America, 1930-1960,* ed. Donald Fleming and Bernard Bailyn (Cambridge: Harvard University Press, 1969), p. 53.

75. Giroux, "Schooling and the Culture of Positivism."

76. Sharp and Green, *Education and Social Control,* p. 221.

77. Young, *Knowledge and Control,* p. 24.

78. I am indebted to Ralph Page for helping me work out this idea.

79. Greene, *Landscapes of Learning,* p. 59.

80. Eisner, *Educational Imagination,* p. 17.

81. D. Huebner, "Curricular Language and Classroom Meanings," in *Curriculum Theorizing,* ed. Pinar.

82. M. Grumet, "Curriculum as Theater: Merely Players," *Curriculum Inquiry* 8 (1978) 37-64; Pinar, *"Currere:* Toward a Reconceptualization."

83. G. Dow, *Learning to Teach, Teaching to Learn* (London: Routledge & Kegan Paul, 1979).